LOCAL
ATTACHMENTS

Creating the North American Landscape

Gregory Conniff
Bonnie Loyd
Edward K. Muller
David Schuyler
Consulting Editors

Published in cooperation with the Center for American Places,
Harrisonburg, Virginia

Woburn

Melrose   Saugus

Lexington

Malden

Medford

Arlington   Revere

Everett

Waltham   Somerville

Belmont

Cambridge   Charles-
                           town   East Boston

Watertown

Allston   North
                           End

Brighton   Back Bay
                           South End

                           South Boston

Brookline   Roxbury

Newton   Jamaica
                 Plain

                           Dorchester

Needham   Roslindale
                West Roxbury

                Hyde Park   Milton   Quincy

Dedham

                                          Braintree

Norwood

Boston

Boston metropolitan area, including Jamaica Plain, c. 1920

LOCAL
ATTACHMENTS

*The Making of an American
Urban Neighborhood,
1850 to 1920*

Alexander von Hoffman

The Johns Hopkins University Press
Baltimore and London

© 1994 The Johns Hopkins University Press
All rights reserved. Published 1994
Printed in the United States of America
on acid-free paper

The Johns Hopkins University Press
2715 North Charles Street
Baltimore, Maryland 21218-4319
The Johns Hopkins Press Ltd., London

Johns Hopkins Paperbacks edition, 1996
05 04 03 02 01 00 99 98 97 96   5 4 3 2 1

ISBN 0-8018-5393-1 (pbk.)

Library of Congress Cataloging-in-Publication Data will
be found at the end of this book.

A catalog record for this book is available from the
British Library.

*Maps by Kenneth Faulkner, Chris Georgiopoulos, and
Glenna Lang*

For Glenna, who knows about Jamaica Plain,
and for Esmé, who learned about it

Contents

Plates appear following Chapters 2, 4, and 6;
maps appear on pages iv, 22, 40, 44, 45, 46, and 118

Acknowledgments

The publication of this book represents the completion of a long intellectual and personal odyssey. I am grateful to all the people who aided this sojourner over the years and beg pardon if for lack of space or lapse of memory I omit someone's name.

For help with research, I am especially grateful to Joan Hamilton, Louise Lane, Christine Peterson, Laura Reyes, and Alice Roberts, of the Jamaica Plain branch of the Boston Public Library, for allowing me the freedom to rummage in their treasure chest. I also thank the librarians at the Boston Public Library, especially Roberta Zonghi in the Rare Books and Manuscripts Department, Henry Scannell in the Microtext Department, and Aaron Schmitt and Sinclair Hitchings in the Print Department. At Harvard University, I thank especially James Hodgson, Christopher Hail, and Hinda Sklar, of the Frances Loeb Library, and Maury Feld and Maryellen P. McCarthy, at Littauer Library. I appreciate the helpful souls at the Massachusetts State Library and at the Boston Landmarks Commission, especially Carol Kennedy. Thanks also to James O'Toole and Ron Patkus at the (Roman Catholic) Archdiocese of Boston Archives, Nora Murphy at the Diocesan Archives of the Episcopal Diocese of Massachusetts, Lorna Condon at the Society for the Preservation of New England Antiquities, Phillip Bergen of The Bostonian Society, and Sally Pierce of the Boston Athenaeum.

For their great help in and about Jamaica Plain, I thank Jamaica Plain's knowledgeable newspaper editor, Sandy Storey, Walter Marx, Henry Keaveny, the Jamaica Plain Historical Society, Nan Haffenreffer, Barbara Kaplan and the Neighborhood Development Corporation, Alice Woodall, Herbert Metten, Hollis Blue, Herb Pierce, Terry Burke, Ellen McGuire, Suzanne Presley, the late James Lenihan, the late August Becker, Karl Ludwig, Madeline Bradley, Walter Bleiler, Marion Cleary, Dorothy Halder, Rudy Cormeil, the late Edward Oberle, Marilyn Oberle, Bradley H.

Clarke, Sister Margaret Patricia Donahue, the Jamaica Plain Neighborhood House Association, and the priests, nuns, ministers, club members, and others who shared their memories and materials.

For the support of the statistical research, I am grateful to the William R. Milton Small Grant Fund, the Joseph H. Clark Fund, and the Harvard University Junior Faculty Research Assistant Program. They made possible the long hours of such helpful assistants as Christopher Duffy, Shelagh Kenney, Carolyn Duffy, Terry Gerstein, and Kathy Poole. I thank the latter two also for the enthusiasm and insights they brought as students, and I thank the members of my seminar on the local community in American urban history as well. For support in producing visual materials for the book, I am grateful to the Department of Urban Planning and Design of the Graduate School of Design at Harvard University.

At the beginning of the journey were the kind neighbors who introduced me to Jamaica Plain and its distinct way of life. For their friendship, I would like to thank Stella Carey, the late Butch Carey, Mary and Joe Jennings and their family, Francis Michael Carey, Maureen Lyons, José Montanez, Tommy O'Donnell, the late Bing O'Donnell, the late Chino Serrano, and the rest of the Creighton Street gang.

Many offered intellectual guidance along the way. In what seems like another epoch, Pauline Maier helped me start the project at the University of Massachusetts at Boston. Later, in the Department of History at Harvard University, I was fortunate to find a dissertation adviser, Stephan Thernstrom, who supported the idea of writing a neighborhood history and who provided astute commentary on the dissertation and later versions of this study. And for their thoughtful editorial advice and rigorous criticism of various versions, I also thank Joseph S. Wood, Chandos Brown, Alex DeGrand, Alan Brinkley, Jeffrey Adler, and Mark Hirsch.

In recent years, colleagues at Harvard University's Graduate School of Design and Department of Visual and Environmental Studies helped me find my way. I have benefited from working with Alex Krieger, Alistair McIntosh, Elizabeth Meyer, Rob Moss, Edward Robbins, Eduard Sekler, John R. Stilgoe, Ellen Whittemore, and many others. I have been particularly blessed with supportive chairmen, Tony Gomez-Ibanez and François Vigier in the Urban Planning and Design department and Alfred Guzzetti and Lou Bakanowsky at the Department of Visual and Environmental Studies. I am especially grateful to Peter Rowe for support he has offered as coteacher, chairman, dean, intellectual sparring partner, and friend.

For aid in the final stages of the journey, I am very grateful to my editor,

George F. Thompson, for his enthusiastic support, as well as my copy editor, Joanne Allen, for her careful work, and to everyone else at the Johns Hopkins University Press for their help in designing, producing, and promoting this book. Also a heartfelt thanks to my mother, Ann Cremin Byrne, for her invaluable help on the index.

In a category by themselves are special persons who saw the voyage through from beginning to end. Among those whom I owe particular debts of gratitude are Kurt and Gladys Engel Lang for their years of unstinting moral support and sage advice about the project. As mentor and friend, Thomas N. Brown provided unflagging encouragement and good-humored patience in the face of countless requests to review this work. Although this book cannot approach either the profundity of his thought or the craftsmanship of his prose, his challenging spirit of inquiry has raised its quality immeasurably.

To my wife, Glenna Lang, for an unwavering belief in the project, for untold hours of editing, design, art consultation, and support, but perhaps most of all for enduring it and me, I owe a debt too great to calculate, let alone repay. Finally, I thank my daughter, Esmé, whose love of history, art, and life has been a special inspiration.

Introduction

"Most men have local attachment so strong," wrote the author of a Massachusetts town history published in 1847, "that it invests some spot, endeared by association, with controlling interest."[1] The observation expressed a prevalent notion of the time. Nineteenth-century Americans conceived of loyalty to place as a basic human emotion, one that justified writing a local history or provoked the wish to be buried near home. The idea of local attachments reflected common experience. For much of the nineteenth century, the United States remained a rural society made up of small face-to-face communities. Founded on the concept of local representation, American government reinforced the localist orientation of the farms, towns, and villages that composed the nation.

During the late nineteenth and early twentieth centuries, however, industrial and communications revolutions transformed the United States into a mighty urban nation. By 1900 New York, Philadelphia, and Chicago had become giant metropolises with over a million in population. Another group of great cities, among the most important of which was Boston, boasted populations of over half a million people. Yet the move to the big city did not erase the locally based community life that characterized the small towns and villages. Rather, the emerging urban majority transferred such localist sentiments to the city neighborhoods where they now lived.

The vigorous intensity of local urban life during the late nineteenth and early twentieth centuries would startle the modern observer. In the era of the shopping mall, our collective memory dimly recollects the corner grocery store and saloon but forgets the carpentry shops, real estate offices, factories, and other enterprises that were once part of the urban neighborhood. In a more religious age than our own, city dwellers not only attended Sunday and weekday church services but also returned to the parish hall for teas, concerts, theatricals, dances, and parties. In the evening, residents scurried along the streets to social clubs, where they competed in bowling and whist tournaments, and fraternal lodges, where they donned exotic robes and chanted mysterious mumbo-jumbo. Politics, too, placed great demands on people's time, with its incessant club meetings, rallies, parades, and annual rounds of elections to party conventions and governmental offices.

Reflecting a broad-based sense of commitment to an urban place, local businessmen, politicians, and other citizens aggressively advanced the cause of their home district. Members of neighborhood clubs clamored for and often obtained improvements in almost every aspect of neighborhood life. Consider, for example, how the neighborhood under study here reacted to a relatively minor nuisance. In February 1911, Jamaica Plain residents and shopkeepers began to complain about noise created by new streetcars on a bend in the tracks along the neighborhood's main thoroughfare. Immediately the neighborhood improvement association organized mass protest meetings and sent a letter of complaint to the president of the streetcar company. Three weeks after the protests began, the company agreed to remedy the situation, and within a few months quieter streetcars had been introduced, to the satisfaction of neighborhood residents. Inhabitants of contemporary American cities would turn green with envy to discover the effective advocacy that once characterized urban life.[2]

The vitality of the neighborhood in this bygone era seems unfamiliar because it does not fit what scholars have taught us. Leading historians have painted bleak portraits of nineteenth-century cities, presenting them as places beset by crisis, much like cities in our own day. Population growth, immigration, and economic instability, according to this influential point of view, registered shocks that urban institutions were unable to absorb. Faced with growing problems of health, disorder, and poverty, uprooted residents focused on achieving personal economic well-being and retreated to private family life. The increasingly popular single-family home expressed the inward-looking attitude of middle-class urban dwellers and further isolated them from their community. Privatism caused or failed to ameliorate uncontrolled urban sprawl, inequalities of wealth, and the lack of effective public institutions and services. Worst of all, these historians concluded, privatism deprived the old city of the civic spirit that could have overcome social and institutional crisis.[3]

From the perspective of other historians, class and ethnicity deeply divided the nineteenth-century city until large-scale institutions began to meld the cultures of the fragmented population into urban mass society. In the late nineteenth century, according to this view, such citywide institutions as the metropolitan daily newspaper and the downtown department store unified the city's many ethnic groups and social classes by providing shared experiences. Similarly, historians of the working class have argued that mass entertainments such as professional baseball and later the movie theater supplanted earlier autonomous forms of working-class leisure culture.[4]

The historians' gloomy view of the late-nineteenth- and early twentieth-century city reflects an uncritical acceptance of early urban sociology. Beginning with the work of Ferdinand Tönnies, sociologists developed a theory about the nature of community in the modern era. The theory held that social life evolved between two poles, referred to as Gemeinschaft and Gesellschaft, or community and society. In the first instance, folk people lived in simple village settings characterized by personal and close-knit relations, fixed social roles, and a strong sense of territorial belonging.

Urban growth and modern technology, social scientists asserted, undermined this communal form of life. Impersonal and distant institutions, ultimately including the nation-state, ruled urban society. The rise of inexpensive transportation and mass communications battered down the barriers that had isolated the inhabitants of the communal village and freed them to move about, less committed to family, friends, and neighborhood and more "instrumental" in their relationships. Only the large bureaucratic institutions and perhaps crude emotional appeals to nationalism or other allegiances could exercise social control over the atomistic citizens of the unbounded society.[5]

For more than a generation, this conception of modern urban life has shaped the way American historians, including eminent scholars such as Oscar Handlin and Robert Wiebe, viewed the city. In a major work of historical synthesis, for example, Robert Wiebe transposed the community-society model to the American experience in the period 1877–1920. Wiebe vividly described the urban neighborhoods and rural towns of nineteenth-century America as "island communities," whose isolation and autonomy were undermined by the expansion of national transportation, communication, and economic networks. Although the island communities fiercely resisted, they could not prevent the creation of a new order. "By contrast to the personal, informal ways of the community," Wiebe explained, "the new scheme was derived from the regulative, hierarchical needs of urban-industrial life."[6]

Despite the community-society model's continuing popularity among historians, urban sociologists have largely abandoned it. A series of empirical research projects revealed the existence of vigorous local communities in twentieth-century Boston, Chicago, St. Louis, and even suburban Los Angeles. Close-knit relations and territorial loyalties, sociologists discovered, had survived in the modern city. Urban residents belonged to what Morris Janowitz labeled the "community of limited liability." They were linked, not by primordial folk ties, but by flexible links that ranged in intensity and number over time and from individual to individual. Going further, the school of network analysis discovered social ties that spread in dispersed geographical patterns. Such far-flung forms of community, however, did not preclude neighborhood associations and loyalties. If, as Gerald Suttles asserts, neighborhood "foreign relations" are a source of local identity, then growth in fact fosters a sense of place by multiplying external ties.[7]

Mindful of the developments in sociological thinking, some historians began to rethink the effects of economic and other forms of growth on traditional forms of community. In an incisive essay, Thomas Bender pointed out that historians illogically had concluded that growth had undermined community in every period of American history from 1630 to the 1920s. Bender theorized that after 1850 both community and society coexisted in the United States. Histories of colonial towns and small mid-nineteenth-century cities now found that the process of growth actually produced social order and local autonomy.[8]

Yet as far as the large cities of the late nineteenth and early twentieth centuries were concerned, the new perspectives on modern society remained largely unexplored. This historiographic silence stems in large part from the fact that historians have only rarely studied the neighborhood as a distinct element in urban society. Borrowing the old sociological definition of the neighborhood as a homogeneous unit, urban historians have conceived of the city neighborhood as a receptacle for a single social or economic group.[9] Thus, a number of historical studies discuss urban neighborhoods, but only as a geographic frame for related topics such as ethnicity, race, class, and religion.[10] As a result, scholars have appealed for new studies to remedy the dearth of neighborhood histories and to explain the significance of place within urban society.[11]

The present work is offered as a first step in exploring how the modern urban neighborhood emerged in the United States during the late nineteenth and early twentieth centuries. The lack of comparable neighborhood histories and the need to scrutinize the subject in sufficient detail required a case study approach to the subject. This book traces the history

Introduction

of a single urban neighborhood, Jamaica Plain, Massachusetts, with an eye to the crucial forces that shaped and defined it. In order to place the local history into the larger context of the history of the modern neighborhood, wherever possible the text compares developments in Jamaica Plain with those in urban communities in Boston and other American cities.

Although the definition of a city neighborhood is problematic, most agree that it is, at the least, an urban spatial unit with generally recognized geographic boundaries, a name, and some sense of psychological unity among its inhabitants. For the purposes of this book, the term *neighborhood* refers to an area greater than a street, block, or other small vicinity (which, confusingly, sometimes also are called neighborhoods) but distinctly smaller than the city as a whole. Thus, in this study the word *neighborhood* is equivalent to the term *local community* as used by sociologists and *district neighborhood* as used by Jane Jacobs in her well-known survey of contemporary urban society, *The Death and Life of Great American Cities*.[12]

The time period covered here spans the development of Jamaica Plain in particular and the emergence of the modern American city in general. It begins in 1850 in order to trace the roots of urbanization that flowered at the end of the century. It ends in 1920, by which time previous growth trends had begun to reverse in Jamaica Plain and a new epoch in the history of the American city, symbolized by the automobile, was clearly under way.

This book focuses on the history of public, not private, life. It attempts to understand the power that could motivate people to stand up and declare allegiance to their neighborhood or act on behalf of it. It is not a study of the sense of community reflected in patterns of friendship and other informal neighborly exchanges. Nor does it intend to explore the intimate lives of men and women in the past, an intriguing topic left for other scholars to pursue. Feelings of community and private lives of individuals appear here only as they express or influence the publicly shared sense of urban place.

In order to recreate the complex history of an urban neighborhood, this work exploited a wide array of primary sources, some of which had lain untouched for decades. Real estate atlases, deed and mortgage records, and historic-landmark surveys illuminated the process of physical development. Census Bureau manuscripts, city directories, and voting lists contained data for statistical profiles of the population and revealed the identities of residents of individual buildings and streets. The records, annals, and memorabilia of parish churches, schools, fraternal lodges, and social clubs told the history of the associational life of the district. An assortment of official documents, including city council minutes and a policeman's work diary, shed light on the relationship of neighborhood residents to each other and their local government. The articles, advertisements, and notices in the local newspapers provided an unequaled source for viewing the fine texture of neighborhood society. Finally, memoirs and oral histories presented personal narratives of neighborhood life.

Although not as well known as some other Boston districts, the subject of this study of the American urban neighborhood constitutes a special and significant part of its city. Jamaica Plain is located in a radius between three and a half miles and five and a half miles from Boston's City Hall.[13] Once a sparsely settled and remote part of the Town of Roxbury, in 1851 Jamaica Plain became the center of the new Town of West Roxbury, and finally in 1874 it was annexed with West Roxbury to the City of Boston. Its population continued to grow and by 1910 exceeded forty thousand, a level at which it remained for much of the twentieth century.

Jamaica Plain has been home to many prominent Bostonians. In the eighteenth century, members of the elite, including John Hancock, kept country houses in Jamaica Plain. During the nineteenth century, such eminences as the historian Francis Parkman lived in estates or summer homes here. In the late nineteenth century, some of Boston's leading political reformers lived in the district. During the twentieth century, Jamaica Plain has been home to several of Boston's mayors and many members of the Boston Symphony Orchestra, including its famous conductor, the late Serge Koussevitsky.

Because it developed as a heterogeneous neighborhood, not as a residence of a single class or ethnic group, Jamaica Plain offers a good opportunity to test allegiances of place independent of class and ethnicity. One of Boston's more diverse neighborhoods, it strikes most observers as a microcosm of the city. "If you took a pair of scissors and cut out Jamaica Plain from Boston," wrote a *Boston Post* journalist in 1941, "you could put it down anywhere and have a big city complete in almost every detail. It has quaint, winding roads lined with trees, . . . brand new homes in which the plaster has hardly dried, and fine looking modern apartments. It also has a congested [industrial] area over which is heard the hum of the elevated or the whistle of freight engines."[14]

Jamaica Plain developed as an outer-city district that combined the characteristics of gold coast, immigrant quarter, working-class slum, and middle-class suburb. Prestigious residential areas sit on the hills and near

Jamaica Pond, an industrial corridor with adjacent working-class districts runs along the Stony Brook valley, and eclectic middle-class areas stretch throughout. The neighborhood boasts a large and varied collection of historic and architecturally significant buildings. In or adjacent to the district are scenic open spaces such as Forest Hills Cemetery and Boston's largest public parks, Franklin Park and Arnold Arboretum, designed by the preeminent nineteenth-century American landscape architect, Frederick Law Olmsted.

During the latter nineteenth and early twentieth centuries, the neighborhood was not an exact statistical microcosm of the city at large, but its diverse population reflected many of the important elements of Boston urban society. From 1880 to 1910 the occupational distribution of white-collar and blue-collar workers in Jamaica Plain approximated that of the city as a whole, although by 1920 the neighborhood was somewhat more heavily white-collar. In ethnic terms, in 1850 the district had a greater proportion of American-born than did the city as a whole; by 1910 it contained more of the foreign-born than did Boston. Ethnic groups rarely distributed themselves evenly throughout the city, however, so that an ethnically representative district would be difficult to find.[15]

In many ways, Jamaica Plain's unique qualities distinguished it from other neighborhoods. In the late nineteenth century, for example, it was home to relatively large numbers of German-Americans, a group frequently overlooked in Boston history, and a surprising number of Boston's leading Progressive reformers and mainstream politicians. In the face of a diverse population, upper-middle-class Protestants, many of them Unitarians, functioned as a local social elite. Moreover, Jamaica Plain managed to escape many of the bitter conflicts and ethnic hostility that disturbed other districts, such as the Boston neighborhood of Charlestown.

Yet despite its unique qualities, Jamaica Plain was shaped by the same urbanizing forces that molded other American city neighborhoods of the nineteenth and early twentieth centuries. Similar forms of demographic, economic, and institutional growth fostered urban development, nurtured local attachments, and strengthened decentralized centers of power across the country. Even the universalist reform movements and other centralizing forces that undercut localism were national in scope. City neighborhoods differed widely in composition and character, but they shared a common urban culture.

Drawing on the conceptual framework offered by revisionist sociological and historical works about the city, this book argues that in the mobile, growing urban society of the late nineteenth and early twentieth centuries, neighborhoods served as important centers of gravity within the complex social organization of the city. It seeks to understand how the American urban neighborhood of the late nineteenth and early twentieth centuries came to exist and to discover the origins of the intense localism that characterized it.

According to the argument presented here, urban neighborhoods were not island communities but vigorously growing substations in a rapidly expanding urban network. Hardly sterile or introspective, neighborhood society produced a colorful public life. Far from declining, civic spirit flourished within the realm of the urban neighborhood. The efforts of Progressive reformers to discipline the neighborhoods were thus not attempts to break down the walls of isolation. After all, reformers could not connect what was already connected. Instead they attempted to gain control of a system that was burgeoning at both the core and the periphery. Not growth, but the limits and erosion of the vital turn-of-the-century neighborhood, contributed to the present urban malaise.

The chapters that follow trace the dramatic transformation of Jamaica Plain into a modern urban neighborhood during the late nineteenth and early twentieth centuries. They demonstrate that growth and connections to the outside world, and not isolation, fostered the development of locally based urban communities. These chapters take a topical rather than narrative form in order to lend coherence to a story involving thousands of characters and numerous centers of activity.

The opening chapter analyzes Jamaica Plain in the mid-nineteenth century and sets the stage for the urban transformation to come. It shows that despite its roots as an agricultural and summer resort area, the territory in 1850 was no longer rural and not yet urban. Instead the district was composed of the typically discordant elements of the early nineteenth-century urban fringe.

Chapter 2 traces the patterns of land development in Jamaica Plain and, in the process, refutes the notion that the late-nineteenth-century expansion of American cities such as Boston created homogeneous, class-segregated bands of residences. In Jamaica Plain, urban migration, neighborhood economic growth, and local real estate development created a heterogeneous urban neighborhood with distinctive land-use patterns. Even as they expanded the neighborhood boundaries to their present dimensions, the processes of urban growth in outer Boston conferred upon Jamaica Plain a sense of identity as an urban community.

The creation of an impressive array of public urban landscapes, examined in chapter 3, was another aspect of Jamaica Plain's physical development. Inspired by universal principles of human psychology and landscape design, the parks of Jamaica Plain represented an exercise in local place-making that ignored the local community. Local-minded neighbors sometimes grew alienated by the large-scale goals of landscape reformers such as Frederick Law Olmsted; in the case of Franklin Park, they undermined Olmsted's plan for the uses of the park. These conflicts anticipated the destructive clashes between universalist political reformers and localist city dwellers.

Chapters 4 and 5 explore in detail the economic and social sources of local attachments in Jamaica Plain. Inside the neighborhood, local institutions created familiar environments that served as buffers against the impersonal scale of the metropolis. Sustained by contacts to the external society, daily neighborhood life spun a dense web of ties that connected local residents to each other and to the local community.

Chapter 4 traces the weave of local relationships that emanated from business activity in the neighborhood. Local business ventures, shared work experiences in local shops and factories, and conversations at the corner store all linked residents to one another and reinforced their connection with the neighborhood. Local economic activity also produced a group of progrowth businessmen who acted as neighborhood leaders. These neighborhood boosters strived to advance both the community at large and local business interests.

Chapter 5 surveys the startling array of neighborhood voluntary associations. Churches, fraternal lodges, social clubs, and other organizations spanned the gamut of neighborhood society. These institutions sponsored meetings, sports contests, street parades, and other events that contributed to the stimulating public life of the neighborhood. Although frequently part of large organizational networks, community branch offices and local chapters created a complex mesh of interrelationships that nurtured local attachments. Expressing their shared sense of community, Jamaica Plain men and women volunteered time, money, and effort to assist "their" poor neighbors and improve the quality of life in their district.

The final chapters examine how Jamaica Plain residents vigorously expressed neighborhood loyalties in the realm of government and politics. Chapter 6 shows how Jamaica Plain citizens' strong support for a progrowth policy helped propel annexation of the district to the City of Boston. Once Jamaica Plain belonged to Boston, a bipartisan coalition successfully pressed the locally based city government for neighborhood improvements. In so doing, Jamaica Plain and other city neighborhoods reversed municipal government philosophy in favor of a progrowth, big-spending agenda. The improvement doctrine had its pitfalls, however, and in the early twentieth century an adjacent neighborhood's pursuit of growth-oriented services, in the form of an elevated rapid-transit station, proved detrimental to Jamaica Plain.

Chapter 7 investigates how the locally based urban political system belonged to the social web of neighborhood society and reinforced local attachments. Because local political party organizations were open to a wide range of neighborhood ethnic and class groups, the political system provided a forum for mediation between the diverse elements of the urban population.

Into this system of assimilation stepped political reformers, including several leading Jamaica Plainers, who declared war on political and governmental localism. Like the park proponents, municipal reformers were guided by universal principles rather than local conditions. Although inspired by the ideals of civic and moral unity, the centralizing measures effected by the reformers hardly unified Bostonians. They made it much more difficult for neighborhood residents to obtain services from the government. Worse, they stirred up bitter class and ethnic hostilities in the climactic mayoral election of 1910 and for decades thereafter.

The concluding chapter of the book summarizes the development of Jamaica Plain and surveys the achievements and later fate of the American urban neighborhood. Even as the classic form of the modern urban neighborhood eroded during the twentieth century, reformers and government officials across the United States used it as a model to cure the ills of the contemporary city.

Finally, because it represents an early effort at examining the history of the local urban community, the book ends with a call for further study of the rise and fall of the historic neighborhood and the urban system to which it belonged. With greater understanding of our past, it is hoped, we will cope with the present problems of the American city.

LOCAL
ATTACHMENTS

1

On the Urban Fringe:
Jamaica Plain in the
Mid-Nineteenth Century

When I first came amongst you (in 1796), this was a
quiet, retired, moral little village.
> —*Thomas Gray, 1842*

Every body who knows Boston knows the neighboring
village of (Jamaica Plain), and its pretty pond, with sloping shores and neat villas and a distant spire.
> —*George William Curtis, 1859*

On the night of June 3, 1851, the
residents of Jamaica Plain celebrated the birth of their new government,
the Town of West Roxbury, by firing cannons, burning bonfires on the
hills, and shooting fireworks from the banks of Jamaica Pond. Jamaica
Plain residents had special reason to smile as they viewed the rockets
soaring over the water. They had spearheaded the effort to emancipate
Jamaica Plain and the other outlying districts from the control of their
former government, the City of Roxbury.

Yet the precise character of the community that led the secessionist
charge remained uncertain. The supporters of independence for their
town argued that, in contrast to the urban sections of Roxbury, Jamaica
Plain and the other sections of West Roxbury constituted a "separate

agricultural town" that deserved its own independent jurisdiction. Their opponents, mainly from old Roxbury, disputed this characterization. They asserted that in fact farming was in decline in the rebellious districts and that the residents there hungered for urban growth and services. They predicted that real estate development would soon fill all the territories with houses and gardens, streets and stores.[1]

Commentators who were not involved in the dispute offered yet another perspective on the character of Jamaica Plain. In his description of the neighborhood in 1842, the Reverend Thomas Gray, pastor of the First Church, emphasized three major population groups, farmers, the wealthy, and businessmen commuters. Writing over a century later, the noted urban historian Sam Bass Warner agreed, describing mid-century Jamaica Plain as a former rural and summer house village that the railroad had transformed into a suburban community of businessmen commuters and their families.[2]

The records of the United States Bureau of the Census further complicate an assessment of the neighborhood's character. In the mid-nineteenth century, according to the census returns, the population of Jamaica Plain had recently grown. In 1840, about 230 households, or 1,540 people, had lived within the boundaries of modern Jamaica Plain. By 1850 the local population had increased by more than 170 percent, to about 2,730. In 1840, federal census takers counted two-thirds of the area's employed male adults in agriculture. In 1850, just over a third (at a maximum) of working heads of households belonged to categories related to farming. At mid-century, the remaining breadwinners were roughly divided between members of the upper middle and middle classes.

The observations of Thomas Gray and data from the 1850 census further suggest that shifts were occurring in the cultural and ethnic character of the population. In the past, Jamaica Plain had had only one church, the First Congregational Society of Jamaica Plain, formerly an established Protestant church and now a voluntary Unitarian church. Gray noted that in recent years adherents of other religious denominations, including Roman Catholics, Baptists, and Methodists, had arrived in the area and begun organizing new religious societies. The mid-century census reported that the local population was predominantly of Protestant American stock but included many out-of-state migrants, including a significant foreign element. In 1850 more than half of the district's heads of households had been born in Massachusetts, more than 15 percent in other New England states, and almost 30 percent outside of the United States (see table 2.5).[3]

A comparison of the occupational levels of the different national groups of local workers, furthermore, reveals economic divisions along ethnic lines that resemble those of American cities today. The American-born heads of households held 97 percent of high-white-collar jobs, 91 percent of low-white-collar jobs, and just under three-quarters of the skilled positions. On the other hand, the foreign-born—primarily Irish, English, Scots, and Canadians—held about a quarter of the skilled positions and three-quarters of the low-blue-collar jobs. The Irish, by far the most numerous immigrant group, were unquestionably the most heavily concentrated in the working class and took a position somewhat analogous to that of groups of African-Americans, Hispanics, and other unskilled recent migrants to the cities in the United States. (See table 2.7.)

The elements that constituted mid-nineteenth-century Jamaica Plain appear as a bewildering and contradictory mix of agricultural village, exclusive suburb, artisan community, and urban ghetto. To reconcile these images, it helps to consider how the booming growth of America's cities refashioned their outlying communities. During the first half of the nineteenth century, the northeastern United States, and especially the New England region, shifted from an agricultural to an industrial economy. The towns and cities of New England became major producers of textiles, shoes, furniture, and sundry other products, which they exported to growing American regional markets. Like the major cities in other regions, Boston, the preeminent port of New England, thrived as a commercial, financial, and manufacturing center.[4]

Similar to the process at work in New York, Philadelphia, and other cities, the economic growth of Boston reverberated over the entire metropolitan area, stimulating new kinds of agricultural, manufacturing, and residential development in nearby suburban towns. In the territory surrounding the city, farmers oriented their production to the city market. Entrepreneurs processed hinterland materials for city buyers in cattle yards, slaughterhouses, grain mills, and other facilities. Others took advantage of inexpensive land on the periphery and operated foundries, machine shops, brickyards, and other factories that produced goods for the urban economy. Meanwhile, first wealthy and later upper-middle-class families took up increasingly larger sections of the periphery and redefined them as pastoral suburban enclaves. The resulting fringe region presented a complex and varied but not very coherent community.[5]

An examination of mid-century Jamaica Plain shows that the divergent assessments of the neighborhood reflected different aspects of a characteristic urban fringe district. The presence of large landholders, predominantly farmers and estate owners, lent some credence to the secessionists' portrayal of their community as an agricultural territory, and white-collar commuters gave the neighborhood a suburban cast. Yet the presence of other local population groups such as artisans, shopkeepers, small manufacturers, and laborers foreshadowed a more urban future. Indeed, only twenty-three years after the establishment of the Town of West Roxbury, Jamaica Plain residents again led the charge to change their government, this time by voting to become part of the great City of Boston.

The topography of Jamaica Plain in 1850 was little changed from what it had been when the Puritans settled the area in the 1640s. The district's most distinctive topographical feature was (and still is) Jamaica Pond, a kettle lake that extended over nearly seventy acres and the largest body of fresh water for several miles south of Boston Bay. A small flatlands called Jamaica Plain (originally Pond Plain) extended south and east of the pond. From there the land began to rise and fall in a succession of small glacial knobs and valleys, typical of the topography of southwestern Boston. In the east the Stony Brook, a small river of irregular width, ran the length of the district in a low marshy valley that extended southwest from lower Roxbury.

Most of the area's important roads were seventeenth-century pathways that wound erratic courses around the drumlins and waterways. The most important thoroughfare, Centre Street, originally called the Highway (or Road) to Dedham, meandered the length of Jamaica Plain from lower Roxbury to its appointed destination. The other main thoroughfare, known in 1850 as the Dedham Turnpike, was a more modern road that ran from Roxbury to Dedham in a straight line down the Stony Brook valley. It had been built by a private corporation as the Norfolk and Bristol Turnpike in 1806; by the late 1850s it would become a public street known first as Shawmut Avenue and later by its present name, Washington Street. Only three short roads, Boylston, South, and Green streets, the last a recently built road, connected Centre Street and the turnpike. The tracks of the Boston and Providence Railroad also ran down the Stony Brook valley, crossing the turnpike at Toll Gate, the turnpike's first gate outside Roxbury, and a railroad station (later known as Forest Hills Station, after the adjacent Forest Hills Cemetery).

The physical appearance of Jamaica Plain in 1850 reflected its mixed character. Farms and country estates, comprising planted fields, orchards, lawns, gardens, and woods, occupied most of the rolling territory. Their green acres gave the initial impression of a rural district. Forest Hills Cemetery, recently built in the southern corner of the district, harmonized with the general landscape.

Local Attachments

On the flatlands south of the pond extended the most densely settled area, the village of Jamaica Plain, referred to here as Pondside. The village center was located at the fork in the road where Centre Street turned west and the appropriately named South Street began. Formerly the location of John Polley's seventeenth-century farm, the intersection was the site of a unified ensemble of late Georgian colonial structures—the Congregational church and parsonage, the Loring-Greenough mansion and its outbuildings, and the Weld Academy. Nearby stood Seaver's, the neighborhood's original general store.

From here a rudimentary webbing of roads and houses extended toward the pond in one direction and toward the railroad and turnpike in the other. Various stores dotted Centre Street, and a string of artisans' shops lined Green Street. Several small manufacturing plants sat here and there along the Stony Brook. Surprising numbers of workers' cottages and boardinghouses were scattered throughout the district and clustered in the more remote areas.

Although a superficial glance seemed to indicate that Jamaica Plain was still a farming community at the middle of the nineteenth century, this was a view rooted more in the past than in the present. During the seventeenth century the English Puritans settled the Town of Roxbury as part of the great migration to the Massachusetts Bay. Similar to the dispersal process in other seventeenth-century New England agricultural towns, as Roxbury's population increased, some of the town's inhabitants moved away from the original cluster of house lots at the town center to farm the unimproved lands in the south and west. As early as 1632, three families, including that of William Heath, staked out homesteads south of Parker Hill on the banks of the Stony Brook. Within a few years William Curtis, John May, and other new settlers had created a string of house lots and farms along the Stony Brook valley.[6]

About the middle of the seventeenth century, John Polley established himself on Pond Plain, the flatlands that stretched between the Great (later Jamaica) Pond and the Stony Brook. For decades afterwards, settlers used Polley's farm (at the intersection of Centre and South streets) as a landmark to demarcate their boundaries. In the following decades the town allotted more lands, creating a swathe of new farms that stretched away from Polley's farm along the Highway to Dedham (Centre Street) to the southwest and southeast.[7]

Just as the Heath and Curtis clans anchored their family homesteads further north, for a century and a half the Weld family controlled a large tract of land between the road to Bear Marsh (South Street) and the

Highway to Dedham. Joseph Weld, an overseas cloth merchant in Roxbury, had received the land for his services in the town artillery. After Joseph Weld's death in 1646, his son John Weld inherited the farm and built a "mansion house," where he lived until his death, in 1691, as the leading citizen of the area.[8]

At some point in the late seventeenth century, the townspeople of Roxbury began to refer to the southwestern section of town as Jamaica. The earliest written records of the district's name were recorded in connection with a drive to start a school, the area's first institution. In October 1676 a resident named John Ruggles donated "to the inhabitants of Jamaica" a piece of land near John Polley's farm for the site of a new school building. The following year, a married couple contributed their local landholdings to the townspeople for the support "of the Schoole newly erected at the end of the Town of Roxbury commonly called Jamaica." In 1689 John Eliot, the Puritan missionary (who did not reside in the area), gave seventy-five acres south of the "Great Pond" to help maintain the school and schoolmaster "at that part of Roxbury, commonly called Jamaica or Pond Plain," for the district's children as well as "such negroes or Indians as may or shall come to said school." Eliot's gift provided the school with a solid financial foundation. In honor of this bequest, the institution, which still exists, became known as the Eliot School.[9]

Neither the name nor the sense of a neighborhood named Jamaica Plain, however, had as yet fully emerged. The name Jamaica at first referred vaguely to the other end of town from the earlier Roxbury settlement. For example, in 1683 the Town of Roxbury granted permission to "our brethren and friends at Jamaco" to make a "buring place," but it was built well to the southwest (near Walter Street) in what is now considered Roslindale. Subsequently the name Jamaica came into common use, but it was attached somewhat inconsistently to the names of sites within the area. The name Jamaica Plain was used as early as 1683, for instance, to refer, not to the neighborhood in general, but to Pond Plain specifically. In 1717 the town records mentioned a Jamaica School. As late as 1739 a petition asked for permission to draw water for a grain mill from Great Pond, although in 1746 a similar request referred to Jamaica Pond.[10]

The settlement of the Spring Street section in the late seventeenth century further delineated the area, but still its boundaries and identity remained indistinct. Named after a stream that ran through the settlement, Spring Street was located far to the southwest, near the Dedham border. (The Spring Street settlement served as the forerunner of the future neighborhood of West Roxbury Village.) In 1706, Joseph Weld and forty-four others living "at the west end of Roxbury towards Dedham, commonly called 'Jamaica End and Spring Street,'" submitted a petition to the General Court of Massachusetts requesting that, since they lived in "an out-part of the town, at great distance from the meeting house," they be allowed to form a separate precinct within the parish of Roxbury and be freed from taxes in support of the church in Roxbury center. This effort finally bore fruit in 1711, after the townspeople of upper Roxbury constructed a church on their own. Located near the burial ground, however, the new church belonged as much, if not more, to Spring Street as to Jamaica End. Only the southwestern section of modern Jamaica Plain was included in the new church district.[11]

During the eighteenth century, if not before, the farmers of Jamaica Plain, like those of other communities surrounding Boston, shifted from the earlier subsistence-and-surplus style of farming to agriculture production geared toward the Boston market. The growing numbers of Boston merchants, artisans, and others engaged in nonagricultural pursuits provided a lucrative market in foodstuffs for farmers in the adjacent territories. Outside Boston, for example, Charlestown's milk row produced dairy products for the port. Tradition holds that Joseph Curtis, whose farmstead was located next to Jamaica Pond, was the first farmer in the Boston area to use a horse-drawn wagon rather than panniers to cart produce to the port.[12]

In the mid-nineteenth century, the green acres and plotted rows of market gardens and farms scattered throughout the neighborhood still gave the district a rural atmosphere. In 1842 Thomas Gray could still describe his parish as "one perfect garden, resembling the best cultivated villages near London," where "wealthy and respectable farmers" raised hay and produce for the Boston market. Like outer Cambridge, Massachusetts, Jamaica Plain still specialized in urban-oriented agriculture. Representatives of the Weld, Curtis, May, and Heath families, descendants of the first Puritan settlers, lent the neighborhood a sense of historic continuity with its seventeenth-century past. Other local agriculturists, such as Leonard Hyde, Amos Holbrook, Isaac Wyman, and Paul Gore, were later arrivals but of similar Yankee stock.[13]

Nonetheless, agriculture in Jamaica Plain had begun to decline sharply. As recently as 1840 the federal census taker had categorized 66 percent of the adult male population within the boundaries of modern Jamaica Plain as working in "agriculture," a figure that included large numbers of agricultural laborers as well as farmers. By 1850, however, the number of people active in local agriculture had shrunk dramatically. In that year, only 10 percent of 436 employed heads of households were listed as farmers. Another 25.5 percent of the working population were laborers, of whom probably most tilled the soil. By the end of the nineteenth century, subdivisions of houses would replace all but a few farms. By then only place names such as Hyde Square and Heath, Wyman, and Paul Gore streets would preserve the memory of the men who had once tilled the Jamaica Plain soil.

At mid-century, the wealthy of Jamaica Plain made up another segment of the local population, one that also contributed to the sense of the district as a rural place and had historic connections to the neighborhood. In 1842 Thomas Gray suggested their importance to the community when, in describing Jamaica Plain, he first pointed to the wealthy persons who inhabited "several gentlemen's elegant seats, beautifully situated on the banks of the lake, and elsewhere," and who crowded into the neighborhood to flee the city heat in the summer. Interspersed among the working farms, the gentlemen's pleasure grounds, orchards, lawns, and gardens contributed significantly to the pastoral image of the neighborhood.[14]

Like the farmers, the wealthy estate owners derived from British-American stock and had lived in Jamaica Plain since the colonial period. Following the fashion prevalent in Great Britain, colonial merchants and government officials created estates in the countryside outside Philadelphia, New York, and other major American towns to use as summer or retirement homes. Although built on a smaller scale than their models in the mother country, these country estates incorporated the architecture and landscaped grounds characteristic of their British counterparts.[15]

During the eighteenth century, numerous Georgian-style country houses and estates sprang up in the towns surrounding the port of Boston. In Medford, Isaac Royall, a West Indian planter, built a handsome mansion; at Unquity Hill, Milton, Thomas Hutchinson, the preeminent Massachusetts provincial official, created a tasteful country home and gardens, and along Brattle Street in Cambridge several prominent Bostonians built a group of country houses that became known as "Tory Row." Lower Roxbury, the section of the town closest to Boston, boasted several similar country estates, the most important of which was Shirley Mansion, built in 1747 by Governor William Shirley, pronounced to be "one of the most formal and imposing houses of the eighteenth century." As in other outlying communities, Boston merchants and high government officials established country houses in Jamaica Plain.[16]

The gentrification of Jamaica Plain began in 1740, when Eleazer May, the great-grandson of the seventeenth-century settler John May, sold a tract between Centre Street and the Stony Brook to Benjamin Faneuil, the nephew of the great Boston merchant Peter Faneuil. Then, in 1745 Joshua Cheever, a "wealthy Bostonian," purchased the old John Polley farm. In 1752 Cheever's heirs sold it to Joshua Loring, a Roxbury resident who had married Mary Curtis, a descendant of the early Jamaica Plain settler William Curtis. After service as a privateer, Loring became a Royal Navy officer, reaching the rank of commodore during the French and Indian War. At the intersection of South and Centre streets Loring built a handsome Georgian mansion (the Loring-Greenough house), where he retired in 1760 after being severely wounded in the war. Other eminent owners of Jamaica Plain country seats included John Troutbeck, a rector of King's Chapel, Boston's Anglican church, and Benjamin Hallowell, a collector, comptroller, and commissioner of customs at Boston. Hallowell acquired his country seat through his wife, Mary Boylston, a member of a family of wealthy Boston merchants.[17]

The creation of a prestigious country-house community in Jamaica Plain reached a climax in 1764, when the provincial governor of Massachusetts, Francis Bernard, built a summer house on the banks of Jamaica Pond. Established on a sixty-acre estate, Bernard's country seat included a coach house, stables, and, to accommodate his horticultural interests, a greenhouse for exotic plants and an orchard, where Bernard reportedly raised orange, lemon, fig, cinnamon, and cork trees. An amateur architect—in 1764 he drew the plan for the new Harvard Hall at Harvard College—Bernard probably designed the three-story country house, with its "elegant hall" that measured twenty-four by fifty feet.[18]

During the Revolution, most of Jamaica Plain's estate owners sided with Great Britain, fled the country, and had their properties confiscated. As elsewhere, after the Revolution new owners, many of them members of the new American elite, replaced the disgraced Loyalists on the country estates in Jamaica Plain. Martin Brimmer, for example, a leading Boston merchant, purchased Francis Bernard's house and lived there until his death in 1804. After John Hancock resigned from the presidency of the Congress of the United States in 1777, he moved to a country seat next to Jamaica Pond. Even spartan Samuel Adams, who succeeded Hancock as governor, succumbed: in 1794 he moved to the Peacock, a former tavern on a forty-acre estate located between Jamaica Plain and West Roxbury.[19]

During the first half of the nineteenth century, the custom of keeping country and summer houses in Jamaica Plain continued to thrive. In 1784 Ann Doane, a wealthy widow, purchased the former Loring mansion and estate and married David Stoddard Greenough, an attorney and son of a member of the revolutionary Committee of Correspondence. Over the next 140 years, five generations of men named David Stoddard Greenough occupied this house. About 1800 John Collins Warren, the eminent Boston surgeon, acquired and rebuilt the country house of Benjamin Pemberton, and Benjamin Hallowell's son, Ward Nicholas Boylston, a wealthy merchant, reclaimed the family tract and created the Hermitage near what became Boylston Street. In 1802, on a hill overlooking Jamaica Pond, James Perkins, a very wealthy China trade merchant, built a summer home, Pinebank, where his descendants would live for much of the nineteenth century.[20]

One of the most remarkable of the new estates was that of Samuel Griswold Goodrich. In 1833 Goodrich, the author of the Peter Parley tales, an extremely successful series of pedagogical children's books, "retired" to Jamaica Plain in order to restore his health. Together with his wife (and trustees), Goodrich assembled a domain from John Collins Warren and others that stretched all the way from Centre Street to Forest Hills Street between the Greenough and Boylston estates. On this great estate the author reportedly cleared over a hundred acres of forest to create Rockland, a landscaped estate of gardens, barn, stables, sheds, and, set far back from Centre Street, an elegant white house with a great piazza. In 1840 Goodrich suffered financial reverses and sold this house and some of his holdings; the family lived in a converted gardener's shed until Goodrich recouped his losses and moved them to a new house on another portion of the property.[21]

Possessed of great wealth, the estate owners exerted a strong influence upon the early development of Jamaica Plain. During the eighteenth century, a time when town life still revolved very much around the local church, estate owners helped organize, endow, and support the area's first religious institution. In 1760 Benjamin Pemberton, a Boston merchant and clerk of the Superior Court of Massachusetts, and his wife Susanna acquired from their relative Benjamin Faneuil his estate, complete with West Indian–style cottage, piazza, and gardens. Once settled in, Susanna Pemberton convinced her husband that local residents needed to have their own church close at hand. In 1769 Benjamin Pemberton helped pay for the construction of the new church building in Jamaica Plain, and in the following years he negotiated with the leaders of Roxbury's First and Second parishes, who were reluctant to lose members and contributions. Pemberton paid out £534 to compensate the Second Parish and took the dispute with the First Parish to the General Court of Massachusetts. The

Local Attachments

new church, originally called the Congregational Society of the Third Parish in Roxbury and later renamed the First Congregational Society of Jamaica Plain, stood opposite the Loring-Greenough mansion, thus anchoring the site as a center of the community.[22]

The First Church, however, represented a limited segment of the community. Although the boundaries of the new church parish coincided closely with the future boundaries of urban Jamaica Plain, most members lived in a much smaller area between Boylston Street and Moss Hill. Furthermore, the institution depended greatly upon its wealthy patrons. The church suffered when its first minister, William Gordon, alienated its chief supporters, Pemberton and Hancock. After Gordon resigned the pastorship to write the history of the American Revolution, for which he is best known, the society drifted for a number of years. In the years following the war, times were generally hard, and without patronage it was difficult to support a minister. Often the church doors were closed, and once some parishioners unsuccessfully attempted to reunite with the Second Parish. Stability returned in 1796 with the arrival of a new pastor, Thomas Gray, who carefully cultivated well-to-do parishioners over his long tenure at the First Church.[23]

During the first half of the nineteenth century, estate owners also asserted leadership in the repeated efforts to separate their community from Roxbury's government. Jamaica Plain's great landholders including Ward N. Boylston, David S. Greenough, Jr., Samuel G. Goodrich, and Joseph Curtis, a prosperous vegetable farmer and property owner, formed local separatist committees. As large property owners, they wanted to minimize their property taxes by avoiding paying for the urban improvements demanded by the growth of lower Roxbury. By placing Jamaica Plain and the rest of upper or southwestern Roxbury under an independent government, they hoped to create and preserve a wealthy suburban enclave for themselves. Similarly, during the nineteenth century the First Congregational Society became an exclusive institution principally controlled by the wealthy landholders and other prominent residents.[24]

At the same time that rich farmers and wealthy estate owners were attempting to preserve Jamaica Plain as a well-to-do rural village, the arrival of upper-middle-class Boston commuters added a distinctly urban element to the local population. Living in "cottages," they were, as Gray described them, "private gentlemen, who retire, every evening, from their business in the city, and pass as much of their time as consists with it, in this delightful spot." Despite the difficulties in distinguishing such commuters from the wealthy of Jamaica Plain, it is clear that at mid-century their numbers had recently increased dramatically. In 1840 the census categorized 13 percent of the adult male population of Jamaica Plain as working in "commerce" and 5 percent as working in the "learned professions" and engineering. In 1850 the proportion of major proprietors and professionals among the working heads of households had risen to 21 percent and 7 percent, respectively. The proportion of business executives represented the second largest percentage of any occupational group. The vast majority of the upper-middle-class men, as well as most of the neighborhood's clerks, commuted to work in Boston.[25]

These commuters and their families were participating in a large suburban movement that had originated in Great Britain but had become popular in New York, Philadelphia, and other American cities. In the United States the preaching of writers such as Andrew Jackson Downing, a promoter of landscape gardening, and Catherine Beecher, the author of women's advice manuals, provided a persuasive rationale for this trend. Strong believers in the influence of the external environment on the individual, they celebrated the domestic life of the middle-class family and expounded the notion that semirural natural settings provided the ideal environment for the family home. As the possibilities for railroad and coach travel into and out of the city increased, growing numbers of urban dwellers answered the siren calls of domesticity and rural surroundings and moved to the periphery.[26]

In the City of Boston, geography added an additional motivation to expand residential areas outward. The city was situated on a narrow peninsula; as the population and commerce of the city grew, land became scarce. Thus, like their counterparts in other cities, increasing numbers of Boston businessmen and professionals sought homes in Cambridge, Somerville, Brookline, and other green towns on the urban periphery. As the innermost community on the land route adjacent to the peninsula, at mid-century Roxbury had the largest proportion of commuters of all the towns surrounding Boston. Many Boston commuters took up residence in Jamaica Plain, where the farms and country estates seemed to offer an ideal form of suburban living.[27]

Like the residents of Roxbury, Charlestown, Cambridge, and other outlying communities, Jamaica Plainers chose from several modes of transportation for trips to Boston. Farmers, laborers, and hucksters usually traveled by horseback, wagon, or, "often heavily laden," on foot. The wealthy traditionally moved about in private carriages. Public transportation came in the form of horse-drawn stagecoaches that initially took either Centre Street or the Norfolk and Bristol Turnpike to Roxbury and

Boston. The coaches came in three main types: accommodation, express, and hourly stages. Favored by occasional travelers and shoppers, the accommodation stages stopped for passengers at their homes when signaled. In 1826 the hourly stages began regular runs from Jamaica Plain to Roxbury, and from there to Boston. The "hourlies," as they were known, became increasingly popular, especially after the introduction of the large omnibus coach in the 1830s. Express stages ran from the New York boat at Providence and took on passengers without heavy luggage for double pay at horse relay stations. Only businessmen could afford the speedy but expensive express stages.[28]

The establishment of regular railroad service to points outside the neighborhood offered another alternative in local transportation. In 1834 the Boston and Providence Railroad began service between its Boston depot and Dedham; the following year service was extended to Providence, Rhode Island. The founders of the Boston and Providence Railroad, like those of other Boston area railroads and the turnpike before them, hoped to capture long-distance traffic. The schedules of the trains were arranged to coincide with the arrivals and departures of New York steamboats in Providence. In Jamaica Plain, the company's track ran along the valley of the Stony Brook. Residents could flag the slow-moving vehicles as they passed through the large estates and farms of the Lowell, Amory, Curtis, and other families.[29]

Despite the conventional assumption that the available means of transport dictated the habits of urban dwellers, the history of Jamaica Plain supports a growing body of evidence that urban residents themselves played a large part in determining metropolitan transportation and settlement patterns. In the 1830s, for example, Boston businessmen living in Jamaica Plain and other places between Boston and Dedham demanded that the Boston and Providence Railroad provide discounted, or *commutation,* fares such as those offered by ferries and omnibus companies. In 1839 the directors of the railroad responded to the demand by inaugurating a special car with low fares for daily round-trip tickets. This practice set a precedent that other Boston-area railroads soon followed and thus helped popularize the term *commuter* to describe an individual who traveled to work. Initially the train was only a single coach, however, and during the first years traffic was light. Robert Morse, Jr., the son of a prosperous Boston businessman, later recalled that during his youth in the early 1840s the train stopped in Jamaica Plain only infrequently; he remembered far more vividly the uncomfortable hourlies, which jiggled their passengers into Boston from Jamaica Plain and Roxbury.[30]

Although carriages, wagons, and coaches continued to be the most popular means of transportation into and out of Boston, by the mid-1840s the rising number of businessmen and professionals living in Jamaica Plain and other communities outside Boston increased the potential profits to be made from short-distance urban railroad travel. The Boston and Providence dropped its commuter fares; by 1850 the trip from Jamaica Plain Station to Boston cost ten cents, two and one-half cents less than the omnibus. As a result of the increased local rail traffic, the company that operated the Norfolk and Bristol Turnpike lost business and profitability. In 1843 the counties through which the road passed purchased the franchise and operated it as the Dedham Turnpike until the 1850s. In 1849 the directors of the Boston and Providence estimated that 320 regular commutation passengers departed and arrived from the eight stations between Dedham and Boston. With depots at Boylston Street, Green Street, and Toll Gate, the Jamaica Plain territory contributed a large portion of this traffic.[31]

Even as they helped to reshape the forms of urban transportation, the new commuters of Jamaica Plain altered the residential character of Jamaica Plain and other outlying communities. Together with the wealthy retirees and summer home residents, the commuters helped to create well-to-do villages that foreshadowed today's rural exurbanite communities.

In Jamaica Plain, most commuters lived near the old village center, at Pondside and Glenvale, usually on smaller house lots than the nearby estates. Many were wholesale merchants, who, though often younger and sometimes less rich than the semiretired estate owners, represented the first wave of commuters into Boston's early suburban communities. In 1842, for example, Thomas W. Seaverns, a thirty-eight-year-old Boston tea merchant, bought Lakeville, an old brick mansion built in Pondside in 1797. Three years later, Franklin Greene, Jr., then also thirty-eight and a Boston merchant (later he became an insurance-company executive), moved nearby into a handsome Italian villa–style house that still stands on Lakeville Place. In 1850 other Pondside residents included William D. Ticknor, president of the well-known Boston publishing house of Ticknor and Fields, and Anson Dexter, a member of a Boston and Roxbury firm that manufactured fringe, tassel, and silk.[32]

Since the 1830s, the new residents had pushed across Centre Street to Glenvale. Here, next to Charles Hill, lived Calvin Young, a lime and building-material merchant in Boston, who purchased portions of the old Warren estate. In 1845 Benjamin Wing, a Boston physician, bought the Ward Nicholas Boylston country seat, and at about the same time, Kilby Page, another wealthy Boston merchant, built a stylish Greek Revival house on Centre Street between Wing and Hill.[33]

Local Attachments

Not all of the new commuters were wealthy. Because they worked bankers' hours, Boston bank officers and employees found that they also were able to commute from Roxbury and other Boston suburbs. Thus, two young bank tellers arrived in Pondside during the early 1840s. Charles H. Smith, a teller at the Grocers' Bank, owned a strikingly picturesque Gothic cottage that still stands today. John B. Witherbee, an ambitious young man who eventually became president of the North National Bank in Boston, built a Greek Revival house, also still extant.[34]

The growth of population in Jamaica Plain encouraged new forms of local economic activity. At first change had come to the neighborhood slowly. In the 1820s two private academies appeared in Pondside to take advantage of the well-to-do neighbors and the prosperous village atmosphere. Charles W. Greene converted Linden Hall, the old eighteenth-century Troutbeck mansion, into a private boarding school. In 1827 Stephen Minot Weld, a former teacher at Greene's school and a member of the old Jamaica Plain family, established Weld Academy in an imposing mansion opposite the Loring-Greenough house. Here he boarded and taught youth from not only the United States but foreign countries as well.[35]

As the new commuters arrived in increasing numbers in the 1840s, they encouraged local economic development of a different nature. Along with the wealthy retirees and summer people, the new arrivals created a vigorous neighborhood market for goods and services. As a result, local artisans, store owners, and lodging house keepers became a major component of the local working population. In 1840, according to the federal census taker, 16 percent of employed males worked in "manufactures and trades"; by 1850 more than 22 percent of Jamaica Plain's employed breadwinners were skilled workers and small store owners.

The most dramatic commercial development took place on Green Street, a thoroughfare that helped to expand the district's physical dimensions by linking Pondside to main transportation lines. Laid out in 1836–37 across Samuel G. Goodrich's lands, Green Street connected Centre Street just above Jamaica Plain Village to the railroad tracks and the Dedham Turnpike (later Washington Street). Although at first "a marsh with a cow-path and bars at the head of it," Green Street provided Jamaica Plain's new commuters with more direct access to Boston. Soon after Green Street was laid out, the Boston and Providence Railroad Company built a station there that became known as Jamaica Plain Station.[36]

Even as the road was being laid out, Goodrich began dividing the land on either side for sale. Such was the demand for lots that by 1842 another road, later known as Seaverns Avenue, was laid out parallel to Green Street. Most of the subdivided lots were purchased by local entrepreneurs who provided goods and services to the growing numbers of businessmen, professionals, and clerks in Jamaica Plain. The location was convenient for those customers who took the train or the old turnpike (Washington Street) to get to Boston. Soon Green Street and Seaverns Avenue were lined with the shops and homes of local artisans such as Isaac Hooper, a shoemaker and native of Maine, George H. and John E. Williams, enterprising harness makers, Alexander Dickson, a wheelwright (who married Susannah May, of the old Jamaica Plain family), and Benjamin Armstrong, Charles Draper, and Paul Lincoln, industrious local carpenters and house builders.[37]

As local residences and workshops multiplied, another commercial strip evolved along Centre Street, Jamaica Plain's main street, between Green and South streets. On Centre Street in Pondside stood a local institution, Seaver's general grocery store, founded in 1796 by Joshua Seaver and conducted from 1833 to 1883 by his son, Robert Seaver. On the corner of Centre and Green streets, George James operated another general store. Both Seaver and James supplied the neighborhood with West Indian goods, teas, coffee, spices, dairy products, and other groceries. Along Centre Street, Jamaica Plain residents could also purchase the wares of provision dealers and a clothing vendor. Two oyster shops provided refreshments for shoppers. In addition, J. Phillips George, the apothecary, ran a post office at the corner of Burroughs Street, and Charles B. Amos, an African-American barber, offered hairdressing.[38]

The growing local population of mid-nineteenth-century Jamaica Plain included many who belonged to faiths other than the Unitarian creed of the First Church of Jamaica Plain. The adherents of different faiths organized the First (St. John's) Episcopal Church in 1841, the First Baptist Church in 1843, and the Central Congregational Church in 1856. Like the stores that dotted Centre Street and like the neighborhood's original church, these new houses of worship were situated along the main thoroughfare, where they would be convenient to the residents of the adjoining Pondside and Glenvale districts.[39]

Manufacturing was common on the urban fringe of American cities of the early and mid-nineteenth century. A variety of factors dictated the placement of certain industries on the fringe. The districts beyond the cities offered advantageous locations to entrepreneurs who wished to process hinterland goods for urban markets. Many types of fringe manufacturing created noxious odors that necessitated sites away from residential areas. Other kinds of manufacturing required water power or large spaces, which were more readily available on the periphery.

Many communities in outer Boston engaged in the industrial production typical of the nineteenth-century urban periphery. Cambridge possessed glassworks that represented fringe manufacturing on a relatively large scale; its tanning, chandlery, and brickmaking characterized small-scale production. The Town of Roxbury built on its eighteenth-century experiences with butchering, tanning, and other processing of hinterland goods to become perhaps Boston's most industrialized early nineteenth-century suburb. Making use of the running water available from the Stony Brook and the Muddy River, lower Roxbury specialized in leather manufacture, shoe factories, machine shops, rope walks, carpet production, rubber companies, and other smaller industries. Although most of Roxbury's industrial activity was concentrated in the inner section of town that was closest to Boston, in the late 1840s an iron foundry, a tannery, and a brewery were established between Parker Hill and the Stony Brook, close to the modern boundaries of Jamaica Plain.[40]

Jamaica Plain also developed manufacturing, which is not surprising given the presence of the Stony Brook and the proximity of industrial enterprises in Roxbury. Although in 1850 the district's manufacturing sector was still relatively small, it contrasted sharply with the suburban image projected by the village at Pondside. Although local manufactures employed relatively few residents in 1850, they represented an important element in the local community. The small factories and other industrial buildings represented a distinct and noticeable form of land use, and one that, as in Cambridge and other suburban communities, would grow in the following years.

As early as the eighteenth century, Samuel "Tanner" Heath, near Heath Street, and John Keyes, near South Street, cashed in on Roxbury's role as a processing center for hinterland goods by using the waters of the Stony Brook to ply the tanning trade. A form of extractive production began in 1795, when the Jamaica Pond Aqueduct Corporation was formed to pump water into Boston. Although not a great financial success, the Aqueduct Corporation supplied Boston until 1848 and afterwards Roxbury, Brookline, and West Roxbury until 1886, when the City of Boston purchased it.[41]

Typical of production on the urban fringe, the early forms of Jamaica Plain manufacturing, such as that of chemicals, glue, tallow, and soap, were activities too noxious to be located close to dense settlements. Two chemical factories were established in 1832 at remote locations along the

Stony Brook and were still operating in 1850. Located far to the north, at Hog's Bridge (where Centre Street and the railroad intersected), the Roxbury Color and Chemical Company had developed by 1850 a small complex with a chimney taller than the Bunker Hill Monument.[42]

Closer to the center of Jamaica Plain, the site of the Norfolk Laboratory, south of Boylston Street, became the center of the Brookside industrial zone. In 1837 Samuel Jackson bought one of Samuel Goodrich's Green Street lots between the railroad tracks and the Stony Brook and later acquired adjacent properties on the aptly named Chemical Avenue (later Brookside Avenue and Cornwall Street). Jackson manufactured leather here and lived nearby in a Greek Revival house on the turnpike. In 1850 the area also contained Daniel Whittaker's soap plant and a chemical works where Epson salts, soda, and saltpeter were produced.[43]

In the 1840s other manufactories appeared elsewhere, creating a nascent industrial corridor. To the south, Edwin Evans and John F. J. Mayo operated a glue factory on the turnpike, west of South Street. To the north, Abijah Merriam ran a leather tannery at Boylston Street and the Stony Brook. Less than a half-mile away, near Egleston Square, Joseph Byron, an Irish currier, and his sons opened another leather-tanning business about 1848.[44]

Unskilled laborers are not usually considered part of suburban society, but they, too, represented an essential part of the economy of the urban fringe in the mid-nineteenth century. In the early stages of American industrialization, large numbers of laborers were needed to run the farms and estates of the periphery of the nation's cities. During the slack season, agricultural workers made up most of the initial labor force for fringe manufacturing. In early nineteenth-century Boston, such laborers were originally of New England stock.

During the middle decades of the nineteenth century, however, masses of Irish immigrants came to Boston looking for unskilled jobs and thus transformed the local labor force. The great bulk of the Irish found employment in the downtown warehouse and factory districts and settled near the waterfront in the crowded North End and Fort Hill sections. But thousands of other Irish immigrants found work as laborers, gardeners, hostlers, and domestic servants in the communities surrounding Boston. In the mid-nineteenth century, Irish immigrants constituted 22 percent of the population of Cambridge, Charlestown, and Somerville and more than 26 percent in Roxbury and West Roxbury. So great were the employment opportunities on estates in the Town of Brookline that Irish residents made up 30 percent of the elite suburb's population, a figure that even exceeded their percentage of Boston's population.[45]

Naturally, then, unskilled laborers represented a very large element of the Jamaica Plain population in 1850. Of the neighborhood's working population, 25.5 percent were laboring men who did the heavy work on the local farms and estates. Near Forest Hills Cemetery, for example, five laborers and three domestics lived with a farmer, John Parkinson. On the Greenough estate, the high-born William H. Sumner, who had married into the Greenough household, employed five laborers and two domestic servants. Some laborers also worked on construction sites, in the shops, and for the small manufactories of the district.

As in other communities, in Jamaica Plain Irish immigrants made up the great preponderance of poor and unskilled workers. Already by mid-century almost 20 percent of Jamaica Plain's heads of households were Irish-born. Of the district's breadwinners, two-thirds of the unskilled and semiskilled workers were Irish-born, and 90 percent of the Irish-born heads of households held unskilled and semiskilled jobs. The neighborhood's Irish population was even greater, however. More than two hundred domestic servants, most of whom were Irish women, helped run the big houses and care for the families of the upper and upper middle classes but were not counted in the out-of-doors work force.

The semiskilled and unskilled Irish and other workers who had their own homes lived in small clusters dispersed around Jamaica Plain. They could be found in Pondside, where, for example, James Flannery, his Irish-born wife, and three children lived. Michael Harney, who probably worked in a foundry, lived with his wife and family near Heath Street. Other Irish laborers, such as Henry McDonald, a resident of Chemical Avenue, dwelt in the embryonic industrial corridor between Egleston Square and Brookside. Still more of the unskilled resided on Green Street around the railroad and along the Dedham Turnpike (Washington Street). Many also lived in the Forest Hills area, near Toll Gate and Walk Hill Street, where they were in walking distance of the farms of Canterbury.

In 1850 Jamaica Plain was a fringe area with a mixed and inchoate personality. Although farmers still persisted in the district, the wealthy and the better-off commuters had come to predominate through their large numbers and extensive financial resources. In their desire to preserve a quiet suburban idyll in Jamaica Plain, these large property holders succeeded in winning the secession of the Town of West Roxbury from Roxbury in 1851. Scattered about the district and preoccupied with getting a secure foothold in their occupations, at mid-century the artisans, factory operatives, and laborers were still marginal to the central character of the place.

A lack of a collective memory demonstrated that the sense of a neighborhood identity still remained relatively undeveloped. Until Thomas Gray wrote his assessment of Jamaica Plain during the first surge of urban growth, no resident had produced a systematic account of the neighborhood's history. When Gray investigated the origin of the neighborhood's name, none of the residents, not even the elders, could produce a credible explanation for it. Gray dismissed as implausible the accounts of mythical summer residents from the Caribbean, legends about an Indian sachem with little connection to the district, and a tall tale about a London woman who found her runaway husband in Jamaica Plain after searching first in Jamaica. So sparse was the historical record that no evidence from earlier times survived to shed light on the question.[46]

Only much later, at the end of the nineteenth century, would residents begin to produce memoirs, reminiscences, and histories of their neighborhood. The authors of these narratives generally would treat the seventeenth century as obscure antiquity and the late eighteenth century as a romantic but forgotten age. In contrast, most would portray the mid-century era (which many remembered from their childhood) as the significant and vivid antecedent age, the fixed point against which later progress and change in Jamaica Plain could be measured. Thus they would attempt to implant in the community's shared consciousness an understanding of the origins of the very different place their neighborhood had become since mid-century.

But such consciousness lay in the future, a future that would endow Jamaica Plain with a new and more coherent identity than it had heretofore possessed. The prosperous owners of Jamaica Plain's estates and suburban villas would not control this future. Less than twenty-five years after they celebrated the establishment of the Town of West Roxbury in 1851, the community would turn the secession into a Pyhrric victory and reject their vision of the district as an elite suburb like neighboring Brookline. Nor would coalitions of upper-middle-class residents, businessmen, and entrepreneurs impose an agenda of controlled growth and independent jurisdiction as they did in the suburban communities of Somerville and Cambridge.[47]

Instead, as the Roxbury critics of secession had predicted, Jamaica Plain would embrace growth and the city. The heirs of those who had been marginal would contribute to the great change. The increasing number of middle- and working-class residents, diverse ethnic and religious groups, and local shopkeepers and factory owners ensured an urban future for the district. In 1873, an alliance of Jamaica Plain businessmen, development-minded property holders, and working-class and foreign-born residents would overcome the slow-growth opposition and vote to join the Town of West Roxbury to the City of Boston. Like Charlestown, Roxbury, and the other districts of West Roxbury, Jamaica Plain would throw its lot with the metropolis. Out of this process of growth and change, Jamaica Plain would shed its urban-fringe character and forge a new and more coherent identity as an urban neighborhood.

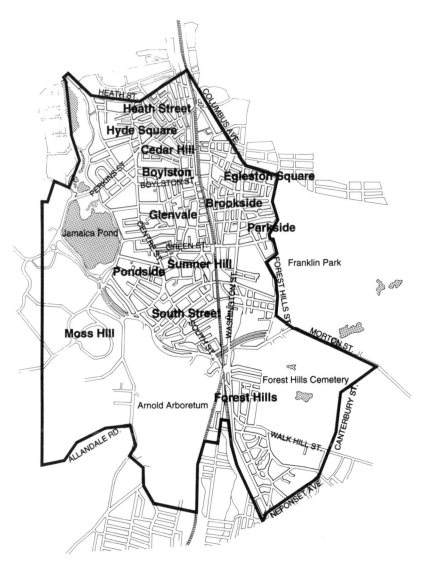

Jamaica Plain, including subdistricts, c. 1920

2

The Making of an Urban Place

The community is now, owing to the growth of Boston, a
very populous one. Electric and steam car lines furnish
cheap and frequent rapid transit. Accordingly, as with
other suburbs, there has been a noticeable increase in
population, in recent years. The consequence is that the
community has now virtually the conditions of city life.
            —*Sumner U. Shearman, 1904*

During the late nineteenth and early
twentieth centuries, soaring rates of economic activity, population growth,
and land development changed the United States from an agricultural
society into an urban nation. Throughout America's expanding urban
territories, the dynamics of growth reorganized space and transformed its
uses. Especially dramatic was the way the city spread, swallowing miles
and miles of the neighboring countryside to create sprawling urban districts. Where once quiet villages sat placidly and farmers raised crops and
grazed herds, now city folk bustled about a vast network of streets to their
homes, offices, factories, shops, churches, and schools.

Extrapolating from Sam Bass Warner's classic study of the development
of outer Boston, most urban historians have concluded that the great urban
expansion of the late nineteenth century sequestered residences from
workplaces, segregated residences by economic and social class, and
eroded community life. In the preindustrial walking city that existed
before 1850, business, commerce, and the residences of the high and low
huddled together in compact settlements. By 1900, according to this analysis, the spatial and social relations of the walking city had been reordered.

23

In the inner city, lower-class workers and immigrants concentrated in crowded tenement districts.[1]

In the outer city and the suburbs, transportation service and other factors separated residential areas into concentric rings that pushed outward as the city expanded. The wealthiest railroad commuters inhabited the band of settlement furthest from the center of the city. Nearer to the center, the provision of regular linear streetcar service created a band of the "central middle class," whose members included small downtown store owners, salesmen, lawyers, and large contractors. Frequent crosstown railway service confined members of the "lower middle class," including small shopkeepers, skilled workers, and clerks, to the territory closest to the center. Historians judged late-nineteenth-century city-building harshly. Warner declared that "nothing in the process [of outer-city construction] built communities or neighborhoods."[2]

Because this model of urban growth was based in part upon Jamaica Plain, the neighborhood's pattern of development illuminates the important question, How did American cities grow? Historians have concluded that late-nineteenth-century Jamaica Plain belonged to the upper-middle- and middle-class residential rings. By 1870, according to Warner, Jamaica Plain had developed a "substantial suburban colony" of the upper middle class. During the building booms of the 1880s and 1890s, the street railways provided only linear service here. Warner concluded that by 1900 Jamaica Plain had become a home for streetcar commuters of the central middle class. Jamaica Plain began life as a residential suburb, another historian declared, and remained one well into the twentieth century.[3]

A close look at Jamaica Plain's development, however, demonstrates that these characterizations do little justice to historical reality. In fact, the territory never constituted a homogeneous segment of the class-segregated city. And although it contained suburban elements, Jamaica Plain never conformed to the usual notions of a suburban community. During the second half of the nineteenth century, Jamaica Plain matured from a fringe district to a heterogeneous city neighborhood, a type of urban area that heretofore has not been generally recognized. It evolved into a local urban community, not as an isolated or segmented district, but as part of the larger growth patterns of Boston.

Transportation did help shape urban growth in Jamaica Plain, but its role was complex. Outer-city residents demanded and received inexpensive and frequent commuter service, which in turn encouraged more residents to settle there. In the latter nineteenth century, only some of the increasing number of commuters shuttled between Jamaica Plain and the downtown business district; many traveled relatively short distances to work in other Boston neighborhoods. Meanwhile, railroad cars filled with freight, not passengers, encouraged the establishment of local factories in and around Jamaica Plain. The growing opportunities for local employment now attracted commuters to Jamaica Plain from *other* neighborhoods.

As the local population grew, its diverse occupational structure and ethnic composition reflected larger trends in Boston as a whole. The presence of upper-middle-class families of downtown professionals and businessmen gave the neighborhood its reputation as a suburban type of community. Long before frequent transportation served the district, however, middle- and working-class people formed a majority of the local population.

In spatial terms, Jamaica Plain simultaneously developed elegant areas for the wealthy, middle-class residential districts, and industrial working-class sections. As the number of Jamaica Plain residents increased, neighborhood entrepreneurs met the growing market for local goods and services. Shops and business offices lined main thoroughfares and clustered in the busy squares adjacent to railroad depots. By the end of the century, Jamaica Plain encompassed numerous subdistricts, which belonged to relatively distinct residential, industrial, and commercial zones but were not arranged in concentric rings dedicated to specialized land uses.

Despite the district's connections to the world outside, as well as its heterogeneous character, urban development fostered a strong sense of neighborhood identity in Jamaica Plain. The construction of new buildings and streets filled in old settlement areas and converted distant and sparsely settled areas into urban territories. Over time, residents by general consensus expanded Jamaica Plain's boundaries by annexing the distant subdistricts to the neighborhood. The process of urban growth in the late nineteenth century created the neighborhood that is still recognized a century later as Jamaica Plain.

During the second half of the nineteenth century, dramatic explosions of growth reshaped most cities in the United States. Improvements in technology, including the increasing ability to tap electric power, expanded industrial capacity. National railroad and telegraph networks accelerated the speed of transportation and communications. As a result, regional and national economies took off, and commercial transactions in urban downtowns multiplied exponentially. America's large cities became great manufacturing centers and immense clearinghouses of wholesale and retail goods.

Exploiting its position as the economic capital of New England, the City of Boston became the leading dealer in the nation's wool and boot, shoe, and leather marts and an important wholesale center for textiles, food-stuffs, and other commodities. Besides creating new fortunes for those in the wholesale trade and related professions, the vigorous commercial activity encouraged new specialization and division of labor, which expanded the employment opportunities for managers, clerks, salesmen, and other white-collar personnel. Commerce and related industries also employed numerous blue-collar workers, including the unskilled (and often immigrant) laborers who moved goods in and out of the city.

At the same time, the Boston metropolitan economy, like that of other large American cities, benefited from a rising tide of urban industrial activity. During the late nineteenth century, Boston built on its early manufacturing activity to rank as one of the nation's leading industrial cities. In contrast to the specialized industrial production of smaller mill towns, the economies of large cities such as Philadelphia, New York, and Chicago rested on a diversified manufacturing base. Thus, Boston's leading manufacturers produced a wide array of goods, including machine-shop products, books and other printed materials, clothing, foodstuffs, furniture, and musical instruments.

Although American big business originated during the late nineteenth and early twentieth centuries, the size of urban manufactures varied widely. During the late nineteenth century, such Boston industries as textiles, boot and shoes, metal products, and distilling grew in numbers, scale, and organization. A range of large factories, from sweatshops to large manufacturing plants, offered thousands of blue-collar jobs and swelled the occupational ranks of the semiskilled factory operative with foreign and native migrants to the city. Paradoxically, however, during the era of corporations and mergers most production in Boston, as in other cities, took place in small-scale workshops and factories. In 1880, for example, the number of hands in Boston's manufacturing workplaces averaged only sixteen.[4]

Thus, even as the growth of the factory undermined their traditional position, urban artisans continued to play a large role in urban manufactures. Some still worked as skilled craftsmen in independent shops, some rose to become owner-entrepreneurs of small and medium-sized factories and retail outlets. Many others worked in larger establishments, either as skilled labor aristocrats or as debased operatives.

Attempting to take advantage of the growing number of urban economic opportunities, masses of people flooded into American cities during the nineteenth century. As historians have shown, not all who came to the city remained there. Cities such as Boston experienced only modest net growth in population relative to the vast tides of humanity that washed in and out. Some elements of the urban population moved away more often than others did. In Boston, those groups lower on the occupational ladder were the most mobile.[5]

However long they stayed, migrants from different parts of the United States and abroad swelled the populations of Boston and other cities. The great numbers of foreign immigrants radically changed the ethnic character of America's cities. Foreign immigrants made up 40 percent or more of the population of such cities as New York, Chicago, Detroit, and San Francisco. During the nineteenth century, the City of Boston attracted American migrants from New England and the foreign-born from the Canadian maritime provinces, Great Britain, Germany, and Scandinavia. By far the largest group of immigrants were the Irish, who poured into Boston not just during the great potato famine but through most of the nineteenth century. Near the turn of the century, members of other nationalities, such as eastern European Jews and Italians, began to arrive in Boston in large numbers.

The people who came to New York, Detroit, Omaha, and other cities discovered that economic opportunity was not evenly distributed among the different ethnic groups in the population. In Boston, native New Englanders and others of American stock tended to capture better-paying and more prestigious jobs. The Germans, British, Canadians, and Scandinavians concentrated in skilled blue-collar and middle-class white-collar jobs. At the other extreme from Yankees, the Irish concentrated heavily in unskilled jobs such as those of laborers and domestics. Their lowly status slowed the economic ascent of the Irish, but over time, as the fathers moved out of unskilled occupations, the following generations of Irish-Americans were able to compete with other ethnic groups.[6]

The increasing economic activity and the growing population in nineteenth-century American cities created new spatial arrangements that contrasted sharply with the extremely compact and mixed physical organization of the colonial port towns. Cities now produced distinct areas in which particular activities, land uses, and types of residences clustered. In the expanding downtowns of America's large cities, financial, legal, wholesale, retail, and subsidiary businesses clustered in special subdistricts. Boston developed specialized leather and textile wholesale districts, a famous banking center on State Street, and its own newspaper row. In Boston and other cities, luxury shops, large department stores, and theaters and concert halls located near the wholesale and administrative districts.

Warehouse and industrial enterprises that fed the urban economy concentrated at the water and rail transportation sites convenient to the downtown. In the late nineteenth century, piers, warehouses, and manufacturing plants filled the waterfront of the Boston peninsula, as well as nearby sites in Charlestown, East Boston, and South Boston.

Inner-city residential development produced clusters that were most discernible at the social extremes. Mansions with landscaped parks, often located in the vicinity of the luxury shopping district, identified the residential areas of the wealthy. Crowded slum buildings for the unskilled laboring classes usually emerged near the warehouse district. In some cities, these areas were surprisingly close to one another. In central Boston, for example, on one side of Beacon Hill a highly prestigious neighborhood looked on the Boston Common, the Charles River, and the fashionable Back Bay district; on the other side, a working-class and transient population faced the immigrant slums of the North End, the West End, and the industrial waterfront. Beyond and between, stretches of row houses, detached homes, and boardinghouses provided residences for a wide range of intermediate income and occupation levels.

During the late nineteenth century, economic activity and population spilled out of the inner cities and transformed the surrounding metropolitan region. Across the Boston metropolitan district, the area of greatest growth, in both percentage terms and absolute numbers, shifted during the second half of the nineteenth century away from the inner peninsula to the city's periphery. This growth created vital subsidiary centers in the outer territory of cities such as Boston.[7]

Physically, outer-city districts usually looked different from the inner-city environs. Here detached frame residences, as opposed to the urban row house, were the dominant element; minimal but separate workers cottages replaced the crowded tenements and subdivided homes of the inner-city slums. In the early stages of their development, outer-city neighborhoods still contained open fields and villas and other elements that projected a suburban and even rural image. But over time they were built up with side streets of single-, double-, and multiunit structures (often cleverly disguised to look like single-family dwellings), corridors of commercial and apartment buildings, and mill complexes along the railroad tracks. Development bestowed upon the outer-city neighborhoods a distinctive but essentially urban character.[8]

With the important exceptions of certain centralized functions such as large-scale banking and wholesale commerce, which remained downtown, outer-city urban growth reflected most of the same land uses and activities that occurred in the inner city. No law of social science, but specific circumstances, dictated the land uses and character of a particular district. Geographic or topological conditions, transportation facilities, employment opportunities, and historic precedents staked out a territory for a particular group or uses. In addition, long-term movements of occupational and ethnic subgroups could alter the population of outer-city districts.

The upper and middle classes, of course, located in the outer as well as the inner city. As historians have carefully documented, a "rural" or "suburban" ideal attracted a broadening base of the population to the urban periphery in the late nineteenth century. In urban centers across the country, the wealthy settled on the edge of the built-up section of the city and in the semirural environs outside the city. Whether in neighborhoods that boasted sumptuous palaces and gracefully landscaped parks or in suburbs lined with lush greenery, the wealthy earned the admiration of the upper middle class, whose members soon followed them to these locales. Wherever they could afford it, the urban middle classes also adopted the detached house, planted yard, and other elements of the suburban ideal that would become institutionalized in the twentieth century. Members of the upper and upper middle classes could be found in genteel railroad commuter suburbs, for example, along the Main Line outside Philadelphia and on Chicago's North Shore. These upper-crust communities usually also housed a laborer population to service the big houses and gardens of the well-to-do.[9]

At the same time, the long-term decentralization of urban manufacturing also brought workers to the urban periphery. In both old eastern manufacturing powerhouses such as Philadelphia and young robust midwestern centers such as Chicago and Detroit, industry pushed outward along rail lines and waterways in search of space and transportation facilities. In Boston as elsewhere, the expansion of industry created irregular geographic patterns that defied idealized models of urban growth.[10]

As studies of nineteenth-century Philadelphia show, most blue-collar workers lived within a mile of their job. Large communities of industrial workers therefore settled in such districts as Spring Garden and Richmond in outer Philadelphia, South Chicago and Pullman outside Chicago, and Ivorydale and Norwood in suburban Cincinnati. A ring of heavily working-class mill towns including New Bedford, Lynn, Lowell, and Lawrence surrounded Boston. Not all working-class immigrants bottled up in inner-city ghettos. They also dispersed to the periphery—the Italians of Chicago's South Side and West Side, for example, and the Poles of east Detroit and Hamtramck—seeking employment wherever it could be found.[11]

Thus, some outer-city districts reflected the same extremes of urban society that could be found in the inner city. As early as the 1890s, prestigious suburban communities waged battles against the working-class saloons and other encroachments of the industrial towns. "The clashing forces of diversity," one historian has written, "were as evident along the urban fringe as in the heart of the metropolis."[12]

More often than has been recognized, however, the multifaceted character of urban development also created heterogeneous outer-city neighborhoods and suburbs. Like the inner sections of the nineteenth-century city, these districts developed residential and industrial clusters often within close proximity to one another. As these diverse neighborhoods grew, so did the residential areas for different social and economic classes within them. In his history of the American suburb, John R. Stilgoe describes the jumbled quality of development in the West Philadelphia neighborhood and in Jefferson Township outside Chicago. Few historians have commented on heterogeneous urban neighborhoods, but research suggests that other diverse districts developed in outer Philadelphia, Milwaukee, and San Francisco.[13]

In the Boston area, heterogeneity abounded during the late nineteenth century. Diverse land uses thrived in Roxbury, whose urban impulses led it to join the City of Boston in 1868. In addition to its many small workshops (such as that of the innovative lithographer Louis Prang), Roxbury acquired numerous manufacturing firms, including breweries and belting, carpet, and oilcloth factories, many of which located in the Stony Brook valley. At the same time, the Roxbury Highlands flourished as a district of estates and homes for solidly middle-class commuters. Even the industrial neighborhood of South Boston, a bastion of the working-class Irish and home of the New England Confectionery Company and the Gillette Razor Company, contained prosperous, suburban-style sections. The independent suburban cities of Cambridge and Somerville also encompassed both industrial development and housing for the upper and middle classes. Far from being unique, Jamaica Plain reflected the heterogeneous tendencies of the outer city in Boston and other urban centers.[14]

The history of transportation services in Jamaica Plain reveals that the role of transportation in outer-city development is more complex than has generally been understood. Rather than being passive objects of inexorable technological forces, outer-city residents themselves often demanded improvements in commuter services. About 1850 the new residents of Jamaica Plain and other outlying communities discovered the commuting possibilities of the railroad. By 1854 the directors of the Boston and Providence Railroad Corporation estimated that two-thirds of its passengers between Boston and Dedham, double the proportion just five years earlier, were paying "commutation" fares and noted that some commuters were making two trips a day. When the company, in concert with other Boston area lines, raised commuter fares, it sparked a protest from residents of outlying sections, who now depended upon the railroad for transportation to and from Boston. In their remonstrance, a group of Dedham residents estimated that four hundred riders, including three hundred commuter fares, regularly embarked from the Roxbury station and the three Jamaica Plain depots, Boylston Street Station, Jamaica Plain Station, and Toll Gate Station (later renamed Forest Hills Station after the nearby cemetery.)[15]

The railroad, however, did not just promote residential areas for prosperous suburban commuters; it also carried freight and thus promoted industrial development in the outer city. As with commuter traffic, demand for better freight rail services prompted improvements in railroad services. In order to save themselves the expense of teaming their wares to the trains, brewers and other Stony Brook factory owners in 1867 persuaded the state legislature to require the railroad to build a new station with loading facilities at Heath Street near Parker Hill. Although the directors of the railroad managed to get the 1867 act repealed, by 1872 they had provided a station at Heath Street, which in turn encouraged the location of more factories along the northern border of Jamaica Plain.[16]

In the following years both commuting and freight traffic increased along the lines of the Boston and Providence Railroad. To handle the additional movement on the rails, the company added a second track by 1860 and, after acquiring from John Amory Lowell some low-lying portions of his estate, a third track in 1870. In 1871 and 1872 all the Jamaica Plain station houses, as well as those at other sites, had to be rebuilt. Although historians have concluded that skilled workers were confined to those parts of the inner city where streetcar fares were low and service was most frequent, at least some Boston artisans could afford to travel to work by railroad. By 1873 the number of piano factory workers commuting to the South End neighborhood of Boston from Jamaica Plain and other stops along the line had grown so numerous that the railroad enlarged its South End station in order to accommodate them. The company named the new station Chickering's, after Chickering and Sons, the great piano manufacturing company that employed the commuters.[17]

As railroad and streetcar service became more frequent in the late nineteenth century, increasing numbers of people traveled into and out of Jamaica Plain for work, recreation, and even worship. In the 1880s the Boston and Providence Railroad Corporation began leasing its tracks to the Old Colony Railroad Company, and in 1893 the New York, New Haven, and Hartford Railroad acquired the Old Colony and the local line. In the 1890s the railroad added a fourth track and ran at least four trains an hour during rush and early evening hours between Boston and the Jamaica Plain stations. (Further away from Boston, suburban branch-line stations at Roslindale, West Roxbury, and Dedham received less frequent service.) In addition, the railroad built new spurs to service neighborhood factories.[18]

The growing demand for commuter service created an incentive to provide alternative means of local transport, and in this, too, local residents played a role in obtaining service. In 1856 the Metropolitan Railroad Company initiated a horse railcar line, the Boston area's second, from downtown Boston to Roxbury. The next year the West Roxbury Railroad Company extended a Jamaica Plain line down Centre Street to a depot on South Street. In 1861 Jamaica Plain residents John Gould Weld and David S. Greenough petitioned the town for a second track to improve service. Although this move failed initially, within a few years the Metropolitan Company took over the line and offered service every half-hour between Boston and Jamaica Plain and every hour between Boston and Forest Hills Station. In 1863 residents of Washington Street cooperated with the Metropolitan Company by petitioning the government to allow service on their street.[19]

The era of rapid transit dawned in 1889, when the West End Street Railway Company, which had absorbed the old streetcar companies two years before, started to electrify its streetcars. Answering the insistent demands of customers for low, five-cent fares and frequent cars, in the 1890s the West End Company provided almost continual service between Jamaica Plain and downtown Boston (every three minutes during rush hours and every eight minutes at other times) and regular service (every ten to fifteen minutes) between Forest Hills Station and Boston. In 1909 the local facilities for mass transit increased when the Boston Elevated Railway extended its elevated tracks from Dudley Street, Roxbury, to new stations at Egleston Square and Forest Hills (after demands from outer-city residents), and in 1912, after pressure from the Jamaica Plain community, it added an elevated station at Green Street.[20]

Urban historians have had little to say about crosstown commuting

Local Attachments

before the automobile era, but the evidence here suggests that the practice dated from the nineteenth century. As early as the 1860s, Jamaica Plain had become a *destination* for some commuters from other parts of the Boston area. Journeymen carpenters from Cambridge, South Boston, Dorchester, Dedham, and Boston, for example, traveled to work at John J. Shaw's large carpentry shop at Green Street, near the railroad depot. Albert Palmer came from his Roxbury home to Pond Street to sell the ice his company harvested from Jamaica Pond. John D. Billings, master of Jamaica Plain's Central School, journeyed all the way from Canton, Massachusetts, and schoolteachers who lived in Roxbury, Dedham, and other nearby communities also came to work at Jamaica Plain schools. By the turn of the century, the growth of neighborhood businesses and institutions, especially large factories of the Thomas G. Plant and B. F. Sturtevant companies, attracted noticeable numbers of streetcar commuters into Jamaica Plain from other Boston neighborhoods. Such streetcar commuting to outer-city factories was common practice in American cities by the early twentieth century.[21]

Spurred by local and regional economic growth, transportation improvements, and the long-term movement of Bostonians away from the center city, the population in Jamaica Plain surged. While under the government of the Town of West Roxbury, the population of Jamaica Plain more than tripled, from more than twenty-seven hundred people to about nine thousand. After annexation to the City of Boston, the number of Jamaica Plainers continued to climb, from nearly thirteen thousand in 1880 to almost thirty-three thousand in 1900. By 1910 the local population had reached forty thousand. (See table 2.1.)

Like the population of Boston as a whole, the population of Jamaica Plain grew in spite of the fact that many inhabitants resided in the neighborhood for relatively brief periods. Analysis of the length of residence of sample individuals drawn from the census manuscripts of 1880 and 1900, for example, indicates that at least a third of the neighborhood population disappeared from the district over a given ten-year period. These rates of geographic mobility matched and perhaps exceeded those of the Boston area as a whole. Unlike the entire Boston population, those who left the neighborhood were relatively evenly distributed among the occupational groups. (See table 2.2.)

A constellation of factors pushed and pulled urban dwellers and influenced their decisions concerning where to live and how long to stay. Proximity to employment, of course, served to attract people to the neigh-

TABLE 2.1

Local Populations, 1850–1910

Year	Jamaica Plain	Roxbury	West Roxbury	Boston
1850	2,730	15,060	3,304	136,811
1865	5,450	28,426	6,912	192,318
1875	9,190	50,429	11,783	341,919
1880	12,810	57,123	14,032	362,839
1900	32,750	105,393	37,263	560,892
1910	40,620	117,727	45,594	670,585

Notes: Jamaica Plain population figures are estimates based on the number of heads of households and the average number of residents in a household for 1850, 1880, 1900, and 1910. The 1875 figure represents 78 percent of the state census figure for West Roxbury, the share the neighborhood had in 1865. Alternatively, the number of 1872 polls (the approximate number of heads of households) multiplied by the average number in households in 1880 yields 9,240 (Town of West Roxbury, *Assessors' Report for the Year 1872,* 2.

The 1850 figures for the Town of West Roxbury (which seceded from the City of Roxbury in 1851) are derived from an estimate from the 1850 census of the population of the territory of West Roxbury (Arthur Austin, *Address at Dedication of the Town House at Jamaica Plain, West Roxbury* [Jamaica Plain, 1868] 33). Other Roxbury and West Roxbury figures are from the Population of Boston by Geographical Subdivisions table of the Decennial Census of Massachusetts.

borhood. In Jamaica Plain, ministers came to live near their churches, teachers came to live near their schools, and untold thousands came to live near the numerous shops and factories of the district.

Family ties also drew outsiders to Jamaica Plain. In 1850 William Minot, Jr., who had recently moved south of Forest Hills to the family estate,

TABLE 2.2

Persistence of Adult Heads of Households,
1880–1890 and 1900–1910

Sample Year	Sample Number	Number after 10 Years	Rate of Persistence (%)
1880	518	262	50
1900	715	335	46

Note: The actual persistence rates may have been higher. For example, if names not listed in either the 1880 or 1881 directory are discarded from the 1880 census sample, 262, or 63 percent of 416 names, were listed in 1890. This 63 percent rate of persistence compares closely with the 64 percent rate for the City of Boston as a whole during the same decade (Stephan Thernstrom, *The Other Bostonians: Poverty and Progress in the American Metropolis, 1880–1970* [Cambridge, Mass., 1973], 19). In both samples, occupations of the unlisted names correlate within 2 percent of the occupational rankings in table 2.4.

Woodbourne, wrote to his father-in-law in order to convince him to move his family nearby. "The only thing I should really like," he wrote, "would be having some member of your family here. . . . Mary Ward has bought a house-lot on Jamaica Pond, and is to be a quasi-neighbor, a new inducement for you to visit Woodbourne."[22] In 1903 Robert T. Fowler and his wife, Alice Barrows, moved from Australia to Jamaica Plain so that Fowler could join the neighborhood real estate firm of his wife's father, Roswell S. Barrows. In 1906 Edgar Achorn, of Newton Highlands, married Alice Gorman Morse, the daughter of a prominent and lifelong Jamaica Plain resident, Robert M. Morse, Jr., and the couple settled in the neighborhood. It was not only upper- and middle-class people who gravitated toward the neighborhood because of family ties. In 1914 August Becker, a recently arrived German immigrant, moved to the bustling Egleston Square district to be near his wife's sister. Undoubtedly hundreds of others moved to the district for similar reasons.[23]

At the same time, similar factors pulled people away from the neighborhood. The genealogies of the Weld, Bowditch, Balch, and other Jamaica Plain families and the newspaper announcements about less affluent citizens reveal a movement of married children away from the home neighborhood. In 1898 George Hills, an agent of the Boston and Portland Steamboat Company, and his wife moved from the Boylston Station area to Brooklyn, New York, because Hills had been appointed superintendent of the New Haven and Hartford Steamboat Company, whose offices were on New York City's East River. The transfer of the Sturtevant Company ventilation factory to Hyde Park removed the neighborhood advantage of proximity for the company's workers. Soon the Jamaica Plain newspaper began to print advertisements aimed at Sturtevant workers for houses in Hyde Park. Illness caused Charles Engstrom, a former state representative, to desert the neighborhood for a more healthful climate.[24]

The movement of people into and out of Jamaica Plain altered the occupational profile of the growing population and created a diverse neighborhood. By 1868 farmers composed a tiny fraction of Jamaica Plain's employed heads of households, and soon they had all but disappeared. Those in the highest social and economic ranks—professionals and wealthy Boston merchants—became a permanent, though influential, minority. The wealthy and the upper middle class were overwhelmingly Protestants from Massachusetts and New England. Although the numbers of prosperous Yankees were diluted by the numbers of their lower-class neighbors in Parkside, their presence dominated the Pondside, Moss Hill, Glenvale, and Sumner Hill sections of Jamaica Plain. Well-to-do families

TABLE 2.3
Work Force Occupations 1850-1922 (in percent)

Occupation	1850 (N=436)	1868[a] (N=1,013)	1880 (N=493)	1900 (N=677)	1910 (N=801)	1922 Men only (N=1,284)	1922 Men and Women[b] (N=1,801)
Professionals	6.7	4.2	3.9	3.5	3.5	6.2	7.0
Major proprietors	21.1	9.0	5.7	3.4	3.0	2.5	1.9
Clerks and salesmen	6.4	10.1	12.4	12.7	12.1	20.5	27.9
Semiprofessionals	0.7	0.9	3.0	5.0	3.6	2.6	3.9
Foremen	0.5	1.9	0.6	2.8	4.7	5.8	4.5
Petty proprietors	7.3	13.9	11.1	7.7	10.2	2.3	1.9
Farmers	10.1	2.0	0	0	0	0	0
Skilled workers	17.2	18.9	27.8	35.5	30.5	26.7	21.6
Semiskilled workers	4.8	4.9	10.8	17.6	20.6	20.3	21.5
Police, mailmen	0	—[c]	2.4	1.2	1.3	3.1	2.2
Unskilled workers	25.5	34.3	22.3	10.3	10.5	9.8	7.4

Note: Petty proprietors and skilled workers are overlapping categories. Only the directory for 1868 and the census of 1910 distinguished employees from employers.

[a] Excluding all 98 Canterbury addresses reduces the proportion of unskilled workers to 28 percent, raises the proportion of skilled workers to 20 percent, and changes all other categories by less than 1 percent.

[b] Includes employed women whose occupations are as follows: professionals, 8.9 percent; clerks, 46.4 percent; semiprofessionals, 7.1 percent; skilled workers, 8.9 percent; semiskilled workers, 24.6 percent.

[c] Included in semiskilled workers.

tended to have numerous children and an extensive entourage of servants, so that as their proportion of the overall population shrank, the size of the average household also declined. Hence, the average number of people in neighborhood households dropped from 5.3 in 1850 to 4.7 in 1880 and 4.2 in 1900. (See table 2.3.)

According to the historians' model of urban growth, the lower middle class did not arrive in the outer city until the 1890s, when streetcar companies initiated frequent service. Yet already by 1868 the number of Jamaica Plainers in middle-class occupations constituted almost half of the number in all occupations. Some of these businessmen, clerks, bookkeepers, and skilled workers traveled to Boston, but others commuted shorter distances, to the South End and especially nearby Roxbury. The numbers of these local commuters undoubtedly increased as service became more frequent. Many other middle-class residents, however, both worked and lived in

Jamaica Plain. Local carpenters, masons, roofers, and house painters built the new residences; plumbers, gas fitters, and furnace and stove dealers equipped them; and local shopkeepers and artisans provided the food, clothing, dishware, and other commodities demanded by the neighborhood's growing number of inhabitants.[25]

Members of the working class, a highly mobile population group, also arrived in the outer city much earlier than expected. Well before the building boom of the 1880s and the onset of the electric trolley and the nickel fare, the proportion of residents who held low-blue-collar jobs increased dramatically. As the number of leather workers and other small manufacturers increased in the late 1860s and 1870s, so did the number of semiskilled factory hands. By 1880, factory operatives and other similar workers made up the same proportion of employed heads of households as farmers had thirty years earlier. New opportunities appeared for unskilled workers as well. Now in addition to work as gardeners and hired hands on neighborhood estates, laborers found jobs in Jamaica Plain on workshop and factory floors, at construction sites, and on road building and other public works projects. (See table 2.3.)

Improvements in transportation and other factors of urban growth did not dramatically alter the neighborhood's basic occupational profile. During the late nineteenth and early twentieth centuries, the overall ratio of blue-collar to white-collar occupations held by Jamaica Plain residents remained approximately two to one (see table 2.4). These proportions made Jamaica Plain slightly more white-collar than Boston as a whole during the same period but more blue-collar than the neighborhood of Brighton or suburbs such as Somerville and Brookline.[26]

Meanwhile, the job structure within the blue-collar and white-collar ranks did change. The number of professionals and big businessmen

TABLE 2.4

Work Force Occupational Groups, 1850–1922 (in percent)

Occupational Group	1850 (N=436)	1868 (N=1,013)	1880 (N=493)	1900 (N=677)	1910 (N=801)	1922[a] (N=1,801)
High-white-collar	27.6	13.1	9.5	7.2	6.5	8.9
Low-white-collar	24.8	28.7	27.2	28.2	30.7	38.3
Skilled	17.2	18.9	27.8	35.5	30.5	21.6
Low-blue-collar	30.3	39.1	35.5	29.1	32.3	31.1

Note: Farmers are included in the low-white-collar category.

[a] See table 2.3 for separate figures for employed men and women in 1922.

The Making of an Urban Place

continued to rise, but not quickly enough to keep pace with other occupational groups. In 1900, skilled workers, including higher-level factory workers, constituted the largest group in the Jamaica Plain labor force—35.5 percent of the sample group—but thereafter began to decline in size. Increasing numbers of clerical occupations, the data suggest, swelled the ranks of low-white-collar employees, especially after 1910. The women who entered the work force during these years were most frequently employed as clerks or factory operatives. At the low end of the occupational ladder, semiskilled jobs replaced unskilled jobs as factories increased in number and size. While the proportion of unskilled jobholders among the sampled heads of households fell to 10 percent of the work force by 1900, the proportion of semiskilled workers rose to 17.6 percent (see table 2.3).

As the number of jobs accessible to Jamaica Plain residents grew, population shifts transformed the ethnic composition of the neighborhood. The proportion of all adult male heads of Jamaica Plain households who had been born in the United States fell from 71.5 percent in 1850 to fewer than 50 percent in 1880 and thereafter. From 1880 to 1910, the proportion of foreign-born heads of households in Jamaica Plain exceeded by about 10 percent their share in the Boston male labor force. Although the size of the local immigrant population was not as great as those of certain inner-city districts, such as the North End, the figures suggest that the degree of foreign ethnicity in Jamaica Plain surpassed that in the city as a whole (see table 2.5).[27]

The movements of different national groups through the Boston region contributed to Jamaica Plain's diverse ethnic makeup. The Irish, Boston's largest group of foreign immigrants, resided in most parts of the metropolitan area, but they concentrated near industrial areas, in neighborhoods such as Charlestown, South Boston, Roxbury, and inner Dorchester. In the late nineteenth century, Irish-Americans in pursuit of employment or better living accommodations expanded their settlements in outer sections

TABLE 2.5

Birthplace of Heads of Households, 1850-1910 (in percent)

Year	N	Massachusetts	Other New England	Other United States	England and Scotland	Canada	Ireland	Germany	Others
1850	513	53.0	16.4	2.1	3.7	2.9	19.4	1.6	0.8
1880	541	31.4	12.2	4.3	6.7	7.8	25.1	10.9	1.7
1900	779	29.3	9.2	5.3	6.0	11.8	18.0	13.7	6.7
1910	923	28.6	7.9	6.3	8.0	10.0	16.7	11.5	11.1

Local Attachments

of the Boston region. One large contingent of Irish moved south, into such districts as Dorchester and West Roxbury. Reflecting this settlement pattern, many Irish moved to Jamaica Plain, where they represented the largest immigrant group. By 1880 the Irish-born heads of household made up 25 percent of all heads of households in Jamaica Plain, while they made up only 18 percent of the entire Boston population. The proportion of Irish-born breadwinners in Jamaica Plain shrank to about 17 percent in 1910, but this percentage was still higher than that of Irish in the city population at large. Within the neighborhood, most Irish residences concentrated in the working- and lower-middle-class sections of Heath Street, Brookside, South Street, and adjacent south Parkside and Forest Hills (see table 2.5 and fig. 2.1).[28]

Over a period of more than a century, the bulk of a much smaller group of foreigners, Boston-area German immigrants, also migrated southward. The nucleus of the German-American population settled in the South End before the Civil War. During the late nineteenth and early twentieth centuries, the German population moved first to Roxbury and then to Jamaica Plain and West Roxbury. Contemporaries at the time attributed the migration to the Germans' love of gardening, but the real reason may have been an economic advancement that allowed them to acquire better housing than was available in the inner city. The arrival of Germans into northern Jamaica Plain during the 1860s and 1870s raised their proportion of heads of households in 1880 to 11 percent. By 1900, the German share of the Jamaica Plain population peaked at just under 14 percent, a figure that declined slightly ten years later. Most Germans lived in Hyde Square, Brookside, and, by 1910, Egleston Square. By the middle decades of the twentieth century the southward movement of German Bostonians had reached Boston's southern suburbs. (See table 2.5 and fig. 2.1.)

During the same period the numbers of other smaller immigrant groups climbed as well. From a mere 3 percent of the total population in 1850, Canadians reached a peak of 12 percent in 1900. The Scots and English, just under 4 percent of the neighborhood population in 1850, grew to almost 7 percent by 1880, and reached 8 percent in 1910. The Canadians settled especially in northern middle-class precincts, such as Hyde Square, Cedar Hill, and Egleston Square. Scottish and English residents of Jamaica Plain were more evenly distributed, with slight concentrations in Hyde Square, Glenvale, and Cedar Hill. By 1910 the number of other foreign-born groups, such as eastern European Jews and Italians, began slowly to rise, although the latter group did not arrive in great numbers until after 1910. (See table 2.5 and fig. 2.1.)

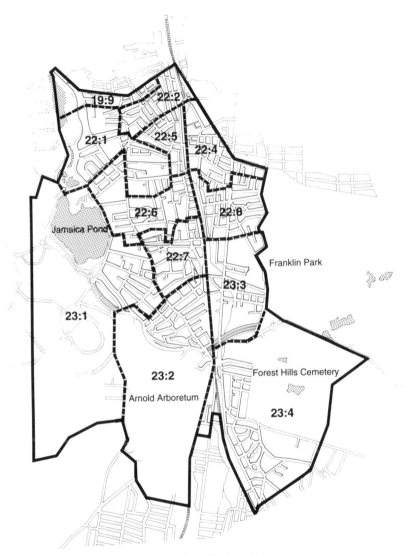

Jamaica Plain ward and precinct boundaries, 1910

Fig. 2.1. Birthplace by Ward and Precinct in Jamaica Plain, 1910
Total $N = 923$. N by ward and precinct: 19:9 = 41, 22:1 = 103, 22:2 = 107, 22:4 = 90, 22:5 = 101, 22:6 = 72, 22:7 = 68, 22:8 = 88, 23:1 = 46, 23:2 = 75, 23:3 = 61, 23:4 = 71.

Fig. 2.2. Occupational Groups by Ward and Precinct in Jamaica Plain, 1910
Total $N = 801$. N by ward and precinct: 19:9 = 39, 22:1 = 91, 22:2 = 90, 22:4 = 76, 22:5 = 88, 22:6 = 59, 22:7 = 55, 22:8 = 83, 23:1 = 37; 23:2 = 69, 23:3 = 52, 23:4 = 62.

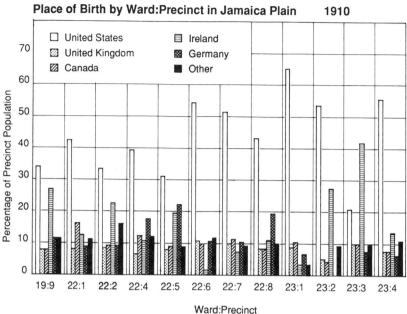

Fig. 2.1.

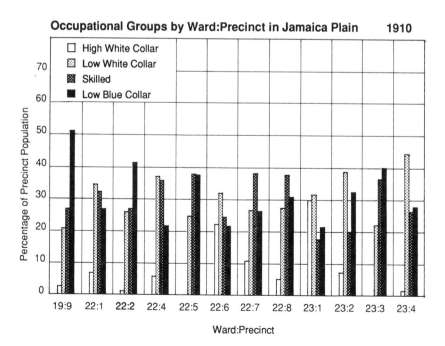

Fig. 2.2.

After 1880, the proportion of the foreign-born rose only slightly, but the increasing numbers of immigrants' children in the neighborhood raised the percentage of heads of households who were of foreign stock. In 1880, 85 percent of the American-born heads of households were sons of American mothers, but by 1900 the proportion had dropped to 65 percent, and by 1910 to only 49 percent. Meanwhile, second-generation Irish-American residents became the next largest ethnic group in the population, making up almost a third of American-born Jamaica Plainers by 1910. The children of German immigrants made up about 7 percent of the native American residents of Jamaica Plain by 1900, but their proportion hardly increased in the following decade. (See table 2.6.)

As in Boston as a whole, the jobs that Jamaica Plainers held were unevenly distributed among different ethnic groups. American-born residents continued to dominate the professions and white-collar occupations, even more than American-born Bostonians as a whole. At the other extreme, the Irish-born heads of households in the neighborhood, as in the city, still held disproportionate numbers of low-level blue-collar jobs. In 1880, with one quarter of the male work force, they held half of the semiskilled and unskilled jobs. By 1910 the Irish tended to work more often as semiskilled factory operatives than as unskilled laborers. In the twentieth century, moreover, second generation Irish-Americans began to take their share of skilled craft and clerical occupations. (See table 2.7.)

During the late nineteenth and early twentieth centuries, the heads of households from Germany, the British Isles (excluding Ireland), and Canada were predominantly skilled and white-collar workers. In 1880 almost half of the employed Germans were skilled workers. Thus, although they made up only 10 percent of Jamaica Plain's male employed heads of households, they held 18 percent of the skilled blue-collar jobs. By 1910 German-born Jamaica Plainers had moved into white-collar occupations at a level commensurate with their share of the population. Canadians also

TABLE 2.6
Birthplace of Mothers of American-born Heads of Households,
1880–1910 (in percent)

	United States	England and Scotland	Canada	Ireland	Germany	Others	N
1880	84.9	3.9	1.2	7.7	1.9	0.4	259
1900	64.9	6.2	2.9	18.3	6.8	0.8	339
1910	48.7	4.8	4.8	31.2	7.4	3.1	394

Local Attachments

TABLE 2.7

Birthplace of Employed Heads of Households by Occupational Group,
1850–1910 (in percent)

Occupational Group	United States	England and Scotland	Canada	Ireland	Germany	Other Countries	N
1850 (N=435)							
High-white-collar	96.8	1.6	0.8	0.0	0.8	0.0	126
Low-white-collar	91.3	1.9	1.9	2.9	1.0	1.0	103
Skilled	73.3	8.0	8.0	8.0	1.3	1.3	75
Low-blue-collar	23.7	5.3	3.1	64.1	3.8	0.0	131
1880 (N=493)							
High-white-collar	87.2	6.4	2.1	0.0	4.3	0.0	47
Low-white-collar	65.7	7.5	5.2	9.7	10.4	1.5	134
Skilled	43.1	8.0	12.4	16.1	18.2	2.2	137
Low-blue-collar	28.6	5.7	6.9	50.9	5.7	2.3	175
1900 (N=677)							
High-white-collar	77.6	0.0	6.1	2.0	12.2	2.0	49
Low-white-collar	59.2	4.7	11.0	9.4	10.5	5.2	191
Skilled	31.7	12.1	12.5	12.1	20.0	11.7	240
Low-blue-collar	38.1	3.0	13.2	28.4	11.2	6.1	197
1910 (N=800)							
High-white-collar	73.1	5.8	3.8	1.9	15.4	0.0	52
Low-white-collar	56.9	6.9	6.1	9.8	9.8	10.6	246
Skilled	30.3	11.1	14.8	10.7	13.9	19.3	244
Low-blue-collar	35.7	6.6	8.9	29.8	8.9	10.1	258

were heavily concentrated in skilled jobs, as were English and Scottish immigrants.

The increase in population and economic activity in Jamaica Plain intensified the early population clusters and strips and produced new pockets of development along the circulation spokes. The construction of streets, houses, and other buildings transformed the old clusters of development into larger subdistricts. Like other sections of both the inner and the outer city, particular types of residential, industrial, and commercial land uses predominated in the subdistricts, creating specialized but informal zones. The evolving internal geography of the neighborhood, however, did not conform to idealized patterns of urban growth any more than

The Making of an Urban Place   43

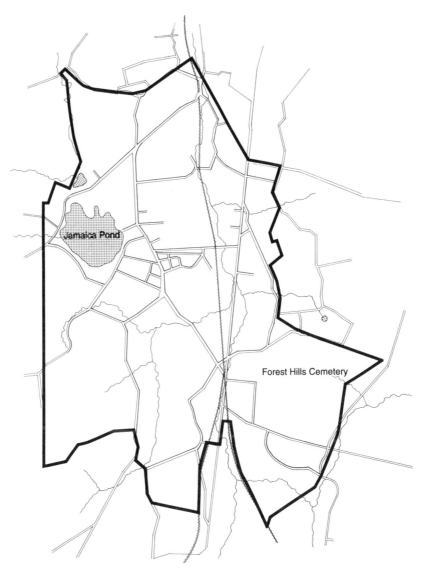

Street map of Jamaica Plain, 1850. *Source:* J. B. Shields, *Map of the City and Vicinity of Boston, Massachusetts* (Boston, 1852).

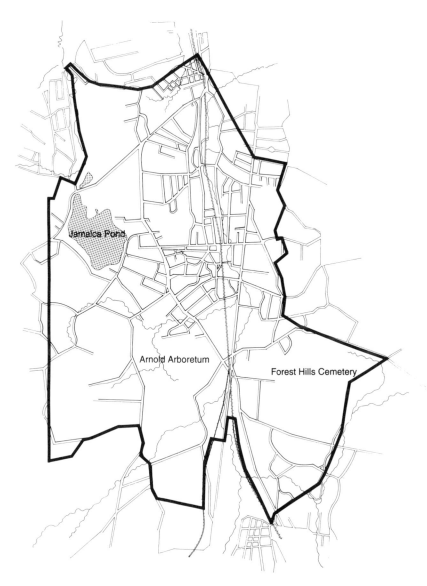

Street map of Jamaica Plain, 1880. *Source:* Sampson, Davenport, and Co., *Map of Boston, for 1880* (Boston, 1880).

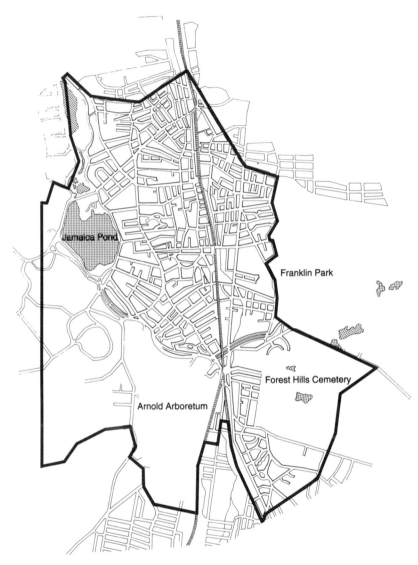

Street map of Jamaica Plain, 1920. *Source:* Sampson and Murdock Co., *Map of the City of Boston* (Boston, 1920).

did the neighborhood as a whole. Instead, subdistricts resulted from the individual decisions of those involved in local real estate development. Local landowners, subdividers, and developers made their decisions based on purely local circumstances, such as the desire for particular kinds of neighbors, topography, the presence of amenities, convenience to transportation, and proximity to employment.

During the late nineteenth and early twentieth centuries, well-to-do districts generally evolved where the wealthy already owned property and wished to preserve their district from alternative land uses or types of residential development. Residences of the predominantly Yankee upper class retreated in the face of industrial and lower-class development in the Stony Brook valley and concentrated in the Pondside, Moss Hill, Sumner Hill, and Parkside subdistricts. These subdistricts did not belong to the most remote band of residential development in either Boston or Jamaica Plain. Only the first three were contiguous, and only one, Moss Hill, was located further from the city center than other residential areas lower on the social scale. (See fig. 2.2.)

Sometimes the emergence of such exclusive areas depended on inherited patterns of property ownership. In much of outer and suburban Boston, the conversion of summer homes to year-round residences and family compounds contributed to the process. About 1850, for example, George R. Minot and William Minot, Jr., followed their father William Minot, a Boston probate judge and insurance businessman, to Forest Hills, where he had recently constructed a summer home called Woodbourne. They built year-round houses there, creating a family compound that, with children, servants, and guests, eventually housed fifty to sixty inhabitants.[29]

Even as industrial and middle-class residential areas spread throughout Jamaica Plain, the scenic qualities of Jamaica Pond continued to lure people of wealth to the Pondside district. During the 1850s and 1860s, for example, Boston businessmen such as Thomas B. Frothingham, near Frothingham Cove, and David Wallace, at Lochstead, joined Francis Parkman, the famous historian, on the shores of the pond. Between Perkins Street and the Town of Brookline extended a line of estates, including those of Quincy Amory Shaw, scion of three old Boston families, and Henry H. Reuter, a Roxbury brewer. On the village plains lived well-to-do Boston brokers and wholesale merchants such as Horace B. Taylor, of the Boston commission firm of Foster and Taylor, who in the 1850s built a splendidly ornate Italianate residence complete with rusticated wood siding, quoins, and roof lantern. New mansions sprang up along Pondside's historic streets during the 1880s and 1890s, and old families such as the Shaws and Bacons provided the area with historic continuity into the twentieth century.[30]

Additions to the Boston park system in the 1890s further enhanced Pondside as a residential area. The creation of Jamaica Park and the Jamaicaway, the adjacent parkway, preserved the natural setting of Jamaica Pond and furnished a stylish carriage drive through the Emerald Necklace, Boston's extensive chain of parks. After the construction of Jamaica Park forced him to abandon his father's home, Robert M. Morse, Jr., said to be the wealthiest attorney in Boston, hired William Ralph Emerson, a nationally known architect, to design an imposing Colonial Revival mansion on the Jamaicaway. In 1896, C. Sidney Waldo, a partner in the Waldo Brothers firm, perhaps the largest supplier of masonry materials in New England, built a majestic neoclassical residence and matching stable near Morse's mansion. In 1915 James Michael Curley, the controversial Boston politician who had been elected the previous year to his first term as mayor, built the most famous home on the Jamaicaway. Reflecting the flamboyant mayor's desires for both respectability and notoriety, the otherwise conservative Georgian-style house was ornamented with bright green window shutters from which shamrock shapes had been cut.[31]

At the same time, Sumner Hill, the uplands of the Greenough estate, developed into another upper- and upper-middle-class residential district. The hill was named after William H. Sumner, the son of a former governor, Massachusetts adjutant general, and East Boston real estate developer, who was a close associate of the Greenough family and married Maria F. Doane, the widow of David S. Greenough II. After Doane's death, Sumner remarried and purchased from his former wife's daughter, Anne Greenough, a parcel of land at the crest of the hill, where in 1852 he built a home for himself and his new wife. The Greek Revival mansion and grounds served as a prestigious anchor for the back of the hill, just as the Loring-Greenough mansion did for the front of the hill, facing Centre Street.[32]

Associations with the Greenough and Sumner families and convenient access to the railroad enabled family members to sell off estate parcels to subdividers and homeowners. In the 1860s and 1870s, for example, George H. Williams, a local real estate investor, and Stephen Heath, a local carpenter, developed Alveston Street into a line of handsome Italianate and mansard-style residences for Boston newspaper owners, attorneys, insurance executives, and other prosperous Jamaica Plain businessmen.[33]

Even when land became less available, Sumner Hill maintained its suburban-style prestige. During the late nineteenth century, well-heeled newcomers took over the dwellings of former residents. For example, Elias Hook, a partner in supposedly the largest organ-manufacturing firm in the United States, bought the house of a retired wholesale wool trader. Other new arrivals built elegant Queen Anne–style residences. In 1880, for instance, Thomas Sherwin, an auditor for a downtown firm, hired the nationally known architectural firm of William R. Ware and Henry Van Brunt to design his home on the former Sumner estate. Nearby, William Ralph Emerson provided Joseph Hardon, a Boston millinery store owner, with a house designed in the Queen Anne and shingle styles, which Emerson helped to popularize. In the 1880s and 1890s similarly imposing houses were crowded into small culs-de-sac laid out on David S. Greenough's holdings. Meanwhile, Sumner Hill evolved as a secondary institutional center with the construction near the Sumner mansion of the neighborhood high school (1868, rebuilt 1900) and three churches, including the Central Congregational Church (1872) and St. John's Episcopal Church (1882), both moved from Centre Street.[34]

At the turn of the century, some of the local well-to-do moved to luxury apartment buildings on Centre Street between Sumner Hill and Pondside. These structures were a local by-product of the fashion that had produced spectacular apartment buildings in Boston's Back Bay and along the central spine of Manhattan in New York City. Unlike the impressive structures of the inner city, outer-city apartment buildings were often built to mediate between inner-city urbanity and the suburban tone of the periphery. The brick edifices were usually limited in height and placed on main thoroughfares, where they would not clash with the wood-frame homes on the side streets. At the foot of Sumner Hill, for example, in 1898 a group of investors including Alfred Bowditch, Jonathan Ingersoll Bowditch's son, developed a relatively plain four-story brick apartment building where wealthy spinsters and stockbrokers came to live. In the early 1900s two Pondside residents, Ella C. Adams and her husband Charles H. Adams, a wholesale grocer in Boston, acquired a neighboring estate, Lakeville, and hired Benjamin Fox, an architect of apartment buildings in the Back Bay and Brookline. Constructed of red brick and rough sandstone in the Richardsonian Romanesque style, the resulting pair of three-story residential blocks nicely expressed the romantic urbanity of the built-up outer city. Inside, Lakeville and Beaufort Terraces provided roomy apartments with hardwood interiors and such conveniences as a telephone system that could ring the front door, the maid's room, or the janitor.[35]

Attracted by scenic views and respectable neighbors on nearby estates, upper-class Bostonians also settled in the Moss Hill district, located on the heights south of Jamaica Pond and across the border from the prosperous Town of Brookline. In 1849 John James Dixwell, who had made a fortune in the India trade and then became president of the Massachusetts National Bank, purchased land parcels from a local farmer to create a carefully cultivated estate, Sunnyside. Dixwell was married to Elizabeth B. Ingersoll Bowditch, the daughter of the famous Salem navigator, Nathaniel Bowditch. By the 1860s, Jonathan Ingersoll Bowditch, Elizabeth's older brother and president of the American Insurance Company, had settled with his family on an adjacent estate. In the 1890s another generation of Bowditches laid out the curvilinear Moss Hill and Woodland roads on family lands.[36]

In the late nineteenth century, this prestigious district extended further south, toward Allandale Road, further enlarging Jamaica Plain. Here lived Harriet Manning Whitcomb, a well-to-do widow who wrote the history of Jamaica Plain, and Marguerite Souther, who ran a dance school in Pondside's Eliot Hall, where she taught deportment and the waltz to generations of well-bred Bostonians. Perhaps the pinnacle of wealth in Jamaica Plain was achieved by the Weld family. William Fletcher Weld, Stephen Minot Weld's brother, was an extremely successful merchant whose Black Horse shipping line helped earn him a fortune of close to $20 million. With their husbands, Edward D. Brandegee, a clothing manufacturer and personal friend of Theodore Roosevelt, and Larz Anderson, a career diplomat, Weld's granddaughters, Mary Bryant Pratt and Isabel Weld Perkins, inherited and purchased great tracts of land along the Brookline–Jamaica Plain border. In the early twentieth century the Weld estates, Faulkner Farm and Weld, were showpieces of landscape design and sources of employment to the Irish laborers of Jamaica Plain and Brookline.[37]

Graceful homes and grounds also appeared in Parkside, a subdistrict whose growth extended the boundaries of Jamaica Plain to the west of the Stony Brook valley. Forest Hills Street had once been a backwoods path called Jube's Lane, the site of a "wretched collection of hovels and sheds occupied by a Moorish-looking man named Jupiter, who kept swine and who had a bevy of wild-eyed children," but in the late 1840s it offered hillside views, the beautiful landscape of Forest Hills Cemetery, and access to Boston via the old turnpike road (Shawmut, later Washington Street). By 1850 Forest Hills Street had become home to such well-to-do Bostonians as Francis Minot Weld, a Boston commission merchant and brother of Stephen Minot and William Fletcher Weld. Nearby, Isaac Cary, the founder of a national ivory and fancy goods import firm, built an estate that boasted an unusual Italianate villa complete with a three-story tower.

Local Attachments

In the 1860s and 1870s the Parkside area continued to attract wealthy gentlemen such as Albert Thompson, a Boston leather dealer, who named his estate Forest Garden.[38]

At the same time, the neighborhood attracted members of the upper middle class, the prosperous commuters who are closely associated with the traditional image of the American suburb. Neighborhood subdividers developed upper-middle-class residences adjacent to and sometimes intermingled with the areas of the wealthy in Pondside, Sumner Hill, Glenvale, and Parkside. In 1848, for example, Stephen Minot Weld created Glenvale Park out of the rocky hills and farmland of Glenvale to sell to businessmen, who could use the Jamaica Plain railroad station nearby. Although construction did not begin in earnest until the 1860s, the stately Italianate and mansard-style houses of Chestnut Avenue, such as the small, villa-style home of Ephraim Merriam, a Boston grocer, attest to his success.[39]

In the 1880s the heirs of Abram French, a wealthy china dealer, converted the family estate, Parley Vale, with its woods, hills, and winding roads (unpaved to this day), into a smaller version of Sumner Hill. In 1896 a group of investors, the Robinwood Associates, took advantage of Parley Vale and next to it developed Robinwood Avenue as a fashionably windy, hilly road; there William W. Dinsmoor, a Boston architect, designed pleasantly eclectic shingle- and Queen Anne–style houses for Boston area professionals and other middle-class citizens.[40]

As the City of Boston prepared the extensive grounds of Franklin Park in the 1880s, Parkside estate owners began to exploit the new amenity by developing their district. Prosperous businessmen bought the first lots. For instance, Francis A. Peters, a Boston bank president, built a spacious Colonial Revival house. Eliot B. Mayo, a Boston-area wood and coal dealer turned industrial real estate agent, lived in a large Queen Anne–style residence designed by the Boston architectural firm of Appleton and Stephenson. In 1893 a group of family members and associates of a Parkside estate owner, George W. Bond, purchased and subdivided Albert Thompson's Forest Gardens to sell to Boston professionals and businessmen. By naming roads in the development Franklin Park Terrace and Olmstead [sic] Street, after the park and its designer, the company directly associated the project with the new park.[41]

Since those in low-white-collar and skilled blue-collar occupations constituted such a large and, until 1900, growing component of the local working population, their homes took up large portions of neighborhood land. Occasionally the families of these middle-class workers lived in partial rows of brick townhouses or respectable three-decker apartments. Most often, however, they chose wood-frame single- or two-family houses whose designs reflected the more ambitious architecture of the suburban wealthy and upper middle class. Because the middle-class homes were abundant and built in the styles of the period, they contributed heavily to the distinctive, if eclectic, appearance of the outer city.

Throughout the second half of the nineteenth century and well into the twentieth century, subdividers usually developed middle-class and lower-middle-class residences on land that had not been otherwise defined by adjacent factories or estates and parklands. Throughout Jamaica Plain—in Bromley Park near Heath Street, on the back slope of Sumner Hill, here and there off Centre Street—one found middle-income residents who commuted to other sections of Boston or earned their livelihood in the neighborhood. As might be expected, the number of commuters in these areas increased as transportation became more available at the end of the century. The precedents for middle-class settlement, however, usually had been set there before frequent transit service arrived.

During the late nineteenth century, for example, a wide range of middle-class residents moved to Pondside, a previously exclusive district, where they settled away from the expensive lands adjacent to Jamaica Pond. In the 1860s and 1870s, local workers and businessmen such as Isaac Jacobs, a town constable, Stephen Heath, a local carpenter-builder, and George Barrett, a Centre Street druggist, moved to wood-frame buildings here. During the 1870s and 1880s, the former Amos Holbrook farm was developed with single-family houses in Italianate and other styles for artisans and businessmen such as James E. McCafferty, the co-owner of a Roxbury brass foundry. Three decades later, the old George and Joseph Curtis farmlands in Pondside were built up with frame structures purchased by salesmen, clerks, doctors, managers, stenographers, skilled workers, and government employees. Many of these were two-family houses, such as the 1914 Colonial Revival residence bought by William Schaehrer, a Jamaica Plain postal carrier.[42]

While Pondside and other districts grew, to the northeast a broad band of territory located closer to the city center remained relatively undeveloped until the annexation of Roxbury to the City of Boston in 1868. Most of this land had been located within the bounds of the City of Roxbury, and even after annexation, official documents classified these districts as parts of the Roxbury section of Boston. During the late nineteenth century, however, the local populace increasingly distinguished the emergent subdistricts from nearby subdistricts in Roxbury.[43] By the turn of the century the popular mind had annexed them to the neighborhood of Jamaica Plain.

These northerly subdistricts—Egleston Square, Boylston, Cedar Hill, and Hyde Square—followed similar patterns of development. During the 1860s and 1870s, there appeared new roads and a few Italianate and mansard-roofed single and double homes owned by workers who commuted varying distances. From the 1880s, more streets and homes were added to accommodate a flood of incoming people. The architectural details on the new houses had changed to reflect the Queen Anne and Colonial Revival styles, but the inhabitants were, for the most part, still white-collar and high-blue-collar families. By the twentieth century these subdistricts had grown somewhat eclectic. Along main streets they included three-decker and other apartment buildings, and in the lowlands they shaded into working-class precincts. Nonetheless, their high concentrations of artisans, clerks, and small businessmen defined these areas as essentially middle- and lower-middle-class residential districts.

In the Boylston subdistrict, for example, in 1868 George H. Williams subdivided Spring Park and sold lots to Boston commuters, including a downtown organ manufacturer (who bought three lots for his house), a piano maker, a bank messenger, and a constable at the Suffolk County courthouse. A Jamaica Plain businessman, Thomas Mayo, co-owner of White and Mayo's hardware store, owned one of the development's more notable buildings, an Italianate edifice constructed with arched porch and railing braces and two types of bays. By 1900, skilled workers, accountants, and professionals had taken over the development.[44]

In the 1860s, two piano makers, a Boston real estate agent, and a carpenter and a grocer, both of whom worked in Roxbury, staked out the Hyde Square area for the middle class. Between 1888 and 1898 Robert Treat Paine, a housing reformer, developed Sunnyside to provide moderate-income housing in Hyde Square. Aimed at the honest workingman, its modest Queen Anne–style homes found instead the lower middle and middle class. Similarly, Cedar Hill in the mid-1870s was home to middle-class commuters, including a South End factory foreman, a partner in a Roxbury painting company, and a minister who worked at the Children's Mission in Boston. Twenty-five years later both Hyde Square and Cedar Hill housed shopkeepers, salesmen, clerks, skilled workers, and factory foremen and operatives.[45]

Many of the home buyers in these subdistricts were rising members of the middle class. Often first- or second-generation immigrants, they attempted to improve their family's standard of living by acquiring a better home. A case in point is Adam Mock, a German immigrant, who in the 1860s worked in a Roxbury rubber factory. In 1868 he purchased a lot on a street in the Hyde Square district and built a modest, two-story house with Italianate details. Eventually Mock was able to quit his factory job and buy a liquor business in downtown Boston. By 1886 he had saved enough money to build a new home on Cedar Hill. Mock hired Jacob Luippold, a Jamaica Plain architect and also a German immigrant, who designed a large Queen Anne–style house complete with arcaded front porch.[46]

Forest Hills, another middle- and lower-middle-class subdistrict, emerged alongside Forest Hills Cemetery, expanding Jamaica Plain's southwestern border. Originally a sparsely settled district of estates, farms, and laborers' homes, Forest Hills offers the clearest support from Jamaica Plain for the theory that transportation improvements brought the middle class to the outer city. Forest Hills Station grew increasingly important as an outer-city and suburban transfer point for trolleys and trains during the 1890s, and with the construction of the electric elevated terminal in 1909. As a result, the adjacent area filled in with single-family houses for clerks, salesmen, and artisans. To the south, Woodbourne was developed as a philanthropic housing project for those with moderate incomes. Ironically, the apartment buildings and English cottages attracted professionals, middle-level white-collar employees, and skilled workers, but hardly any members of the working class, to Forest Hills. Thus, outer-city development at Forest Hills actually raised the economic standing of the district by diluting the presence of low-blue-collar workers with large numbers of middle-class residents.[47]

The quickening rhythms of economic activity throughout the Boston metropolitan region fostered the growth of neighborhood production in Jamaica Plain. In the late nineteenth century, Jamaica Plain continued to provide commodities, services, and processing of hinterland goods typical of urban fringe areas. As they had since the colonial period, Jamaica Plain's farmers practiced market gardening for the urban market. For much of the nineteenth century, for example, members of the Curtis family who owned lands near Jamaica Pond prospered as market gardeners and maintained a stall in Faneuil Hall Market. As late as 1868, Jamaica Plain store owners such as Robert Seaver weighed hay and wood for farmers from Dedham and other parts of the countryside traveling to Boston. Even in the early twentieth century the Whittemore family maintained a Washington Street outlet to sell hay and other goods from their West Roxbury farm. Exploiting a hinterland commodity first discovered early in the century at

Fresh Pond in Cambridge, ice companies harvested ice from Jamaica Pond for sale in Jamaica Plain and Boston from the 1850s until the Boston Park commissioners took control of the area in the 1890s.[48]

The decentralization of industries in American cities also brought factories and workers to Jamaica Plain. In the late nineteenth and early twentieth centuries, Jamaica Plain developed small-scale factories that sold in the Boston region and larger industrial plants that served national and even international markets. Among the small factories, tanneries and other leather shops processed New England hides for sale or resale in the downtown Boston leather trade, and breweries distributed their products to a Boston-area market. Most of the large factories fabricated goods such as industrial fans and ventilation equipment, surveying tools, automobile parts, plumbing tools, and electric motors for the national producers' market. One exceptional but important enterprise, the giant Thomas G. Plant Company, manufactured ladies' shoes for national retail distribution.

Thus, at the same time that neighborhood upper- and middle-class residential districts evolved, industrial areas with factories and working-class residences vigorously expanded up and down the length of the neighborhood. Jamaica Plain's oldest industrial zone, Brookside, located in the lowlands over the Stony Brook, was developed originally for its remote location and its access to water. In 1856 the Jamaica Plain Improvement Company auctioned forty-one lots near the railroad depot and Brookside Avenue for "stores, factories, and houses." Within three years this area included a soap factory, a currying shop, oil, boiling, and stock houses, and two factories of the Boston Japan Leather Company. In the 1860s and early 1870s the district gained the Jamaica Plain Dye House, operated by F. Kohlhepp, the masonry business of D. E. Handy, the tannery of an Irishman, Charles Dolan, and the mills of the Aetna and Eagle rubber companies. In 1871 Rudolf Haffenreffer, a German immigrant and former Roxbury brewery worker, started the Boylston Lager Beer Brewery, which went on to prosper in Boston's competitive beer market.[49]

In the 1880s, Frederick W. Dahl built a factory where he operated first a leather business and later a silver-plating company, and Patrick Meehan, an Irish-born contractor, built a handsome four-story, brick carriage factory. In 1898 the Buff and Buff Manufacturing Company expanded this industrial cluster to the other side of the railroad tracks. Although a small factory, the Buff and Buff Company built finely calibrated transits and other surveying instruments, which it shipped to mining, construction, and engineering sites across the United States and abroad.[50]

At the same time, the Brookside industrial belt expanded along the railroad tracks south of the Jamaica Plain Station at Green Street. In 1878 Benjamin F. Sturtevant, the inventor and manufacturer of a shoe-pegging machine, brought large-scale manufacturing to Jamaica Plain when he opened an industrial-use exhaust fan factory. By the 1890s the Sturtevant company, which produced ventilation equipment necessary for the operation of power plants in factories and ocean liners, employed five hundred workmen in a great industrial building complex. Although in 1904 the company moved to a still larger complex in Hyde Park, Jamaica Plain factory workers petitioned the New York, New Haven, and Hartford Railroad for an express train to the new works, and soon other firms, such as the United Machinery Company, offered employment at the old plant.[51]

Although it was located further from the city center than many better-off districts, the South Street area, once home to a few laborers, blacksmiths, and wheelwrights, evolved into an industrial and working-class Irish residential neighborhood. Jamaica Plain's old families aided the transformation. In 1850 David S. Greenough III subdivided the southern portion of his family estate south of the village center into sixty lots and four new roads, including Keyes (now McBride) Street. Located in a low-lying section near a spring, these lots were filled with workers' cottages, most of which were purchased by people of Irish origin. Greenough attempted through deed restrictions to limit construction to "not more than one dwelling house" per lot, but economic considerations often led to more buildings than the deeds allowed. In 1866, for example, Greenough sold a lot to John Ryan, an Irish immigrant laborer, who built three small cottages there. Across from Greenough's development, in 1853 Christopher Weld, a physician and another brother of Stephen Minot Weld, laid out a curvilinear path on a hill where over the next decades modest cottages and houses appeared. Here in 1900 lived city laborers, a teamster, a produce peddler, and Margaret Horan, a forty-five-year-old Irish widow, with her seven children, including Frank, a twenty-six-year-old carpenter, and Mary and John, both in their twenties, who worked as twine makers.[52]

Nonresidential development of the South Street area soon followed. In 1853 Greenough sold a tract along the railroad tracks at Keyes Street, where the directors of the Jamaica Plain Gas Light Company built their gasworks. A few years later, the West Roxbury Railroad Company built a depot and stables for its horse railroad at the corner of South and Keyes streets. By the 1860s the number of Irish Catholics in the area had grown to such an extent that the Roman Catholic Diocese of Boston felt it necessary to provide them with a church. In 1867 the diocese purchased a site from Abner Child, a member of the First Church of Jamaica Plain, and the

Local Attachments

following year began construction of St. Thomas Aquinas Church. With a growing number of parishioners and the addition of a parish grammar school in 1873, St. Thomas Aquinas became a major Jamaica Plain institution.[53]

The South Street district extended to the south and west. By the 1890s it had merged with the spreading Brookside factory zone. At the intersection of the two subdistricts, south of the gasworks, the Boston Thread and Twine Company operated its factory. On the other side of Washington Street, along the Stony Brook, were the local processing plant of the Naptha Cleansing Works, a Roxbury cleansing and dye company, and the car barn for the West End Street Railway Company's Washington Street line.[54]

In northern Jamaica Plain, factories and breweries spread southwest from Roxbury along the Stony Brook to create the Heath Street industrial and working-class district. From the late 1840s, an iron foundry, a tannery, a silk manufactory, and several breweries filled the land north of Jamaica Plain between Parker Hill and the Stony Brook. The boundary of modern Jamaica Plain was breached in 1867 by the opening of Henry H. Reuter and John R. Alley's Highland Spring Brewery at New Heath Street and soon thereafter by the opening of the Alley and Nichols Brewery off Heath Street, nearby. By 1872 the Heath Street area had become a working-class district with so many saloons that a Protestant minister, William Bradley, and his wife were inspired to found a mission at the Heath Street railroad station.[55]

The mushrooming industrial activity in the Heath Street vicinity extended Jamaica Plain northward. In 1885 John R. Alley went into business on his own and hired a Philadelphia brewery architect to build the Eblana Brewery. James W. Kenney, an Irish immigrant and Roxbury wholesale liquor merchant, built two breweries, the Park Brewery in 1882 and the American Brewing Company, elegantly ornamented with stained glass, a corner bay turret, and arched portals, in 1892. In the late 1890s industrial construction reached a climax when Thomas G. Plant built a giant shoe factory at Centre and Bickford streets. Completed in 1900, it employed from three thousand to five thousand workers, some of whom commuted from other neighborhoods, and was said to be the largest women's shoe manufactory in the United States. The streets and buildings of the Heath Street subdistrict blended with those of the Hyde Square area but were separated from Roxbury by the natural boundary of Parker Hill. By the turn of the century, Heath Street had become Jamaica Plain's northern border.[56]

During the late nineteenth and early twentieth centuries, this industrial sector advanced along the Stony Brook and the railroad tracks eastward into the Egleston Square subdistrict and southward to Brookside. In 1877 James Kenney built another brewery on Amory Street, which to some seemed "sadly out of place in (the) sylvan retreat" of the Amory family estate. Nearby the Suffolk Foundry Company established its works; it was succeeded in the mid-1880s by the Robinson Brewery. About 1906 the Trimount Manufacturing Company, makers of plumbers tools, purchased the factory building, where it employed some 250 workers. Businesses based on new technologies kept the local industrial impulse vital well into the twentieth century. In the 1910s the Randall-Faichney Company, a producer of automobile parts such as horns and spark plugs, and the Holtzer-Cabot Electric Motor Company opened plants that linked the northern industrial belt with Brookside to the south.[57]

The creation of a chain of factories that extended virtually the length of Jamaica Plain swelled the numbers of factory operatives and other workers living in the neighborhood. Brookside factories already had attracted numerous laborers when in 1869 Charles J. Page, a Jamaica Plain man, began building workers' cottages near the railroad tracks and the Stony Brook. By 1880 Brookside had become a major concentration point for Irish laborers and factory hands and German operatives, skilled workers, and entrepreneurs. In the twentieth century, Brookside evolved into a heavily working-class district known as "the Jungle" for its unruly youth.[58]

In the 1890s the working-class residences of the South Street district expanded across the railroad tracks toward Franklin Park, invading the suburban-style Parkside district. Only the obstacle of the park and bordering estates halted the neighborhood's advance. The Heath Street breweries and factories helped attract thousands of Irish Catholics to the Heath Street and Hyde Square areas. In response to their presence, in 1892 the Roman Catholic Diocese of Boston founded the Blessed Sacrament Church in Hyde Square. Between 1910 and 1917 a monumental church in the Italian Renaissance style was constructed to accommodate the massive numbers of parishioners. In 1916 the opening of the Holtzer-Cabot factory caused an influx of workers that spread as far as Brookline.[59]

Until the late nineteenth century, members of Jamaica Plain's lower-middle and working classes tended to live in small double houses, cottages, or even smaller structures of one or two rooms. The poor and the working-class often lived in unhealthy conditions, because their residences were located in marshy lowlands, exposing them to damp rooms or, worse, contaminated water supplies. The construction of drainage-sewer and water-supply systems by the City of Boston represented progress for the poor living in Jamaica Plain's valleys.

Increasingly during the late nineteenth century, the residential building of choice for those of limited means was "Boston's weed," the three-decker. A peculiarly New England building type, the three-decker combined the detached character and eclectic stylistic devices of the wood-frame one- or two-family house with the vertical orientation of the apartment building. Often endowed with front porches, it contained three full floors, each floor being an apartment of from four to seven rooms. Some three-deckers were eminently respectable—for example, the "exuberant Queen Anne/Shingle Style 'double' three-decker" on the corner of Centre and Holbrook streets in Pondside—but most were relatively inexpensive to build. They provided adequate light and air, and with two rents to ensure the payback of mortgage loans, they furnished working-class or lower-middle-class families with decent, if modest, living quarters. First appearing in the 1870s, three-deckers caught on in the 1890s and grew more popular thereafter. Sometimes they were inserted individually among one- and two-family houses; other times they were grouped along a street. In the twentieth century, when developers began to work on a larger scale, they lined entire blocks. Three-deckers spread throughout most of Jamaica Plain, but especially in the working-class and eclectic lower-middle-class districts.[60]

In contrast to Jamaica Plain's processing and manufacturing, which thrived because of the neighborhood's proximity to Boston's vigorous producer and consumer markets, locally oriented goods and service ventures expanded in the face of competition from Boston-area outlets. At no time could Jamaica Plain merchants and artisans monopolize the neighborhood market. By the 1850s, nearby Roxbury offered the same goods and services available in Jamaica Plain, as well as shops that satisfied specialized wants, such as for daguerreotype miniatures and watches, then unavailable in Jamaica Plain. Moreover, the wives and children of Jamaica Plain's commuting businessmen were already accustomed to taking shopping trips to Boston, where they could choose from an even greater assortment of consumer items. Besides possessing a wide variety of dry goods outlets, Boston offered mainstays of the middle-class household that were rare or unavailable in the suburbs, such as pianofortes and other musical instruments, books, art paintings, and prints.[61]

In the late nineteenth century, transportation improvements and population expansion created overlapping suburban markets. Roving butchers' and grocery store delivery trucks, based inside and outside Jamaica Plain, traveled over territories that included more than one neighborhood. Roxbury's commercial center at Dudley Street continued to grow as a secondary downtown district to which the residents of Jamaica Plain had easy access.

Meanwhile, the marketplaces, shops, and department stores in downtown Boston continued to aggressively compete for the patronage of Boston-area consumers. In the early years of the twentieth century, officials of the New York, New Haven, and Hartford Railroad became frustrated with outer-city women who disguised their downtown shopping purchases and thus deprived the express company or the railroad of freight charges. The women hid their goods in clothing trunks and checked them to their home station (where they then made use of a wheelbarrow). One Jamaica Plain woman got her just deserts, according to the officials, when a baggage handler mistakenly dropped her trunk and a can of blueberries oozed out.[62]

Despite the attractions of stores outside the neighborhood, many neighborhood residents preferred the great convenience of shopping close to home. Thus, as the population of Jamaica Plain multiplied, the neighborhood generated a thriving "domestic" market for local stores and service shops. In the 1850s local entrepreneurs such as grocers, blacksmiths, carpenters, dry goods store owners, tailors, apothecaries, and a billiard-room operator served the growing number of Boston commuters and other residents of the neighborhood. In addition, wheelwrights, carriage shops, and harness makers literally catered to the local carriage trade. By the late 1860s this group of enterprises had diversified to include a variety of food, clothing, and hardware stores, as well as Boston express services, stationery shops, a photography studio, and a toy store. In the early twentieth century, new specialized services such as rug cleaners and hand laundries joined the established core of outlets. Throughout the period, the process of selling, subdividing, and building upon local lands created numerous opportunities for local real estate brokers, contractors, and builders.[63]

As in the outer-city territories of other cities, such enterprises tended to concentrate on main thoroughfares and around transportation hubs. Located along the seams of the residential zones, the local commercial districts served as neighborhood meeting places and included important community institutions. Along Green Street, small artisan and service shops continued to flourish during the late nineteenth century. In the 1890s the strip offered various skilled services, including those of Cornelius Sheehan, slate and tin roofer, Rowen Brothers, plumbers and gasfitters, a vacuum rug-cleaning company, and G. T. Jaques's hand laundry.[64]

By 1870 a string of food markets, bakeries, dry goods stores, and other shops stretched out along Centre Street, Jamaica Plain's "Main Street."

Here one could find Seaver's, James's, and Norcross and Myrick's grocery stores, butcher and provision stores, and other establishments that provided the domestic necessities. In their neighborhood apothecary shops, George N. Barrett and John C. Howard sold a wide range of goods, including medicines, "foreign leeches," stationery, snuff, cigars, perfumes, towels, and other toiletries. They also offered liquors such as brandies, aged bourbon whiskey, and brand-name wines, allegedly for "medicinal purposes." The Centre Street strip also included tailors, dressmakers, hardware stores, and gentlemen's clothing shops.[65]

The increasing number of retail shops encouraged local entrepreneurs to build commercial blocks along Centre Street. In the early 1870s, for example, Isaac Myrick, of the Myrick and Norcross grocery business, built a one-and-a-half-story structure, and Cyrus White built White's Block, a two-story frame building that housed his stove and hardware store and the businesses of a jeweler, dressmaker, carpenter, and hairdresser-undertaker.

In the following years, modern brick commercial and commercial-residential buildings upgraded sections of the Centre Street strip. In 1875 the Seaver family rebuilt Jamaica Plain's oldest establishment, Seaver's grocery store, as a three-story panel brick commercial building with residential apartments upstairs. In the 1880s other larger structures followed. In 1888 W. F. Fallon, a Centre Street fish and oyster dealer, developed a Romanesque brick building that was the site of Charles B. Rogers's drugstore, a neighborhood establishment for more than a century. In Hyde Square, the construction of more frame and masonry commercial-apartment buildings contributed to another line of stores on lower Centre Street.[66]

As railroad traffic increased, bustling centers of commercial activity emerged around the neighborhood's railroad stations. By the late 1860s one could find Leopold Vogel's shoe store, D. A. Brown's grocery and crockery business, John J. Shaw's carpentry shop, Hattie Chase's fancy goods, stationery, and toy store, and other enterprises grouped around the Jamaica Plain depot on Green Street. Woolsey Square, the space opposite the railroad station, acquired its first commercial block, the Elson Building, by 1873, and another commercial building, the Woolsey Block, a large post office building, and the Hotel Gordon by the turn of the century. On the other side of the station stood Bartlett's Building, where first Alden Bartlett and later Roswell S. Barrows, publisher of the *Jamaica Plain News,* pursued an insurance and real estate business. By the early twentieth century, Forest Hills Station, the focus of the booming residential districts nearby, had generated in its immediate vicinity several saloons, a restaurant, a realtor, a stoves and furnace store, a pharmacist, and an undertaker, as well as commercial buildings such as the Minton Block and the Forest Hills Hotel.[67]

The commercial districts of Jamaica Plain, typical of such outer-city strips and clusters, represented mixed land use, not tightly defined zones of activity. In the commercial-apartment buildings and houses along Centre Street, residences were interspersed with stores. Businesses also located in Green Street's new apartment buildings. Upholsterers, bellhangers, and gaslighting services operated in the Hotel Morse, and George A. Cahill, a Jamaica Plain resident and architect, kept his office in the Hotel McKinley. By the same token, wood-frame apartment buildings with storefronts for local grocers, butchers, or general stores were scattered here and there in residential areas such as Hyde Square, Egleston Square, and Heath Street.[68]

Contrary to the conventional view, the process of constructing the outer city did indeed build a neighborhood. During the late nineteenth and early twentieth centuries, powerful surges of urban growth, pausing only during economic depressions in the 1870s and 1890s, transformed Jamaica Plain from a rudimentary fringe settlement into a major urban district. In the process, the boundaries of what was commonly recognized as Jamaica Plain were pushed outward from the early compact settlement near Jamaica Pond. By the early twentieth century the neighborhood encompassed almost four square miles of territory, including previously unassociated areas and areas that once "belonged" to other districts. The extension of boundaries rendered the name Jamaica Plain inappropriate. The neighborhood had become a place of hills and valleys; in the larger context, the flatlands near the pond were now unique.

The place that emerged from the process of urban development did not conform to a homogeneous band in a city segregated by class. Instead Jamaica Plain became an extensive and distinctly heterogeneous neighborhood. As the neighborhood incorporated disparate subdistricts, tens of thousands of people of diverse backgrounds and circumstances came to think of Jamaica Plain as their home. Jamaica Plainers ranged from the independently wealthy to the indigent, from downtown professionals and businessmen to local artisans and laborers, from prosperous wives and widows to hard-working domestic servants. Puritan-stock Yankees, Irish-Americans, German-Americans, and other immigrant ethnic groups shared a sense of belonging to the community. The diverse peoples of the neighborhood, wherever they lived and whatever their station in life, all belonged to a place called Jamaica Plain.

Local Attachments

Despite the fact that the territory never constituted an independent town or other official governmental jurisdiction, both inhabitants and outsiders recognized and affirmed the existence of Jamaica Plain during the late nineteenth and early twentieth centuries. The *West Roxbury News,* founded about 1855 and regularly published from the mid-1870s, focused most of its attention on Jamaica Plain, the most populous and booming district of the old Town of West Roxbury. The growth of the local population and business community merited a more locally targeted newspaper, and from 1893 the paper was published as the *Jamaica Plain News.* By covering the events, people, and businesses of the neighborhood, the *News* communicated a sense of the district's importance to its inhabitants.

Out of a sense of local attachments, local citizens wrote histories and recorded memoirs that traced and preserved the early days of their home district. In 1897 Harriet Manning Whitcomb published a book on the history of the neighborhood, *Annals and Reminiscences of Jamaica Plain.* Local clubs invited elderly residents to offer recollections of the neighborhood as they had known it in their youth. On important anniversaries, the *Jamaica Plain News* printed the histories of neighborhood churches, schools, and other institutions.

Large outside agencies certified Jamaica Plain as a distinct neighborhood with its own identity. About 1870 the U.S. Postal Service provided the neighborhood with a post office to serve the neighborhood postal district. Even today envelopes addressed to a street in "Jamaica Plain, Massachusetts," will find their destination. Similarly, when telephone services were established in Boston at the turn of the century, *Jamaica,* later shortened to the prefix *JA,* became the telephone exchange for the district.[69]

Thus, out of the building process of the late nineteenth and early twentieth centuries, people came to live in an urban place called Jamaica Plain. They believed that the neighborhood in some sense belonged to them. Another aspect of the neighborhood's physical development, however, put such proprietary feelings to the test. For the public green spaces that lined Jamaica Plain's borders were created in the name of universal principles, not local places. To further understand the making of America's urban neighborhoods, then, we must now ponder the paradox of parks.

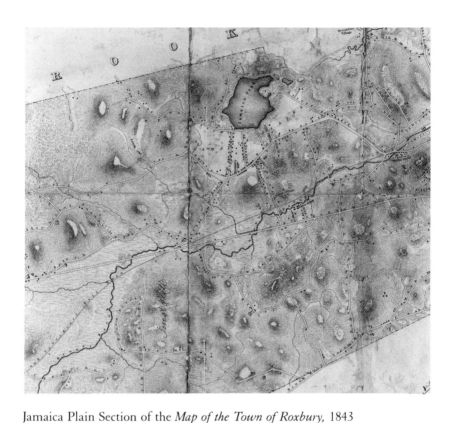

Jamaica Plain Section of the *Map of the Town of Roxbury,* 1843

Drawn nine years after the building of the railroad (running diagonally from bottom left), the map shows Jamaica Pond, the Stony Brook, and nearby drumlins—Parker Hill at the upper right, Cedar Hill near the brook, Sumner Hill, Moss Hill and the Bussey Farm hills on the left. The map reveals the early road and settlement pattern, with most residences yet clustered in the village of Jamaica Plain. It also shows the fringe industries—the Norfolk Laboratory between the turnpike and the brook and the Roxbury chemical works (the cluster of buildings on the right). The neighborhood's name, Jamaica Plains, is plural here because most still considered the district to be located on the flatlands adjacent to the pond, not on the rolling lands beyond.

Map by Charles Whitney, Boston, 1843, courtesy of the Harvard Map Collection, Harvard University.

The Jamaica Plain Station at Green Street, ca. 1905

Railroad stations created other centers of activity in outer-city neighborhoods such as Jamaica Plain. The station houses on either side are flanked by substantial residential and commercial structures.

Postcard courtesy of Suzanne Presley.

Jamaica Plain Village, 1815

The historic center of Jamaica Plain was located at the intersection of Centre Street and South Street (along the wall). Originally the First Church (Third Congregational of Roxbury) and the Loring-Greenough house anchored the site; Seaver's general store, just beyond, is obscured by the trees. Despite the pastoral vision symbolized by a farmer plowing the fields, the owner of both the mansion and the fields, David S. Greenough, was a prominent Boston attorney.

Painting, *View of the Revd. Thos. Grays Church and Parsonage and the Home of D. S. Greenough Esq.,* by W. Dobbins, 1815, courtesy of the Society for the Preservation of New England Antiquities.

Pinebank, ca. 1840

Andrew Jackson Downing, the renowned landscape gardener, considered the Perkins estate at Jamaica Pond to be among the admirable examples of American suburban landscape. The house depicted here was built in 1802 but was soon replaced by a French-style mansion and then, in 1870, by an English Victorian brick structure. Note the wooded grove, winding road, and pond on the right.

Lithograph from Andrew Jackson Downing, *Treatise on Landscape Gardening* (New York, 1841).

The Chemical Works, Roxbury, 1853

On the urban fringe, one found such industrial compounds as the Roxbury Chemical and Color Manufacturing Company. Despite the company's claim that no employee had ever died of lung problems, such factories were considered noxious places and hence located away from middle-class residential areas.

Wood engraving by John H. Schenk from *Gleason's Pictorial*, courtesy of the Boston Athenaeum.

Jamaica Plain, Ward 23, City of Boston, 1891

This bird's-eye view of Jamaica Plain reveals the diversity of outer-city develop-
ment. In the foreground are the woodsy estates of Parkside and Forest Hills Street.
Beyond them is the industrial railroad corridor, with the large factory complexes of
the Boston Thread and Twine Company and the Gas Company works (left), the
B. F. Sturtevant industrial fan company (center), and Brookside's Cable Rubber
Company and Haffenreffer's brewery (right). Working-class cottages are located in
Brookside along the railroad and between the thread factory and South Street.
Across the tracks from Sturtevant's factory, the tall spire of Central Congregational
Church marks the entrance to upper-middle-class Sumner Hill. To the right, the
Jamaica Plain Station commercial buildings are next to Green Street; middle-class
residences are scattered on either side. In the background is Pondside, with the Sol-
diers Monument on an island in Centre Street (left), the First Church just beyond,
and the Baptist Church (center).

Lithograph by O. H. Bailey, 1891, courtesy of the Jamaica Plain Tuesday Club.

Heath Street and Parker Hill, ca. 1890

Along the northern border of Jamaica Plain, New Heath Street crosses the railroad
close to the Highland Spring Brewery, and Heath Street, with its working-class
residences and factories, sweeps along the foot of Parker Hill and the Lowell family estate. Bromley Park, a middle-class row house development, is on the left.

Photograph by from *Jamaica Plain Boston 200* (Boston, 1976), courtesy of the Boston Public
Library Print Department.

Belmore Terrace, ca. 1905

The winding road and handsome two-family houses were part of a Cedar Hill development of the 1890s.

Postcard courtesy of the Jamaica Plain Historical Society.

Family at 89 Mozart Street, ca. 1890

Evidence suggests that this photograph, found among the papers of Jacob Luippold, shows the German immigrant architect and his family in front of their new but modest house in the growing Hyde Square subdistrict.

Photograph courtesy of the Society for the Preservation of New England Antiquities.

Hyde Square, ca. 1910

In northern Jamaica Plain, Hyde Square provided a secondary center of activity
with its own commercial-residential blocks. The lawn in the foreground belongs to
the rectory of the Blessed Sacrament Church.

Postcard published by Reichner Brothers, courtesy of Suzanne Presley.

Washington Street near Egleston Square, ca. 1870

The drawing sketches daily life in a respectable middle-class area of the outer city. A top-hatted businessman commuter chases a Metropolitan Railroad Company horsecar, baseball players banter on the corner, a couple strolls past a row of one- and two-family houses, and a woman takes her two children to church, probably the Egleston Square Methodist-Episcopalian Church.

Pen and ink drawing courtesy of Beth Anne Bower.

Burroughs Street, ca. 1915

The comfortable homes of a main Pondside street.

Postcard courtesy of Suzanne Presley.

The Eliza Dixwell House, Moss Hill, ca. 1885

Here two women of the Bowditch-Dixwell family enjoy the pleasant life at the Sunnyside estate on Moss Hill.

Photograph by Thomson and Thomson, courtesy of the Society for the Preservation of New England Antiquities.

Governor Foss's House on Revere Street, ca. 1910

Sumner Hill contained residences of upper-middle-class families such as this one, occupied by Eugene Foss, the son-in-law of Benjamin F. Sturtevant, heir to the ventilation company fortune and eventually governor of Massachusetts.

Photograph courtesy of the Society for the Preservation of New England Antiquities.

The S. G. Thaxter Residence, 22 Sigourney Street, ca. 1890

The creation of Franklin Park inspired the development of Parkside as an upper-middle-class residential area. In the 1880s Sigourney Street was developed with houses such as this one designed by the well-known Boston architect Edmund M. Wheelwright.

Photograph by the Soule Photograph Company, courtesy of the Society for the Preservation of New England Antiquities.

South Street and Car Stables, ca. 1914

South Street was the commercial thoroughfare for a predominantly working-class district. From the 1850s the horses of the streetcar line were stabled here, and the neighborhood gasworks was situated at the railroad nearby. In the background looms the spire of St. Thomas Aquinas Church, built to accommodate the large Irish Catholic population in the South Street area.

Postcard published by A. Kagan, courtesy of Suzanne Presley.

The West Side of Washington Street, Looking North from Keyes Street, May 1906

Here Washington Street, a commercial and residential thoroughfare, connects the southern extension of industrial Brookside with the eastern extension of the working-class South Street district. Note the stables in the left foreground, J. M. Fallon's saloon next-door, and Curley's saloon down the street.

Photograph by the Boston Elevated Railway Company, courtesy of the Society for the Preservation of New England Antiquities.

Hyde Park Avenue at Forest Hills, August 1905

Forest Hills began as a stop on the railroad and later became a terminus for Boston streetcars and a transfer point for remote neighborhoods and suburbs. Even before the elevated terminal was built there, the area generated considerable commercial activity. Here were poolrooms, cleaners, a local real estate and insurance agent, and, across from the handsome brick commercial block, the popular Forest Hills grocery market.

Photograph by the Boston Elevated Railway Company, courtesy of the Society for the Preservation of New England Antiquities.

3

The Paradox of Parks:
Universal Landscapes in
the Local Community

The stillness of the woods is broken only by the unfre-
quent note of some lingering bird or the whisper of the
dying leaves. But to the soul there are voices, O how elo-
quent and impressive! breathing in the very silence, and
in harmony with the faint song of bird and sigh of
leaf,—voices that utter not, yet are full of lessons.

—*William Augustus Crafts,*
"Reveries at Forest Hills," 1855

Large parks are not created in order to provide flower
gardens, zoological gardens, eating houses, race courses,
football fields, or any other such things . . . but primarily
that the public may have access to interesting scenery.

—*Olmsted, Olmsted, and Eliot*
to the Boston Commissioners of Parks, 1896

Even as Jamaica Plain developed
into an urban district of residences, factories, and shops, a significant
portion of neighborhood territory was converted to public open spaces.
Almost twelve hundred acres of landscaped parklands, the greatest concentration of parks in Boston, are located in or adjacent to Jamaica Plain.
This impressive array of nineteenth-century open spaces includes Forest

Hills Cemetery, laid out by the designer of America's first rural cemetery, and Arnold Arboretum, Franklin Park, and Jamaica Park, designed wholly or in part by the renowned landscape architect, Frederick Law Olmsted.

A national movement to create public urban landscapes produced these green spaces and others like them during the nineteenth and early twentieth centuries. It arose from the private efforts at gardening and landscape gardening and the related public campaigns for scientific agriculture and horticulture. In cities across the United States it fostered landscaped cemeteries, botanical gardens, arboreta, public parks, parkways, and the green milieu of suburbia.

Sweeping and sophisticated reform goals informed the public landscape movement. Inspired by associationist philosophy, landscape reformers believed strongly that natural settings designed especially in the tradition of English landscape gardening could uplift the minds and souls of American urban dwellers. If designed properly, green spaces would raise the level of national civilization by improving aesthetic taste and advancing the knowledge of science. What was most important, the reformers believed, these parklands would elevate the moral faculties of the urban public. Viewing public landscapes as a means of urban reform, they aimed to develop an alternative physical environment to the congested residential and busy commercial sections of the inner city. They strove to create, in the words of the historian David Schuyler, a "new urban landscape."[1]

Paradoxically, the creation of public landscapes represented an exercise in local place-making that usually ignored the local community. Beyond measuring the physical attributes of the site, designers of large parks rarely gave much thought to the immediate neighbors of the new green spaces. The creators and proponents of public landscapes did not believe that parks should express the local character or uniqueness of Jamaica Plain or any other individual neighborhood. Inspired by the universal principles of moral and aesthetic philosophy, park proponents and designers instead hoped to uplift whole cities and refine the entire nation. They believed that public landscapes should conform in purpose, function, and style to particular types of parks. These templates of intent and design could, with due respect for topography and climate, be applied to any community.

Not surprisingly, the plans of urban landscape reformers conflicted with the wishes of local residents in cities such as Boston, Worcester, and Pittsburgh. In Jamaica Plain, most local residents received the public open spaces willingly, but the large-scale goals of the landscape reformers tended to alienate the parklands from their neighbors. As Forest Hills Cemetery and Arnold Arboretum began to serve metropolitan and national constituencies, they became dissociated from the life of the local community. Jamaica Plainers asserted a proprietary interest in Franklin Park and Jamaica Park that undermined the universal principles of public parks proponents. As in other neighborhoods, the desire of Jamaica Plain residents for ready access to local green spaces and for active forms of recreation clashed with the reformers' plans to create quiet sanctuaries from urban life.[2] → want to keep local activity out of parks

The urban landscape reform movement originated in the activities of wealthy city dwellers who established private country and suburban estates near America's major urban centers. From the eighteenth century, men of wealth established country seats as summer or retirement homes in the villages and along the highways outside Boston, New York, and Philadelphia. Inspired by the high status and wealth of the landed gentry in Great Britain and on the Continent, they built elegant country houses and created lush estates around them.

In the early nineteenth century, wealthy Americans moved to the country, not to adopt the local life of villagers and farmers, but rather to achieve grand cosmopolitan goals. Influenced by British literature, especially in the Whig tradition, wealthy urban merchants and professionals perceived the acquisition of a country estate as a means to eschew aristocratic indulgence and cultivate private virtue. American urban gentlemen greatly admired British businessmen who retired to the country to study arts and letters. Ever conscious of their membership in a parochial society, the owners of country seats also felt a mission to create in the United States a great civilization equal to those across the Atlantic. They pursued wealth in the name of increasing the nation's prosperity, and they donated time and money to a wide range of cultural, educational, and philanthropic institutions.[3]

The urban gentleman practiced scientific agriculture, horticulture, and landscape gardening in this patriotic spirit. Because they believed that the progress of American agriculture would determine the fate of the nation, like Thomas Jefferson, gentlemen farmers studied and experimented with methods of growing crops, raising livestock, and other agricultural techniques. In order to advance and disseminate the knowledge of farming, the estate owners joined scientific agriculture societies. Leading literary and learned journals of the early Republic published articles on agriculture and related topics.[4]

By the 1820s, horticulture, the practice of growing fruits and flowers, began to capture the attention of America's urban cultivators. Unlike agriculture, horticulture was directly related to ornamental and landscape gardening and thus more suitable to the urban estates of the wealthy. During the decades before the Civil War, well-to-do gentlemen and their hired gardeners worked determinedly, and often at great expense, to raise and improve fruit trees and flowering plants in the suburbs of America's cities. Urban gentlemen subscribed to gardening periodicals and organized societies in their hometowns to further fruit and floral gardening. Each year they sent bouquets of flowers and baskets of fruits to compete for the prizes at the annual exhibitions of their horticultural societies.[5]

Horticulture fulfilled the urban gentlemen's patriotic aspirations as much if not more than scientific agriculture did. If agriculture was the foundation of a civilized nation, the gardeners asserted, horticulture represented the highest accomplishment of an advanced society. Only after a society had developed its agriculture, military skills, arts, and science, explained Henry Alexander Scammel Dearborn, the president of the Massachusetts Horticultural Society, could it reach the ultimate stage of civilization represented by horticulture. Thus, Philadelphia's Pennsylvania Horticultural Society complimented the contributors to its annual exhibition on their "patriotic zeal."[6]

To its sophisticated adherents, horticulture was both a science and an art. As a branch of science, horticulture represented a kind of applied botany; from the perspective of one gardening enthusiast, botany was theoretical horticulture. The gentlemen gardeners also considered horticulture to be a fine art, like painting and sculpture. Horticulture was indispensable to the practice of landscape gardening, which in turn derived from the genre of landscape painting.[7]

The gentlemen gardeners, moreover, assumed that horticulture and landscape gardening acted as agents of moral reform, an assumption that rested on the belief in the relationship between inner and outer nature. Following a long line of British and Scottish writers, educated Americans held that one's innate moral sense and aesthetic taste were closely related through the mental impressions or "associations" that connected a person's experiences. Thus, they believed that environments could elevate or debase the mental and moral faculties. The exercise of the mental faculties upon objects of great beauty, such as paintings or natural scenery, improved the imagination (or "taste," as it was sometimes called) and satisfied the moral sense. During the eighteenth century, moreover, the idea of the natural sublime had evolved into a belief that all nature was a projection of the divine mind. The contemplation of the infinite universe, the atomistic substructure of rocks and plants, or natural scenery refined the moral sense by bringing the individual closer to God.[8]

Urban horticulturists applied these assumptions to their avocation. Gardening, according to one horticulturist, was "conducive to moral and intellectual refinement," because "Horticulture is Art co-operating with Nature." "A student of nature, who should become sensual and debased," another declared, "would present as strange an anomaly as an undevout astronomer." "He who will walk in the garden with humility," explained a Boston horticulturist, "may yet hear the voice of God in its bowers."[9]

For similar reasons, estate owners were enthusiastic about landscape gardening, the large-scale arrangement of natural elements. They consciously designed their grounds according to cosmopolitan principles that contrasted with indigenous practices and local context. Following British practices of landscape gardening, nineteenth-century American estate owners increasingly turned away from the formal and symmetrical style in favor of the "natural" curving lines and asymmetrical plantings associated with the English landscape gardening movement. Within this movement, the picturesque school emphasized irregular and somewhat wild-appearing forms, including dark woods, rocky areas, and shaded pools of water. The beautiful or pastoral style, often associated with the landscape gardener Lancelot "Capability" Brown, presented curvilinear but more regular lines, usually containing broad sweeps of lawn and meadow, ponds, and clusters of trees rather than dense woods. Although the settings for American estates often favored the picturesque, many estates combined elements of both schools, especially when extensive grounds were available. The more recent gardenesque style, with its obviously ornamental displays of flowers and plants, also made inroads on American estates.[10]

As elsewhere, estate owners in Jamaica Plain participated actively in the agriculture and horticulture movements of the nineteenth century. An especially prominent leader was John Lowell, a retired lawyer from one of Boston's first families who planted groves of trees and experimented with exotic plants at Bromley Vale, his estate in northern Jamaica Plain. Lowell served as corresponding secretary and journal editor of the Massachusetts Society for the Promotion of Agriculture and helped to found the Massachusetts Horticulture Society. Several other members of the Massachusetts Horticulture Society lived in Jamaica Plain, including Francis Parkman, who indulged his passion for gardening at his summer home on the banks of Jamaica Pond. Parkman wrote the standard manual on growing roses, developed a double-blossomed crab apple and a lily, both of which were named for him, and became as famous for horticultural work as for historical writing.[11]

Jamaica Plain estate owners also transformed their properties by using the sophisticated principles of landscape design. Rockland, created in the 1830s by Samuel G. Goodrich, included wide lawns, ornamental trees, flowering shrubs with loopholes cut out for attractive views, and his personally designed rose garden, located behind the house. The Jonas Chickering country seat, "with its lovely water-front, its unique gothic buildings, its vine-covered lodge, and its deer-park," was one of several estates that graced the banks of Jamaica Pond. On the opposite shore stood Pinebank, the recently rebuilt house and estate of Edward Newton Perkins. In his survey of American estate grounds, Andrew Jackson Downing singled out Pinebank as "one of the most beautiful residences near Boston. . . . The perfect order of the grounds; the beauty of the walks, sometimes skirting the smooth open lawn, enriched with rare plants and shrubs, and then winding by the shadowy banks of the water; the soft and quiet character of the lake itself . . . all these features make this place a little gem of natural and artistical harmony, and beauty."[12]

The case of Benjamin Bussey, an important local property holder, exemplifies how estate owners created planned environments based on grand goals, not local concerns. A former goldsmith and back-country merchant, Bussey earned a fortune in the lucrative export fur trade, moved to Boston, and by the 1830s counted among his friends a former president of the United States, John Quincy Adams. In 1806 he moved to Jamaica Plain and began the process of creating a great country estate, Woodland Hills, about a mile south of Jamaica Pond. Here in 1815 he built and lavishly furnished a magnificent country house. Although he had received little formal education, Bussey greatly respected education and culture. At Woodland Hills Bussey kept an extensive collection of prints, sculptures, and paintings, including family portraits by Gilbert Stuart. Bussey owned shares in the Boston Athenaeum and at the time of his death possessed a personal library of eighteen hundred volumes. Outside his mansion, Bussey kept a furnished observatory with a large telescope.[13]

Although he supported Jamaica Plain's church, Bussey, like other wealthy philanthropists, was chiefly concerned with "the prosperity and happiness of our country." In his will he bequeathed to Harvard College funds for scholarships and professorships in the fields of agriculture, law, and theology. In particular, Bussey believed that rural pursuits, as they were known, would raise the level of American civilization. The greatest proportion of his bequest to Harvard College went to fund "instruction in practical agriculture, in useful and ornamental gardening, in botany, and in . . . other branches of natural science." In order to establish the Bussey Institution for lecture courses in agriculture and related subjects, Bussey willed that Woodland Hills, in "its high state of cultivation and improvement," be transferred to Harvard College after his heirs no longer wished to occupy it.[14]

As the bequest indicates, Bussey did not draw any hard distinctions between agriculture, horticulture, and landscape gardening. His estate contained a working farm with its own farmhouse, and he helped to introduce Merino sheep to the area, a great cause among the leaders of New England scientific agriculture. A member of the Massachusetts Horticultural Society, Bussey also experimented with horticulture in his orchard and gardens. Bussey transformed much of Woodland Hills into carefully crafted pleasure grounds that included such picturesque features as a forest crossed by winding paths, a rustic bridge over a brook, and a willow-bordered pond stocked with gold and silver fish. Broad and distant vistas of town and country were thought to expand the mind, and Bussey placed at the summit of Hemlock Hill an arbor where one could sit and view the surrounding valley and hills.[15]

Anticipating later public parks in Jamaica Plain, Bussey kept Woodland Hills as a semipublic park by opening the gates to the population at large. Among the visitors who strolled the grounds of Woodland Hills was Margaret Fuller, the editor of the transcendentalist journal *Dial,* whose family lived nearby. Ironically, Fuller used the contrived picturesque environment of Bussey's park as a place to contemplate nature and discuss natural philosophy with friends such as William Henry Channing and Ralph Waldo Emerson.[16]

Twenty-nine years after Bussey's death in 1842, his granddaughter, Maria Bussey, released the estate lands, and the Bussey Institution was established. In the fall of 1871 it began offering courses in agricultural chemistry, horticulture, and farming to teach "young men who propose to be farmers or gardeners, or who expect to have charge of large landed estates or ornamental grounds, whether private or public." The faculty members of the new institute included Francis Parkman, professor of horticulture, and Maria Bussey's husband, Thomas Motley, instructor in farming.[17]

The Bussey Institution eventually failed, but the founder's larger goals for the estate survived. Suburban scientific agriculture proved to be unpopular among both Harvard's students and its donors; in addition, the value of the Bussey Trust's downtown real estate holdings plummeted in the years after Boston's Great Fire of 1872. In the twentieth century the school was closed. In the meantime, Woodland Hills was transferred to the Arnold Arboretum, thus preserving in different form Bussey's bequest and parklands.[18]

More immediately, Woodland Hills set a precedent for Jamaica Plain's first large public landscape, Forest Hills Cemetery. Forest Hills Cemetery exemplified the rural cemetery, a new type of fully landscaped burial ground that became popular in American cities before the Civil War. The national efforts on behalf of horticulture and landscape gardening inspired the rural cemetery movement. In 1831 the Massachusetts Horticultural Society opened the country's first rural cemetery, Mount Auburn Cemetery, in the Boston suburb of Cambridge. Promoted by estate owners, horticulturists, and landscape gardeners, the idea of landscaped burial grounds soon spread to other American cities. Within a few years Philadelphia, Brooklyn, Rochester, Baltimore, and Worcester had opened their own landscaped burial grounds, and in the following decades rural cemeteries spread to cities and towns all over the United States.[19]

As part of this trend, in 1848 the City of Roxbury established Forest Hills Cemetery in southern Jamaica Plain. The officials of Roxbury had not intended to create a rural cemetery until Henry Alexander Scammel Dearborn, the designer of Mount Auburn Cemetery, launched a campaign to convince them to do so. As the city council deliberated the matter in 1846, Dearborn submitted a petition in favor of a rural cemetery. The following year Dearborn was elected mayor of Roxbury and joined the city council's committee on burial grounds. From this influential position he wrote the committee's report in favor of a landscaped cemetery. When a battle in the city council over finances threatened the project, Dearborn called a public rally, where he and others spoke on behalf of the proposed rural cemetery.[20]

For the site of the new rural cemetery, Dearborn sought a locale suitable for landscaping in the picturesque style. He chose a hilly tract of eighty-five acres near Toll Gate in southeastern Jamaica Plain, owned by Joel Seaverns, Esquire. Less than half a mile away, Benjamin Bussey had created his attractive pleasure grounds on similar terrain. Although much of the land was rugged, Dearborn reported, it had great potential for landscape gardening.[21]

Dearborn's vision reveals how landscape reformers focused upon universal laws and national civilization, not the peculiarities of local place. Dearborn, an active figure in Massachusetts politics and a man of great enthusiasms, was obsessed with creating an American civilization as great as those of classic antiquity. To show how the United States could acquire the wealth of the great empires, Dearborn wrote about the trade of the Black Sea and the effects of internal improvements in the American West. To encourage moral and cultural refinement, he wrote works on ancient burial practices and a study of Grecian architecture. In other books he celebrated the heroism of Jesus and of John Eliot, the Puritan missionary. To commemorate the great deeds of the American Revolution, Dearborn helped preserve the Bunker Hill battlegrounds in Charlestown. He organized the Roxbury Athenaeum and declared that despite its initially modest book collection, the institution would soon join the "triumphant march of civilization and refinement."[22]

As a builder of a great civilization, Dearborn pursued horticulture and landscape gardening, or what he called his "love of ornamental cultivation." "The culture of the earth is the basis of all the progressive movements of man, in the march of civilization," Dearborn declared. For many years he practiced horticulture and landscape gardening at Brinley Place, his inherited country seat in Roxbury, not far from the estate of his fellow cultivator John Lowell. Dearborn contributed to scientific agricultural journals and helped organize the Massachusetts Horticultural Society, serving as its first president.[23]

Concentrating always on the grand scale and universal laws, Dearborn seldom contemplated the individuality and particularism of local place. In 1830 Dearborn delivered a lengthy address celebrating the bicentennial of the founding of Roxbury but paid scant attention to the place he was commemorating. Like Emerson at Concord in 1835 and other commemorative speakers of the day, Dearborn focused upon the great sweep of history and civilization. With the glorious American past as his theme, Dearborn launched into the saga of the English Puritans and the Massachusetts Bay Colony. He duly noted the settlement of Roxbury but soon moved on to the early democratic achievements of the provincial government. He recalled briefly Roxbury's "chivalric ancestors" and their contributions to the "general weal" and then invoked George Washington's military leadership in South Boston (not Roxbury) and the great leader's sacrifices for "national existence." Dearborn spent the last quarter of the address comparing the virtues of the American republic to those of Phoenicia, Egypt, Africa, Greece, Gaul, and Britain.[24]

Dearborn thus thought of local places as the small but necessary cogs in the great machinery of civilization. Neighborhoods such as Jamaica Plain and towns such as Roxbury merely provided the background for heroic individuals to perform great deeds, whose transcendent importance was manifested elsewhere, in the political capitals of the empire. Since its founder held such views, it is not surprising that Forest Hills Cemetery was essentially Mount Auburn Cemetery transposed to the terrain of Jamaica Plain, an institution cut from the same mold as rural cemeteries in cities all over the United States.

The design pattern for rural cemeteries was derived from the landscape gardening traditions of the country and suburban estates. Drawing from the English landscape style that the wealthy employed on their estates, Dearborn, with the help of a civil engineer, designed Mount Auburn Cemetery to achieve a "picturesque effect" composed of serpentine walks and paths, groves of dark woods, ponds, clearings, ornamental plantings of trees, shrubs, and flowers, and plenty of border space between the burial lots. The picturesque style at Mount Auburn Cemetery set the pattern for the designs of Philadelphia's Laurel Hill Cemetery, Brooklyn's Greenwood Cemetery, and other rural cemeteries.[25]

At Forest Hills Cemetery, Dearborn recreated the landscape that typified Mount Auburn and other American rural cemeteries. After studying the site, Dearborn arranged winding roads, trees, shrubs, and flower beds in a plan that he hoped would place the flora in the best setting. He hired Daniel Brims, a gardener who had managed several Boston-area "country residences," to supervise construction and plantings. Like the horticulturists, Dearborn and Brims ordered plants from abroad (including eight thousand trees from England) and transplanted popular garden trophies such as rhododendrons and kalmias. Although the rolling terrain of southwestern Roxbury differed from the high hills of Mount Auburn, the defining design elements of the two cemeteries—winding roads, dark groves, and a body of water—were nonetheless identical. The mental image of the rural cemetery was so firmly fixed that the engraved scenes in guidebooks for Forest Hills Cemetery and other cemeteries were virtually interchangeable.[26]

The philosophical underpinnings of Forest Hills Cemetery were the same as those that had inspired Mount Auburn and other rural cemeteries. The proponents of the rural cemetery saw it as a natural sanctuary, like the private estate where the city dweller could recuperate from the stresses of urban life. They, like the horticulturists, believed in moral environmentalism based upon the doctrine of associations. Besides commemorating the dead, the new style of burial grounds would refine the taste, inculcate patriotism, and elevate the morals of the public at large.[27]

Proponents of the rural cemetery felt that the cemetery's defining elements—graves, monuments, and natural landscape—provided the public with edifying associations. From the early eighteenth century, British and American writers had described graves as reminders of death that purified the inner soul. Cemetery reformers, however, felt that the rural cemeteries such as Mount Auburn and Forest Hills were more conducive to mourning and quiet meditation than traditional burial sites.[28]

Dearborn hoped that Forest Hills Cemetery would contain the same kinds of historic and patriotic monuments that had helped define Mount Auburn and other rural cemeteries. Dearborn named hills in Roxbury's cemetery after two former Roxbury inhabitants, John Eliot, the Puritan divine, and General Joseph Warren, a hero of the American Revolution. He attempted to have their remains transferred to Forest Hills and monuments built in their honor, although he succeeded only in Warren's case. Forest Hills Cemetery never seriously competed with its Cambridge predecessor for prestigious tenants, but it did eventually receive the remains of William Lloyd Garrison, Edward Everett Hale, and Dearborn himself.[29]

As at other rural cemeteries, most of the columns, obelisks, and other funereal monuments built at Forest Hills were simple memorials constructed by family and friends to preserve the memory of the departed. Reflecting middle-class ideals of domesticity, these monuments, like the "consolation literature" of the period, portrayed heaven as a place where family life continued as it had on earth. Many inscriptions simply identified the buried person's position in the family—father, mother, son, or daughter. One monument, for example, displayed the words, "My Husband and Child," under a statue of a woman in ancient garb weeping over an urn with flowers and a funeral torch. Perhaps the most extreme expression of domesticity was the red sandstone sculpture of a sleeping Newfoundland dog with the simple inscription "Lotty."[30]

The natural landscape differentiated the rural cemetery from its graveyard predecessor. As at Mount Auburn and other cemeteries, the landscape and plantings at Forest Hills Cemetery were intended to comfort mourners and elevate the public. Each season at Forest Hills, wrote William Augustus Crafts in his guidebook, "has some peculiar charm which leads the mind to tender associations and to high and solemn thought." The cemetery's beautiful displays of nature might even benefit the poor, who "may . . . receive impressions never to be forgotten, which shall purify their hearts, awaken aspirations which they never felt before, or open new and pure sources of pleasure."[31]

As large numbers of people flocked to Forest Hills Cemetery, its commissioners concluded that the cemetery was having its intended effect. In

1851 the commissioners reported that "the immensely increased number" of visitors illustrated "the instructive, refined, moral, and pious influence of this sacred Receptacle of the Dead." The institution of a regularly scheduled omnibus to accommodate cemetery traffic seemed to substantiate the commissioners' belief that Forest Hills would attract not only the bereaved but those with the "taste to discern and sensibility to appreciate its quiet loveliness."[32]

Most of the thousands who visited Forest Hills, like those who congregated in other rural cemeteries, however, were not gentlemen and ladies in search of aesthetic refinement. They were ordinary people, "weary from the toil and anxieties of the daily routine," bringing "thoughts of recreation and pleasure only to fill the little gap between the hours of money-getting or household cares." Many of these were local residents who came to stroll, picnic, feed the ducks and English swans at Lake Hibiscus, and otherwise enjoy the scenery. Some evidently practiced behavior deemed inappropriate by cemetery officials, who accordingly issued regulations against admitting dogs, picking flowers, defacing monuments, discharging firearms, and making "unseemly noises." As Andrew Jackson Downing observed, most people came to the rural cemeteries, not because of their monuments, their role as "solemn places of meditation," or even because they were burial grounds, but because they offered substitutes for landscaped public parks, which America lacked.[33]

Despite the initial popularity of Forest Hills Cemetery, its relationship to the neighborhood in which it was located was somewhat distant. Although the cemetery commissioners felt that the neighborhood provided pleasant scenery on the drive to the burial grounds, Forest Hills Cemetery was originally an institution of the City of Roxbury, not Jamaica Plain. Then when the City of Boston annexed Roxbury in 1868, Forest Hills Cemetery became a private corporation, further attenuating its local connections. Roxbury and Boston men outnumbered the few wealthy Jamaica Plainers who served as trustees of the cemetery. To boost the income of the cemetery, the directors began selling only perpetual-care lots. This raised the cost of the lots, limiting the number of Jamaica Plain residents who could afford to buy into the burial grounds.[34]

By the turn-of-the-century, Forest Hills Cemetery had become a private metropolitan institution. It maintained an office in downtown Boston and received the remains of those, such as playwright Eugene O'Neill, whose lives belonged to communities far from Jamaica Plain. Forest Hills Cemetery was still a pleasant place to stroll, but by then authentic public parks attracted local residents who wished to enjoy landscaped scenery.

With the encouragement of Andrew Jackson Downing and others, from the 1850s large public parks had eclipsed the rural cemetery as the focus of urban landscape reform. In 1851 Downing prepared a plan for a large public grounds in Washington, D.C., and the following year the government of New York City declared its intention to create Central Park. In 1858 Philadelphia's city council embarked upon a plan to greatly enlarge Fairmount Park, and soon thereafter Baltimore officials created Druid Park. In the late nineteenth century the leaders of any city of substantial size felt the necessity of a large-scale public park as a matter of civic pride.[35]

In Boston, Arnold Arboretum was one of the first components in the city's new system of public parks, and it was the first such park to be built in Jamaica Plain. It was the forerunner of the urban arboretum parks, which spread across the country, from Washington, D.C., to Seattle, Washington. Traditionally Americans had felt affection and respect for certain trees that they associated with the local community or patriotic events. Landscape gardeners used trees as a key element in their designs in the form of small stands, dark groves, or deep woods. The arrangements and choice of trees were a matter of pride to the creators of estate landscapes and rural cemeteries such as Forest Hills Cemetery. Others, including Frederick Law Olmsted, had proposed creating arboreta before, but no plans had gotten beyond the drawing board. With no American precedents to draw upon, Arnold Arboretum presented the public park as a tree and plant museum, suburban estate, and resource for private horticultural and landscape gardening.[36]

Arnold Arboretum eventually came to represent the scientific and aesthetic branches of the parks-and-landscape movement, but it was rooted in the traditions of philanthropy and moral reform. In 1867 James Arnold, a wealthy New Bedford merchant, drew up a will in which he bequeathed a share of his wealth to Harvard College. Like Bussey, Dearborn, and other antebellum gentlemen, Arnold believed that "rural pursuits" promoted moral refinement. With his wife he created a "very interesting and instructive suburban seat" on their New Bedford estate. In his will, Arnold set aside a share of his wealth to advance "Agricultural or Horticultural improvements, or other Philosophical, or Philanthropic purposes." Arnold left the precise method and means of executing the bequest to three trustees—George Barrell Emerson, his brother-in-law, John J. Dixwell, the president of the Massachusetts National Bank and a resident of Jamaica Plain, and Francis E. Parker, an attorney.[37]

It was Emerson who translated the Arnold gift into an arboretum on the Bussey estate in Jamaica Plain. Emerson had originally suggested to his brother-in-law that he establish an arboretum to help the work of the Harvard botanist Asa Gray. After Arnold died in 1868, Emerson led the negotiations with President Eliot of Harvard that established the new arboretum and determined its location. Gray hoped that the new arboretum would be located next to the Botanic Garden in Cambridge so that he could oversee them both, but Emerson vetoed the idea because of high land prices. In 1869 Emerson chose the site of the Bussey estate because Woodland Hills was available to Harvard and already possessed a forest-park landscape and because the Bussey Institution had established a precedent for a research organization there. In addition, nearby, on Moss Hill, fellow Arnold trustee John J. Dixwell, a member of the Massachusetts Horticultural Society, boasted an estate with "one of the largest and best collections of native and foreign trees in New England."[38]

Unlike philanthropic businessmen such as Bussey or Arnold, Emerson was an educator and reformer. A Harvard College graduate, in 1821 he became the first principal of English Classical School (now English High School) in Boston. Two years later he opened his own private school for girls, which he presided over until 1855. A strong supporter of the public-school advocate Horace Mann, Emerson helped organize the American Institute of Instruction and worked for the education of artisans and southern freedmen. As a reformer like Mann, Emerson believed in the importance of "moral education" and delivered lectures on the subject.[39]

Like other educated members of his generation, Emerson linked the study of nature to universalist moral philosophy and reform. A founder and former president of the Boston Society of Natural History, Emerson greatly admired Louis Agassiz, the geologist and well-known exponent of the belief in the divine meaning of natural history. As a result of his work on the zoological and botanical survey of Massachusetts, in 1846 Emerson published a study of the trees and shrubs of Massachusetts that became a standard work on the subject. In his list of the uses of trees, Emerson cited their important role in the art of landscape gardening, their contribution to a country's beauty, and the pleasure they brought the "contemplative man" who possessed "the eye of a painter and the feelings of a poet, or those of a worshiper of the Author of those beauties."[40]

The first director of the Arnold Arboretum, Charles Sprague Sargent, placed the institution at the service of science and art. Sargent was an elitist blue blood whose aloofness typified the personality "cold roast Boston." In 1868 Sargent returned from a European tour to manage Holm Lea, the large family estate located on the Brookline side of Jamaica Pond. His success in reshaping Holm Lea gained him local recognition, especially from Horatio Hollis Hunnewell, an influential friend of the family and the owner of a breathtaking estate in what is now Wellesley, Massachusetts. Four years later, in May 1872, Sargent replaced Francis Parkman as professor of horticulture at the Bussey Institution. The next month he was named curator of Arnold Arboretum, and the following year he was promoted to director. Although Sargent lacked academic qualifications for these appointments, his friendship with Hunnewell, a benefactor of the Harvard botany department, and his own fortune commended him for the leadership of the poorly endowed institution.[41]

In order to ensure Arnold Arboretum a permanent existence, Sargent orchestrated a campaign to bring it into the emerging Boston park system. He hoped an agreement between the college and the city would safeguard the future of the institution (eventually a 999-year compact was signed) and free it from city taxes. There followed years "of exceedingly disagreeable semipolitical work" in which Sargent lobbied officials of Harvard and Boston, who were highly suspicious of each other. Sargent persuaded Eliot, who jealously guarded the school's administrative powers, to relinquish some nominal jurisdiction in return for landscape design, paved carriage drives, park police, and an additional piece of land at no cost. Some Boston councilmen charged, not without reason, that the park would be an "aesthetic farm" whose carriage paths would serve only the wealthy. The opportunity to acquire a park at a greatly reduced price, however, finally convinced the city council to appropriate the funds for the new park. In 1882 Arnold Arboretum became one of the links in Boston's chain of parks.[42]

Sargent shaped Arnold Arboretum into an institution that would further universalist principles of science and art. The Arboretum functioned on the one hand as a tree and shrub research center, where experts would collect and study forms of plant life and instruct in their uses, and on the other hand as a resource for those interested in the art of landscape gardening. Sargent allowed "students, landscape-gardeners and nurserymen" to compare the shrubs "available for planting in the Northern states." His exhibits of exotic and domestic plants were of great interest to horticulturists such as H. H. Hunnewell, and Sargent even provided advice on gardening to those who inquired.[43]

Sargent's weekly publication *Garden and Forest* expressed the dual role of Arnold Arboretum. Sargent placed explanations of botanical principles and a column devoted to the taxonomic features of "New and Little Known Plants" next to such articles as "The Artistic Aspects of Trees."

The "aesthetic ideals" that Sargent touted in *Garden and Forest* exemplified the high-culture branch of the landscape reform movement. According to Sargent, an important function of park landscapes was to teach the public artistic taste.[44]

In collaboration with Frederick Law Olmsted, Sargent planned the design of the park to "facilitate the comprehensive study of the collections, both in their scientific and picturesque aspects." Although he had originally planned to group trees according to morphological categories, after consulting with Olmsted, Sargent compromised the botanical arrangement to meet artistic standards. The central circulation feature of the arboretum was a winding carriage path lined with eye-catching shrubs such as azaleas, lilacs, and mountain laurel. Thus, Holm Lea as much as Linnaeus inspired the layout of Arnold Arboretum.[45]

Although Sargent believed that public parks provided the urban population with a place to repose and enjoy healthful air and sunshine, more than a little sense of noblesse oblige informed his thinking. Sargent presented the high science and art of landscape to the public as a way for the common people to enjoy a taste of the finer things in life. Although he opened Holm Lea to the public on weekends and organized guided tours of Arnold Arboretum for schoolchildren, he grumbled about the conduct of his visitors. He fought to insulate the administration of the arboretum and other public parks from the authority of municipal government. He raised funds for the arboretum from a small number of wealthy Bostonians, not from the populace at large.[46]

Needless to say, because of the philosophy of its director, Arnold Arboretum was *in* Jamaica Plain but not *of* Jamaica Plain. As a collection center for tree and other plant specimens, the arboretum was a national and even international institution. It also served as a remote branch of Harvard University's botanical studies and a resource for the estate owners and gardeners in the Boston area. Employees of the arboretum lived in Jamaica Plain, and Sargent's publicity releases about Lilac or Crab apple Sundays were dutifully used to fill space in the local papers, but that was the extent of the Arnold Arboretum's affiliation with the neighborhood in which it was located.

The protection extended by Harvard University and wealthy patrons enabled Sargent to manage Arnold Arboretum with little regard for the wishes of neighboring Jamaica Plain residents. This isolation was for the most part of little consequence. Most Jamaica Plainers probably accepted Arnold Arboretum as a pleasant place to visit on special occasions such as Lilac Sunday. But there was also a sense of the Arnold Arboretum as an esoteric institution with little relevance to the community. Indeed many Jamaica Plain residents were unaware that the arboretum was a Boston park. In the early twentieth century some local citizens actually proposed subdividing the arboretum and developing houses on its site. Nothing came of the demand, for Sargent had succeeded in safeguarding his institution, but such a proposal in relation to the area's other parks would have been unthinkable.[47]

Franklin Park, the largest of the parks in Jamaica Plain, was not intended as a neighborhood institution either. Bostonians supported public parks for reasons that ranged from pure moral reform to civic boosterism, but all agreed that a park should exist for the city as a whole. As part of the planned park system for Boston, in 1876 the park commissioners proposed the creation of "the chief park of the city," on the model of New York's Central Park. For this city park they chose a site located adjacent to Forest Hills Cemetery, between Jamaica Plain and Dorchester.[48]

Frederick Law Olmsted, the influential landscape designer who was hired to lay out the Boston park system, agreed that parks were city, not just neighborhood, institutions. He hoped that Franklin Park would be the crowning jewel in the chain of parks that became known as Boston's "Emerald Necklace." Given a relatively free hand in the creation of the park system by the Boston park commissioners, Olmsted both designed and shaped the initial policies governing the use of Franklin Park. Olmsted saw the creation of Franklin Park as an opportunity to bring sophisticated moral reform to the City of Boston as a whole.[49]

Olmsted carried the idealistic values of the antebellum movements for scientific agriculture and horticulture into the profession of landscape design. While a young man, Olmsted had been a gentleman farmer in Connecticut and then on Staten Island. Influenced by moral associationist philosophy, he felt that "rural pursuits . . . tend to elevate and enlarge the ideas." Like other antebellum gentlemen farmers, Olmsted practiced agriculture in the hope of raising the level of American civilization. He aimed to become, in his words, a "country squire" who would improve "the education of the ignobile vulgus."[50]

Olmsted combined the zeal of the urban reformer with the practice of landscape gardening. While in New York during the 1850s and 1860s, Olmsted belonged to a circle of leading social and political reformers that included Charles Loring Brace, an old friend and the founder of New York's Children's Aid Society, E. L. Godkin, the editor of the reform journal *The Nation,* and George William Curtis, the crusading journalist.

Local Attachments

With these men, Olmsted promoted tariff and civil-service reform and helped found the American Social Science Association, an organization that took on the "responsibilities of the gifted and educated classes for the weak, the witless, and the ignorant."[51]

With the help of his reformer friends, Olmsted obtained a job as superintendent of New York City's proposed Central Park. In this capacity in 1857 he collaborated with architect Calvert Vaux on the winning proposal for the design of the park. After trying out other occupations in the 1860s, Olmsted launched a successful career in landscape design and in the process helped to found the landscape architecture profession in the United States. Although Olmsted won a wide range of public and private commissions, he considered large urban public parks to be the highest and most socially significant form of his art. Besides Central Park and Franklin Park, Olmsted designed similar large parks in Brooklyn, Buffalo, Chicago, and Detroit.[52]

Like the proponents of horticulture and rural cemeteries, Olmsted derived his concept of the effect of park scenery from associationist philosophy. Olmsted had discovered moral associationism and the powerful effect of the environment on the human psyche from nineteenth-century Romantic writers. "A great object of all that is done in a park, of *all* the art of a park," wrote Olmsted, "is to influence the mind of men through their imagination."[53]

Olmsted believed that parks helped to uplift and reform the urban population in a variety of ways. Like the rural cemetery advocates and public landscape proponents such as Sargent, Olmsted believed that the beauty of park landscapes elevated American culture by improving public taste. When his design for Central Park was accepted, Olmsted declared that the new park represented a significant "democratic development" upon which "much of the progress of art & esthetic culture in this country is dependent." Parks, according to Olmsted, stimulated "the development of talent in landscape painting and . . . the demand for education in landscape judgment."[54]

Olmsted was convinced that the large public park served a unique function as a psychological sanctuary from modern urban life. Like the supporters of rural cemeteries, Olmsted was not anti-urban. He accepted cities as products of an advanced and cultured civilization. Yet Olmsted believed that advances in civilization brought on new and more complex problems. Combining associationist logic with the nineteenth-century notion that modern society could cause madness, Olmsted concluded that the formal designs and crowded conditions of cities produced mental and moral debilitation, or, as he put it, "degeneration and demoralization." Fortunately, according to Olmsted, appropriate park landscapes would remedy this condition. The "soothing and reposeful influences" of large park landscapes antidoted the "vital exhaustion, nervous irritation and constitutional depression" brought on by the growth of cities. Thus, in 1880 Olmsted declared that the surge in interest in parks over the previous twenty-five years demonstrated civilization's "self-preserving instinct."[55]

Like other supporters of public parks, Olmsted felt that a crucial mission of the public park was to uplift and reform the urban working classes. Central Park, thought Olmsted, "exercises a distinctly harmonizing and refining influence upon the most unfortunate and most lawless classes of the city." In his plans for Franklin Park, Olmsted targeted the families of workers and clerks. The toiling mothers in these families, Olmsted observed, were confined and subject to nervous fatigue, a fact which exerted "stinting" and "materialistic" influences on every member of the family. Franklin Park, Olmsted believed, would benefit these women and their families by "tranquillizing and refreshing" them.[56]

Olmsted realized that a large gap existed between the sophisticated aesthetics of landscape gardening and the public reform mission of Franklin Park and other urban parks. The appreciation of natural beauty, according to most authorities, had to be consciously cultivated. Thus, education and refinement seemed to be prerequisites for benefiting from natural scenery. Only "the more worldly fortunate," Olmsted observed, usually possessed the "refined culture" necessary "to enjoy the charm of rural scenery sympathetically with Wordsworth, Emerson, Ruskin, and Lowell."[57]

How would uneducated members of the public benefit from the big city parks that were intended to help them? To solve this problem, Olmsted returned to the familiar idea that nature exerted an unconscious influence on the mind. Working-class people might not appreciate the surroundings intellectually, argued Olmsted, but they were still affected—"made healthier, better, happier"—even without knowing it. To prove his case, Olmsted pointed to the humble origins of nineteenth-century writers and artists who had spread "the poetic enjoyment of nature." He quoted a description from the 1840s of the moral influence of park scenery on weary factory workers in Manchester, England, and asserted that similar scenes could be witnessed in the parks of Brooklyn, Buffalo, and Philadelphia.[58]

In order to achieve the universalist ends the park served, Olmsted developed a basic design formula for the large urban public park and applied it to sites in a number of different cities. Olmsted held that the ideal park environment represented the antithesis of urban "conditions of corruption, physical and mental." Reflecting a shift in taste away from antebellum estate and cemetery design, he declared that only the pastoral style of English landscape gardening would be appropriate. Thus, he defined the ideal park landscape as "a simple, broad open space of clean greensward, with sufficient play of surface and a sufficient number of trees about it to supply a variety of light and shade." Formal designs in either buildings or grounds, which had often been found in and around the mansion of the traditional country estate, were to be prohibited or restricted to the periphery of the park. Going further than many horticulturists and even park designers, Olmsted attempted to exclude exotic flowers, formal plantings, or what he considered obtrusive architecture from the sanctuary of his parks.[59]

In his plan for Franklin Park, published in 1886, when the park was officially opened, Olmsted divided the new pleasure grounds into two sections, the Country Park and the Ante-Park. Believing that only "tame and homely" scenery in the pastoral style offered relief from "the restraining and confining conditions of town life," he designed the Country Park, the main body of Franklin Park, as an open expanse of sloping lawn encircled by woods. A visitor standing at the center of the Country Park, where its two principal meadows met, could see in all four directions "broad, open views . . . between simple bodies of forest, the foliage growing upon ground higher than that on and near the centre lines." This simple, pastoral scenery, Olmsted believed, would give Franklin Park the "soothing charm which lies in the qualities of breadth, distance, depth, intricacy, atmospheric perspective, and mystery."[60]

In order to avoid "scenery . . . that would induce sensational effects" at Franklin Park, Olmsted made minimal use of the rugged grounds, abrupt hills, caverns, and other features associated with the picturesque style of landscape. The design for the Country Park did include picturesque "passages," but these rocky hills and wooded areas were intended to offset and emphasize the park's dominant sweeps of meadow. Even Scarboro Pond, created in 1891, was not part of Olmsted's original plan. The park commissioners requested that Olmsted's firm add it after they received petitions for a pond from local citizens.[61]

On the other hand, Olmsted prohibited formal plantings or ornate gardenesque-style features in the Country Park. He insisted that within the Country Park, "nothing shall be built, nothing set up, nothing planted as a decorative feature." Because the "beauty of rural scenery" appealed to "a different class of human sensibilities" than did decorative flowers,

Olmsted prescribed only native field flowers, not exotic hybrids, for the Country Park. The landscape architect even preferred the uneven but natural-looking lawns created by grazing sheep over the too-elegant neatness of the lawn mower.[62]

Olmsted designed Franklin Park such that nothing would disturb the quiet contemplation of the Country Park's serene landscape. With the exceptions of small areas near the picnic grounds that he set aside for tennis, croquet, and archery, Olmsted prohibited all active sports and large-scale amusements from the Country Park. As he had elsewhere, he sequestered the park from surrounding streets with a dense border of trees because, as he explained, the city conflicted with the park "in expression, sentiment, and association." In order to divert noisy and crowded activities from the asylum of the Country Park, Olmsted created the Ante-Park, a subsidiary park whose subdivisions included a formal promenade for carriages; an outdoor music amphitheater; a children's play lot and amusement park; and the Playstead, a playing field for young boys' athletics and large official ceremonies. Foreseeing the inevitable pressure for a zoo at the park, Olmsted designated a section known as Long Crouch Woods for a collection of small and domestic animals; he hoped no "sulky lions" would ever live there. The Ante-Park, like the city, would be hidden by a wall of greenery from the visitor to the Country Park.[63]

Like Dearborn's and Sargent's visions of the public landscape, Olmsted's conception of Franklin Park had little to do with the particulars of place. True, Olmsted attempted to evoke the area's past by giving historical names to sections of the park. Scarboro Hill and Ellicottdale were named after old Roxbury settlers, and Schoolmaster Hill commemorated Ralph Waldo Emerson's former residence in the area. Yet Olmsted intended neither to accommodate present neighbors nor to create a local institution but rather to establish a park for the use of Bostonians from all over the city and all different walks of life. Nor was the concept of Franklin Park unique to the City of Boston. Adjusting for terrain and climate, Olmsted attempted to apply the same principles of policy and design to large parks in other cities.[64]

Not surprisingly, given such universalist intentions, conflict arose between Olmsted's lofty goals and local citizens who took a proprietary interest in Franklin Park. In 1899, for example, when the park commissioners tried to realize Olmsted's goal of a landscaped asylum isolated from the surrounding cityscape by building a wall around Franklin Park, they ran into a buzz saw of community opposition. The owners of the expensive homes on the streets bordering the park were particularly incensed because the project involved closing convenient park entrances. They complained that the walls were lowering the value of their properties, that the city could not afford such costly measures, and that the artistic beauty of the park would suffer irremediable damage because of them. During a hearing of the Board of Aldermen on the Parks Department's activities at Franklin Park and Jamaica Park, the alderman from Jamaica Plain, Elbridge Gerry, attacked Olmsted's policy of sequestering the park and criticized Sargent, who supported the policy, as a member of an "extreme school" of landscape architecture. The park's neighbors eventually halted the construction of the wall.[65]

Although Olmsted tried to accommodate proponents of active recreation by providing sports facilities at Franklin Field and other sites, Jamaica Plainers, like neighborhood residents in Worcester and elsewhere, persistently challenged Olmsted's policy of repose and quiet recreation for Franklin Park. As early as 1888, Olmsted's firm complained that baseball games were ruining the turf of the Playstead. The following year, Boston's park commissioners announced a new policy banning all sports and active recreation from the park, with the exceptions of the Playstead, where only boys under sixteen years old were allowed, and a section of the Country Park set aside for the quiet young ladies' games of lawn tennis and croquet. Nonetheless, in 1890 George Wright, a local sporting goods merchant, received permission to set up a golf course on the Country Park's scenic meadows and began to offer lessons. In the late 1890s golf had become so popular that for safety's sake park officials banned nongolfers from the course on holidays and Saturday afternoons. Many of the golfers were residents of Jamaica Plain, and the neighborhood's newspaper duly noted their comings and goings, as well as the opening of the course every spring.[66]

During the 1890s local bicyclists also helped to undermine the solitude of Franklin Park. Jamaica Plain residents, including the members of the Jamaica Cycle Club, regularly rode through the park. Large races and holiday cycling in Franklin Park created the kind of mass spectacles that Olmsted deplored. On the Fourth of July in 1891 thousands of spectators who came to watch the bicycle races had to be held back by police officers. One Sunday in April 1895, it was reported, twenty-five thousand cyclists pedaled along the park paths. So it was that in 1899, when the park commissioners attempted to regulate cyclists by requiring that bicycles in Franklin Park be equipped with lamps, local residents, supported by the *Jamaica Plain News,* howled in protest. When the commissioners threatened to file a bill in the state legislature requiring lamps on bicycles, neighborhood legislators declared their opposition to the law to the local consul of the League of American Wheelmen.[67]

Despite the new Franklin Field's success as the most popular playground in the city, Jamaica Plain residents preferred the more conveniently located Playstead in Franklin Park. The neighborhood went "baseball crazy," and in the early twentieth century fielded a half-dozen teams of young men, including the Lowells, the Boylston Athletics, and the team of the Thomas G. Plant shoe company. Thus in 1903 citizens of Jamaica Plain vigorously protested the park commissioners' refusal to allow young men's football and baseball on the Playstead. This policy, too, was abandoned, and that fall hundreds of residents of the Egleston Square and Boylston Station areas came to Franklin Park to watch the local baseball championship, in which the Boylstons squared off against the Boylston Athletics. In the wintertime local residents flocked to the park for tobogganing on Schoolmaster Hill.[68]

In the late nineteenth century some reformers defected from the movement for contemplative landscapes and began to press for playgrounds and active recreation. The alternative playground movement combined with the clashes between local sports enthusiasts and the park commissioners over park policy to produce an anti–Franklin Park sentiment. In 1909, for example, the *Jamaica Plain News* complained that Franklin Park was "aesthetic," and not "practically useful" as a play area. With no other neighborhood playgrounds available, its editors claimed, local boys had been forced to resort to the streets, where they learned to shoot craps, steal fruit, and sneak rides on streetcars. Local residents did not wish to do away with the park. Rather, they wanted to open its facilities to sports and garner playgrounds and athletic fields for neighborhood youth.[69]

Acquired by 1892 and constructed in the mid-1890s, Jamaica Park was the last of the Jamaica Plain parks to be developed. In 1900 it was joined with neighboring Leverett Park and renamed Olmsted Park in honor of the designer of Boston's park system. Jamaica Park was built around Jamaica Pond and thus exemplified the type of park centered on a body of water. Although Olmsted felt that the water park, like the large city park, could function as a quiet asylum, the historic connection of Jamaica Pond to the community of Jamaica Plain challenged his assumption.[70]

Jamaica Pond had long been a place of recreation and an extension of the gentlemen's landscape on water. By the second half of the eighteenth century, when Massachusetts governors built summer houses there, boating and fishing had become a popular activity, and probably "the ancient custom of sliding and skating on the pond" had also been established.

Local Attachments

During the nineteenth century, as estates spread along its shores, Jamaica Pond continued to serve as a local recreation site for boating, fishing, and ice-skating. At their estate on Frothingham's Cove, the Frothingham family kept a sailboat, which they enjoyed racing against their neighbors' boats, and from the 1850s Jamaica Plain residents held rowing regattas on the Fourth of July. After the young men of Pondside raced their single and double sculls, neighborhood children competed in washtub races. The pond was also popular as a fishing hole, and freshwater smelts and other fish flourished there. Several nineteenth-century lithographs, including a print by Winslow Homer, document the continuing popularity of ice-skating on the pond during the winter.[71]

A desire to preserve a neighborhood recreational site and the estate landscape that adjoined it motivated the creation of a park at Jamaica Pond. In 1876 the Boston park commissioners first proposed the creation of Jamaica Park, including the pond and adjacent lands, with facilities for boating and skating. The commissioners described the western shore of the pond as "a somewhat steep hill-side, well planted with trees and shrubbery, and mostly occupied by private dwellings, with their adjacent ornamental grounds," and the eastern shore as "occupied by private dwellings, with their lawns and shrubberies, and with some fine trees." Ice harvesting, however, had given rise to a number of drab wooden icehouses on the western shore. The commissioners predicted that if the land surrounding the pond was not taken by the city, the "rural character of the scenery" would be replaced by icehouses, horse stables, and tenement buildings, causing a danger to public health through pollution of the pond. It is unclear how real the threat of industrial development at Jamaica Pond was, since the commissioners repeated the same argument for the following fifteen years.[72]

In 1891 the city council of Boston finally appropriated funds for the purchase of the Jamaica Pond and neighboring lands, and the following year Olmsted drew up the plan for Jamaica Park. By January 1893 park commissioners had taken control of Jamaica Pond and purchased three neighboring estates, but the high cost of the estate properties prevented acquisition of more than a thin strip of lands around the perimeter of the pond. Although Olmsted deemed the preservation of all the private homes on the pond impractical for a public park, his park plan did call for the preservation of two homes as "refectories" or refreshment stands. Significantly, the houses to be saved were two elegant mansions, the Prince Street home of Robert M. Morse, Sr., and Pinebank, the home of Edward Newton Perkins.[73]

Because it was essentially a preservation project, Jamaica Park, of all the parks of Jamaica Plain, most clearly reflected its local context. The grounds of Jamaica Park did not require extensive rehabilitation to be made into a public park. Olmsted merely replaced some buildings with plantings, built an embankment along parts of the pond's shore, and completed a walking path around the pond. He also proposed building, at different sites along the border of the pond, a boathouse to facilitate the traditional recreational use of the pond and a bathhouse, an expression of late-nineteenth-century public-health reform.[74]

Yet even at Jamaica Park there was a formulaic element. By the time he designed Jamaica Park, Olmsted had incorporated water scenes into his definition of the public landscape as an antidote to modern civilization. "An expanse of water," Olmsted wrote in 1886, "can never fail to have a refreshing counter interest to the inner parts of a city; it supplies a tonic change at times even from the finest churches, libraries, picture galleries, conservatories, gardens, soldiers' monuments, parks and landward outskirts." Thus, after they had taken control of Jamaica Pond in 1892, the park commissioners instituted a policy prohibiting from Jamaica Park large public events and celebrations, the kind of mass entertainments that Olmsted felt disrupted the repose of the ideal park environment.[75]

The long tradition of private residences and public recreation at Jamaica Pond counterpoised such universalist intentions. Like Franklin Park, Jamaica Park inspired strong feelings of local proprietary interest. As at Franklin Park, neighbors objected strenuously to the park commissioners' policy of shutting out the city from the parkland. The abutters criticized the construction of walls along Prince and Pond streets as a detriment to the beauty of the park. When park workers were seen throwing large stones into Jamaica Pond, the atmosphere of suspicion gave rise to charges of scandal and to a city council investigation, led by local politicians, of the Boston Parks Department. In 1899 the Jamaica Plain Carnival Association, a group of neighborhood businessmen, persuaded the commissioners to reverse their previous policy against public celebrations in the park and began conducting annual Fourth of July festivities there that included swimming, boating, the ever-popular tub races, and a spectacular evening fireworks display.[76]

Community opinion divided over the proposed swimming area and bathhouse at Jamaica Park. In 1900 the park commissioners vetoed the bathhouse on the grounds that public bathing—like the icehouses— would spoil the "sylvan beauty of Jamaica Pond" and disrupt "the quiet neighborhood of suburban residences." Jamaica Plain supporters of active recreation continued to agitate for public bathing, but the wealthy abutters

of the park were adamantly opposed. When some Jamaica Plain businessmen again proposed a bathhouse in 1904, Robert M. Morse, Charles F.
Farrington, and other Pondside property owners decried the idea. They
claimed that Pondside owners had paid dearly to maintain their estates "in
harmony with the beautiful park which the city has created." The Town of
West Roxbury once had demolished public bathhouses as a nuisance, they
asserted, and new bathhouses would drastically lower their real estate
values. Bathhouses would attract disorderly elements, charged Morse and
his neighbors, and be the center of "noise, vulgar and profane talk and
rowdyism." "The public parks are for all the people," they concluded,
"and no use of them should be allowed that is offensive to a large body of
intelligent and respectable citizens." With the aestheticism of the park
commissioners and the abutting neighbors' opinions for once in congru-
ence, the quiet of the park landscape at Jamaica Pond was preserved.[77]

The efforts to create universalist landscapes in the local community of
Jamaica Plain produced ambiguous results. They succeeded in creating a
remarkable set of landscaped open spaces and a pastoral image for many, if
not all, sections of Jamaica Plain. Reflecting the high value the upper class
placed on landscaped greenery, most Jamaica Plainers considered the adjacent parklands as neighborhood amenities. Yet the far-reaching universalist ideals that propelled the urban landscape movement often did not
synchronize with the particular interests of neighborhood residents. Especially in the case of Franklin Park, an aroused localism challenged the
fundamental assumptions of the park builders and undermined their far-
reaching goals. Such skirmishes foreshadowed the disastrous struggles
between universalist political reformers and locally oriented politicians
during the early twentieth century.

Before investigating that monumental conflict, we need to examine how
neighborhood residents came to feel such a strong sense of local attachment. Both the expanding sense of neighborhood identity and the readi-
ness to contest landscape reformers and park commissioners attest to the
strength of local ties but do not explain its source. In order to better
understand the powerful force of localism, we shall turn in the following
chapters to the economic, social, and political dimensions of neighborhood
life. We shall begin by exploring the obscure but crucial world of business
in the urban neighborhood of the late nineteenth century.

4

Neighborhood Business Ties

The Directors of this Company [the Jamaica Plain Gas
Light Company] are well known to you, they are your
neighbors . . . they have every incentive to deal fairly
with their customers, and preserve and maintain the
most pleasant relations with them.

—*John C. Pratt, 1886*

Economic enterprise played a crucial role in the historic development of the modern American city. During the nineteenth century, trade, later supplemented by manufacturing, propelled the growth of the great cities of the United States. City entrepreneurs dramatically expanded the scale and scope of urban wholesale, retail, and manufacturing enterprises. The transfer of capital and goods and the production of commodities provided livelihoods for masses of urban residents and, by attracting migrants to the city, increased the urban population. As economic activity expanded and demand for space soared, businessmen speculated in downtown real estate, realizing great profits even as they reshaped the urban core.

Downtown business leaders strongly identified with their cities and exerted great influence over their affairs. Acting as aggressive city boosters, leading businessmen and their political allies promoted local economic growth and attempted to aggrandize advantages for their towns. Businessmen were heavily involved in urban politics and government as candidates, party patrons, or political reformers. Leading downtown business figures also organized and participated in the great mercantile, financial, and cultural institutions of the city.

90

Scholars have long recognized the importance of economic activity to urban centers, but surprisingly few have examined the impact of enterprises and entrepreneurs on city neighborhoods. Since the days of Robert Park and Ernest Burgess, urban sociologists have been fascinated by the nature of community in the modern urban setting. Consequently, they have tended to study neighborhood social relations, institutions, and land uses but not local business establishments. Similarly, urban economists and geographers have tended to explore metropolitan scale economies, patterns of industrial and residential location, and regional urban hierarchies rather than neighborhood economies. Interested in understanding the city as a whole, historians examined downtown merchants, large manufacturers, and the economic structure of entire cities. As a result, they, too, have given neighborhood businesses and business persons only passing notice.[1]

Economic enterprises and entrepreneurs, however, affected the urban neighborhood as profoundly as they influenced the downtown and the city as a whole. Economic activity, of course, enabled the urban neighborhood to thrive and grow. More than that, as the history of Jamaica Plain reveals, it encouraged urban residents to form attachments to their neighborhood in at least three different ways. First, economic activity fostered business relationships between residents of Jamaica Plain. As a part of the larger metropolitan capital market, the neighborhood capital market linked members of the community to one another and to their neighborhood. Those with resources loaned or otherwise made capital available to neighborhood proprietors. Such loans allowed local businesses to expand and linked neighborhood investors and businessmen to one another, even across religious and ethnic barriers.

Second, once established, neighborhood businesses encouraged local social ties and neighborhood allegiances. Functioning as community institutions, manufactures projected the intimate patterns of mill town life onto the city neighborhood. Factory owners and managers lived near their plants, frequently adopted paternalist attitudes toward their workers, and took part in the public life of the neighborhood. By bringing workers together under one factory roof, manufacturing establishments indirectly fostered social ties and, often, worker solidarity among their employees, most of whom lived near the plants. Similarly, local retail shops often functioned as community social centers, and as a consequence successful local businessmen emerged as neighborhood leaders. By sustaining a wide range of local business activity, real estate development involved great numbers of neighborhood residents and gave them an economic interest in the future of their community.

Finally, local business activity produced individuals who articulated and championed the interests of the neighborhood. Perceiving the potential for local economic opportunities, Jamaica Plain boosters promoted economic and population growth through real estate development, transportation and utility companies, savings and loan banks, and the local newspaper. Through their activities and organizations, Jamaica Plain businessmen articulated the vision of a booming community and fought for the neighborhood interest as they saw it. When local businessmen founded a Jamaica Plain improvement association at the turn of the century, they institutionalized their efforts to achieve the twin goals of local business prosperity and the advancement of the neighborhood.

Commerce, manufacturing, and other kinds of urban enterprise depend upon the availability of capital. During much of the nineteenth century, however, investment banking in New England was devoted primarily to large-scale commercial and manufacturing enterprises, many of them in other regions of the United States. At the same time, Boston's commercial banks and other large financial institutions were located in the downtown financial district, not in urban neighborhoods such as Jamaica Plain. With banks and other financial institutions frequently closed to them, beginning or small-scale urban entrepreneurs had to look to individual investors for the capital to inaugurate and expand their operations.[2]

The participation of individuals in the capital markets of nineteenth-century Boston enabled residential neighborhoods to function as small capital-exchange zones. Despite its lack of a commercial bank, Jamaica Plain contained both sources of capital and opportunities for investment. On the one hand, some neighborhood residents possessed reserves of capital that could be loaned. On the other hand, a growing number of neighborhood entrepreneurs needed resources to launch or expand manufactures, workshops, stores, and other enterprises.

Although nineteenth-century business investments are generally difficult to trace, records of chattel property mortgages in the Town of West Roxbury provide a window through which to view the neighborhood capital market. Unlike the mortgages used to finance purchases of real estate property, these transactions were business or personal loans with movable property held as collateral. A survey of the chattel mortgage records pertaining to Jamaica Plain businesses reveals the basic patterns of neighborhood flows of capital. Jamaica Plain residents exported capital to businesses outside the neighborhood; business associates, relatives, and others from elsewhere extended credit to local businesses; and neighborhood residents, who learned of local investment opportunities through neighborhood channels, lent financial backing to home enterprises.[3]

In some instances, local capital traveled outside the neighborhood, although often both investors and borrowers resided in Jamaica Plain. Among neighborhood residents, downtown commission merchants generally commanded the largest amounts of surplus capital and belonged to a group known for its predilections toward investment. Several helped finance the activities of neighbors who were themselves wholesale merchants or large manufacturers in other parts of Boston. In 1857, for example, one extremely wealthy Jamaica Plain resident, James W. Converse, the founder and copartner of Field and Converse, a leading Boston boot and leather company, and president of the Mechanics' Bank of Boston, loaned the formidable sum of $18,900 to Donald McKay, the famous shipbuilder of East Boston. McKay put up for collateral the equipment and supplies of both his old and his new shipyards, the contents of his East Boston house, and his house, stables, carriages, and boats on Jamaica Pond. In 1856 Robert Morse, a wholesale grocer in Boston who lived on Pond Street, applied to Samuel May, a wealthy Boston merchant and banker who lived in Roxbury, for a loan of $5,000 and to his Pondside neighbor Melancthon Smith, another Boston merchant, for an additional $2,000.[4]

Yet the neighborhood also attracted capital from external sources. Unable to tap into the affluent mercantile network, some small-scale local entrepreneurs, like immigrant and small businessmen in San Francisco and elsewhere, were forced to rely upon savings or loans from relatives and countrymen. Thus, the West Roxbury records include numerous transactions between Jamaica Plain businessmen and individuals of the same last name who resided in locations remote from the neighborhood. In 1851 the grocer Daniel A. Brown, for example, put up twenty boxes of sugar, two hogsheads of molasses, one lot of cigars, six barrels of oil, and sundry other items in stock in his Green Street store for a loan of two thousand dollars from Daniel Brown of Danvers, Massachusetts. In 1857 Thomas Decatur, the proprietor of a Green Street provisions store, used ice chests, chopping blocks, marble slabs, and the horse and wagon he used in his business as the collateral for a two-thousand-dollar loan from John and Horace Decatur of Barrington, New Hampshire. In 1866 William Wood used the equipment of his cotton-bleaching plant on Brookside Avenue as collateral to obtain a loan of four hundred dollars from James R. Wood of Lawrence, Massachusetts.[5]

Just as manufacturers sometimes tapped the downtown wholesale merchants who traded their products, Jamaica Plain entrepreneurs obtained extra-neighborhood capital from individuals or firms in the same field of business. In 1857, for example, Charles G. Farnum, a cutter, received a mortgage worth $950 from a wholesale tailor in Boston, and Edward Stone, a provisions dealer in Jamaica Plain, obtained a mortgage of $600 from the partners in a Brighton butcher firm. Sometimes such transactions represented advances on sales from supplying companies. James Richardson and Maurice Foucar, copartners in a Jamaica Plain billiard saloon, received an $800 loan from Amasa Bailey, of Boston, using as collateral the mahogany billiard tables, "now in the saloon," which Bailey had made. Similarly, in 1860 the owners of a Boston lumber firm loaned Levi P. Dudley, a Jamaica Plain carpenter, $68.20 and used his carpenter's shop and stable as collateral.[6]

Within Jamaica Plain, geographic proximity combined with economic opportunity to encourage local capital transfers between neighborhood residents and entrepreneurs. Because they lived in the neighborhood, local investors could discover and observe nearby economic enterprises. Eight years after he mortgaged his store, for example, Daniel A. Brown was able to loan a thousand dollars to Joseph Byron, a local currier. Byron put up as collateral the fixtures in his leather factory and all his household goods, including a pianoforte, china, and four oil paintings. In 1863 John E. Williams, a Green Street harness maker, loaned three hundred dollars to the owner of a nearby clothing store, John Buchanan.[7]

At times, this local capital market bridged the gap between neighbors who belonged to different social classes. In 1865, for example, an Egleston Square milkman, Melzer C. Waterman, received a loan of six hundred dollars from a neighbor, Boston wholesale merchant Charles Merriam. In February 1862 Nelson Curtis, an extremely wealthy mason, gave an eight-hundred-dollar, one-year mortgage to Levi Champion, the owner of a delivery service between Jamaica Plain and Boston. In return Champion put up all his business equipment, including eight wagons, three double sleighs, three sets of harnesses, and eleven horses, among which were "two large bay horses named 'Tiger and Sam,' one Roan horse named 'Billy,' two gray horses named 'Ned and Sam,'" and a bobtailed bay horse and a plain bay horse, both named Charlie. Like most of the mortgagees, Champion was slow to repay his debt, but in August 1863 Curtis canceled the mortgage.[8]

The evidence suggests that business ventures in Jamaica Plain, like those of nineteenth-century Poughkeepsie and other American cities, were precarious affairs at best. The tendency of local mortgagees of the 1850s and 1860s to be late in repayments indicates the difficulties they experienced in starting and running businesses. Indeed, some businessmen were foreclosed upon by their mortgagors, and most neighborhood businesses were small or short-lived.[9]

Success in a neighborhood business depended upon a confluence of factors, including entrepreneurial skills, access to capital, the existence of a market for the business product, a good location, and a certain amount of luck. The story of how Rudolf F. Haffenreffer, an immigrant entrepreneur, established the Boylston Lager Beer Company provides a case study of the elements necessary for a neighborhood business to succeed. It further demonstrates how the urban neighborhood provided an economic nexus for enterprising individuals of diverse religious and national backgrounds.

At first glance Haffenreffer's story appears to be a rags-to-riches tale, but a closer look suggests that he inherited middle-class values and aspirations from his family. In 1847 Haffenreffer was born the youngest of four children of a Lutheran family in Heidenheim an der Brenz, Württemberg. His father was an attorney, but in 1861 the elder Haffenreffer lost all his property, including a substantial home, because of financial obligations to a brother-in-law whose business failed.

With access to a profession closed off, Rudolf began to acquire artisanal skills in the brewery trade. In 1861 he was apprenticed at a Wasseralfingen brewery as a brewery worker and waiter in the adjacent inn. Three years later he moved to a local cooperage, where he learned the cooper's trade. Later that year Haffenreffer acquired his first job as a brewer in Bavaria and then worked his way up to head maltster, which position he held until August 1865. Over the next three years Haffenreffer worked in various capacities in breweries in Nürnberg, Strasbourg, and other sites in France and Germany. He found each job unsatisfactory for one reason or another, but he furthered his knowledge of the beer trade in the process.[10]

Historically, push-and-pull factors have influenced the movements of immigrants to the United States. In Haffenreffer's case, the fear of fighting in the German army pushed him to migrate, and the opportunity for employment pulled him to Boston. Although he was not enthusiastic about moving to America, Haffenreffer considered it to be the only reasonable alternative to imminent conscription. In August 1868 he departed from Bremen on the steamer *Deutschland,* bound for New York. Arriving in New York City on August 22, Haffenreffer, an experienced European traveler, was greatly impressed. "What a beautiful sight!" he wrote to his parents. "Here on the coast stood palaces and gardens such as I have never seen." On August 24, after only one day in New York, he traveled by ship to

Boston, "a very lovely city about five times as large as Stuttgart." Upon his arrival, Haffenreffer took a job at Gottlieb Burkhardt's brewery in Roxbury.[11]

Whether by wit or luck, Haffenreffer arrived in the Boston area just as brewing and beer consumption had begun to increase. Traditionally Bostonians had drunk British ales and stouts, and in the early nineteenth century ale breweries were established in South Boston and Charlestown. As in New York, Cincinnati, Milwaukee, and other cities, however, a large influx of German-speaking immigrants in the mid-century decades expanded the market for brewed beverages and helped popularize lager beers. Taking advantage of the water source provided by the Stony Brook (and perhaps the presence of skilled German workers), immigrant entrepreneurs began setting up new breweries in Roxbury. In 1847 Charles Roessle and Matthias Kramer bought a facility for brewing small beer in Roxbury and moved the operation to a pond created by the Stony Brook. The next year, Roessle and Kramer hired Gottlieb Burkhardt, a recently arrived immigrant, who began brewing the first German lager beer in the Boston area. Boston brewers commonly followed the artisanal tradition that journeymen should establish themselves as independent masters, and Burkhardt soon left to start his own brewery on Parker Street in Roxbury.[12]

American breweries grew in scale and number as the urban market for beer expanded beyond the German-American population. Breweries in Boston, most of which were devoted to lager beer production, proliferated in Roxbury and northern Jamaica Plain during the following decades. In the 1850s, Burkhardt, Roessle, Joseph Hechinger, and Henry and Jacob Pfaff started lager beer breweries just north of Jamaica Plain along the Stony Brook. In 1862 Burkhardt hired Henry H. Reuter, a native of Westphalia, to administer his growing business. But in 1867 Rueter quit and, with John R. Alley, founded the Highland Spring Brewery along the Jamaica Plain border at Heath Street. By 1880 the brewing business, centered in the Stony Brook area of Jamaica Plain and Roxbury, had become one of Boston's major industries in terms of both capital invested and workers employed.[13]

Blessed with skills, determination, and a middle-class background, Rudolf Haffenreffer exploited the opportunities offered by the growing brewing industry. Although he began work in 1868 at Burkhardt's brewery as the cellar man at a wage of eight dollars a week, his knowledge of brewing and his work habits brought him regular promotions and raises in pay. The following year, Haffenreffer worked his way up to the position of brewmaster in charge of more than fifty employees, and in October 1870 he was earning a hundred dollars per month. Meanwhile Burkhardt's business boomed, enabling its owner to build a large brewery complex that also contained a brandy distillery. When he started to work for Burkhardt, Haffenreffer reported, the brewery shipped its beer in three wagons, but by the summer of 1870 it took fourteen wagons to ship between thirty thousand and forty thousand dollars' worth of beer a month.[14]

Haffenreffer soon concluded that unlike in Germany, "here you can still earn something with beer." Now he, too, began planning to strike out on his own. Like other budding entrepreneurs, Haffenreffer looked first to savings and family for start-up capital. He saved money by boarding with Gottlieb Burkhardt's widowed sister-in-law and soon began to court her daughter Katherine. His employer approved of the match and promised, should Haffenreffer marry his niece, to assist the young brewer in starting an independent business. Haffenreffer, however, was wary of Burkhardt, who had a reputation of exploiting those in his debt. Thus in 1871 Haffenreffer went to Germany to acquire capital from his relatives and received a loan of five thousand dollars from his sister. The seed money from Haffenreffer's family, however, also came with a price: until he repaid his sister's loan, Haffenreffer was subjected to the nagging of his uncles, who apparently managed her money, for the interest and repayment.[15]

Despite the support from his family, Haffenreffer needed more capital. In order to get funds, he made use of ethnic and business connections. After rejecting his first preference for a site in South Boston because it cost too much, in 1871 he chose a site along the Stony Brook near Boylston Station in Jamaica Plain, "where it is ten times lovelier than in Germany." Haffenreffer then joined with Franz von Euw, a German Swiss carpenter who lived near Burkhardt's brewery, to buy the land and start the company, but the expenses of starting up were great. The brewery site cost four thousand dollars; then there was the equipment, including brewing casks in eight-, ten-, sixteen-, and twenty-barrel sizes, which he financed with a six-hundred-dollar, four-month mortgage from the Boston coopers Henry Hill and George Wright; and there were construction and other costs. Although von Euw and Haffenreffer had put all of their available money into the business, it seemed that there were always more workmen to be paid. When he received no more additional money from Germany, Haffenreffer became desperate.[16]

Fortunately for his venture, Haffenreffer was able to tap into the Jamaica Plain capital market. Like other local businessmen, the young brewer from Württemberg discovered that the common bonds of neighborhood and economic opportunity overcame barriers interposed by ethnic and religious differences. In December 1871 Charles Dolan, an Irish immigrant and currier in the Egleston Square area, became a partner in the Boylston Lager Beer Company and advanced Haffenreffer as much money as he needed to complete his contracts and begin delivering beer. Demand for Haffenreffer's lager beer was brisk, however, and by June 1872 he needed to buy two more horses and a new double-yoked wagon and to build a new ice cellar. To finance the cellar and again expand his capacity, Haffenreffer mortgaged the brewery for a twenty-thousand-dollar loan, half to be repaid in ten years, from Patrick Meehan, a wealthy Irish-born contractor and real estate investor who belonged to the group of land investors who had sold Haffenreffer the brewery site.

Saddled with this great debt, Haffenreffer was unable to repay his family's loan (it would take him eight years), but in November 1872 Francis A. Peters, "a rich American," bought out von Euw and Dolan. Peters, a Yankee broker in the Boston firm of Peters and Parkinson (and later president of the Webster National Bank), lived in the Pondside district and was investing in Brookside real estate. Haffenreffer now took sole control of the business and paid Peters his "per cent." Soon thereafter Patrick Meehan, perhaps as a way of obtaining his mortgage payments, also joined the partnership of the Boylston Lager Beer Company.[17]

With access to the deep pockets of his Jamaica Plain neighbors, Haffenreffer was able to make the Boylston Lager Beer Company succeed. During the 1870s and 1880s he increased production of his beer, which he claimed Bostonians preferred to any other. In November 1873, after expenses and the cost of new equipment were subtracted, the company showed a net profit of five thousand dollars, which Haffenreffer decided to use to enlarge the business still more. In June 1874 Haffenreffer bought new equipment, and by 1876 production was up to four hundred barrels a week in the summer. Three years later Haffenreffer was using seventeen horses and employing more than forty men in the brewery. During the first decades of operation he added a boiler house, a cold-storage building, an office, a bottling facility, and other structures, in the process creating an enclosed brick factory complex at Bismarck and Germania streets. In 1890 Haffenreffer sold the brewery to the New England Brewing Company, a syndicate of Massachusetts breweries, but he managed the brewery until his retirement in 1905, after which his son Theodore took over.[18]

Jamaica Plain manufacturers such as Rudolf Haffenreffer profited from local affiliations, but they also encouraged local residents to form local

Local Attachments

attachments. Like small businesses everywhere, the factories of Jamaica Plain were local institutions, for the most part owned and operated by neighborhood residents. Most Jamaica Plain manufacturers, from the immigrant owners of small workshops to the directors of large industrial plants, practiced what might be called a "mill and mansion" form of personal supervision of their enterprises. Paternalism ruled even at the Thomas G. Plant Company, by far the largest of the neighborhood's factories. When the company founder retired in 1910, for example, he rewarded employee loyalty by giving workers five dollars for every year they had worked for the company.[19]

Like the paternalist factory owners in nineteenth-century mill towns and elsewhere, Jamaica Plain manufacturers lived adjacent or near their factories and thus could know and be known to their workers. Some even lived with their workers. During the early artisanal stage of Jamaica Plain's industrial development, it was not unusual for craftsmen to board apprentices or younger employees. Joseph Byron, for example, lived adjacent to his leather tannery in the Egleston Square area; in 1850 he boarded two seventeen-year-old leather workers at his home, and he subsequently developed a set of modest houses nearby as residences for his curriers (including his son) and other workers. In order to save money in the early years of his brewery, Rudolf Haffenreffer and his wife also took on several boarders at their home next to the brewery.[20]

Even those factory owners who did not board their workers lived close to their enterprises. For example, Haffenreffer rented quarters near his brewery until 1876, when he built a new house on Brookside Avenue adjacent to the brewery complex. In the early 1870s Benjamin F. Sturtevant moved to Sumner Hill and built his great industrial fan and ventilation factory in the Stony Brook valley below. In the late 1890s, when George Buff founded his surveying instruments factory on Lamartine Street, he took up residence almost directly behind the workshop. Soon thereafter his brother and cofounder, Louis Buff, bought a handsome mansard-style home located a block away from the factory.

Not all manufacturers lived so close to their factories. Henry Reuter lived on Perkins Street, about a half-mile from his Highland Spring Brewery. Thomas G. Plant, the very wealthy owner of the Thomas G. Plant shoe factory, also an exception, chose to live in the Back Bay. William L. Ratcliffe, the company's treasurer and Plant's successor (in 1911) as president, however, did live in Jamaica Plain, in Glenvale, about a mile and a half from the giant factory.[21]

By participating in the public life of the neighborhood, Jamaica Plain manufacturers expressed a commitment to place as well as to profit. Under town government, local manufacturers held offices, perhaps in part to defend themselves against those who hoped to restrict manufacturing from residential areas. Nathan B. Prescott, a dealer in Jamaica Pond ice, and Samuel Jackson and Charles Dolan, local leather manufacturers, served as selectmen for the Town of West Roxbury.[22]

Later, when the neighborhood became part of the City of Boston, manufacturers looked to state government and the courts to defend their interests and participated less in local politics, acting instead as leaders in local church and social organizations. Rudolf Haffenreffer, for example, was a prominent member of the German Lutheran Trinity Church and supported local German social clubs such as the Boylston Schul Verein. Benjamin F. Sturtevant took an active role in the affairs of the First Baptist Church of Jamaica Plain and contributed significant sums to the religious society. William L. Ratcliffe, the vice-president, treasurer, and then president of the Thomas G. Plant Company, belonged to the Eliot Club of Jamaica Plain and held the office of junior warden at St. John's Episcopal Church.[23]

The workplaces that manufacturers and other local business persons established nurtured neighborhood community life. The neighborhood workshops provided a primary point of social contact for workers, who, like their employers, usually lived near the source of their livelihood. Increasingly during the nineteenth century, the artisan system of work organization shifted from the traditional master-journeyman-apprentice shop to a workplace characterized by a permanent division of labor between managers and workers. Although the new relationships created a conflict of interest between boss and employees, it also brought a sense of commonality to workers in the urban trades.

In Jamaica Plain, as elsewhere, participation in labor organizations most visibly expressed the sense of shared experience among workers. Boston trade union directories listed Jamaica Plain as the residence for a multitude of union agents. The officers of the neighborhood carpenters, railroad trainmen, cigar tobacco strippers, coopers, waiters, musicians, horseshoers, bakers, plasterers, plumbers, and other locals revealed only the tip of a large iceberg of Jamaica Plain trade unionists. Like many neighborhood social organizations, some union locals clustered people by occupation, wealth, and ethnicity. The brewery workers, for example, were divided into two locals, one for the better-paid, predominantly German inside men, the other for the less skilled, mainly Irish teamsters.[24]

The labor disputes that broke out periodically in neighborhood factories demonstrated the extent of worker solidarity. In 1885 and 1902, for example, neighborhood brewery workers walked off the job as part of citywide strikes; in 1899 workers struck the Temple Glove Factory and the Plant shoe factory; and in 1906 a labor dispute broke out at the Napier Motor Company, an automobile parts factory. As in Paterson, New Jersey, and many other urban communities, neighborhood ties encouraged local residents and businessmen to support striking workers. During the brief but bitter brewery strike of 1902, for example, Jamaica Plain saloon keepers refused to serve union-boycotted beer. When drivers of nonunion teams attempted to deliver the product, Jamaica Plain boys harassed them by halting their horses.[25]

The same shared work experiences that produced union solidarity also fostered social bonds, which the neighborhood context reinforced. In 1903, for example, employees of the Sturtevant ventilator factory threw a surprise birthday party for their fellow worker William Cropper at the plant. In 1907 nearly fifty current and former employees of the E. W. Clark dry goods store gathered at Clark's house for a reunion, and in 1909 local telephone operators organized a social club named Entre Nous.[26]

Even more than manufacturers, neighborhood retail merchants were strongly identified with the public life of the district. Observers of twentieth-century urban neighborhoods have noted how retail businesses contribute to neighborhood identity and organization. In his analysis of the West End, a working-class neighborhood in Boston, Herbert Gans revealed how stores, taverns, and restaurants functioned as "ganglia in the area's extensive communication network" and how their proprietors served as caretakers of the neighborhood. Similarly, in Jamaica Plain the owners of locally oriented businesses cultivated good relationships with neighborhood residents, and in turn their customers came to see them as important to the life of the community.[27]

Although many small establishments eventually went out of business, those stores that survived became prominent neighborhood institutions. Two of Jamaica Plain's longest-lived enterprises, for example, persisted for more than a century. Three generations of the same family ran Seaver's grocery store from 1796 to 1928, and a succession of business partners operated Charles B. Rogers's pharmacy from 1867 to the 1970s. Successful proprietors ran their businesses for many years or sold them as going concerns to former clerks. For example, in 1867 J. Phillips George sold his drugstore, already more than twenty years old, to his former clerk George Barrett, who ran the business until the turn of the century. In 1866 Cyrus White helped found a general hardware, stove, and furnace business on

Centre Street. Sewall D. Balkam, a former clerk, took over White's hardware store in 1891 and operated it until his death in 1912. Longtime proprietors announced their longevity in signs and advertisements; their successors emphasized continuity rather than change, advertising that the business would carry on "as before" "in the old stand."[28]

In many nineteenth-century American cities, local businesses offered a way for some working-class and first- and second-generation immigrant city dwellers to climb the ladder to social and economic respectability. In Jamaica Plain also, German, Irish, and other ethnic entrepreneurs followed the example of Yankee storekeepers and exploited the economic opportunities offered by the growing neighborhood. As in other cities, the long-term success of their establishments bestowed local status upon their proprietors. For example, Leopold Vogel, the son of German immigrants, opened a boot and shoe store near the Jamaica Plain railroad station in 1861 and operated the business for close to forty years before turning it over to his son. About 1880 William Rooney, born in America of Irish parents, opened a shoe store in White's Block; in 1889 he relocated the business in the Centre Street commercial building, which he built with Michael F. Dolan, an Irish-American fruit and confection dealer. As late as 1925 Rooney's boot and shoe store was still operating. Such local businesses helped to broaden the definition of neighborhood community to include residents of diverse religious and national backgrounds.[29]

Neighborhood stores did more than dispense goods to the community: they linked customers to the urban place in which they lived. Just as the traditional general store, with its potbellied stove and cracker barrels, functioned as an important center of country town life, so the urban grocery store provided a neighborhood gathering place. Seaver's, a typical example of the urban general store, sold, among other items, eggs, sugar, groceries, wooden ware, oil for lighting fuel, and bottled liquor. Looking back in 1931, Fred Seaver remembered Seaver's as "a community store [that] sold everything. After supper the gang would collect there, sit around the old stove and discuss everything from politics to women, and believe me, they could gossip." One Jamaica Plain resident remembered the elder Robert Seaver in the 1840s as "everybody's friend, interested in every Jamaica Plain happening, past and present."[30]

Like their country town cousins, the proprietors of local stores provided loans and goods on credit to their customers. Debtors whose accounts fell too far in arrears sometimes had to pass on their earnings until they had repaid their debt. In 1873, for example, Thomas Garraty, a laborer employed by the Town of West Roxbury, agreed to give over his wages to the

Centre Street grocers Isaac Norcross and Edward Myrick.[31]

The grocery stores of German and Irish entrepreneurs also served as community centers, especially for the neighborhood's immigrant population. Frederick Bleiler, a native of the Schwabia section of Bavaria, provides a good example of the immigrant grocer. His father, a butcher, brought his family to the United States in the mid-1840s, moved to Roxbury in 1852, and in 1860 opened a butcher shop there. Bleiler followed his father into the butcher trade, and by the 1880s he and his wife Rosa had opened their own butcher and provision shop near Heath Street. (He drove a meat truck about town while she butchered in the shop.) Success in the business allowed Bleiler to buy the former estate of Moses Day, a Roxbury cordage manufacturer, in 1890, and about 1892 he moved the store to a nearby site. Like Seaver's, Bleiler's store was a place where local people congregated. Chairs were provided, and one resident remembered that "the gang from the Schwaben Hall," a Schwabian social club, liked to meet there. The Bleilers, too, extended credit to their neighbors. Also like the Seavers, Bleiler was a gregarious sort. In later years he was known to invite a friend to join him in his yard for a few schnapps.[32]

Like the neighborhood saloons in Boston, Chicago, and other American cities, the taverns scattered about industrial Brookside and South Street also served as meeting places for the inhabitants of those districts. Taverns such as the ones operated in Brookside by German-born A. Huber in the 1880s and the Irish-American William Parlon in the 1890s provided a place to socialize for working-class and lower-middle-class residents; the patrons, like the tavern proprietors, were often Irish and German immigrants. However, the taint of impropriety that hung around Boston saloon keepers, especially in areas with large Protestant populations such as Jamaica Plain, prevented them from taking positions of visible leadership.[33]

Many proprietors of respectable local businesses, however, did emerge as neighborhood leaders. As a rule, Jamaica Plain store and shop owners lived in the neighborhood, sometimes in the building that housed their shop, and therefore almost by definition had a double stake in the welfare of the community. Well known to their neighbors, the owners of local concerns easily assumed the role of neighborhood leader. Besides acting as official weigher of hay and wood for the Town of West Roxbury, Robert Seaver served as Jamaica Plain's postmaster in the 1840s and state representative in 1872 and 1873. Jamaica Plain provisions dealer Alden Bartlett was elected as an assessor and selectman for the Town of West Roxbury. A member of the Roxbury Horse Guards during the Civil War, Frederick Bleiler served as a Democratic member of the Boston Common Council from 1871 to 1873 and presided over local Democratic political rallies as late as 1900. Eugene W. Clark, the owner of a Centre Street dry goods store for forty years, was the deacon of St. Paul's Universalist Church, and Sewall D. Balkam, the hardware store proprietor, was an active member of the Central Congregational Church and treasurer of the Jamaica Plain Fraternal Council of Churches. In the 1890s both Clark and Balkam emerged as leaders in neighborhood improvement organizations.[34]

Far more than any other area of business activity, real estate development involved Jamaica Plain residents, gave them a stake in the neighborhood, and gave them a common interest in the future of their community. Although historically real estate in most residential neighborhoods has not been as valuable as prime downtown lands, during boom periods neighborhood real estate development was a thriving business that yielded handsome profits. A study of Chicago land values during the nineteenth and early twentieth centuries showed that upswings in real estate cycles lured many ordinary citizens and small operators, including dishonest "curbstoners," to speculate in neighborhood lands.[35]

Like other forms of local economic activity, the field of real estate nurtured local attachments by tying a wide range of people to their neighborhood. The process of developing homes, stores, and factories on open agricultural or estate lands may be understood as a complex and fragmented form of production. Landowners sell the raw material, land; investors and subdividers act as wholesale merchants by overseeing primary processing and resale; architects, builders, and contractors perform tasks related to final processing and manufacturing; real estate agents sell the finished product on the retail level, and homeowners and other buyers are consumers.

The complexity of real estate projects involved so many individuals that, as Warner pointed out, "a development could easily generate more agents than houses."[36] Yet despite the complexity, real estate development was deeply rooted in the neighborhood at each stage in the process. And because of the complexity, residents from across the social and economic spectrum of Jamaica Plain society participated in it.

During the nineteenth and early twentieth centuries, the original holders of undeveloped tracts of land in Jamaica Plain were either the resident owners of suburban estates or farms or heirs to them. These owners tended to be relatively wealthy, and even when they were not, they possessed assets made valuable by rising urban land values. In some cases local investors had purchased the land to earn a profit from it. Sometimes landowners, even if they were investors, chose not to develop the land immediately but to enjoy it or wait for a more opportune time. The transfer of property to heirs, the need for immediate funds, or the desire to ensure future income might trigger the process.

Except during periods of intense price inflation, urban landowners in outer-city neighborhoods such as Jamaica Plain held real estate as a long-term investment rather than a short-term speculation. Local investors bought up neighborhood lands and held on to them in anticipation of the day that demand would raise their value. Even after the lands had been subdivided into streets and house lots, landowners frequently reinvested in newly created parcels to await still further rises in land values. Thus real estate development was more often an investment in the future of the neighborhood than a way of cashing in and moving out.

The availability of real estate properties in Jamaica Plain and a growing demand for urban lands in the Boston area opened the way for investors to subdivide tracts for sale as individual parcels. With few exceptions, the investors and subdividers were residents of Jamaica Plain. Like Jamaica Plain residents who invested in commercial and industrial ventures, neighborhood real estate investors were in an advantageous position to hear about and appraise local properties.

Most of the early land merchants in Jamaica Plain were well-off local residents who speculated in neighborhood lands as a secondary, albeit lucrative, career. For example, Stephen Minot Weld, founder of Weld Academy in 1827, earned a "substantial pecuniary reward" from the 1830s to the 1860s by buying large parcels when they were low in value, holding on to them for years if necessary, and then selling them as individual lots. In 1865 George F. Woodman, a resident of Sumner Hill, retired at the age of forty from his woolen house with "a handsome competency" and took up real estate development. From the early 1870s Woodman subdivided properties on Sumner Hill, creating dozens of lots along recently laid-out roads. In 1880 J. Alba Davis, a wholesale hide and leather dealer in Boston, took part in a number of real estate subdivisions, including the subdivision of his former estate grounds on Chestnut Avenue. Similarly, in the 1880s George William Bond, a wealthy wool wholesale dealer who lived in Parkside, subdivided a part of his estate and also bought five lots from an adjacent estate.[37]

As the market in Jamaica Plain lands grew more brisk, the neighborhood real estate business began to produce full-time specialists, who were often of more modest background. The career of George H. Williams illustrates the transition of the neighborhood real estate business. Williams began his business career as a partner with his brother John E. Williams in a saddle and harness making business at the corner of Centre and Green streets. From 1838 to the 1870s George Williams accumulated and sold properties in the Sumner Hill, Pondside, Glenvale, and Boylston sub-districts. He gave up the harness business to be an insurance agent and real estate broker. His departure from commercial Green Street to an imposing house in the Pondside area in the 1860s symbolized his rise to wealth and respectability. Similarly, in 1869 Charles J. Page, the son of the owner of a Boston hat and cap shop, began to develop land near his home in Brookside for single and double workers' cottages and industrial buildings. His career launched, in 1879 Page moved to Boston and became involved in real estate operations over a wide range of territory in outer and suburban Boston.[38]

In the late nineteenth century, real estate subdividers in Jamaica Plain often formed partnerships and land companies comprising shareholders for a particular development project. As a rule, the membership of a local speculative land company included a Jamaica Plain resident. For example, the membership of the Robinwood Associates, a company formed in 1892 to develop a Glenvale tract, included Abraham T. Rogers, an assistant inspector of buildings for the City of Boston, who lived close to the development site, Thomas Minton, a well-known Jamaica Plain contractor, as well as two Roxbury insurance agents, a Roxbury dentist, and investors from various locales.[39] In 1893 George Sturgis Bond, a wholesale wool trader like his father, the late George William Bond, bought Forest Gardens, a former estate located near his Parkside home. He then sold it to the Peter Parley Land Company, whose members included Bond, his two brothers, his brother-in-law George W. Wheelwright, Jr., a large paper manufacturer, and Wheelwright's mother, all of whom lived next to one another in the family compound.[40]

The subdivision of land parcels and construction upon the resulting lots created new opportunities for investment in both lots and buildings. At first only wealthy men and those with a particular interest in real estate invested in local lots and houses. In the early 1870s the greatest real estate property owners were men such as George H. Williams, Robert Scott, a wholesale cotton broker in Boston, and Isaac Cary, a wealthy import merchant. At the turn of the century, men of wealth were still active in real estate development. For example, Charles F. Farrington, like his father a Jamaica Plain resident and wholesale grocer in Boston, developed a Pond-side estate with houses and an apartment block, invested in land in the Forest Hills section, and, along with Benjamin F. Sturtevant, the Jamaica

Plain industrialist, purchased lots in the Jamaica Plain Land Company's development in South Street. Patrick Meehan, the well-to-do contractor who invested in Haffenreffer's brewery, aggrandized so many tracts of land that he was accused of being a land baron.[41]

But by the late nineteenth century the increasing number of subdivisions and structures also enabled middle-class neighborhood residents to invest in the local real estate market. In the mid-1870s Alexander Dickson, an aging local artisan who worked as a carriage smith, blacksmith, and builder, developed eleven Italianate-style single-family and double houses off Green Street, apparently as a nest egg for his heirs. From 1872 Frederick Bleiler, the grocer, bought and sold property in the Heath Street district, and by 1885 his holdings, which included his home and store, eight houses, and one lot, were valued at $22,800. For those of lesser means, real estate investments might be limited to only one or two properties. In 1893 Kate Fallon and her husband Michael, an Irish-born laborer, purchased the foreclosed mortgage of a two-family house around the corner from their Heath Street area house and rented it out for their remaining years.[42]

The experience of local growth taught ordinary Jamaica Plainers that there were profits to be had in their own backyard and that if they failed to act, they could only rue a lost opportunity. One resident remembered his father in 1912 pointing to the recently erected brick apartment buildings and charitable institutions on South Huntington Avenue and saying, "You ought to give me a good kick in the ass. I could have bought all this land for two and a half cents (a square foot) in the 1890s." His father did not miss out altogether, however; instead he invested in two three-deckers near Hyde Square.[43]

Construction followed the subdivision and the sale of individual lots, and here, too, a strong local flavor can be detected. Often investors sold lots and gave mortgages to small-scale builders or contractors. These men, generally unassuming artisans of the working or middle class, would sell a completed house to the individual who would occupy it. In the late nineteenth century, as Warner has shown, builders in outer Boston operated chiefly in the neighborhoods in which they lived, and Jamaica Plain carpenters such as Benjamin Armstrong, Paul Lincoln, and J. J. Shaw were no exception. Stephen Heath, a carpenter who built houses in the Pondside, Sumner Hill, and Green Street districts, became so widely recognized that when his son ran for political office, the campaign literature identified the candidate not only as a neighborhood druggist but also as the son of Stephen Heath, the "well known contractor and builder." Even where outside investors had subdivided properties, local influences were exerted upon the development. For example, after a Boston lawyer subdivided a large parcel on Cedar Hill in 1868, Timothy F. Bowe, a mason and builder who resided on Cedar Hill, bought up many of the subdivided lots and constructed mansard-style row houses upon them.[44]

As the number of local real estate transactions increased, Jamaica Plain acquired its own full-time real estate agents and brokers, several of whom entered the field from other neighborhood small businesses. In 1868 J. Phillips George left his apothecary business to become a real estate broker. Soon thereafter Alden Bartlett, the owner of a commercial block near the Jamaica Plain railroad depot, shifted from groceries to real estate services such as auctioneering, brokering, mortgage negotiations, and insurance. These concerns became established neighborhood mainstays when in 1878 Roswell Barrows took over Bartlett's business and later George W. Kenyon succeeded George. In the 1880s John Scales, an upholsterer and cabinetmaker on Cedar Hill, and Baily L. Page, who started as a clerk and bookkeeper for local hardware stores, opened real estate offices.[45]

Contractors who constructed neighborhood streets, sidewalks, and other parts of the physical infrastructure were also generally local residents. Property subdividers usually were responsible for the preliminary work of laying out roads and grading the land, whereas the city government generally paved the streets, put in sidewalks, and connected the sewers and water pipes. For the most part, these and related jobs went to local contractors, who hired unskilled laborers from the neighborhood to do the work. Frequently Irish businessmen, local contractors did a lucrative business when they received government contracts. Owen Nawn, for example, earned large sums from the City of Boston and lived in a mansion near Hyde Square. In the 1890s Thomas Minton, a Forest Hills resident, kept an office near Jamaica Plain Station and supplied sand and gravel from a sandbank near Franklin Park. Minton's company received a steady stream of contracts from the City of Boston, especially street construction projects. On a lesser scale, contractors such as Thomas O'Leary laid concrete and asphalt paving for streets, sidewalks, brewery floors, and cellars.[46]

Although most of those involved in Jamaica Plain real estate development were based locally, there were some exceptions. Some did not live in the neighborhood or, if they did, did not confine their activities to the immediate vicinity. Some professionals, such as civil engineers, surveyors, conveyance attorneys, and mortgagors, needed a larger market for their services than a single neighborhood could provide. During the middle decades of the nineteenth century Theodore B. Moses, for example, surveyed numerous subdivisions in Jamaica Plain, but Moses, a resident of West Roxbury Village, worked throughout Norfolk County. Jamaica Plain real estate lawyers often hung their shingles downtown. Among insurance and real estate agents who lived in Jamaica Plain, L. L. P. Atwood had offices in downtown Boston, at Jamaica Plain Station, and in suburban Roslindale, and Asa Spaulding Weld, a pillar of St. John's Episcopal Church, kept offices downtown and on Centre Street. Although a great deal of building financing came from neighborhood sources, in the late nineteenth century the bustling metropolitan-area mortgage market centered in Boston.[47]

In general, however, a close relationship existed between the neighborhood and the real estate development process. As a result, local developers usually tried to uphold community standards. Middle-class businessmen and residents considered industrial and inexpensive residential development appropriate to the marshy areas but preferred "first class" residential or commercial development for other sections. To protect middle- and upper-class parts of the neighborhood from inappropriate growth, developers attached restrictions to property deeds. Typically these deed restrictions prohibited industrial uses, ensured against the crowding of buildings, or set a minimum value for the future structure. For example, on Seaverns Avenue, a road parallel to Green Street's artisan strip, George H. Williams helped develop and sell modest homes for craftsmen on lots under four thousand square feet. The properties he sold a few blocks away on Sumner Hill, however, were on much larger lots, most exceeding twelve thousand square feet. The deeds required that houses be set twenty feet from the street and prohibited public stables, slaughterhouses, distilleries, or other workshops.[48]

Evidence suggests that community opinion was not to be taken lightly. When the First Congregational Society of Jamaica Plain built a new meeting house in 1853, for example, Stephen Minot Weld bought the old church, moved it across the street, and began to remodel it as a stable. Just before the structure was ready for occupancy, it caught fire and was destroyed. Many believed that an unknown neighborhood resident or residents had committed arson to prevent the desecration of the old church. Whether or not this was the case, some Jamaica Plainers believed that Weld had paid a price for defying the will of the neighborhood. Similarly, neighborhood business investors also took into account the opinions of the community. At a time when many neighborhood residents supported temperance reform, for example, Francis A. Peters and Patrick Meehan attempted to keep their investment in Haffenreffer's brewery secret because of "the moral view which some may take in account of the nature of the business."[49]

Because Jamaica Plainers were so involved in local real estate development, neighborhood residents often perceived real estate projects that violated community standards as the work of outsiders. Expressing their identification with the neighborhood, they used xenophobic terms to condemn inexpensive development in "respectable" subdistricts. When three-decker apartment buildings went up on hitherto exclusive Glen Road near Franklin Park, the local newspaper likened their arrival to an invasion of "Northern hordes of Barbarians pouring in upon the classic beauties of Rome" and accused an outside Jewish syndicate of being the "cold blooded" culprit. The same local writer who admired the garden of a "Guinea" junk collector expressed dismay at the construction of three-deckers and storefronts for fruit dealers and tailors as "extending Italy" into Jamaica Plain. When the Arboretum Land Company persuaded the Boston Common Council to remove deed restrictions in order to develop property near the Arborway, the normally pro-growth and discreet *Jamaica Plain News* condemned the company's primary agent, a man who lived outside the neighborhood, for high-handed maneuvers.[50]

The economic opportunities in real estate and other forms of economic development gave businessmen and other residents a stake in local economic growth and a reason to identify with the interests of the neighborhood. Thus, Jamaica Plain spawned energetic neighborhood boosters equivalent to the tireless optimists who promoted nineteenth-century towns and cities across the United States. In the early nineteenth century, for example, Dr. Daniel Drake of Cincinnati and William B. Ogden of Chicago confidently envisioned a booming future and strove to acquire railroads, factories, and other advantages for their communities. In the late nineteenth and twentieth centuries, Harrison Gray Otis, the publisher of the *Los Angeles Times* and a founder of the Los Angeles Chamber of Commerce, and his son-in-law Harry Chandler trumpeted the destiny of Los Angeles, aggressively promoted local real estate development, and fought to obtain control of a freshwater port and access to inland water for the city. Like these city boosters, neighborhood boosters pushed to gain facilities and improvements for their communities. They, too, saw no conflict between their public leadership and their efforts to reap the benefits of growth. From the perspective of the businessman promoter, the two goals coincided.[51]

Stephen Minot Weld was an early, prominent Jamaica Plain booster. Despite his outside activities on behalf of Harvard College and the Northern cause during the Civil War, Weld worked assiduously to build up his home neighborhood. In addition to investing heavily in local real estate, Weld served as a local justice of the peace and sat on the board of directors of the Jamaica Plain Gas Light Company. As a representative of the West Roxbury Horse Railroad Company, he petitioned the West Roxbury Board of Selectmen to allow the company to lay tracks along Centre Street through Jamaica Plain. In 1858 Weld became the president of the Metropolitan Railroad Company, which had leased the Jamaica Plain tracks of the West Roxbury Company to run its own horsecars.[52]

Weld pursued policies both as a civic leader and a businessman, promoted the growth of Jamaica Plain, and benefited his own economic interests. In 1859, for example, Weld served on a Town of West Roxbury committee to resolve the problem created by the increasing number of ice company buildings on the banks of Jamaica Pond. Asserting that the recent period of "unparalleled prosperity" indicated that Jamaica Plain would soon grow crowded, the three-person committee moved to defend the recreational privileges of its residents. Staking out the town's ownership of the pond and its right to regulate the ice houses, Weld and his fellow committee members argued that the use of the pond for skating, sledding, and other forms of recreation attracted new residents, added to the present residents' health and pleasure, and increased "the advantages of the town as a residence."[53]

As president of the Metropolitan Horse Railroad Company, Weld attempted to boost neighborhood growth with his efforts to attract ice skaters to Jamaica Pond. First, a Jamaica Plain resident later recalled, he used large signs on the horsecars to advertise "Good Skating" at the pond. Second, he had the pond cleared of snow at company expense. Taken together, these policies enhanced the residential qualities of the neighborhood, attracted more riders on the cars, and advertised the neighborhood to potential buyers of local real estate.[54]

Among local businessmen who championed the neighborhood and local growth in the late nineteenth and early twentieth centuries, Roswell S. Barrows emerged as perhaps the most important neighborhood booster. Originally from Providence, Rhode Island, Barrows moved to Boston in 1869 and entered the fire insurance business there. In 1878 he bought Alden Bartlett's real estate and insurance business and moved to Jamaica Plain. As a subdivider, builder (he built more than thirty houses in Jamaica Plain before 1900), and most frequently as a mortgage and property broker, Barrows took a leading part in Jamaica Plain real estate development. In 1881 Barrows helped found the West Roxbury Co-operative Bank in Jamaica Plain and bought the *West Roxbury News,* also located in Jamaica Plain, which he published either by himself or with a partner until 1899. When in 1893 he renamed the newspaper the *Jamaica Plain News,* he also distributed editions under Roslindale and West Roxbury headings for those neighborhoods. In addition, Barrows led the neighborhood lobbying efforts to acquire local improvements from the city and state governments.[55]

Jamaica Plain boosters joined together to form businesses that benefited from and promoted neighborhood growth. In 1853, for example, a group of downtown businessmen and neighborhood entrepreneurs organized the Jamaica Plain Gas Light Company to produce gas and coke for the local market. John C. Pratt, a Boston businessman and president of the Ogdensburg and Lake Champlain Railroad, helped found the company and served as president until his death in 1888. A Pondside resident and strong neighborhood booster, Pratt served on the board of selectmen in the West Roxbury government, where he bitterly opposed the slow-growth leadership of Arthur Austin. Other early directors of the Gas Light Company included such leading Jamaica Plain real estate developers as Stephen Minot Weld, Charles Brewer, a prominent Boston merchant, and Ebeneezer T. Farrington, a wholesale grocer and one of the wealthiest men in the district. In the 1890s Francis A. Peters, the local real estate investor and financial backer of the Haffenreffer brewery, succeeded to the presidency of the Gas Light Company. The neighborhood real estate agents J. Phillips George and George Kenyon served as successive treasurers.[56]

Like the horse railroads and local retail stores, the Jamaica Plain Gas Light Company depended upon the growth of the Jamaica Plain community to increase its profits. The company sold fuel to the local government to light public buildings and street lamps and to home and business owners to illuminate private residences and shops. From the time of its founding, the company earned steadily rising profits, which by the mid-1880s reached close to eighteen thousand dollars a year. As a public utility company, however, the Gas Light Company felt extreme pressure both to pay dividends to stockholders and to keep prices to residential customers low. With constraints on the prices it charged, the only avenue left to the company was to increase the number of customers, a policy that dovetailed nicely with local real estate development.[57]

To directly promote neighborhood growth, downtown and local businessmen organized savings banks to issue real estate mortgages. In the early 1870s a group of local residents closely connected to the Jamaica Plain Gas Light Company initiated the Jamaica Plain Savings Bank. In 1872, at the annual corporate election meeting held in the Gas Light Company's offices, John C. Pratt, the head of the Gas Light Company, was elected president of the bank, J. Phillips George, the treasurer of the Gas Light Company, was elected secretary of the bank, and Charles Brewer, a Gas Light Company director, was elected as one of the bank's vice-presidents. Other prominent businessmen, including local citizens such as Joseph W. Balch, Robert Seaver, and Alden Bartlett, filled the remaining offices and trusteeships of the bank. Despite the support of Jamaica Plainers, the Jamaica Plain Savings Bank faced financial difficulties brought on by the panic of 1873 and the subsequent slump in Boston-area real estate and thus survived only a few years.[58]

In 1881 another group of businessmen, bolstered by the support for cooperative banks as a tool of housing reform and by a new state law authorizing their establishment, organized a new local savings bank, the West Roxbury Co-operative Bank. Meeting at the office of Roswell S. Barrows, the founders included John Pearce, a Roslindale resident who became the bank's first president, and Charles G. Keyes, a Jamaica Plain resident and Boston lawyer who served as the bank's attorney. In the 1890s Eugene W. Clark, the owner of a local dry goods firm, became vice-president of the bank, and in 1896 Stephen F. Woodman, a Boston insurance man and a Jamaica Plainer, succeeded Pearce as president of the bank.[59]

Although based in Jamaica Plain—its office was at Woolsey Square, at the Jamaica Plain depot—the new bank cast its net over neighboring residential districts as well. Its investments went predominantly to "home seekers and persons of moderate incomes" who wished to purchase homes in the outer-city neighborhoods, such as Jamaica Plain, Roslindale, West Roxbury, and Dorchester. Because of the economic depression of the early 1880s, the bank's business grew slowly at first, but after 1885 it began to thrive. By the early twentieth century the assets of the West Roxbury Co-operative Bank had reached over a half-million dollars.

Other cooperative banks with local ties supplemented the efforts of the West Roxbury Co-operative Bank to provide home mortgages in Jamaica Plain. The Germania Co-operative Bank, for example, was based in Boston's South End and served the German-American community of Boston, but it had close ties to Jamaica Plain, where in the early twentieth century its president, vice-president, and two directors lived. Frederick Bleiler, the grocer and real estate investor, served as a director of the Roxbury Co-operative Bank, located on Columbus Avenue along the Jamaica Plain border, and thus was in a position to help grant mortgages to other prospective buyers of local property.[60]

More than other local growth-oriented businesses, Jamaica Plain's weekly newspaper transmitted and cultivated the sense of neighborhood identity. Typical of the modern local community newspaper in Chicago and other cities, the *Jamaica Plain News* spoke for neighborhood residents and informed them about each other and their neighborhood. Like other local newspapers, the *News* was closely linked to local retail and service businesses, upon which it depended for the majority of its advertising revenue. Also like other local weeklies, it reported local news almost to the exclusion of items concerning the city or nation, recounted and celebrated the history of the community, took the side of neighborhood residents in any conflicts with the outside world, and attempted to avoid or quiet controversies within the neighborhood.[61]

Like big-city newspapers, the local newspaper loudly trumpeted local boosterism. Under Barrows and his successor, Ledru J. Brackett, the *Jamaica Plain News* consistently acted as a cheerleader for neighborhood growth. Besides listing local events and the activities of the neighborhood's residents, the *News* recorded the real estate transactions of the week, aired complaints about neighborhood services and street conditions, and published suggestions to improve neighborhood life. The columns of the newspaper urged Jamaica Plainers to shop locally and to feel proud of their neighborhood and its businesses, including the newspaper itself. The paper celebrated the opening of new stores and factories and, as one might expect a periodical published by a real estate agent to do, informed its readers of all progress in the area of real estate development. In 1883, for example, the paper proclaimed the laying of curbstones on Glen Road as "evidence of an advance in civilization."[62]

In a 1903 address Samuel B. Capen, a local political reformer, declared the importance of the local newspaper to neighborhood society. Unlike the city daily papers, he explained, the neighborhood paper could not serve scandals, adventures, and world news with breakfast. But by agitating for local improvements, shaping local public opinion, and reporting the activities of local organizations, it could do what the city dailies could not. He had described the *Jamaica Plain News* with its booster ethos perfectly.[63]

At the end of the nineteenth century, the increasing number of local businesses, widespread participation in real estate development, activities of neighborhood boosters, and the drumbeating of the *Jamaica Plain News* culminated in the creation of the Jamaica Plain Carnival Association and the Jamaica Plain Businessmen's Association. On the one hand, these businessmen's organizations gave an institutional form to the shared interest of those entrepreneurs, real estate investors, and others with a stake in the economic welfare of the neighborhood. On the other hand, they were devoted to the interests of the neighborhood as a whole, and like the boosters and the neighborhood newspaper, they intensified the sense of neighborhood identity in Jamaica Plain.

In 1897 the neighborhood businessmen Sewall D. Balkam, Eugene W. Clark, and Roswell S. Barrows organized and directed a communitywide organization, the Jamaica Plain Carnival Association, to run the neighborhood's Fourth of July celebrations. The Carnival Association leaders coordinated the massive parades of floats, marching bands, drill corps, and other groups, the day's biking, boating, and swimming contests, and the evening fireworks displays at Jamaica Pond. Although a variety of callings were represented in the Carnival Association, the dominant element in the organization were small businessmen such as Frederick Bleiler and Michael S. Morton, both grocers, William G. Roemer, a plumber, and Charles A. Underwood, a bicycle store proprietor. The Carnival Association's Fourth of July celebrations not only expressed national patriotism; they also celebrated the neighborhood of Jamaica Plain and through the floats of the various neighborhood firms served to advertise local merchants.[64]

Inspired by the success of their Carnival Association and the establishment of improvement associations in neighboring communities, Jamaica Plain business leaders created the neighborhood equivalent of a downtown chamber of commerce. In February 1899 Jamaica Plain businessmen met in the office of George W. Kenyon, the local insurance and real estate agent, and organized the Jamaica Plain Businessmen's Association. At its second meeting, chaired by Roswell S. Barrows, the group adopted a constitution and elected Eugene W. Clark as president, Timothy J. McLaughlin, an upholsterer and later an express agent, as treasurer, and Howell Thomas Wood, a Boston attorney, as secretary. Besides William Rooney, the boot and shoe store owner, and J. W. Goodnow, a prosperous baker and confectioner, founding members included the three Jamaica Plain Carnival Association leaders. By 1900 the membership had grown from ten to more than sixty members, almost all of whom were local businessmen.[65] The organization was by no means unique. During the same period businessmen's organizations could be found in towns and cities across the country, notably in New York City, where local merchants, builders, and real estate agents formed neighborhood chambers of commerce that effectively lobbied for governmental services.[66]

From the start, the founders of the Jamaica Plain Businessmen's Association proposed to address both the needs of local merchants and the "interest of the whole community." The problem of how to increase local trade in the face of competition from downtown department stores had provided the immediate catalyst for forming the organization. During its first year of existence, the group's efforts to establish a local branch of a national bank, deal with customers who kept delinquent accounts, and inaugurate a weekday half-holiday during the summer for local shops reflected the occupational interests of the membership. In order to advance "the improvement of Jamaica Plain as a business and residential district," the organization also tackled neighborhood issues such as widening South Street, combating the vandalism and rowdy behavior of local youth, and obtaining new recreational facilities.[67]

Within three years of its founding, the Businessmen's Association had evolved into a civic improvement organization for the neighborhood. The group changed its name to Jamaica Plain Citizens' Association and invited neighborhood clergy, professionals, and other prominent citizens (but not women) to join. Although the new members broadened the base of the organization, local businessmen remained an important part of the membership, and such proprietors as E. W. Clark, Sewall Balkam, and Roswell Barrows continued to play leading roles in the organization over the following decade.

Although it was not always effective—the attempt to establish a national bank came to naught—the Jamaica Plain Citizens' Association became an important neighborhood institution. By 1903 it encompassed nearly every facet of public life in Jamaica Plain. The Committee on Facilities and Convenience of Transportation monitored the city's transit companies and campaigned for useful streetcar transfer points and local stations. The streets and public works committee pushed for street improvements and other large-scale improvement projects. Absorbing the functions of the Carnival Association, the public occasions committee managed the neighborhood celebrations of Memorial Day, the Fourth of July, and other holidays. A public parks and grounds committee led the neighborhood's crusades for playgrounds and other recreational facilities. The public entertainment committee organized lectures on neighborhood history and other social events. Other committees dealt with schools, police and public order, and fire protection; one lobbied the government to pass legislation helpful to the district. In the following years, the Citizens' Association most frequently pursued local street, transportation, and recreation improvements, but it also grappled with many other neighborhood issues, ranging from the threat of a typhoid epidemic to the depredations of the gypsy moth.[68]

Local economic activity, then, helped to forge local attachments by linking members of the community to one another and to their neighborhood. It created common economic interests that tied neighborhood inhabitants to one another, and it nurtured the workshops and stores where neighborhood people came together. Successful manufacturers and shopkeepers became respected members of the neighborhood, and they in turn often participated in community organizations. Jamaica Plain residents with a stake in growth promoted it through real estate development, utility companies, savings and loan banks, and the local newspaper. Finally, Jamaica Plain businessmen banded together with other prominent Jamaica Plain residents to protect their common interests and those of the neighborhood. For them, as for earlier local boosters, neighborhood loyalties and economic self-interest were intimately related. Thus, throughout the nineteenth century the pursuit of economic rewards gave shape and momentum to the efforts to define the neighborhood to which its inhabitants belonged.

Yet if local economic growth and neighborhood improvement helped to define a neighborhood interest, they also helped to further fragment Jamaica Plain society by increasing and further diversifying the population. Factories attracted workers, population growth created opportunities for new shopkeepers, real estate development gave residences to blue-collar and white-collar, immigrants and native-born people alike. It is true that the ties of business functioned as a backbone and central nerve column for the complex society of Jamaica Plain, but in order for that society to cohere, the neighborhood of Jamaica Plain needed other kinds of social ties to act as sinew, ligament, and tissue.

The Entrance to Forest Hills Cemetery, ca. 1900

The gate to the Forest Hills Cemetery reflected the romantic landscape within.

Postcard published by the Hugh C. Leighton Company, courtesy of the Boston Public Library Print Department.

Ice Men from the Jamaica Pond Ice Company, ca. 1885

The deliveries of local ice men, coal men, butchers, and other vendors were part of the daily rhythms of neighborhood life.

Photograph courtesy of the Bostonian Society.

Skating on Jamaica Pond, ca. 1920

This twentieth-century portrait of skaters on Jamaica Pond was one in a long line that stretched back to Winslow Homer's lithograph for *Harper's Weekly*. For residents of Jamaica Plain, the pond was a natural resource of infinite charm and recreation.

Glass plate negative by Leon Abdalian, courtesy of the Boston Public Library Print Department.

The Country Park in Franklin Park, July 1904

A Boston Parks Department photograph portrays the aesthetic and tranquil emptiness that Frederick Law Olmsted strived to create in the Country Park. Barely visible in the distance, herds of sheep share the meadow with golfers putting on the green.

Photograph courtesy of the National Park Service, Frederick Law Olmsted National Historic Site.

The *Syringa* (lilac) Collection in Bloom, Arnold Arboretum, May 1908

While a gardener tends the lilacs, genteel visitors, including carriage riders, a lady with a parasol, and a lone bicyclist, enjoy the aesthetic views offered by the tree museum.

Photograph by Thomas E. Marr, courtesy of the Arnold Arboretum of Harvard University, Photographic Archives.

Wheeling in Franklin Park, 1890

For Jamaica Plainers and other Bostonians, Franklin Park represented a space for active recreation. Much to the dismay of the Olmsted firm and the Boston Parks Department, hordes of bicyclists from the Jamaica Cycle Club and elsewhere liked to wheel through the park.

Drawing in the *Boston Globe*.

The Centre Street Business Section, Looking South, ca. 1912

A quiet hour in downtown Jamaica Plain. Across the street from Keazer's grocery is the C. B. Rogers & Co. drugstore, a neighborhood fixture until the 1970s. In the left foreground, White's Block houses Jamaica Hardware and Plumbing, owned until 1909 by Sewall D. Balkam; Margot the florist; and the real estate firm (still operating today) of Robert T. Fowler, the son-in-law of Roswell S. Barrows. In the background is an upscale apartment building at the foot of Sumner Hill.

Photograph by Thomson & Thomson, courtesy of the Society for the Preservation of New England Antiquities.

Robert Seaver & Sons, Grocers, Established 1796, ca. 1900

Located for over a century on Centre Street, close to the village center, Seaver's represented an urban version of the American general store found in the small towns of New England. Like the other local grocery stores, Seaver's served as a community social center, a function as important as food distribution.

Photograph courtesy of the Bostonian Society.

Woolsey Block, 1895

The Jamaica Plain railroad station (out of view at the left) generated substantial commercial blocks, such as Woolsey Block, which contained the rooms of the West Roxbury Co-operative Bank, real estate agents, and the news depot where the *Jamaica Plain News* and other newspapers were sold.

Photograph from *Picturesque Boston Highlands* (Boston, 1895), courtesy of the Bostonian Society.

Rudolph Haffenreffer's Boylston Lager Beer Company Workers, 1891
Haffenreffer's brewery was one of the main institutions in the industrial Brookside subdistrict. Here Haffenreffer's employees pose with the company product.
Photograph courtesy of the Boston Public Library Print Department.

The Thomas G. Plant Company's Manufacturing Establishment, ca. 1900
The mammoth factory of the Thomas G. Plant Company had a private park where the employees could stroll and the company sports teams could play. The houses and stores on Centre Street can be seen on the right; the tenements of the Heath Street subdistrict on the left.
Photograph courtesy of Marilyn Oberle.

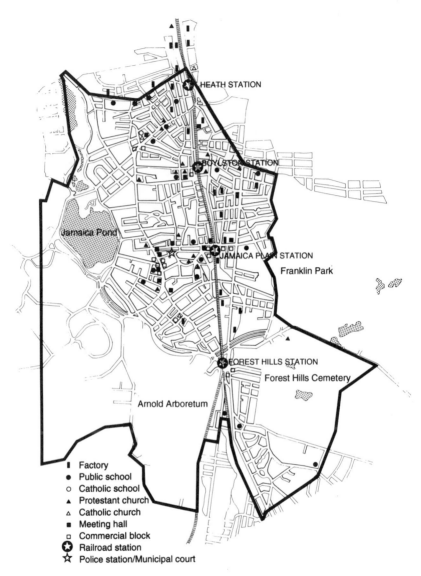

HEATH STATION

BOYLSTON STATION

Jamaica Pond

JAMAICA PLAIN STATION

Franklin Park

FOREST HILLS STATION

Forest Hills Cemetery

Arnold Arboretum

▮ Factory
● Public school
○ Catholic school
▲ Protestant church
△ Catholic church
■ Meeting hall
□ Commercial block
✪ Railroad station
☆ Police station/Municipal court

Jamaica Plain, including major institutions, c. 1900

5

The Web of
Neighborhood Society

There is a little suburb, it is called Jamaica Plain,
But some of its best citizens are still out in the rain.
Now, if they wish to get on board and be distinctly in it,
Why don't they join the Jamaica Club before we reach our limit?

—*Fred Seaver as "Susy,"*
Jamaica Club Minstrel Show, 1900

In the nineteenth and early twentieth centuries the neighborhood was the cornerstone of American urban society. It served as a fundamental unit for much of the organized social life of the city. Paradoxically, external relations nurtured the internal growth of neighborhood society and promoted neighborhood identity of place within the urban matrix. Because of its location within larger networks of people, places, and organizations, the neighborhood provided a stable way station for a mobile urban population.

Focusing on the downtown or the city as a whole, historians have tended to overlook the neighborhood's crucial function in the late-nineteenth- and early twentieth-century city. Some historians have concluded that private interest undermined urban public life and the formation of a citywide communal identity. Others believe that large institutions such as the metropolitan daily newspaper, the vaudeville house, and the professional major-league ballpark helped to create a mass culture that unified the diverse urban population.[1] These analyses neglect the far-flung nature of urban activity and culture. City dwellers often sought entertainment downtown (as well as in garden amusement parks on the suburban rim), but they also read their neighborhood newspaper and frequently attended theater and sports events in their local community.

Indeed, the neighborhoods of America's cities generated a startling array of local organizations and institutions. As urban women and men enjoyed increasing amounts of leisure time, they flocked to local churches, schools, charitable organizations, unions, fraternal lodges, and social and other types of clubs. Here neighborhood residents came together in lively rounds of religious services, meetings, theatrical performances, lectures, dance balls, and sports events. The urge to join a group became so powerful in Jamaica Plain that at the turn of the century several families living in the same apartment building banded together as a club and began holding monthly "reunions."[2]

Drawing upon a diverse and shifting local population, Jamaica Plain's institutions and organizations linked residents according to cultural identity. Generally neighborhood groups regulated their membership through requirements or by committee, but the degree of social exclusivity varied from group to group and over time. Local associations constituted neither a set of impermeable and isolated social cells nor a group of component parts whose integrated membership reflected the characteristics of the neighborhood population at large. Instead these groups composed a complex set of overlapping layers of religious, ethnic, class, gender, and other identities within the neighborhood context.

Despite the differences in membership and function, each type of association contributed to a common neighborhood culture that expressed a broadly middle-class perspective. As in Providence and other cities, in Jamaica Plain many types of organizations originated among the elite and then spread across the neighborhood social spectrum. Other types derived from working-class or ethnic traditions. As their numbers multiplied, however, neighborhood societies adopted remarkably similar organizational structures and rules of conduct. Moreover, as the urban joiner trend gathered momentum in the 1880s, the forms of activities held by local organizations began to converge into a relatively uniform set of entertainment formats. Thus, although some elements of Jamaica Plain society remained remote and even alienated from one another, common organizational forms and social rituals allowed some Jamaica Plainers to cross the lines of religion, class, and ethnicity.[3]

The result of the complex associational activity was a rich public life centered, not downtown, but in the city neighborhood. As the residents of Jamaica Plain organized and scurried to fairs, lectures, teas, recitals, dances, lodge meetings, and other events, they developed bonds to one another and to the neighborhood where they lived. Historians have demonstrated that the formation and activities of voluntary associations promoted a public life and communal identity in medium-sized nineteenth-century American cities. The history of Jamaica Plain also suggests that urban neighborhoods of the late nineteenth and early twentieth centuries fostered local attachments.[4]

Sustained by both internal and external links, local institutions and organizations may best be understood as branch offices and local chapters. As local manifestations of the national proclivity toward voluntary associations, they functioned as the building blocks of a "nation of joiners." Over the course of the nineteenth and early twentieth centuries, millions of Americans enlisted in local church groups, fraternal lodges, clubs, and other organizations that belonged to nationwide networks. The sprawling organizational empires fed the local branches in Jamaica Plain and other neighborhoods by creating a large pool of people who could transfer into local organizations from similar ones outside.[5]

These branch offices and local chapters were not parts of tightly organized bureaucratic systems. The organizational links and relationships between neighborhood groups and similar external organizations varied greatly. Some groups, particularly churches, were the progeny of outside parent organizations; others, such as sport clubs, depended on kindred organizations located elsewhere to carry out their purpose. Even those organizations that belonged to hierarchical structures, such as local Episcopal and Roman Catholic churches, emerged and grew during the nineteenth century as relatively autonomous bodies.

The histories of local institutions and organizations reflect their own life cycles and abilities to cope with the changing and mobile neighborhood society to which they belonged. As with neighborhood population movements, neighborhood groups did not automatically profit from participation in an interdependent urban system of organizations. Neighborhood residents often joined or became affiliated with institutions outside the neighborhood either because there was no such organization available locally or because individuals preferred to participate elsewhere. In order to counter competition from outside and other neighborhood groups, neighborhood organizations had to be wary of the problems posed by aging memberships, weak or unstable leadership, and excessive financial burdens.

Perhaps the most important voluntary institutions in any late-nineteenth-century American community, and especially in the historic land of the Puritan, were those connected with religion. Religious affiliation was a fundamental part of the individual ethnocultural identity, and religious matters were taken no less seriously than grave political issues. During the nineteenth century the disestablished status of religion in the United States seemed to energize America's churches, and especially the Protestant denominations, to attract the voluntary support of the population.[6]

Voluntarism, a central component of nineteenth-century Protestant religious life, had an enormous impact on American society, particularly in the North. At the local level, the dynamic of "voluntaryism" encouraged the establishment of and participation in auxiliary religious and charitable organizations. On a larger scale, it produced the great domestic missionary and reform movements of the antebellum period. The effort to organize and coordinate denominational church societies as well as missionary tract, Sunday school, temperance, and other moral reform movements produced loosely affiliated institutional networks. These efforts, as Gregory Singleton points out, provided the organizational model for secular enterprises in commerce, industry, and government that emerged in the late nineteenth century. More important for present purposes, however, is the fact that the local-chapter structure elaborated first by Protestant church members was adopted by a wide range of religious and secular neighborhood organizations.[7]

Church-related activity also provided an opportunity for women to play a significant public role in American community life. From the start, American women responded in large numbers to the fervent religious revivals of the nineteenth century. During the first half of the century, they redefined church-related activities as a respectable public extension of the domestic sphere to which women were thought to belong. As a result, in the late nineteenth century men primarily staffed Protestant vestries and parish committees, while neighborhood women constituted the backbone of the church and related voluntary charitable and missionary associations.[8]

In Jamaica Plain, as in other urban neighborhoods, religious zeal blossomed into a profusion of institutions. During the late eighteenth century the area's only church had struggled to survive, but by the early 1900s Jamaica Plain residents came together to worship in at least eighteen local churches of Christian denomination.[9] In general, churches allowed all to attend religious services but required some kind of profession of faith for active membership. Although churches divided the neighborhood population along religious, class, ethnic, and gender lines, they also crossed these lines by means of heterogeneous memberships and interdenominational cooperation. Thus, like other local organizations, religious institutions both linked and separated neighborhood residents.

Founded in 1769 as a New England Congregational church, the First Congregational Society of Jamaica Plain was the community's oldest and most prestigious religious organization. Early in the nineteenth century the First Church evolved from New England religious orthodoxy toward more moderate Unitarian dogma. Born in Boston in the late eighteenth century, New England Unitarianism represented a liberal reform of orthodox Congregationalism (for example, it stressed the doctrine of free will rather than predestination) and had strong associations with the social elite.[10]

Like other neighborhood religious societies, the First Church represented a local chapter in a larger organizational network. Although historically New England Protestants believed in the ideal of the autonomous congregation, even during the early colonial period ministers of different churches had formed denominational synods. As early as the 1830s the First Church of Jamaica Plain had joined a conference of New England Unitarian churches, and in the latter nineteenth century it belonged to the American Unitarian Association, which functioned as a national coordinating body of Unitarian churches.[11]

In the late nineteenth century the First Church of Jamaica Plain upheld the Unitarian traditions of liberalism and elitism.[12] Under the leadership of Charles Fletcher Dole, who joined the church in 1876, became pastor in 1881, and served until 1916, the church became a forceful advocate of the social gospel, the tide of liberal Protestant reform that rose during the last decades of the nineteenth century. Despite its liberalism, the First Church was run as an exclusive organization dominated by the neighborhood "gentry," who rented their pews at premium rates. Indeed, when Dole attempted to reform the system of pew rental by creating a "free church," the parishioners, led by Robert M. Morse, Jr., the preeminent Boston attorney who headed the Parish Committee, overwhelmed the motion.[13]

The exclusivity meant that in social terms the First Church congregation was distinguished by the presence of many members of the neighborhood elite. Throughout the nineteenth and early twentieth centuries, members of Jamaica Plain's oldest and wealthiest families, such as the Balches, Bowditches, Curtises, Greenoughs, and Welds, attended and supported the First Church. In 1880 about half of the male parishioners were prosperous wholesale merchants and professionals who commuted to

TABLE 5.1

Members of the First Congregational Society of Jamaica Plain
(First Church), 1880 and 1915

Members	1880	1915
Households	200	278
Total members	586	506

Sources: Manual of the First Congregational Society, of Jamaica Plain (1880); First Congregational Society Manual and Parish List (1915).

work from Jamaica Plain to downtown Boston. The remainder were by and large respectable Yankees, aspiring downtown business clerks and a few local shopkeepers. (See tables 5.1 and 5.2.)[14]

Unlike the First Church, St. John's Episcopal Church, Jamaica Plain's second major religious institution, belonged to a denomination with a hierarchical administration. From its inception, St. John's was a member of the New England Episcopal network known as the Eastern Diocese. The benefits of these external connections were demonstrated in 1841, when the Episcopal bishop and William R. and Amos Lawrence, residents of the Town of Brookline and heirs to a great New England textile fortune, contributed financial support that enabled the small group of local Episcopalians to build a small chapel. On the issues of ritual that deeply divided nineteenth-century Episcopalians, St. John's took an emphatically Low Church stand.

From its colonial beginnings as the American Anglican church, the Episcopal church had traditionally been associated with the upper class, and in the nineteenth century the emergent urban elite reaffirmed the

TABLE 5.2

Male Members of the First Church by Occupational Group,
1880 and 1915 (in percent)

Occupational Group	1880	1915
High-white-collar	58	49
Low-white-collar	38	34
Skilled	5	10
Low-blue-collar	1	7

Sources: See table 5.1.

Note: For 1880, $N = 127$, or 79 percent of all listed men; for 1915, $N = 130$, or 70 percent of all listed men.

connection. The congregation of St. John's, like that of the First Church, reflected these aristocratic associations. The first Episcopalian services in Jamaica Plain were held at Lakeville, the Pondside estate of a wealthy Englishman, Charles Beaumont, and in the mid-nineteenth century other wealthy residents, such as Edward N. Perkins and William H. Sumner, also supported the institution. A parishioner described the congregation of the 1860s as "a fine-looking, aristocratic set . . . who drove to church in their carriages." At the turn of the century, well-to-do Boston businessmen such as Asa Spaulding Weld and Andrew J. Peters, Sr., preserved the prestige of St. John's.[15]

  Yet the congregation of St. John's Church also illustrates how neighborhood institutions could bring members of different socioeconomic groups together. Perhaps reflecting the movement among some Episcopalian leaders to broaden the appeal of the Episcopal church, from mid-century St. John's in Jamaica Plain attracted local businessmen and artisans. In the late nineteenth century numerous clerks, agents, and foremen joined the local shopkeepers and skilled workers to give the St. John's congregation a decidedly middle-class aspect. (The parish even included a few working-class members, such as George H. Dyer, the janitor at Eliot Hall, and William E. Fischer, a gardener at Franklin Park.) Although the congregation was probably dominated by New Englanders, by the early twentieth century it had attracted a number of first- and second-generation immigrants of English, Irish, Canadian (especially from the Maritime Provinces), and occasionally Swedish background. (See table 5.3.)[16]

Evangelical Protestantism was the bedrock of New England religious culture. Encouraged by Jonathan Edwards, Timothy Dwight, and their heirs, from the eighteenth century onward religious revivals had erupted

TABLE 5.3

Male Members of the St. John's Episcopal Church, by Occupational Group, 1903–1911 (in percent)

Occupational Group	%
High-white-collar	24
Low-white-collar	50
Skilled	13
Low-blue-collar	12

Source: Episcopal Diocesan Archives, St. John's List of Families, 1903-11.

Note: N = 67 (traced in the *Boston City Directory* for 1907), or 50 percent of all listed men.

periodically across the region. During the first half of the nineteenth century strict preaching and ecstatic revivals invigorated New England fundamentalist churches and propelled a sense of mission that sent New England doctrines and culture westward across the United States. Not surprisingly, as the population of Jamaica Plain swelled during the late nineteenth century a number of fundamentalist Protestant churches sank roots in the neighborhood. Unlike the First Church, these churches appealed especially to women and to the middle- and lower-middle-class elements of the local population.

The oldest of these was the First Baptist Church of Jamaica Plain, which originated in 1840 when a group of local Baptists who had been holding prayer meetings in their homes began renting the Village Hall for services. A Boston-area religious revival added to the roll of local Baptists, who in 1843 had grown numerous enough to construct a new church and choose a pastor. Two years after a fire destroyed the original building, a new structure was completed on Centre Street, and in 1892 church members added a commodious parsonage next-door.[17]

Despite a large building debt, the ranks of local Baptists grew during the late nineteenth century. As part of an evangelical denomination, the First Baptist Church of Jamaica Plain appealed strongly to women, who made up the majority of the members. Initially the congregation was primarily middle-class and New Englander in character, although immigrants from Scotland and Nova Scotia also joined the religious band. In the late nineteenth century the membership included wealthy men such as the deacon, James W. Converse, a prominent Boston shoe and leather dealer and banker, but most of the employed men were artisans, clerks, or local businessmen, such as George James, the Centre Street grocer, and John D. Wester, a local builder. (See tables 5.4 and 5.5.)[18]

As in the case of other neighborhood organizations, links to the outside world aided the establishment of a local branch of conservative Congregationalism, still a vital creed in late-nineteenth-century New England. In

TABLE 5.4
Members of the First Baptist Church of Jamaica Plain, 1842–1871

Members	1842	1871	1842–71
Female	42	139	287
Male	17	72	157

Source: "Historical Catalogue of Present Members," *A Brief History of the Jamaica Plain Baptist Church of West Roxbury* (Boston, 1871), 36–48.

TABLE 5.5

Male Members of the First Baptist Church of Jamaica Plain,
by Occupational Group, 1842–1871 (in percent)

Occupational Group	%
High-white-collar	32
Low-white-collar	37
Skilled	22
Low-blue-collar	8

Source: "Historical Catalogue of Present Members," *A Brief History of the Jamaica Plain Baptist Church, of West Roxbury* (Boston, 1871), 36–48.
Note: N = 88, or 56 percent of all listed men.

1852 four prosperous Jamaica Plain men who were unhappy with the liberal Unitarianism of the First Congregational Church met to establish "an Orthodox ministry" in the neighborhood. Soon the growing group of members began holding services in the West Roxbury Town Hall. Despite the relative autonomy of traditional evangelical congregations, however, a body of Congregationalist churches had to approve the organization of a formal church. In February 1853 a council of eleven churches from Boston and neighboring towns convened and, after listening to testimony, approved the establishment of the Central Congregational Church. With contributions from Jamaica Plain, Boston, Dorchester, and Roxbury, the Congregationalists built a church on Centre Street in 1856. As Congregationalists continued to arrive in Jamaica Plain, the society soon outgrew the church. Fearful of losing the new arrivals to churches of other denominations, the society sold the old building in 1871 and built a new church on Sumner Hill, one of three at that location.[19]

Like the Baptist congregation, the fundamentalist Central Congregational attracted more female than male church members. Although some members believed that Central Congregational did not include the truly rich, the upper middle class, if not the elite, was well represented in the church by physicians, lawyers, and downtown merchants and manufacturers. For example, the church deacon for forty-five years and teacher of the men's Bible class was Samuel B. Capen, a partner in a Boston carpet manufacturing firm. (Capen became a leader in the national Congregational Sunday school movement and, as we will see, the movements for municipal school and government reform.) Local businessmen, salesmen and clerks, and local artisans made up the predominant middle-class male element in the congregation. (See tables 5.6 and 5.7.)

TABLE 5.6

Members of the Central Congregational Church, 1870 and 1877

Members	1870	1877
Female	128	236
Male	73	135

Source: Rules . . . Central Congregational Church, Jamaica Plain, Massachusetts with a Catalogue of its Officers and Members (1870 and 1878).

Although strongly New Englander in composition, the Central Congregational Church also attracted immigrants, especially Scots, whose Presbyterian traditions were closely allied with Congregationalism. The church became so closely associated with Scottish culture that in 1912, 150 Scottish members of the church gave an ethnic surprise party for their pastor, complete with Scottish menu, dress, and bagpiper.[20]

Other middle-class Protestant denominations were not able to build large congregations. Although local Methodists had gathered for services since the 1850s, it was not until 1870 that, with financial backing from Boston Methodists and Jamaica Plain Unitarians, they were able to build their stone church on Sumner Hill. In 1891 church membership peaked at 190, but plagued by an instability in the pastorate, by 1909 the church dropped to 104 active communicants. Another small but hardy band was the Universalists, who in 1871 organized a parish in the former Congregationalist Church at Greenough Avenue and Centre Street and, bolstered by the commitment of a few leading members, such as Eugene W. Clark, the dry goods store owner, survived into the twentieth century.[21]

TABLE 5.7

Male Members of the Central Congregational Church, by Occupational Group,
1853–1870 and 1870–1877 (in percent)

Occupational Group	1853–1870	1870–1877
High-white-collar	30	29
Low-white-collar	40	36
Skilled	26	24
Low-blue-collar	4	11

Source: Rules . . . Central Congregational Church, Jamaica Plain, Massachusetts with a Catalogue of Its Officers and Members (1870 and 1878).
Note: For 1853–1870, $N = 50$, or 48 percent of all listed men; for 1870–1877, $N = 66$, or 60.5 percent of all listed men.

While neighborhood Protestant churches counted their adherents in the hundreds, local Roman Catholic congregations numbered in the thousands, with many working-class members. Roman Catholics had arrived in the neighborhood by the 1840s, but it was not until 1867 that a parish was established to serve the swelling Catholic population. In that year the pastor of St. Joseph's Church in Roxbury, whose jurisdiction encompassed Jamaica Plain, purchased land on South Street, in the heart of a working-class Irish residential district. In 1869 the archbishop of the Roman Catholic Diocese of Boston appointed Thomas L. Magennis, a native of Lowell, Massachusetts, and recently ordained priest who had been working at the Roxbury church, to organize the new parish in Jamaica Plain. Magennis persuaded the selectmen of the Town of West Roxbury to allow him to hold services nearby in Curtis Hall, the new town hall, which he did until 1873, when St. Thomas Aquinas Church was completed and consecrated.[22]

Magennis was an energetic pastor who, like the neighborhood's strong Protestant pastors, provided his church with leadership and stability. His situation also resembled that of the Protestant pastors in that in the 1870s the Roman Catholic Diocese of Boston, a New England institution that had accommodated itself to its Yankee environment, was still in a rudimentary stage of development. It was only beginning to absorb the massive numbers of recently arrived Irish and other immigrants. Much of the task of adjusting the newcomers to Boston and the church was left to parish priests such as Magennis, who as a result had much of the same autonomy as their Protestant brethren. By the time he died in 1912, Magennis had been elevated to the position of monsignor and had built up a parish of well over six thousand parishioners. (See tables 5.8 and 5.9.)[23]

During the late nineteenth and early twentieth centuries the growth of population in secondary areas of development– Forest Hills in the south and a northern belt that encompassed Hyde Square, Cedar Hill, and Egleston Square—stimulated further church-building. Although these later churches usually included wealthy parishioners, their membership also reflected the large numbers of middle- and working-class residents of immigrant stock in the population of these subdistricts.

In these areas wealthy longtime residents shared in services and church activities with their newly arrived neighbors. After a successful experiment with a Sunday school at the Boylston railroad depot, some prominent members of the Central Congregational Church built the Danforth Street Chapel in 1870 with the assistance of their home church and the Old South Church in Boston. After two failed attempts, in 1879 the local Congrega-

TABLE 5.8

Fathers in Roman Catholic Baptism Records, by Occupational Group,
1900 (in percent)

Occupational Group	St. Thomas Aquinas	Blessed Sacrament
High-white-collar	0	0
Low-white-collar	24	30
Skilled	26	20
Low-blue-collar	50	50

Source: Archives, Archdiocese of Boston, parish records.

Note: For St. Thomas Aquinas, $N = 38$ (traced from 1 in 4 random sample of fathers' names), or 17 percent of 230 listed; for Blessed Sacrament, $N = 30$ (traced from 1 in 6 random sample of fathers' names), or 10 percent of 294 listed.

tionalists established a formal church society with a minister, and in 1885 they built the Boylston Congregational Church adjacent to Boylston Station. Drawing from northern Jamaica Plain and nearby sections of Roxbury, by 1896 the Boylston Congregational Church had increased its membership to more than 205, 75 percent of whom were women. More middle-class than the Central Church, Boylston Congregational attracted not only New Englanders such as Frederick J. Leighton, an Egleston Square plasterer from Maine, but also Canadians such as Henry Doherty, a Hyde Square machinist, and European ethnics such as William H. Nitz, a bookkeeper, and Olaf Olsen, a bank messenger. (See table 5.10.)[24]

Jamaica Plain's second Episcopalian church took root with help from both inside and outside the neighborhood. In 1889 Sumner Shearman, the pastor of St. John's, Phillips Brooks, Boston's Episcopalian bishop, and the

TABLE 5.9

Birthplace of Fathers and Father's parents in St. Thomas Aquinas Baptism
Records, 1900 (in percent)

Birthplace	%
Father and both parents United States	18
Father United States and 1 or more parents Ireland	18
Father and both parents Ireland	58
Father and both parents Germany	3
Father, Scotland and both parents Ireland	3

Source: Archives, Archdiocese of Boston, parish records.

Note: $N = 38$ (traced from 1 in 4 random sample of fathers' names), or 17 percent of 230 listed.

Local Attachments

TABLE 5.10

Male Members of the Boylston Congregational Church, by Occupational
Group, 1896 (in percent)

Occupational Group	%
High-white-collar	10
Low-white-collar	40
Skilled	40
Low-blue-collar	10

Source: Manual of the Boylston Congregational Church, Boston, Mass., 1896.
Note: N = 42, or 82 percent of 51 men listed (205 total membership).

Episcopal City Mission helped organize St. Peter's Church as a mission
near Boylston Station. In five years the congregation grew to about two
hundred active members, acquired a minister, and built a granite church.
The predominantly middle-class congregation included second-generation
immigrants such as William C. Krauth, the son of German parents and a
cashier at Rudolph Haffenreffer's Boylston Lager Beer Company, and
George Dakin, a Boston civil engineer of Canadian and Irish parentage.[25]

Evangelical denominations also tapped the growing population in the
outer sections of Jamaica Plain. Those Methodists who did not belong to
the First Methodist Church were dispersed among several churches, including Egleston Square Methodist Episcopal Church, founded in the
1870s, St. Andrew's Methodist Episcopal Church, organized in 1891 on
Heath Street out of a former working-class mission church, and, to the
south, the Forest Hills Upham Methodist Church, established in 1893. The
Boston Baptist Church Union, a confederation of Baptist churches, helped
found the Centre Street Baptist Church (1892) in Hyde Square and the
Franklin Park Baptist Mission to spread the gospel to newcomers.

The Roman Catholic Diocese of Boston looked to the new settlements
to serve the swelling numbers of Catholic residents there. In 1892 it organized the Church of the Blessed Sacrament in Hyde Square with a school-
house and a chapel for a thousand communicants. By 1910, when construction of an imposing Italianate church building was begun, the size of the
parish had reached eleven hundred families and six thousand souls. In 1896
the pastor of St. Thomas Aquinas Church, Thomas Magennis, started the
Church of Our Lady of Lourdes in the industrial Brookside section. As at
St. Thomas Aquinas, working- and lower-middle-class Irish-Americans
predominated in the newer parishes. (See tables 5.8 and 5.11.)[26]

TABLE 5.11

Birthplaces of Marriage Partners, Church of the Blessed Sacrament,
1900, (in percent)

Birthplace	%	Birthplace	%
United States / United States	33	Ireland / Ireland	38
United States / Canada	15	Ireland / Other	3
United States / Ireland	5	Canada / Canada	3
United States / Other	3		

Source: Archives, Archdiocese of Boston, parish records.

Note: N = 40, or 100 percent of listed marriages.

In Boston, as in Milwaukee and other cities with large German populations, German ethnic solidarity splintered along religious lines, and religious solidarity foundered on ethnic allegiances. German-speaking residents of Jamaica Plain, free to select their own institutions, often chose to
attend German-language churches, even if it meant going outside the
neighborhood. For example, to serve outer-city Lutherans, a one-story
wooden chapel was constructed on Parker Hill in Roxbury in 1871. In 1892
members of the German Evangelical Lutheran Trinity Church added a
large brick Gothic church to the chapel. Despite the distance from their
homes, some of Jamaica Plain's leading German businessmen, including
Adam Mock, the owner of a liquor store in Boston, and Rudolf F. Haffenreffer, the Jamaica Plain brewer, were strong supporters of the Lutheran
Trinity Church. Such loyalty persisted in the twentieth century even as the
number of German speakers in the congregation dropped and the church
shifted to English-language services.[27]

In response to the new church building of their Lutheran rivals, local
German Catholics attempted to acquire a new German Catholic church.
During the nineteenth century a complex of German Catholic institutions
grew up around the Holy Trinity Roman Catholic Church, founded in
1844 in Boston's South End. In 1893 a group of German-speaking Catholics in Roxbury and West Roxbury, including more than three hundred
from Jamaica Plain, attempted to persuade John J. Williams, the archbishop of Boston, to establish a German-language church closer to their
residences. Mindful of the sums recently expended in the South End and
perhaps doubtful that the size of the German Catholic population could
sustain another church, Williams refused the request. Thus, many Jamaica
Plain German Catholics continued to travel to the South End for religious
services, and the Irish dominated the neighborhood Catholic churches.[28]

Local Attachments

The movement of German-Americans toward Jamaica Plain and West Roxbury produced other German-language Protestant churches. In order to keep up with its adherents, a Roxbury German Baptist church in 1893 established a German Baptist mission in lower Jamaica Plain and in 1901 sold their original Roxbury church in order to build a new church near Hyde Square in Jamaica Plain. Similarly, a German Methodist church in lower Roxbury followed the German-American population and in 1900 built a church in the area of Boylston Station.[29]

The religious institutions of Jamaica Plain differed in several ways. Most fundamentally, they diverged on church polity, ritual, and principles of dogma such as infant baptism and papal infallibility. Each congregation presented its own unique social, economic, and ethnic complexion. The Protestant churches, moreover, maintained an aloofness toward the Catholics.[30]

Yet interdenominational cooperation was also in evidence in Jamaica Plain. It was a tradition among the neighborhood churches to help each other in time of need, for example, by offering the use of a church building when fire or other disaster struck. Neighborhood charitable work also involved interdenominational cooperation. Faced with an overwhelmingly working-class congregation and a lack of financial resources to support the construction of a church, Thomas Magennis, the pastor of Catholic St. Thomas Aquinas, turned for support to local Protestants. Despite later generations' belief in a traditional enmity between wealthy Protestants and working-class Irish Catholics, these Unitarians and Episcopalians aided him in his efforts. The treasurer of the First Church, Abner Child, took a special interest in the progress of St. Thomas and bequeathed a substantial amount of money to the poor of the parish. A small plaque in Child's memory still located inside the main door of the church expresses the parish's gratitude.[31]

Whatever their denomination, class, or ethnic character, neighborhood religious institutions spawned clusters of auxiliary organizations, most of which were staffed by women. At the First Church, for example, the Sunday school, directed for many years by Ellen C. Morse, Robert M. Morse's sister, by 1916 was run by a three-person administrative staff, a musical director, and ten teachers. Other women's parish groups included a sewing circle to produce clothing for the needy and a Post Office Mission to correspond with interested souls in other states and countries. In 1888 the phalanx of women's auxiliary groups whose purpose was "to quicken the religious life of the church; to bring the women into closer acquaintance, co-operation, and fellowship; and to promote denominational, missionary, and philanthropic work," was reorganized in a denominational network of similar groups as the Jamaica Plain Branch of the Alliance of Unitarian and other Liberal Women. The women of the parish also raised the money to build and furnish the new Parish House, opened in 1890 to accommodate the Sunday school, parish meetings, and sundry other church activities.[32]

Other churches developed similar parish organizations. The Central Congregational Church, for example, combined religious with social life in organizations such as the Senior and Junior Christian Endeavor societies, the Woman's Foreign Missionary Society, the Woman's Home Missionary Auxiliary, the Thimble Club, the Daughters of the Covenant, and the Young Men's Congress. The neighborhood's Catholic churches, too, brought parishioners back to participate in the local chapters of the St. Vincent de Paul Conference, a group whose purpose was to assist the parish priest with school activities, bake sales, and other parish events. In July 1910 a picnic organized for the Church of the Blessed Sacrament attracted a crowd of two thousand people.[33]

Like Jamaica Plain's churches, local educational institutions also linked neighborhood residents to one another. Reflecting the nineteenth-century growing taste of the urban elite in Boston and other cities for exclusive private schools, many upper- and upper-middle-class Jamaica Plain residents sent their young children to private schools in the neighborhood. In the public schools, young children enrolled up to the third grade in one of several small primary schools scattered throughout the district.

Within the public schools, social experiences varied. The primary schools reflected the school-age population, minus the children in private and parochial institutions, of the immediate area in which they were located. Thus, schools in the industrial Heath Street area concentrated children of working-class and Irish families, and schools in heterogeneous Boylston Station mixed children of different ethnic, religious, and, within limits, economic backgrounds. In September 1904 the local newspaper reported the opening of the Ellis Mendell Primary School near Boylston Station in positive, if grossly stereotyped, images: "Here a sturdy German woman with her golden-haired blue-eyed 'kin-kin' chatted affably with a rosy-cheeked Irish-woman, who had two bright looking children to register, while the cutest little pickaninnies you ever saw clung shyly to their mammies. . . . A stylish little chap . . . doffs his cap and hands his card to the principal with the air of the little gentleman he is. His (American-born) parentage is unmistakable."[34] Local children in the fourth to ninth grades attended the neighborhood's large district grammar schools, which offered a potentially broader spectrum of social contacts.

Once beyond the age of compulsory schooling, young people and their parents could choose from a complex of educational institutions throughout the metropolitan area. Many working-class students were unable or did not wish to continue on to high school. The privileged or academically gifted, on the other hand, often left the neighborhood to prepare for college at the Roxbury Latin School (whose charter admitted qualified Jamaica Plain residents without tuition), Boston's Boys' and Girls' Latin schools, or exclusive private preparatory academies such as Phillip's and St. Paul's, many of which were located outside the city.

From the 1840s Jamaica Plain's own public high school, Eliot High School, renamed West Roxbury High School in 1874, appealed especially to middle-class families. A product of the antebellum high-school movement in Massachusetts, it provided a college preparatory course, a new "English" curriculum that taught science and practical education, and, from the early twentieth century, a commercial track that emphasized office skills. As in high schools in neighboring communities, the increasing curricular emphasis on white-collar training helped boost enrollments.[35]

Just as Boston's public-school officials hoped to mold the minds of immigrants' and workers' children, neighborhood priests aimed to acculturate and assimilate their predominantly Irish and blue-collar parishioners through a Catholic education. In the face of opposition from some Protestants and the lack of public enthusiasm of Archbishop Williams for parochial schools, in 1873 Thomas Magennis, of St. Thomas Aquinas, started the Leo XIII (grammar) School, where hundreds of local children soon enrolled. In 1893 Arthur T. Connolly, the pastor of the Blessed Sacrament Church, founded the Cheverus School. In 1901 the school enrolled more than five hundred students, by 1911 almost a thousand. Connolly added a two-year girls' commercial high school, whose program of bookkeeping, stenography, and other clerical skills was aimed, according to one graduate, at keeping local girls from working in the Plant Company shoe factory.[36]

Although neighborhood schools often represented distinct cultural clusters, shared experiences within the institution also created new kinds of bonds. This was most clearly the case at the West Roxbury High School, which became a popular local institution under the leadership of George C. Mann, the son of the Massachusetts educational reformer Horace Mann and the school's principal from 1879 to 1915. Like students in Somerville and other urban locales, West Roxbury High School students participated in school activities that reflected their sense of belonging to a distinct peer group. With feelings of communality promoted as school spirit, young Jamaica Plainers played on and watched school basketball and other athletic teams, joined school fraternities, and published the annual school yearbook and the school newspaper, the *Clarion*. Such experiences could significantly influence the lives of students. One woman from a German Catholic family, for example, testified that she joined the Boylston Congregational Church because the girls she befriended at the West Roxbury High School attended that church.[37]

The activities of school alumni groups reflected the strength of the social ties formed by shared curricular and extracurricular activities. During the nineteenth century the celebration of membership in a college class took on ever more elaborate forms. The collegiate class dinner, held while in school, soon became a preamble for the reunion dinners and festivals, which featured speeches, the class poem, and even the class song. About mid-century college alumni began to organize themselves formally and produced commemorative rings, napkin holders, mugs, and other memorabilia of their gatherings.[38]

The rising sense of "class" consciousness in nineteenth-century colleges then spread to neighborhood high schools and even grammar schools. Starting in 1884, for example, the alumni of West Roxbury High School started the West Roxbury High School Association, which staged an annual reunion and dance that became progressively more popular as the years went on. Thereafter the interest in school reunions spread to the alumni of grammar schools such as the Bowditch School and the Lowell School, who began holding their own reunion balls. In 1907 graduates of local Catholic grammar schools joined the movement by forming the Leo XIII Parochial School Association of St. Thomas Aquinas Church.[39]

In the late nineteenth century, the fraternal lodge, a distinctive type of voluntary association, rippled across the different elements of neighborhood society. Freemasonry, the original fraternal order and the model for subsequent orders, began in the early eighteenth century as an English stonemasons' society and spread to America during the colonial period. At first the lodges functioned essentially as drinking and eating clubs, but a growing contingent of members worked to elaborate the Masonic rituals, ceremonies that were loosely derived from the traditions of the medieval guild.

During the antebellum period, the anti-Masonic movement struck heavy blows against the order, allowing middle-class and professional members to transform it into a bastion of sobriety and self-improvement. For those not wishing to be associated with Freemasonry, the International Order of Odd Fellows, originally an English working-class drinking and aid society, became an alternative. In the mid-nineteenth century the Order of Odd Fellows inherited many former Masons and was similarly transformed into a sober, middle-class organization with an intricate set of rituals.[40]

From the time of the Civil War, the popularity of fraternalism revived dramatically. It is estimated that in the last third of the nineteenth century millions of American men joined the lodges of the Masons, Odd Fellows, and other recently founded brotherhoods, such as the Knights of Pythias and the Ancient Order of United Workmen. Like America's churches, the fraternal orders were structured along hierarchical lines with varying degrees of centralized authority. Constituting a classic case of branch-office and local-chapter structure, Jamaica Plain's fraternal lodges were neighborhood sections belonging to regional and national networks of similar organizations.[41]

Based on the concepts of brotherhood, mutual aid, and sociability, fraternal lodges were defined by their esoteric quasi-religious rituals. Especially important was the "work" in which exotically costumed members earned "degrees" by learning secret code words and gestures, such as hand grips, which symbolized the inner mysteries of the order. Although the past cultures invoked by the rituals varied from order to order, they bore a strong familial resemblance, in many cases having been adapted from one another.

The precise significance of these ceremonies is elusive, but as the fraternal orders were coterminous with the onset of modern society in the nineteenth century, they clearly helped Americans adjust in some way. Recent scholarship is divided regarding whether they offered American Protestant males a ritualistic way to cope with changing class relations, the absence of the father in the Victorian family, or the loneliness brought on by life in a mobile urban society. Religious in tone, the lodges may also have offered Protestant men a refuge from both work and the female-dominated churches. Whatever their subliminal symbolic significance, as a practical matter, the lodges brought urban dwellers together socially in a communal setting. In addition, they often provided useful services such as health insurance, funeral expenses, and support for widows of deceased members.[42]

The two oldest fraternal lodges in Jamaica Plain were the Eliot Masonic Lodge and the Quinobequin Lodge of Odd Fellows. The Eliot Lodge was founded in 1866 in the post–Civil War Masonic revival. The Quinobequin Lodge of Odd Fellows moved to Jamaica Plain from the Town of Dedham in 1855, went out of business in 1862, and was revived in 1869. Perhaps due to lingering anti-Masonic opposition from followers of fundamentalist religions, both lodges grew slowly. In the early 1870s, for example, the Quinobequin Lodge had only fifty members. In the early 1890s the Eliot Lodge reached "a low ebb," and the two organizations shared a number of members. Soon after moving to the large Masonic Hall on Centre Street in 1899, the Eliot Lodge began to attract younger members, and the membership rolls climbed to 225. The Quinobequin did even better and by the early 1900s had surpassed the Eliot Lodge in the number of members.[43]

At the local level, fraternal lodges regulated the admission of new members through a process of internal nomination and committees. The available evidence suggests that Jamaica Plain lodges, like those elsewhere, were somewhat heterogeneous in social and occupational terms, but middle-class respectability was a principal thrust of lodge participation. Reflecting the general prestige of the Masonic order, the Eliot Lodge was securely located in the Protestant Yankee environment of the neighborhood's middle- and upper-middle-class commercial and professional residents. Nonetheless, the Eliot Lodge was not a strictly exclusive club. Like Freemason lodges in New York, Boston, and other places, it admitted German immigrants; at times, it even administered degree rites in German. It was estimated that the Eliot Lodge contained more German members than any other Massachusetts lodge except Boston's Germanian Lodge, a specifically German branch.[44]

Similarly, immigrants and blue-collar workers penetrated the ranks of local Odd Fellows. By the turn of the century, the leaders of the Quinobequin Lodge were worried that their membership had stopped growing and that its character was too working-class. They then launched a membership drive that would gain the lodge middle-class respectability. In an effort to "improve the personnel," the Quinobequin Lodge made a conscious effort to attract physicians, lawyers, businessmen, and other "men of public note." The drive was a great success, and in 1907 the membership of the lodge, now one of the largest Odd Fellows chapters in the state, swelled to three hundred, including six doctors, six lawyers, and numerous former and present government officials and political-party activists.[45]

As in other communities, the reproduction of Masonic-type organizations allowed members of other class and ethnic groups and even women to participate in the lodge style of life. The Ancient Order of United Workmen (A.O.U.W.), for example, was founded in 1869 to provide life insurance to working men who could not ordinarily have afforded it. The evidence suggests that, true to its origins, the Marion Lodge, Jamaica Plain's branch of the A.O.U.W., was solidly blue-collar. A similar insurance order was the United Order of Pilgrim Fathers, organized in New England in 1878, which utilized colonial symbolism in its rituals. The leadership of the local chapter, the General Warren Colony, was made up primarily of skilled workers and clerks. The Royal Arcanum order, founded in Boston in 1877, was represented by two lodges, the Jamaica Plain Council, a prosperous group that included skilled workers and downtown lawyers and businessmen, and the Forest Council, whose officers included local businessmen, clerks, and mailmen.[46]

Although Roman Catholics were prohibited by papal edicts from joining fraternal orders such as the Masons, a fraternal order of Catholic men, the Knights of Columbus, was founded in Connecticut in 1882 and spread rapidly over the United States. In 1895 Jamaica Plain Catholics organized the Jamaica Plain Council of the Knights of Columbus. It quickly became an important local lodge distinguished by an original flair in its ritual and social activities. Although many working-class Irish Catholics lived in the neighborhood, the most active members of the Jamaica Plain Council were middle-class men such as John M. Minton, a Boston lawyer who lived in Forest Hills, Michael S. Morton, a successful Forest Hills grocer, and James M. Ryan, a Roxbury real estate agent who lived on Cedar Hill.[47]

Some fraternal orders were organized more along ethnic than along religious lines. The Ancient Order of Hibernians (A.O.H.) retained some Masonic trappings and provided insurance benefits for the Irish. Although association with the Molly Maguires had hurt the reputation of the order, it was quite popular in Jamaica Plain. Division 15, the local Hibernian group, was organized in 1894 and within a few years could claim four hundred members, dwarfing even the Quinobequin Lodge. The low-white-collar and blue-collar occupations of active members in 1899 suggests that, in striking contrast to Jamaica Plain's Knights of Columbus, the neighborhood Hibernians, like the A.O.H. chapters in Worcester, Massachusetts, were strongly working-class. Fraternalism could also express Scottish ethnicity. In 1898 local Scots organized Clan Gordon No. 8 of the American Order of Scottish Clans. The composition of the committees in charge of their annual social in 1899 indicates that the members of the Clan Gordon were overwhelmingly skilled workers.[48]

Most of the fraternal lodges were all-male, but Jamaica Plain had its version of the women's auxiliary lodges that, despite their diluted versions of fraternalism, spread across the country in the late nineteenth century.

Within the ranks of the local Odd Fellows, for example, there was the female William Parkman Lodge of the Daughters of Rebekah; in addition, there was the Columbia Lodge of the imitative but unaffiliated Order of Odd Ladies. Belonging to the United Order of Pilgrim Fathers, an exceptional lodge in regard to segregation by sex, the General Warren Colony included both men and women.[49]

Clubs, another popular form of local association, also linked neighborhood residents to one another. Like lodges, clubs were social organizations modeled on societies formed earlier in the eighteenth and nineteenth centuries. Clubs, however, lacked the exotic trappings of the fraternal orders and varied widely in origins, purpose, and degree of exclusivity. Some promoted learning and self-improvement, some focused on games and sports, while others aimed at simply socializing. As with other forms of neighborhood organizations, upper- and upper-middle-class residents tended to concentrate in their own relatively exclusive clubs, but other groups emulated the examples set by those higher on the socioeconomic ladder.

In Jamaica Plain as in other communities, the social gatherings of the neighborhood elite provided a basis for later, more formal organization. Out of such roots, for example, emerged the Footlight Club, perhaps the oldest continuously running amateur theater group in the United States. Beginning in 1850, an enthusiasm for parlor theater swept through American polite society, and thus some Jamaica Plain residents kept a tradition of staging "private theatricals" in their homes.[50]

In December 1876 a group of well-born young friends including Thomas B. Ticknor, a Harvard graduate who worked at his father's well-known publishing house, Ticknor and Fields, and Frances Goodwin, daughter of the Boston merchant William H. Goodwin, decided to regularize the local theatrical tradition by organizing a neighborhood amateur drama club. Led by Caroline H. Morse, in January 1877 they formally organized the Footlight Club "to promote friendly and social intercourse and to furnish pleasant and useful entertainment by the aid of the drama."[51] In February the players presented their first production at the German Theater, near the Boylston railroad station, but in 1878 a growing following led the club to move to the larger Eliot Hall, around the corner from the First Church of Jamaica Plain.

The Footlight Club admitted two types of members: active members presented the light comedies that were the club's stock in trade; associate members supported the proceedings and, dressed in black-tie formality, attended the shows. The club grew in popularity as numerous members of prominent Jamaica Plain families, such as the Ticknors, Welds, and Wheelwrights, threw themselves into the amateur productions. In 1902 a Footlight Orchestra was added to the productions, and in 1906 the Footlight Club reached a high-water mark of 65 active members and 275 associates.[52]

Local traditions of a different sort produced elite literary clubs. Beginning in the 1820s, many New England communities began holding public lectures for the moral and intellectual advancement of their residents, and the idea of the lyceum then spread across the country. Jamaica Plain was a part of the New England lecture circuit, and in the antebellum period distinguished Harvard professors such as Oliver Wendell Holmes and Louis Agassiz delivered lectures at the old Village Hall. After the lectures, all retired for a pleasant evening of refreshments and socializing at one of the graceful Pondside homes. Reflecting a widening interest in knowledge and high culture in Boston and other cities, during the nineteenth century a stream of experts and musicians gave lectures and musical recitals at Jamaica Plain halls and sometimes private homes.[53]

The growth of the neighborhood population, as well as the proliferation of churches and other organizations, however, left some of the neighborhood's well-to-do railroad commuters feeling that they had less opportunity to meet with one another socially. "The morning train to Boston was losing its character as a social event." As a consequence, in 1882 Charles F. Dole, the pastor of the First Church, and some of the "older residents" formed the Eliot Club to serve as a "common meeting ground and a vigilance committee to guard the interests of the community."[54]

The founders of the new club probably drew inspiration from the long tradition in Boston proper of exclusive gentlemen's clubs such as the Wednesday Evening Club, Somerset, Thursday Evening, and St. Botolph, where members mixed serious intellectual matters with conviviality. The all-male Eliot Club met once a month for a banquet and lecture on some subject of historical, literary, scientific, or topical interest and took part in neighborhood and governmental affairs, regularly petitioning the government and other bodies on matters of interest. At the turn of the century the most active members of the Eliot Club were wealthy executives, prominent Boston lawyers, and neighborhood physicians, ministers, and businessmen.[55]

Many upper-middle-class American women, denied a career or formal education outside the domestic sphere, had a special thirst for learning. In the early nineteenth century women had made up a large part of lyceum audiences. After the Civil War, Jane C. Croly and Julia Ward Howe started a national movement to form women's study and literary clubs, which spread to towns and cities from Massachusetts to California. Until the establishment of women's colleges and the gradual acceptance of the career woman rendered them redundant, these clubs provided a sense of sorority and intellectual attainment to generations of upper-middle-class American women.[56]

In 1896, at a high-water mark in the women's study-club movement, Jamaica Plain women formed the Jamaica Plain Tuesday Club. Tuesday Club members included such pillars of the neighborhood as Ellen C. Morse, Mrs. Thomas Sherwin, whose husband was the president of the New England Telephone and Telegraph Company and an active Eliot Club member, and the energetic Annie Coffin Weld, wife of a wealthy Boston wholesale broker, Aaron Davis Weld.

The bimonthly meetings of the club were chiefly dedicated to lectures and concerts, but the group also supported nonpartisan causes, which were often neighborhood-related. At a typical meeting in February 1900, Ellen Morse's sister-in-law, Mrs. Robert M. Morse, presided. She first announced a petition, brought in by members who belonged to the Consumers' League of Massachusetts, that called on the state legislature to reduce the work week for women and minors to fifty-two hours. The club then voted to launch an individual subscription drive to fund interior decorations for the new West Roxbury High School, a gift deemed appropriate because it dealt with "the artistic and educational element in life for which the club stands." The speaker of the day, Dr. Louis Kelterborn, delivered a lecture titled "The German 'Lied' in Olden and Modern Times." A recital of songs by the doctor's wife followed the lecture, and then all retired to another room to enjoy tea and refreshments.[57]

Culture and improvement were only part of urban club life, of course; from the eighteenth century much of the activity in British and American gentlemen's clubs centered on less edifying forms of recreation. In Boston and other American cities men of wealth and distinction enjoyed fellowship at their clubs over dinners, drinking, billiards, and cards.[58]

The Jamaica Club represented a neighborhood version of this type of gentlemen's club, but politics provided the immediate catalyst for its organization. The idea originated in the fall of 1884 with the officers of the local Ward 23 Battalion in the campaign of James G. Blaine and John A. Logan, the Republican party candidates for president and vice-president. While waiting in Boston to march in the great torchlight parade, the Jamaica Plain men discussed forming a club that would "keep alive the spirit of fraternity and good fellowship which had grown up among them." Soon thereafter twenty-five neighborhood men rented a room, acquired the basic equipment for their purposes—a half-dozen card tables, two dozen chairs, and a stove—and elected their officers. Within six months of its founding, the number of members rose to about 150, a level it maintained until about 1889, when it rose again, necessitating the construction of a clubhouse.[59]

The chief business of the Jamaica Club (and many other neighborhood clubs) was play. Despite the club's origins in a political campaign, no political discussion was allowed. Instead, on Saturday nights club members enjoyed a generous spread of food and then concentrated on card and other indoor games. Like most of the other local social organizations, the Jamaica Club was connected to an extra-neighborhood network. Participation in the Suburban Interclub League allowed Jamaica Club members to do battle at home and away with their counterparts from similar outer-city clubs in tournaments of whist, table tennis, billiards, pool, and bowling. In addition, the club put on public theatrical productions, such as its popular minstrel shows, and held a variety of other entertainments and social events.[60]

Although perhaps not quite as prestigious as the elite Footlight Club or the Tuesday Club, the Jamaica Club adopted a membership policy that leaned toward upper-middle- and middle-class men. The great majority of the club's founding members were young downtown clerks, such as William J. Cable of the Cable Rubber Company, who expected to have an upwardly mobile career track in wholesale and manufacturing firms. At the turn of the century the active membership was still dominated by white-collar types, including bookkeepers, local merchants, downtown businessmen, and professionals.[61]

In Boston and other cities the nineteenth-century Anglo-American campaigns for Muscular Christianity fed the rising respectability of sports. From the antebellum period, some elite clubs focused primarily on sporting activity. While the wealthy of New York formed the New York Yacht Club, Bostonians organized the Union Boat Club (1851) and the Boston Yacht Club (1866). Like their counterparts elsewhere, during the nineteenth century well-to-do families who lived near Jamaica Pond held rowing and sailing regattas. By the early 1880s Boston newspapers reported that the Fourth of July regattas at Jamaica Pond were attracting audiences of about two thousand people, including many ladies in carriages. Out of these races developed the Jamaica Boat Club, organized by respectable local young men such as George B. Ager, Jr., and Russell S. Hyde, both downtown business clerks.[62]

Members of the urban elite across the United States organized sports clubs devoted to activities such as hunting and polo, cricket and baseball, and various forms of tennis. In 1882 J. Murray Forbes, a Boston railroad tycoon, invented the idea of an exclusive all-purpose sporting club, soon realized as the Country Club, the prototype of this popular institution of the American well-to-do. Established on an extensive tract in neighboring Brookline, the Country Club offered its members facilities for equestrian sports, cards, billiards, curling, and tennis, but beginning in 1892 it became associated primarily with the newly introduced sport of golf. Not surprisingly, wealthy citizens of Jamaica Plain such as Robert M. Morse, Quincy Amory Adams, and Charles P. Bowditch became members of the Country Club, which was located a short distance from their homes.[63]

Of course, wealthy residents did not monopolize club life any more than they did churches or lodges. During the late nineteenth century, clubs for middle- and working-class urban dwellers proliferated across the country. Sports clubs, for example, were popular across the socioeconomic spectrum of Jamaica Plain society. Local residents took part in the late-nineteenth-century bicycle-club craze by forming first the Jamaica Wheel Club and then, in 1893, its successor, the Jamaica Cycle Club. By the end of the century, the Jamaica Cycle Club had become a general sports club whose seventy-odd members contended in bowling, pool, and whist sections with teams from other Boston neighborhoods. The Cycle Club brought together New England and immigrant-stock skilled workers and store clerks, such as Charles A. Coombs, a bicycle repairman from Maine, William R. (Billy) Cole, a Canadian-born printer, Harry Hulme, an English machinist, Henry E. Hudson, a jewelry store salesman of German and French parentage, and John H. Egan and A. W. McLean, clerks of Irish descent.[64]

Once a predominantly urban, white-collar sport, baseball became thoroughly democratized and decentralized in the late nineteenth century. Middle- and working-class baseball clubs abounded in Jamaica Plain. Young men from the various sections of the neighborhood assembled as the Lowells, the Vine Rocks, the Boylston Athletics, and the Boylston Baseball Club to square off against one another and teams from other neighborhoods. Nonsports organizations formed their own local teams, such as the Jamaica Plain Grocery Clerks Ball Team and the Boylston Congregational Church Nine Baseball Club. Sometimes a local boy did well enough to play for an outside team. In 1899, for example, the Sharon (Massachusetts) Athletic Association in the Norfolk County League ran up an 18-2 record on the strength of their star left-handed pitcher from Sharon, their catcher from Foxboro, and the team's second baseman, "big,

Local Attachments

modest Simeon A. Murch, the well-known plumber of Jamaica Plain," who covered "a lot of ground" at second base and was "the heavy batter of the team."[65]

All neighborhood organizations performed a social function for their members, but some clubs existed specifically to bring people together, usually by means of the "social dance," the popular version of the traditional dance ball. Throughout the nineteenth century, fancy-dress balls had been a feature of American urban upper-class life. During the later decades the ball supplemented the social register as an avenue by which guardians of high society certified the membership of new entrants, especially young women making their "debuts." The fabulous cotillions of the Four Hundred in New York and the Newport aristocracy had their counterparts in Boston, Chicago, and other cities. Yet during the same period, ethnic organizations in Boston and other cities also threw balls, public ceremonies to socialize and celebrate their group identity. Less respectable but still popular, the working-class dance hall, often attached to a saloon, also indulged the American urge to move to music.[66]

The residents of urban neighborhoods shared this taste for dance, and in the late nineteenth and early twentieth centuries instructors offered classes in ballroom dancing in Jamaica Plain and adjacent districts. Many local organizations held dances, but by the turn of the century social clubs that specialized in dances began to appear. The Hubklub, founded in 1899 by middle-class Yankees, regularly attracted scores of couples to its annual dance. Other neighborhood social clubs included the Violet Club, for "young Catholic ladies"; the Alpine Social Club, which failed to survive and sent a number of its members to the Eliot Social Club (not the Eliot Club); the Franklin Social Club; and the carefree-sounding Flickamaroo Club, formed by young people in the northern part of the district.[67]

Even in a nation of joiners, German-speaking immigrants in nineteenth-century cities such as Milwaukee and Cincinnati stood out for their associational tendencies, or *Vereinswesen*. In late-nineteenth-century Boston there were a number of German organizations, such as the German Aid Society, the Harugari Society, a fraternal order, and the Fidelia Club, as well as a German-language newspaper, the *Germania*. Similarly, Jamaica Plain German-Americans developed clubs devoted to activities that paralleled those of other neighborhood groups. In 1871, for example, residents of the Boylston Station area organized the most prominent of the local German clubs, the Boylston Schul Verein. A German cultural society akin to the Eliot Club, the Boylston Schul Verein was intended "to stimulate an interest in politics and problems of government," establish a German-language school for members' children, and develop the intellectual and physical culture of its members.[68]

The athletic club, or Turnverein, was a favorite German institution. In Germany during the early nineteenth century the Turners had combined gymnastic exercise with a sense of German nationalism. After the failed revolt of 1848, they fell out of favor with the governmental authorities. From the 1850s onward, German immigrants, many of them political refugees, spread the Turner movement to American cities and helped popularize gymnastics and athletics in the United States. In Boston they founded the Arbeiter Turnverein in the Brookside section of Jamaica Plain, as well as a citywide organization, the Boston Turnverein.[69]

Like other neighborhood groups, the German clubs possessed distinct occupational and ethnic characteristics that were important to members. Businessmen and other white-collar workers dominated the Boylston Schul Verein. The core of the Arbeiter Turnverein membership was a group of relatively well-paid members of the cigar workers' union. Immigrants from the region of Schwabia organized another German club, the Schwaben Verein, near Heath Street. Jamaica Plain residents remembered it as a social club of skilled workers and shopkeepers such as barbers, bakers, and butchers.[70]

Among the numerous late-nineteenth-century voluntary associations there also existed neighborhood military-drill and patriotic groups. Veterans' organizations included not only Boston Post 200 of the Grand Army of the Republic but also, in the absence of a recent major war, the Sons of Veterans, Joseph Stedman Camp (named after a local physician), and the Daughters of Veterans, Betsy Ross Tent. In 1896 the Mary Draper chapter of the Daughters of the American Revolution was organized, and in 1909 the members somewhat belatedly placed next to the Civil War monument a memorial stone and plaque to the men of Jamaica Plain who had served in the Revolutionary War.[71]

Located within a diverse matrix of numerous neighborhood and city voluntary associations, local organizations had to compete for the time of local residents. As we have seen, many local residents traveled outside the neighborhood to attend church or school and to seek out a variety of leisure-time amusements. Like other local Protestant ministers at the turn of the century, Sumner U. Shearman complained that neighborhood people were commuting to the Episcopalian churches in Boston rather than attending nearby St. John's. Furthermore, Shearman wondered why "men failed to attend church and yet in large numbers were to be met at Masonic meetings, which all knew were largely gatherings of a religious nature." As both the pastor of St. John's Episcopal Church and the chaplain of the local Eliot Masonic Lodge, Shearman must have been familiar with the problem.[72]

Yet because local residents participated in citywide networks, the whirl of local activity also attracted participants from outside the neighborhood. Social events such as dances regularly pulled outsiders from Roxbury, Dorchester, and other locales. At the surprise twenty-first birthday party for Fred J. Conant, a local resident who took part in Boston-area institutions such as the Gordon Training School, the Immanuel Praying Band, and the Boston YMCA, guests included not only Jamaica Plainers but also friends and fellow students from Roxbury, Boston, South Boston, Cambridge, and Providence, Rhode Island. If successful enough, a local institution might become a central place within urban social networks. By the turn of the century, for example, the Footlight Club attracted both players (such as Parkman Dexter, a Boston salesman who became the club's president) and audience from the Boston area.[73]

Not everyone was incorporated into the complex of local social organizations. Members of the working class, particularly young men, represented an element that dissented from the middle-class order of club life. To some extent, saloon culture, with its air of disrepute, exemplified the alternative style. Even more annoying to some were the gangs that harassed passers-by on the street, vandalized property, and took part in raucous parties at Curtis Hall. It was this group that the local social reformers hoped to tame first in the South Street area, later in Brookside, where philanthropic ladies encountered "the toughest boy proposition" they had ever seen. Although these behavior patterns contained little if any political content, they did have implications of place. Territoriality, one of the most basic forms of local attachments, is of defining importance to members of street gangs.[74]

Despite seeming to separate the neighborhood population along the lines of gender, religion, class, occupation, or leisure-time interests, local voluntary associations shared a common urban culture. Beneath the bewildering array of urban neighborhood associations, strikingly similar organizational structures and forms expressed collectively held middle-class values. The diverse local groups sponsored increasingly similar types of recreational activities. These common traits allowed the neighborhood branch offices and local chapters to absorb new arrivals, function internally, and participate in larger networks. The many activities of the local organizations created a communal public life at the neighborhood level rather than the city level.

The democratic political culture of nineteenth-century America clearly exerted a strong influence on the internal organizational form of the neighborhood branch office. With few exceptions, most organizations made use of the structure and processes of the legislative body, namely, an annual election of officers, regular meetings, the creation of committees, and standard rules of order. The members of church charitable associations, literary societies, and sports clubs alike elected a president, vice-president, secretary, and treasurer, the slate of officers common to American political, governmental, or other corporate bodies. The nomenclature of fraternal lodge officials differed according to the prevailing ritual, but whether the officers were known as senior and junior wardens, noble and vice grands, or chief patriarch, high priest, and scribe, they performed functions equivalent to those in other societies.[75]

Aided by the increasing dissemination of legislative rules of order, democratic political bodies also influenced the conduct of meetings of local organizations. Although detailed legislative rules of order were originally published in oversized tomes, from the time of the antebellum period new editions began to appear as pocket-size manuals. The late-nineteenth-century editions of rules of order increasingly addressed not only legislative assemblies but also religious groups, citizens' societies, and social clubs. Besides setting forth rules for meetings, they offered model constitutions of voluntary associations.

In the highly organized society of the nineteenth century, urban Americans needed to know how to carry on their public business. "It matters not whether a meeting be held to form a singing-choir, or a base-ball club, or an excursion party, or a society for amusement or improvement," the author of a popular press manual declared; the meeting should be conducted in an orderly fashion "so that every one interested may have an opportunity to hear and be heard." By the 1890s the growing number of women's clubs and societies induced publishers to print rules-of-order manuals specifically for women.[76]

The adoption of common forms and rules of order facilitated transfers of members from one organization to another. Henry M. Robert, the author of the most successful of the late-nineteenth-century manuals, explicitly attempted to assist affiliated Americans to adapt to branch-office and local-chapter society. The purpose of *Robert's Rules of Order* was to "enable civic-minded people to belong to several organizations or to move to new localities without constantly encountering different parliamentary rules." Masonic-style rites, albeit with sundry variations, provided a similar continuity to the ritual work of the local lodges; after the rituals the lodges also used parliamentary rules to conduct business meetings.[77]

From the 1880s, Jamaica Plain organizations, like those in Providence and elsewhere, also adopted similar forms of entertainment. Whatever their original purpose or identity, neighborhood societies chose their entertainment fare from a menu of lectures, concerts, dances or other kinds of parties, light theatricals, vaudeville shows, and games. Competition among the different groups for the free time of neighborhood residents probably encouraged the spread of common recreational activities. Whatever the cause, multiplication of local entertainments had the effect of enriching the public life of the neighborhood.[78]

Since the society and club entertainments and socials also followed prescribed forms, the leisure part of an association's program was just as familiar as the business meeting. Lectures were accompanied by a short musical recital and followed by refreshments. Dances, too, were accompanied by refreshments, and the more respectable ones had patronesses to chaperone and assist the proceedings. Proper social etiquette ruled at neighborhood teas and garden parties. Smoke talks, theme parties, and theatricals all had their formats.

Just as rules-of-order manuals promoted consistency in club meetings, other types of printed matter assisted urban residents with recreation. The publication of sheet music provided the melodies and arrangements for local recitals and dance orchestras. Low-cost script and production books made possible locally produced minstrel shows and other theatrical performances. Whether for whist or baseball, books that spelled out the rules of the game helped establish order among the players.[79]

Not surprisingly, clubs whose primary purpose was social offered the full range of prototypical recreational activities. Over the first twenty years of its existence the Jamaica Club, for example, staged, in addition to its very popular minstrel shows, an annual New Year's ball, a mock trial, an operetta, band concerts, ladies' nights, men's smoker nights, and a prize military drill. The German clubs in particular offered a wide range of popular entertainments. The drama groups of the Schwaben Verein, the Boylston Schul Verein, and the German Young Ladies Club performed plays in German. The Schwaben Verein had an active singing group, and in 1904 the Schul Verein organized its own orchestra, which performed monthly concerts. The Arbeiter Turnverein was primarily a gymnastic club, but the other clubs also had athletic activities. The Boylston Schul Verein celebrated the immigrants' native culture in traditional German costume, or *Faschings,* balls and *Stiftungsfest,* or anniversary parties.[80]

At the same time, however, local churches adopted similar forms of entertainment and, as a result, created religious social centers. In the name of what became known as the institutional church, local churches sprouted parish halls, and ministers and priests added buildings to serve extra-religious functions. Until 1885, local Protestant churches convened the church elders annually for a quiet business meeting. In 1885, however, the pastor of the Central Congregational Church, George M. Boynton, transformed the annual meeting into a rally in which all the church members were invited for a reception and supper, followed by a public roll call and reports from the various church organizations. This innovation proved to be so successful that it became the customary practice at Central Congregational and at other neighborhood churches.[81]

The pastor of the Boylston Congregational Church, Ellis Mendell, took the social ideal further. In 1889 he organized a Boy's Club, which soon enrolled over one hundred boys. In 1893 it became the Boys' Brigade and focused on both Bible and military drill. Other youth groups included the Junior Christian Endeavor Society (1892), the Young Women's Missionary Society (1889), and the Whatsoever Circle of the King's Daughters (1893). In 1890 Mendell built a gymnasium and began offering classes for young people and businessmen. The purchase of a church printing press enabled the Young People's Society of Christian Endeavor (founded in 1885) to begin publishing a monthly newspaper, the *Boylston Messenger,* in 1893. The Boylston Church also maintained reading and game rooms. First the Boylston Lyceum League and soon thereafter the Junior Lyceum were assembled to debate "questions of public interest." Later the church added still more groups, such as the Bicycle Club, founded in 1898.[82]

Catholic clerics also pursued the ideal of the institutional church. Thomas Magennis, the pastor of St. Thomas Aquinas, organized the first parish fair even before he had completed building the church. In 1897 he initiated an annual parish Harvest Party, which in 1907 drew twelve hundred people. Arthur T. Connolly, the pastor of the Church of the Blessed Sacrament, started a parish school in 1893, and in 1894 he built Columbia Hall to house parish social activities. In the following years, Connolly added a day-care center and a children's medical dispensary.[83]

On St. Patrick's Day, Jamaica Plain Irish Catholics celebrated Irish culture with lectures and musical performances, often held at Curtis Hall to accommodate the large audiences. In the early 1900s they flocked to hear Michael J. Dwyer, a lawyer of Irish parentage and a parishioner of the St. Thomas Aquinas Church, recite Irish poetry and sing Celtic ballads. In

1907 Father Connolly, who had visited the Emerald Isle several times, spoke on Irish art and scenery and displayed lantern slides, after which a vocal quartet performed Irish songs.[84]

Thus, neighborhood religious institutions presented a range of entertainments. Sometimes church groups produced theatricals, such as the romantic comedies staged by members of St. John's Episcopal Church in 1899. At other times the churches functioned as literary clubs. The same year, for example, the Central Congregational Church offered the People's Course, a series of lectures on topics ranging from the role of the United States in the Philippines to the character of South Africa. At their annual dinner in 1910 the members of the Unitarian First Church Union heard a recital by a contralto soloist and a talk entitled "The English in India." In the twentieth century church groups further expanded their undertakings to include music lessons and cinema, among other activities.[85]

Anticipating the evolution of fraternal orders into fun-loving social clubs during the 1920s, Jamaica Plain fraternal lodges, like those in Providence and elsewhere, also appended club-style entertainments to their traditional activities. During its turn-of-the-century membership drive, the Quinobequin Lodge was transformed into a fraternal version of the institutional church. Besides the regular weekly evening meetings, the lodge initiated a year-round social program that included an autumn roll call with social hour, a children's day with Punch-and-Judy shows and other entertainments, ladies' night, "farmers' parties" and other theme parties, men's smoke talks, and illustrated lectures. The Quinobequin season was climaxed by the annual spring ball, a mammoth affair that frequently attracted a thousand people, including in 1902 the governor of Massachusetts.[86]

Announcements of lodge entertainments testified to the changing function of the orders in the neighborhood from fraternalism to club-style sociability. A leader in this respect was the Jamaica Plain Council of the Knights of Columbus, which soon after it was founded in 1895 became distinguished by an original flair in its social activities. Soon other Knights of Columbus councils imitated Jamaica Plain Council events such as the annual anniversary banquet held at a Boston hotel or the ladies' night with whist games. So, too, other lodges, such as the Royal Arcanum Jamaica Council, held whist and dancing parties and other entertainments. When the Beethoven Lodge No. 333 of the New England Order of Protection was established in 1899, its founders did not speak of its ritual; rather, they promised that it would be "one of the strong social organizations" in the Egleston Square area.[87]

Social entertainments were also important to the ethnic fraternal groups. In April 1899 the fifth annual social dance of the Ancient Order of Hibernians drew three hundred persons to a local hall decorated with a screen of palms, ferns, and evergreens, behind which played the Hobbs Orchestra. After several musical concert selections, the crowd danced until two o'clock in the morning. The annual social of the Scottish Clan Gordon No. 8 followed a similar program, except that the Scots demonstrated the Highland fling and the bagpipes before taking to the dance floor.[88]

Reflecting the national progressive reform movement to create neighborhood social centers in urban public schools, in the early twentieth century Jamaica Plain schools also began to offer a range of entertainment activities for adults. In Boston reformers conducted the social-center campaign in order to inculcate good citizenship in the working class and end the supposed isolation of urban dwellers. Since many local residents already participated in neighborhood churches, clubs, and other groups, however, the school department had to compete for the public's leisure time.[89]

The educational component of the social-center program comprised evening classes and lectures for adults. In 1902 the Boston School Department established the Lowell Educational Centre at the Lowell School, and by 1904 some six hundred men and women per night were taking manual-training and vocational-education courses there. Besides enrolling in subjects such as dressmaking, civil-service examinations, and practical electricity, hundreds also attended the Lowell Centre lectures on a variety of historical and literary topics. In 1902–3 the subjects of the Lowell Centre lecture series ranged from imperial India to Evangeline. (The top draw, however, was Michael J. Dwyer, whose talk "The Poems and Songs of Thomas Moore" brought out over twelve hundred people on a rainy night in November.)[90]

In the same vein, the school system promoted the growth of neighborhood parent associations. The activities of the parent associations echoed the entertainments of other neighborhood groups. A typical monthly meeting of the Bowditch-Agassiz Parents Association was held in the Bowditch School hall on the night of January 2, 1907. Edith Whitmore, the president of the Public Health Club, spoke on the topics "Household Economics" and "Diet and Disease"; a sixth grader, Gertrude Baldwin, gave two recitations; two teachers performed music on the violin and piano; and then refreshments were served on tables decorated in pink and adorned with narcissi. On a Friday evening in February of the same year about seven hundred parents of children in the Lowell Grammar School braved stormy weather to attend an entertainment program in which the seventh graders sang to the accompaniment of the school orchestra; an assistant Boston school superintendent, Mrs. E. C. Ripley, spoke on the topic "Parents' Cooperation"; and coffee and cake were served at a social hour before all dispersed at eleven o'clock.[91]

Even the workplace could function as a social center if it commanded the resources of the Thomas G. Plant Company. Because of his previous troubles with unions in Lynn, Massachusetts, at the turn of the century Plant attempted to suppress union activity in his giant women's shoe factory. Plant instituted an innovative program of welfare capitalism, a management policy that became popular with American companies in the 1920s. To encourage discipline and productivity among his approximately thirty-five hundred workers, he established a Profit-Sharing and Saving Fund and a disability and death-benefits fund.

Besides providing economic work incentives (and a nine-hour work day), Plant created an industrial counterpart to the institutional church and the school social center. He named the remarkable domain Queen Quality City, after the company's product. Among the factory's extensive recreational facilities were a landscaped park, a women's recreation room furnished with piano, separate game rooms with bowling alleys, card tables, and pool tables for the foremen and other employees, and a fully equipped gymnasium with sixty showers and a salaried instructor to offer classes for both sexes. The company fielded its own basketball and baseball teams (the Queen Qualities) and presented smoke talks, vaudeville shows, Saturday-afternoon music concerts, and dances. In addition, it provided a circulating library and a weekly newspaper, *Queen Quality Topics*.[92]

The similarity of local chapter rules, rituals, and activities smoothed the membership transitions that ensued from the mobility of urban dwellers. Organizational networks of Protestant churches and fraternal orders assisted the movement of members through the institution of transfer letters or cards. From 1853 to 1903, for example, the Central Congregational Church accepted 803 new members with letters of transfer from other churches and dismissed 624 members to go elsewhere.[93]

Internal organizational similarities enabled neighborhood residents to move from one organization to another, and there are numerous cases of duplicate memberships, even including two lodges within the same fraternal order. A joiner such as Sewall C. Brackett, a lawyer in downtown Boston, belonged to the Quinobequin and Charles Hayden Odd Fellow lodges, the Knights of Pythias, the Knights of Honor, the Eliot Club, the Jamaica Club, and the Jamaica Plain Citizens' Association. Immersed in local social life, Brackett easily crossed the religious divide between Protestants and Catholics in February 1903 by delivering a stereopticon lecture on Havana first at a smoke talk at the Quinobequin Lodge of Odd Fellows and the following week at a meeting of the Jamaica Plain Council of the Knights of Columbus.[94]

Over time some local associations incorporated members of different ethnic, religious, and, to a certain extent, economic groups. For example, Joseph J. Leonard, a Catholic who served as a state representative in 1904 and 1905, became a leading member of the predominantly Protestant Jamaica Club. Faced with a shrinking of their base of support, local institutions would at times replenish their membership with members of groups passed over formerly. By 1915 the hitherto exclusive congregation of the First Church had begun to include immigrants and their offspring, mostly German and Scandinavian in origin, such as the families of Peter J. Imberger, the German-born owner of a Centre Street paint and wallpaper store, and his son, Edward H. Imberger, a painter. The Blessed Sacrament Church recorded a small but steady stream of marriages between Roman Catholics and Protestants, usually of different ethnic backgrounds. By World War I the Boylston Schul Verein admitted non-Germans such as Joseph Chalifoux, a French-Canadian Plant shoe factory foreman, and Petro Alemi, an Italian edge trimmer at the same factory.[95]

Yet the shared middle-class culture expressed by group rituals and activities also built barriers of gender and race that proved difficult to overcome. Local groups reflected the doctrine that men and women belonged to separate spheres. For most men of the middle class, the ideal, if not always the reality, was that women should keep house and not take outside employment. Women staffed and ran most of the church and charitable voluntary associations, and most fraternal organizations and social clubs were segregated by sex. Among the literary clubs, the Eliot Club was male and the Tuesday Club was female, the fraternal lodges were generally all-male, although the Odd Fellows lodges had female auxiliaries. There were German-American women's clubs—the Koffee Klatches, Frau Vereins, and the *Damenzwieg des Boylston Schul Verein*— whose benefits and social events contrasted with the drinking and card-playing routine of the male clubs.[96]

Some local women chafed at the inequities, and reformer circles agitated the idea of women's suffrage. The Jamaica Plain Citizens' Association barred women from membership on the grounds that women were not interested in neighborhood uplift. Thus, when the association asked the women of the Tuesday Club to help them suppress rowdy behavior at

Curtis Hall, one Tuesday Club member, Mary E. Starbuck, publicly chastised the group for its double standard. One neighborhood resident, Mrs. Pauline Agassiz Shaw, served as president of the Boston Equal Suffrage Association for Good Government; another, George A. O. Ernst, a reformer attorney, proposed laws to allow women to sue at court.[97]

Local racial attitudes mixed liberal tendencies with bigotry, all the more deeply felt for its unconsciousness. Reflecting New England reformer traditions, white Jamaica Plain residents displayed public attitudes of tolerance and even sympathy for African-Americans. Charles F. Dole, the Unitarian First Church pastor, was a friend of Booker T. Washington and a strong supporter of Tuskegee Institute. Jamaica Plain women helped put on a benefit for the Harriet Tubman House to help unemployed black girls. Sometimes local pride transcended stereotyped racial attitudes. In the 1880s the principal of the George Putnam School encouraged Lucilla Smith, the school's only African-American student. Seventeen years later, when Smith returned to address the school's graduating class, the neighborhood applauded her accomplishments in educating the poor of North Carolina. Similarly, the local newspaper applauded Henry Poy, the Chinese-American owner of the Boylston Station laundry, when he won the two-mile bicycle race at the Chinese picnic at Walden Pond.[98]

Although Irish and German comic skits were not unusual, a steady stream of locally produced minstrel shows and other blackface comic routines betrayed a condescending presumption of caste that exceeded vaudevillian stereotypes. Even the Young People's Union of Dole's First Church staged a minstrel show. Occasionally local racist assumptions found more direct expression. In 1908, for example, the neighborhood newspaper, which as a rule tried to avoid controversy, printed on the front page a mocking interview with a local charwoman who was an evangelical Christian. The article consisted mainly of quotations rendered in dialect and included racist comments such as the allusion to "the wild barbaric grace characteristic of the African." While not as extreme, local attitudes toward Chinese residents similarly mixed tolerance with condescension.[99]

Of course, an important function of the branch offices and local chapters, whatever their ostensible purpose, was to bring people together. In a letter of thanks for the award of a commemorative cup from the Footlight Club, Thomas Ticknor acknowledged how the social function of club life lent stability and reinforced commitment to the organization. "The Club, which has brought us all so much pleasure," wrote Ticknor, "has done far more than prove a source of entertainment. It has formed and cemented valued friendships, which will always last, and which will under-lie and make strong the whole organization." The celebrations and memorial histories of local organizations represented more than self-congratulations; they represented a shared pride in obstacles overcome and good deeds accomplished. Members of St. Thomas Aquinas Church, the Footlight Club, and the Boylston Schul Verein alike noted with satisfaction the "traditions" that helped to define their institutions.[100]

Not surprisingly, strong affective feelings sometimes arose from people working and clubbing together. Elderly members of the German clubs remembered the card tables, parties, and picnics where, perhaps over a round of drinks, one made close friends, got loans, and heard of job openings in the nearby factories. August Becker recalled meeting Otto Heidrich at the Arbeiter Turnverein not long after Becker moved to Jamaica Plain, the beginning of a friendship between the two active clubmen that lasted until Heidrich's death more than six decades later. Becker also met his second wife at one of the dances held by the Boylston Schul Verein. Similarly, at a Footlight Club rehearsal William Stanley Parker, a leading player, met Elizabeth Porter, a violinist in the club orchestra, and later the two married.[101]

Neighborhood residents sometimes became devoted to the leaders of their local organizations. Several neighborhood ministers developed close relationships with their congregations. In 1907, a public testimonial to Thomas Magennis at Curtis Hall, Jamaica Plain's town hall, celebrated the fortieth anniversary of his ordination and honored his work for St. Thomas Aquinas. More than a thousand people from the parish and neighborhood attended. Thirty-three years after he resigned the pastorship of the Central Congregational Church of Jamaica Plain, Francis Perkins looked back at his pastorate from distant Sonoma, California, and vividly expressed feelings for a people and a place long gone. "No other church has ever taken such hold on my affections as that at Jamaica Plain. There are such hallowed associations as cluster around no other spot when I think of my life among you."[102]

The unexpected death of Ellis Mendell, the pastor of the Boylston Congregational Church, in 1903 reverberated in the community. Local businesses closed during his funeral, and Boylston Church members circulated a petition to name a newly constructed public school in Mendell's honor. Some four hundred Jamaica Plain residents, including prominent neighborhood figures such as Michael J. Murray, a Catholic, and E. Peabody Gerry, a Unitarian, signed the petition. At a hearing of the Boston School Committee, Jamaica Plain politicians and residents asserted that a city school should have a "local name." They declared that the name previously proposed for the school, Alexander Hamilton, was obnoxious to the community and had led many to ask, Who was Alexander Hamilton? In contrast, Mendell had worked day and night for the community, said the petitioners, and "persons of all races and creeds" wished to see him so honored.[103]

The rich variety of neighborhood associational activities did more than link neighborhood residents to one another, however important the deep bonds may have been to individuals. The undertakings of Jamaica Plain's local chapters and branch offices created a communal public life that heightened the sense of neighborhood identity and kindled feelings of loyalty to Jamaica Plain.

The several elite charitable reform groups vividly demonstrated the sense of local attachment to Jamaica Plain. Refuting the notion that the urban upper middle class turned its back on the city, the historical record shows that in Jamaica Plain such people were actively involved in their local community. Although they tended to be elitist in outlook and socially aloof from other neighborhood residents, members of the upper and upper middle class in Jamaica Plain expended both time and money to take care of and instruct "their own," their poor and working-class neighbors. Cosmopolitan ideas inspired district charitable groups, but local allegiances defined such organizations as the Jamaica Plain Friendly Society, the Jamaica Plain Dispensary, and the Jamaica Plain Neighborhood House.[104]

In Jamaica Plain as in other communities, neighborhood churchwomen traditionally took on the responsibility of caring for the local poor and needy. Throughout the nineteenth century, Jamaica Plain's churches, usually led by women parishioners, donated clothing, food, and other aid to the parish poor (and supported missionary ventures for the underprivileged near and far). It was natural, then, for local Protestant women to take up the cause of the poor of the neighborhood as a whole. For example, the Needle Woman's Friend Society, founded in 1847, hired needy women to sew clothing and linens, a nineteenth-century approach to charity that was intended to provide support without undermining independence. At the turn of the century, the Needle Woman's Friend Society still flourished. With two wealthy Unitarian ladies, Annie Coffin Weld and Mrs. George W. Wheelwright, the wife of a paper manufacturer, as president and secretary, it hired sixty women every week to produce sheets, towels, and underwear.[105]

In 1871, after an ad hoc committee of "ladies and gentlemen" had finished aiding the victims of the great Chicago fire, its leaders called for a similar organization to assist the increasing numbers of local poor people. Encouraged by the Town of West Roxbury's overseer of the poor and chief of police, in December 1871 they organized the West Roxbury Relief Society in order to implement "the best methods of relieving suffering, encouraging the industrious poor, and improving the character and habits of the degraded and ignorant classes." Although the directors of the society represented Catholic St. Thomas Aquinas as well as neighborhood Protestant churches, the local Unitarian elite held firm control of the organization.[106]

The officers and directors of the West Roxbury Relief Society soon discovered that the tasks related to administering poor relief were far greater than they had expected. Thus in 1874 the remaining members of the society and other neighborhood residents formed a larger, more structured organization, the Jamaica Plain Employment and Temporary Relief Society, which in 1885 was renamed the Jamaica Plain Friendly Society. Besides a president, treasurer, and secretary, the new group had six vice-presidents, an executive committee, and a substantial team of donation solicitors, who annually collected amounts in excess of a thousand dollars.[107]

Although the Friendly Society officers and workers were earnestly nonsectarian and the recipients of support were predominantly Irish Catholic (more than two-thirds of the families visited in 1877 were Irish), a stable group of upper- and upper-middle-class Protestants dominated the relief organization. Mrs. David S. Greenough, who had helped lead the society's predecessor organization, and other women of well-to-do families, such as Caroline Chickering, Ellen C. Morse, and Mrs. Thomas B. Frothingham, held executive positions for many years. Both the vice-president, Charles P. Bowditch, an independently wealthy trustee from Moss Hill, and the treasurer, Eugene W. Clark, the Centre Street clothier and community leader, served the society for more than twenty-five years. Local Protestant ministers and physicians also played key roles in the society.

The society's visitors, the group's chief workers, as a rule were women, generally the daughters and occasionally the wives of downtown wholesale merchants and insurance executives who lived in Pondside, Sumner Hill, and Moss Hill. They were accompanied, presumably for safety, by male "associates," who were sometimes their husbands. Sometimes the associate was a local businessman such as Patrick McMorrow, an Irish-born paving contractor, or William Rooney, an Irish-American proprietor of a boot and shoe store, but most were Protestant ministers and doctors.

Even a cursory examination of the process of financial support clearly demonstrates the female nature of the society's enterprise. With few exceptions, the donor solicitors were women, usually individuals other than the visitors and officers, but of the same family or class. Leopold Vogel sent shoes from his shoe store, and John C. Pratt sent coal from the Jamaica Plain Gas Light Company, but the neighborhood's society ladies provided most of the annual donations, most in the form of clothing. Cash donors, numbering from 450 to 550 each year, included some immigrant and immigrant-stock residents but were predominantly Protestant and overwhelmingly women.

Espousing a philosophy popularized by Boston's Joseph Tuckerman, New York's Robert Hartley, and American Social Science Association reformers, among others, the neighborhood relief society adamantly opposed "indiscriminate almsgiving" on the grounds that it weakened character, undermined self-reliance, and led to pauperism. Inspired by the British social reformer Octavia Hill, the society instead began with the idea that it would investigate and assess each case carefully, provide short-term and minimal relief to those who truly deserved it, and remedy the underlying causes of the distress of the rest. The society pioneered the approach taken by the urban Charity Organization Society in the late 1870s and 1880s. Beginning in 1874, it divided the neighborhood into districts, in which assigned workers systematically investigated cases of distress and took what they considered to be appropriate action. In 1888 a special committee was created to process cases.[108]

One of the society's basic tenets was the importance of giving work to all who were able-bodied. At its inception the society assigned sewing work to indigent women under the supervision of a hired agent, Mrs. Bradley. Under Mrs. Bradley, a strict disciplinarian who would not accept dirty or inferior-quality work, and her successors, dozens of neighborhood women produced clothing and other sewn articles which the society sold to neighborhood residents and Boston-area hospitals and orphanages.[109]

Despite the vast differences in perspective between the society's visitors and their hosts (and the authority wielded by caseworkers over aid recipients), the experience of Friendly Society workers taught them something about the lives of their less-well-off neighbors. Although society visitors found cases involving intemperance, they also found numerous cases of distress that could not be blamed on weak character. Like social workers elsewhere, they discovered that external circumstances such as the coal shortage of 1902 and the depression of 1907 contributed to the problem of urban poverty. Thus, despite the rhetoric of moral reformation repeated in the annual appeals for donations, the society regularly increased the proportion of the annual budget expended on donations of coal, food, clothing, and money for rent and other needs. Physical proximity may have contributed to an understanding of the plight of the poor: as a rule, Friendly Society visitors lived less than a ten-minute walk from the homes of the families they considered "our poor people."[110]

In trying to solve the financial problems of the local poor, the affluent workers of the Jamaica Plain Friendly Society also tapped into the diverse networks of philanthropic, religious, ethnic, and occupational aid societies that crisscrossed the neighborhood. In chronic cases where temporary aid did not seem appropriate, the society served originally as a conduit for private charity, by interesting individual donors in particular cases, and later as an umbrella charitable or social-work organization that referred cases to the appropriate, albeit sometimes sectarian, agencies. From an early date, the Friendly Society relied upon the St. Vincent de Paul Society to take over cases involving Catholic residents of the neighborhood, and the list quickly expanded to include such groups as the Jamaica Plain Dispensary, the German Aid Society, and Boston-area hospitals and asylums. In 1912, for example, the society discovered the four children and wife of an Irish plasterer who was in a sanatorium with tuberculosis. After providing groceries to the family, the society's worker contacted the local priest, the Knights of Columbus, and the Plasterers Union, among others, and sent the wife to the Boston Dispensary for care and treatment.[111]

Blaming alcoholism for much of the impoverishment, in 1881 the Friendly Society tried unsuccessfully to persuade the police commissioners to close all the neighborhood saloons. Then in February 1883 local Methodists and Baptists organized the Jamaica Plain Women's Christian Temperance Union (W.C.T.U.). Although more middle-class in character than the Friendly Society, the local W.C.T.U. chapter was a fervent Protestant reform organization. Its work consisted chiefly in organizing local temperance lectures and socials, distributing temperance tracts, and collecting for a wide variety of temperance and charitable causes. In the early twentieth century some 150 members of the local chapter raised money for the perennial campaigns for district option (for local prohibition) and settlement houses in Jamaica Plain and Boston's West End.[112]

The upper crust of Jamaica Plain society strongly supported local charitable medical organizations. After the Civil War, social-minded physicians in Boston and other cities established small clinics where they donated their services and medical supplies to the urban poor. As part of this movement, in 1877 George Faulkner, E. Peabody Gerry, and other local physicians instituted the Jamaica Plain Dispensary in order to provide free health care and medicine for the "sick and worthy poor." Well-to-do Friendly Society supporters and other prestigious residents supported the dispensary.[113]

In 1900 George Faulkner founded Faulkner Hospital, one of several neighborhood and parochial medical institutions that helped to popularize the concept of the modern hospital among the middle classes in Boston. The son of a wool manufacturer, Faulkner graduated from Harvard and moved to Jamaica Plain, where he took over the practice of Luther M. Harris, another longtime Jamaica Plain doctor. In establishing the hospital to treat the sick of Jamaica Plain and adjacent neighborhoods, Faulkner institutionalized the mission and work of local medical practitioners. Prominent local Unitarians and Friendly Society figures served on its board of trustees and on the Faulkner Hospital Aid Association, a women's auxiliary. For the first twenty-seven years of the hospital's existence, Franklin G. Balch, son of Joseph W. Balch, a prominent Jamaica Plain resident and insurance executive, served as chief surgeon.[114]

The commitment of well-to-do Jamaica Plainers to help and uplift their less fortunate neighbors took other forms as well. In the late nineteenth century, young residents brought the international movement to create youth clubs and settlement houses for the urban working class to Jamaica Plain. In 1889, the year that Jane Addams started the Hull House settlement in Chicago, Emily Green Balch, the daughter of a distinguished Boston attorney, pioneered similar local endeavors. Responding to the call of her pastor, Charles F. Dole, of the First Church, Balch dedicated herself to "the service of goodness," a mission that eventually led her to Europe and a Nobel peace prize. During her childhood in Jamaica Plain, the only working-class people whom Balch had known were her family's Irish domestic servants. Nevertheless, when she graduated from Bryn Mawr College the twenty-two-year-old Balch and a friend, Sophie F. Baylor, founded the Jamaica Plain Working Girls' Club to aid the young women who labored in local factories. To serve younger children, Mabel Bond and Alba Davis, the scions of two other leading neighborhood families, then organized the Junior Girls' Club. In 1895 Helen C. Weld, the daughter of Annie Coffin Weld, and Katherine P. Bowditch, a daughter of Charles P. Bowditch, started the Agassiz Boys' Club, which met in the same Green Street quarters at alternate times.[115]

When Helen Weld died in 1897 at the age of twenty-eight, her friends founded the Helen Weld House in her honor and soon afterwards consolidated the three youth clubs in a central clubhouse. In 1900 the widow of William H. Goodwin rented a building on her estate to the new organization. Through donations, bequests, garden parties, and benefit entertainments, the Helen Weld House drew on the same pool of affluent Jamaica Plain citizens who supported the Friendly Society and other local charities.[116]

Similar to neighborhood settlement houses in London, Boston, New York, and other cities, the Helen Weld House emphasized, not the relief offered by charitable organizations, but educational and recreational opportunities that would build the character of the working-class children in the neighborhood. Like the clubs started by Hull House, the Jamaica Plain youth clubs mixed classes with recreation such as gymnastics and baseball. The workers at the house maintained a supervised playground, a key element in the national reform movement for organized recreation, and taught manual-training classes, a program that incorporated popular late-nineteenth-century educational innovations. Like their counterparts elsewhere, Weld House workers organized summer visits for club members to country vacation houses, ran a flower mission for distribution to the city's sick and poor, lobbied for child-labor laws, and took part in municipal crusades.[117]

Also like settlement-house workers elsewhere, Weld'House workers tried both to bridge the cultural gap between the diverse elements of the urban neighborhood population and to impart their own, presumably superior values. Thus Weld House was supposed to "find the common human interest underlying all differences of worldly conditions or of religious faiths" while at the same time promoting "the civic welfare" and offering "opportunities to those who are deprived of much of what makes life happy." Were it not for "this philanthropy," wrote the Weld House workers in 1903, the children who took part in the house activities would be "much in the streets, acquiring most undesirable habits of indolence, if not vice."[118]

Although the Helen Weld House resembled a settlement house in many respects, it was not a place where educated young people from distant places came to live in the slums among the lower classes. After all, both groups resided in the same neighborhood. Instead, at Weld House Jamaica Plain inhabitants reproduced middle-class club society for the benefit of their working-class neighbors. Within a few years Weld House evolved into a neighborhood educational and social center, much like those in neighborhood churches and schools, and was increasingly staffed by full-time teachers and settlement-house professionals. Thus in 1907, in order to better express the "neighborly spirit" for which it stood, the officers of the Helen Weld House renamed the organization the Jamaica Plain Neighborhood House Association.

A sense of commitment to neighborhood was not restricted to the well-to-do; local attachments spanned the entire spectrum of branch-office and local-chapter society in Jamaica Plain. The names of institutions and clubs such as the Jamaica Plain Friendly Society, the Jamaica Club, the Star of Jamaica Veteran Firemen, and the Jamaica Cycle Club expressed at a basic level the sense of place that was integrally related to the identity of neighborhood organizations. Sports clubs, often autonomous organizations, flew the banner of neighborhood pride in contests with similar clubs from other sections of the city. Participation in local lodges engendered feelings of loyalty to their own local chapter and the neighborhood to which it belonged. In 1900 at their annual banquet, the assembled members of the Jamaica Plain Council of the Knights of Columbus sang the following anthem, written by a member to the tune of "My Maryland":

Jamaica Plain! Jamaica Plain!
To thee we pledge our hearts again;
Our thoughts are thine on sea or plain,
Our Order's star, Jamaica Plain.[119]

As in other American communities, holiday ceremonies served as a vehicle to celebrate both national patriotism and local identity. Starting in 1897, Sewall D. Balkam, the local businessman, and the Jamaica Plain Carnival Association organized communitywide celebrations of the Fourth of July in which the neighborhood celebrated itself. While the Jamaica Club and other local clubs festooned their headquarters and held open house for hundreds of visitors, a massive parade wound its way through the different sections of the neighborhood. In the procession, military and drill units, veterans (and sons of veterans) groups, neighborhood cycle clubs, Catholic and public schools, church societies, neighborhood political figures, government officials, and numerous individuals, many dressed in vaudevillian costumes, marched or rode on decorated floats to the huzzas of the residents.

Memorial Day offered another opportunity for members of local organizations to present themselves to their neighbors. On Memorial Day in 1903, for example, the Unitarian First Church of Jamaica Plain, the Central Congregational Church, the First Baptist of Jamaica Plain, St. Paul's Universalist, St. Thomas Aquinas (Roman Catholic), the Quinobequin and Daniel Hersey Odd Fellows lodges, the Masonic Eliot Lodge, the

Catholic Knights of Columbus, the Boylston Schul Verein, the Egleston Club, and the Jamaica Club all sent representatives to escort the Grand Army of the Republic Post 200 in solemn procession and public commemoration of the wartime dead. In a happier vein, in 1907 Old Home Week explicitly celebrated local history and historic sites. A huge ceremony and a fireworks display put on by Jamaica Plain's Odd Fellows lodges capped a week of neighborhood nostalgia.[120]

Neighborhood theatrical events also celebrated the neighborhood. Like the Fourth of July floats, the roles played by politicians and other prominent citizens in mock trials and other humorous productions both evoked a sense of local solidarity and reaffirmed the superior position of neighborhood leaders.

The crowds that attended public spectacles and entertainments were especially fond of "local hits," references to local people and places that expressed the shared experience of neighborhood life. For example, the 1897 Fourth of July parade gave the prize for the "Most Amusing Local Hit" to the Egleston Square Push Club for its float, "The Jamaica Plain Club Punch," and in 1900 another group parodied the unfruitful efforts of the Business Men's Association with a giant windmill float. In the Jamaica Club minstrel show of 1900, Fred Seaver, dressed in blackface as a woman named Susy, brought the house down with a musical number, "The Best in the House is None Too Good for Riley!" In the song, Seaver shifted from topical references to Admiral Dewey and the Boer War to spoofs of such well-known neighborhood figures as Captain Riley of the local fire department, local alderman E. Peabody Gerry, and local newspaper publisher Roswell S. Barrows. In one verse Seaver ribbed the Tuesday Club, and in the following verse he poked fun at the district's perambulating physicians.

> There's Dr. Jameson, Winkler, Broughton, Tompkins, Gerry, Ernst and
>   Cross,
> And some of them ride on bicycles and others drive a horse;
> What is it that makes the horses shy, the drivers swear so freely;
> It must be Dr. Stedman with his new automobily.

> CHORUS:

> For he steers it through the streets just like a madman;
> If any one crosses his path, he'll be a deadman;
> But won't there be jar, if he strikes a trolley car;
> There'll be work for the rest on Dr. Stedman.[121]

The *Jamaica Plain News* reflected the increase in the number of organizations and the growing strength of local sentiments. As late as 1891, the editor of the local newspaper had expressed feelings of urban inferiority and begged subscribers to contribute items to fill its pages. "It is a Jamaica Plain characteristic to disparage home industries and institutions. It is in the atmosphere, the doings of a great city of which we are a part, almost overshadow our small achievement. So we find people who instead of feeling local pride in their local paper, mourn because it is not as big and full of news as the city dailies." By the end of the decade, however, the *Jamaica Plain News*'s weekly coverage of the local scene had expanded to include a front page on subjects of general interest, another page devoted to editorials and local political activity, and numerous stories and regular columns crammed with notices of local events in the district's subsections of Jamaica Plain, Boylston Station and Hyde Square, Egleston Square, and Forest Hills.[122]

During the late nineteenth and early twentieth centuries, urban life allowed neighborhood residents to construct an almost infinitely varied number of personal orbits of public activity. Affiliations with the diverse groups of urban society determined the trajectory of many of these orbits. The lists of group affiliations routinely included in biographies, memorials, tributes, and obituaries attest to the importance of associational life.[123]

Of course, there were those who did not or could not participate fully in neighborhood social life. Some were too busy. Patrick Ward ran a local teaming and contracting company (which he passed on to his son) and lived for almost fifty years on South Street. When he died in 1906, the local newspaper reported somewhat wistfully that he "belonged to no organizations, being immersed in his home and business."[124]

Family or other competing demands caused many church, club, and lodge members to drop out of or become less active in their voluntary associations.[125] A significant number of local residents spent only part of their life in the neighborhood. Some, like Emily Greene Balch, spent only their youth in Jamaica Plain; others were adults who came, participated for a while, and then moved on.

Yet it was a rare inhabitant of Jamaica Plain who did not at some point participate actively in neighborhood society. The diverse and numerous opportunities for personal interactions offered by the neighborhood's branch offices and local chapters engaged virtually everyone who lived in the district. Churchgoers, schoolchildren, fraternalists, clubmen and women, and charitable workers all had ties to the neighborhood. (Even

Patrick Ward belonged to the parish of St. Thomas Aquinas Church.)

The routes traveled by individuals varied greatly. Some were confined to the neighborhood. For example, working-class residents might work at a local factory, patronize a local saloon, belong to a local church, marry and die in Jamaica Plain. At the other extreme, Isabel Weld Perkins, heiress to the William F. Weld fortune, and her husband Larz Anderson, a diplomat, lived out their lives in global networks, touching down occasionally at Weld, their lavish country estate on the Jamaica Plain–Brookline border.[126]

The social orbits of most neighborhood residents probably fell somewhere in between, mapped out within the metropolitan area. Members of local clubs traveled outside the neighborhood to compete in various activities, such as whist, baseball, and German chorales. Some residents, such as John M. Minton, a Grand Knight in the Boston Knights of Columbus, rose from the local ranks to prominence in a central organization. Other residents had affiliations in more than one locale. John McKim, a longtime member of St. John's Church and the Masonic Eliot Lodge in Jamaica Plain, for example, also belonged to Charlestown organizations. Indeed, the modern city dwellers who lived in Jamaica Plain were hardly secluded from the world outside. They knew that workplaces, entertainments, vacation spots, and friends and relatives could be found in the lands beyond the neighborhood borders.[127]

Connections to such larger networks fostered neighborhood identity and a loyalty of place. They defined the home district in relation to other parts of the urban system and produced a sense of a shared life in a particular locale. Despite the fact that no official document or charter had ever validated its corporate existence, Jamaica Plain became, as twentieth-century residents affectionately referred to the neighborhood, the old hometown.[128]

Inevitably, strong feelings of local attachment to Jamaica Plain were not confined to economic and social life. They spilled into the realm of politics and government, where local residents struggled to advance the cause of their neighborhood. There Jamaica Plainers were forced to defend the interests of their community against those of other districts similarly held together by the web of neighborhood society.

6

Improvement and the
Politics of Place

As sure as the sun rises every morning, as the city grows
in size it needs improvements.

—*"For a Better Boston,"*
Walter A. Webster, 1908

Now, first of all we need a man
  With concentrated gall
Who'll go with us at any time
  To visit City Hall.
The Mayor must tremble when he sees
  Him enter at the door
And jump to grant him all he asks
  And sometimes give him more.

Now, such a man we'll surely make
  The chairman of the ward.
We'll vote for him through thick and thin,
  And send him to the "Board" [of Aldermen].

—*"Wanted: A Ward Committee,"*
F. A. Wood, October 4, 1900

During the late nineteenth and early
twentieth centuries the processes of urban growth that sustained the
neighborhood economy and society also shaped the perception of a local
political interest. The problems of urban growth raised issues of impor-

167

tance to the neighborhood as a whole and thus defined the terms under which local residents fought for their community. Across the United States, urban neighborhood residents who were linked together spatially, economically, and socially expressed a sense of local attachments in the political realm. Citizens demonstrated a commitment to their home district by debating, petitioning, rallying, and lobbying the government about issues affecting the welfare of their neighborhood.

In the process, neighborhood residents helped bring about a radical transformation in municipal governmental policies. In the early nineteenth century, city officials generally limited the amount of municipal spending and the scope of governmental activity. Following traditions that dated from the colonial period, they relied upon wealthy taxpayers and private companies to provide improvements and services to the community. Volunteer fire brigades, sponsored police forces, and private water companies exemplified the style of urban administration characterized by individual subscriptions and corporate charters. Large landholders, who paid the greatest share of property taxes, usually opposed government expenditures if the measures seemed expensive and of little advantage to themselves. As a result, city government budgets tended to be parsimonious, and urban services disproportionately benefited the wealthy.[1]

In the late nineteenth century, city officials reversed tracks and began spending freely to build America's cities. Organized in neighborhood improvement and other associations, neighborhood residents became a powerful force that overcame the opposition of wealthy property holders committed to limiting the role of government. Strongly progrowth, local citizens demanded large-scale improvements, schools, streets, sewers, utilities, and convenient and inexpensive means of transportation and communication. The local basis of city government ensured that neighborhood residents found cooperative officials to provide services and sponsor local projects.

As neighborhoods competed and negotiated with one another to obtain local improvements, they recast urban government along activist and egalitarian lines. Many city dwellers began to perceive urban services and facilities as a necessity for the general populace, not a luxury for the wealthy. They began to assume that city governments would provide police and fire forces, sewer systems, and street-paving to all sections of the city. At city hall, the problem became how to mollify the growth-hungry neighborhoods when resources were limited or claims of one district conflicted with those of another. In the outlying suburbs, progrowth citizens agitated for annexation of their communities as a way of obtaining services from large municipal governments.

Historians have noted the activities of neighborhood residents and their lobby groups, the local improvement associations, in numerous cities including New York and Houston.[2] Some have criticized the neighborhood efforts for an "irresponsible parochialism" that led to unplanned and inefficient management of city resources. Oriented toward the downtown, however, scholars have rarely examined the political impact of the neighborhoods at the local level. As in other areas of urban life, the history of the Jamaica Plain neighborhood encapsulates many of the themes that were central to the politics of growth in the neighborhoods of Boston and other American cities. It demonstrates how issues of growth galvanized neighborhood residents to overturn the traditional philosophy of municipal government.

In Jamaica Plain, well-off property holders had sought to escape paying the costs of growth by separating the Town of West Roxbury from the booming City of Roxbury. After succeeding in establishing the new town in 1851, they convinced the town government to adopt the traditional urban policies of slow growth, low taxes, and minimal services. Increasing population and demand for government services, however, strained the capacities of town government and exacerbated sectional jealousies within the town. A broad-based coalition of well-to-do businessmen, middle-class entrepreneurs, and workers united to champion growth-related measures in Jamaica Plain. In 1874 the coalition overcame fiscally conservative taxpayers and town officials and achieved the annexation of the Town of West Roxbury to the City of Boston.

Once they had become citizens of Boston, progrowth Jamaica Plainers, like their counterparts in urban neighborhoods across the country, worked to obtain a wide range of local services and other enhancements of neighborhood life. During the following decades, the government of the City of Boston responded to local supporters of "improvement" by spending millions of dollars on Jamaica Plain and other Boston neighborhoods. By the twentieth century, outlying districts that had once opposed the growth of Jamaica Plain now competed vigorously with the neighborhood for goods and services. This shift became apparent in 1903 during the heated dispute over the construction of an elevated train down one of Jamaica Plain's most important thoroughfares, Washington Street. The fight over the elevated forced neighborhood residents to oppose improvement and foreshadowed the period of the later twentieth century, when the expression of neighborhood interest would become sporadic and defensive.

In the nineteenth century, well-to-do Americans who wished to live on estates in romantic suburbs often supported the incorporation of their communities as autonomous jurisdictions. Whether outside Chicago or Boston, anti-improvement suburbanites felt that small independent towns were more likely than larger jurisdictions to limit government spending, keep property taxes low, and preserve the exclusive tone of their communities.[3] Thus, during the first half of the nineteenth century, wealthy Jamaica Plain estate owners spearheaded several campaigns to separate their district from the Town of Roxbury. Content with the slow growth of their own estate district, these large property holders resented paying taxes for the infrastructure and services that went to "Roxbury proper."[4]

In 1838 a Jamaica Plain committee analyzed the town's accounts to argue that the outlying sections were paying unfairly for the urban growth of lower Roxbury. The wealthy Jamaica Plainers asserted that the town government expended sums for "paving streets, lighting streets, building reservoirs, and supporting a town watch, though their services are confined to first parish exclusively."[5] Not only did most of the beneficiaries of poor relief live in lower Roxbury, complained the committee, but the labor that the poor provided to the town in the form of road-building went solely to the central part of town. It could not be otherwise, since the anti-growth leaders of Jamaica Plain saw no need for a new road in their section.[6]

During the 1840s, prosperous Jamaica Plain residents sent forth new petitions for separation. Leaders in Roxbury opposed to the separation movement responded to the secessionist effort by proposing to change the form of Roxbury's government. This change entailed a shift from a town form characterized by the town meeting, the celebrated example of traditional New England democracy, to a city structure made up of a mayor and a legislature whose members represented the city's different wards. In 1846 the General Court of Massachusetts acceded to the majority's request for a city charter, but the secession movement continued to gather strength in upper Roxbury.[7]

The Jamaica Plain separatists persuaded Arthur W. Austin, a wealthy Boston lawyer, to lead the movement. Austin convinced the Jamaica Plainers that success depended upon accomplishing two goals. The first was to achieve support throughout all of southwestern Roxbury, especially in the West Roxbury district, where opposition to secession had stymied the movement. This goal became attainable because as the number and size of expenditures on lower Roxbury increased, the large property holders in West Roxbury came around to the same jealous perspective held by those in Jamaica Plain. Second, the secessionists had to make the principle of local self-government, not tax grievances, their primary issue. Following Austin's advice, the secessionists submitted a petition to the state legislature under the name of Samuel D. Bradford, a Boston merchant who lived in West Roxbury, in favor of setting off the southern wards of Roxbury as a "separate agricultural town."[8]

Austin and Rufus Choate, a well-known lawyer and legislator, argued the separatist cause in hearings before the Joint Legislative Committee on Towns. In a forceful presentation before the joint committee, Choate emphasized the difference between the two parts of town, one urban, the other agricultural. While admitting that Jamaica Plain had estates and that a number of residents commuted by railroad to Boston, Choate insisted that upper Roxbury was a single agricultural district whose market was Boston. He dismissed the mechanics and artisans of the area as being like those found "in every farming town in Massachusetts." Having established a great divergence of interest between the sections and the overwhelming political dominance of the lower part of town, Choate stressed the need for separate governments.[9]

Although Choate and Austin persuaded the General Court to approve the secession of West Roxbury, their arguments masked the resentments of residents of Jamaica Plain and upper Roxbury about paying taxes ear-marked for improvements and services in lower Roxbury. Secessionists were not against growth altogether. They complained that they were unable to sell their lands under the official jurisdiction of a city. But they desired a controlled and exclusive kind of suburban growth. They wanted to sell to wealthy individuals like themselves who could afford to keep up and improve large properties but did not wish to pay high taxes.[10]

The citizens of the new Town of West Roxbury adopted a town form of government. An informal and personal type of administration, town government worked best when public business was limited. Although in theory town government embodied the will of the entire community, in practice elected officials and appointed department heads ran the government. Most important of these was the five-member Board of Selectmen, which decided a wide range of issues. Citizens who wished to make a request of town government usually petitioned the Board of Selectmen (or other government body). Because of the disorganized nature of town meeting discussions, the selectmen tried to keep divisive issues out of the town meeting. Its actual functions were to elect town officers, appropriate town expenditures, and on occasion decide certain matters of policy.

At first, under the leadership of Arthur W. Austin, the Town of West Roxbury followed a slow-growth policy that was consistent with the secessionist arguments. Austin's role in establishing the Town of West Roxbury earned him an honored place in local government, and although he was a

Democrat, for eight years he was elected over Know-Nothing and Republican candidates to the Board of Selectmen. As chairman of the Board of Selectmen, which included wealthy estate owners and Yankee farmers, Austin attempted to keep tax rates low. According to Austin, the town's relatively low tax rate made it attractive to large property holders, and he therefore adopted a gradual scheme of improvements attuned to suburban ideals. West Roxbury, he declared in 1854, possesses "regions that must be forever rural."[11]

Austin also was able to suppress or smooth over disputes related to neighborhood localism. Soon after the town was established, for example, a controversy over the location of a town hall, known as the Town House, broke out. The people of the southwestern area proposed the area of Taft's Tavern (later Roslindale) for the seat of town government, but residents of the more populous Jamaica Plain opposed the plan. In the afterglow of the successful campaign for independence, and with promises of future considerations, Austin was able to defeat the proposal of a new town hall outside Jamaica Plain without too much rancor.[12]

Town government reflected the rudimentary stage of urban administration that did little except where it benefited the wealthy. The provision of street improvements, annually among the largest items of appropriation in the town budget, demonstrated the geographic and class biases of town government. The lion's share of street construction appropriations regularly went to the town's most populous section, Jamaica Plain. Within Jamaica Plain, expenditures were directed not only to heavily trafficked thoroughfares such as Centre Street but also to roads such as Greenough Avenue and Chestnut Avenue, where tax-paying property holders lived. Thus, it was little problem for large Jamaica Plain property holders, such as Moses Williams and Stephen Minot Weld, to have their streets accepted by the selectmen, after which the town would pave the roads (generally with gravel) and later add sidewalks and gutters.

As the town population grew in the late 1860s, the amount of road work increased noticeably. In 1866 the selectmen hired a road commissioner to oversee street construction. Support for street improvements broadened as townspeople discovered that providing local working-class families with employment in road-building and related tasks both improved the town roads and cut down the number of applications for poor relief. By the early 1870s local laborers provided the bulk of votes for town appropriations for street improvements in Jamaica Plain.[13]

Nonetheless, the town's infrastructure remained relatively rudimentary. The town had no sewer system, but relied upon street gutters for surface drainage. An ongoing problem was the Stony Brook, which flooded periodically and was polluted by industrial and residential waste. Austin, who perceived the problem of the Stony Brook as an aesthetic issue, did little about it. In the late 1860s a group of townspeople prodded the town to tackle the problem of diverting and containing the waters. During the early 1870s the town surveyed lands, paid damages to abutters, and attempted to deepen the channel of the brook, but the effort was slow, expensive, and marred by poor workmanship. For water the townspeople relied primarily upon wells, but a combination of the increasing number of wells and a drought in the 1860s lowered the water table and made town residents, especially the newcomers to Jamaica Plain, increasingly insecure about their future water supply.[14]

Nor were town services very elaborate. The government offered little in the way of waste disposal. Garbage collection depended upon the sale of offal for feed to livestock, primarily hogs. The town paid its official collector of offal, a farmer named Artemas Winchester, a small salary and all the offal he could gather. Despite Winchester's official position, numerous freelance collectors, many of whom lived in the poor and congested districts, collected offal for sale or feed for their own hogs. This lowered the cost of the service, but the local board of health found the existence of "piggeries" among the crowded human quarters to be unhealthy.[15]

Similarly, the volunteer fire department operated inefficiently, and its members had been known to drink in the engine houses. Nonetheless, little attention was paid to the problem until 1867, when a disastrous fire destroyed the Perkins mansion, Pinebank, at Jamaica Pond. In the hope of making the system more efficient, the town acquired a new steam engine and got rid of the system by which it relied upon bystanders at a fire to run equipment.[16]

The town police were also ineffective. The most spectacular murder of the time, the mysterious killing in 1866 of two children on the Bussey estate, went unsolved without so much as a clue. The chief problem was the lack of manpower. Before 1871 the entire constabulary consisted of only seven policemen. As late as 1872 only ten men guarded the seventy miles of town roads, with the six night watchmen responsible for over twelve miles of territory each.[17]

Along with street improvements, the town's greatest expenditures were on schools, whose purpose, according to the school committee, was "to instruct and elevate the masses." The town's public grammar schools had a reputation for mediocrity, so that despite the pleadings of local school officials, those who could afford to usually sent their children to private schools. As with the local police force, some of the problems of town schools were due to understaffing. In the 1860s, for example, it was not unusual for one teacher to instruct fifty students in a classroom. Such large classes not surprisingly led to discipline problems, which were met by stern physical punishment, a controversial policy that failed to endear the schools to either students or their parents.[18]

In the context of an overwhelmingly Protestant school system and an increasing number of Catholic students, the discipline of Catholic children by Protestant teachers raised issues of culture and class. In October 1858, in retaliation for her severe punishment of their son, Mr. and Mrs. Joseph Byron assaulted a Central School teacher, Rebecca Drake, who did not return to her classroom for a full year after the beating. Byron, an established Jamaica Plain currier of Irish descent, claimed that Drake's behavior was only the latest in a series of unprovoked chastisements for which there was no hope of appeal. The superintendent and the school committee backed the teacher, and in 1860 the school committee, claiming full power in relation to school expenditures, attempted to allocate funds to pay Drake for the time she was absent from her duties. The selectmen, apparently more sensitive to the general perception of the schools as overly harsh, disagreed over the substantive issue whether Drake was at fault and successfully disputed the legal right of the school committee to make appropriations. In another incident in 1873 two men, John M. Galvin and Thomas Magennis, the pastor of the St. Thomas Church, who represented Catholic interests on the school committee, resigned in protest when the committee reversed its stand and rehired a recently dismissed primary-school teacher.[19]

Despite these problems, the undersupply of alternative schools and the growth of the school-age population boosted the demand for accommodations in the public schools. Given the sense of mission associated with the common school, the town had little choice but to appropriate larger and larger sums for new schoolhouses and teachers' and masters' salaries. Unlike the early grade schools, the town high school, which for a time had benefited from the Eliot School bequest, had an excellent reputation that argued for its appropriations. In addition, by the 1870s school reformers and improvers had expanded the scope of the school system to include evening schools, sewing schools, and drawing and music classes and in 1872 proposed that the schools offer industrial training to ensure that all students would be equipped to earn a livelihood.[20]

Beginning in the late 1860s the growth of the town and the widening scope of government business led to the construction of new institutional buildings. The great number of additional citizens made town meetings uncomfortably overcrowded. Furthermore, the town lacked a fixed seat of government where the increasingly busy treasurer and a growing number of paid town officers could work. The Board of Overseers of the Poor, for example, desired a permanent room where a case officer could accept applications of poor relief. Responding to these pressures, in 1868 the town built a new town hall (Curtis Hall) adjacent to the Greenough mansion. In order to accommodate the growing number of public-school students, in 1867–68 the school committee spent more than forty-six thousand dollars to build a new public high school on Sumner Hill. During the early 1870s, the increase in police business led Alexander McDonald, the chief of police, with the assistance of Robert M. Morse, the prominent attorney, to campaign for a new building to house the local court, the police station, and the lockup. In 1873, on the eve of the town's annexation, the handsome Gothic police station was constructed on Seaverns Street in the bustling Green Street subdistrict.[21]

Although the new buildings and government enterprises represented accomplishments, the flaws of town government complicated responses to urban growth. The strong influence of property holders in town management meant that wealth and property played a disproportionate role in town decisions. In 1861, for example, the wealthy estate and store owners on Centre Street were able to persuade the selectmen to veto the petition of the West Roxbury Railroad Company for a double track along the neighborhood's main road. Two years later the selectmen approved a railroad's request to run their tracks along Keyes Street, despite the objections of the residents of this working-class Irish Catholic street, who feared for the safety of their children.[22]

The personal, almost informal style of town leadership represented by the Board of Selectmen led to official arrangements that smacked of the kind of conflict of interest that later Boston reformers would have considered scandalous. In 1856 the town hired Arthur W. Austin, while he was serving as selectman, to represent the legal interests of West Roxbury in a number of cases concerning the town's rights, privileges, and finances. For one such case, concerning the Boston Water Power Company, Austin earned a tidy two thousand dollars. Nelson Curtis, a wealthy masonry contractor who kept on good terms with the selectmen, won several large contracts, sometimes without bids, to build water reservoirs, the new Town House, the Town House fence, and the Civil War Soldiers Monument. In choosing a design for the new town hall, the Town House Committee chose the entry of a local resident over the plans submitted by three out-of-town architects. The disgruntled architects filed a lawsuit against the town on the grounds that the decision process had been rigged.[23]

Far from being neutral instruments of the town meeting, town selectmen jealously guarded their prerogatives. Even after the town hired a road commissioner, for example, one selectman insisted upon keeping control of the street appropriations in his district. In 1872 a reform group won a majority on the Board of Selectmen, replacing a clique that had ruled for several years. The new men undertook to improve on the old inefficient methods and professionalize town government. They instituted new methods of bookkeeping, reorganized the fire department, and, in an attempt to keep pace with "the rapid settlement of many districts," pushed through the purchase of sixty new street lamps. Because they felt that road construction was too expensive to be left to selectmen, who were chosen "on mere political grounds," they hired a civil engineer to oversee all street improvements.[24]

The following year the old selectmen were reelected, demonstrating the vulnerability of the town meeting to organized political activity. Bent on recovering their powers, the selectmen threw out virtually all of the reforms adopted the previous year. They also pursued a policy of vigorous retrenchment, stripping the town's fire and police departments of employees.[25]

Neighborhood jealousies often fueled such disputes. In 1866 the choice of a site for the town hall stirred up the issue of neighborhood prerogatives. Throwing out an 1852 town meeting decision to place the hall near the town's territorial center (outside Jamaica Plain), the members of the Town House Committee decided that the location of the population center (in Jamaica Plain) would guide their choice. The majority favored an expensive site located at the intersection of the town's busiest thoroughfares, Centre and Green streets. The minority preferred two other locations near the railroad station as more convenient for residents from the distant sections of town. Foreseeing conflict, the committee hoped that those whose preferences did not prevail would "yield with good grace." The dispute over the site was made moot by a donation from David S. Greenough of land near his home on South Street near Centre Street. In order to allay persistent suspicions about the decision and Greenough's motives, however, the selectmen felt impelled to publish Greenough's deed giving the land to the town.[26]

History repeated itself as Jamaica Plain now played the role of the growing, budget-hungry section that lower Roxbury had played before the

Local Attachments

town secession. As the most populous and therefore politically dominant neighborhood in the Town of West Roxbury, Jamaica Plain received all of the town's major public institutions, including the new town hall (1868), the high school (1868), and the police station and court building (1873). As Jamaica Plain had once done, the West Roxbury and Roslindale sections now took an arbitrary oppositional stance against Jamaica Plain. "This line of action," commented one observer, "leads voters from other villages, particularly West Roxbury, the one farthest remote, to act on much the same principle as did Jefferson Scattering Batkins, the gentleman from Cranberry Centre (Cape Cod), who was instructed by his constituents to oppose Boston members first, last, and always, whatever the issue."[27]

Such contrariness led to strained attempts to ensure more equal expenditures among neighborhoods despite the disparities in population. The town purchased a steam engine for the sparsely settled district because Jamaica Plain, the "thickly settled suburb to a large city," required one. West Roxbury residents opposed needed street straightening and widening because they would benefit only Jamaica Plain.[28]

During the late nineteenth century, the desire of suburban communities to obtain services and develop local real estate propelled a wave of jurisdictional consolidation across the United States. From Philadelphia to Los Angeles, large urban centers annexed their suburban neighbors. As part of this trend, in 1868 the City of Roxbury joined the City of Boston. While the Town of West Roxbury wrestled with growth-related issues, increasing numbers of Roxbury citizens had come to believe that the best method to promote local development and services was to unite with Boston. After years of agitation, in 1867 a vote registered the first solid majority in favor of annexation. By then, even Roxbury city officials believed that only Boston could solve their problems of water supply and complete the landfill and drainage of the Back Bay and South Bay lands along the border between Boston and Roxbury.[29]

In Jamaica Plain, the example of Roxbury and local issues of growth fed support for the annexation of the Town of West Roxbury to the City of Boston. By 1871 West Roxbury residents had begun to complain that the increase in population had rendered the town meeting too cumbersome. At first residents proposed forming a city government, but by early 1872 the sentiment in favor of annexation was strong enough for a vote to be called on the matter. Although annexation was defeated by a margin of 623 to 409, its proponents continued to raise the subject.[30]

Like annexationists elsewhere, Jamaica Plain proponents of consolidation hoped to obtain expensive infrastructure and inexpensive transportation. First on the list was a secure and ample water supply to replace the old system of private wells. Water had been a concern since the drought of the 1860s, and in 1871 the town formed a committee to investigate the best way of supplying the town. Second, they were interested in petitioning for a good sewer system, but this depended upon the solution of the vexing Stony Brook problem. Because of the grade of Jamaica Plain, any underground system of sewers would need to connect with the Stony Brook channel. Furthermore, many working-class families were moving to the inexpensive but damp Stony Brook lowlands, creating a health hazard. Patrick Meehan, the wealthy contractor and real estate investor, believed that the Irish in the Brookside area had no money to move and would die if the area was not drained. Finally, annexationists hoped to acquire better and cheaper horse railroad transportation to and from locales in town.[31]

In Jamaica Plain commuter businessmen, entrepreneurs, real estate investors, and members of the working class came together in favor of growth and annexation. The leaders included downtown executives such as John C. Pratt and Charles Brewer and local businessmen such as Robert Seaver, owner of Seaver's grocery, Charles Dolan, an Egleston Square currier, and Joseph Rowe, a South Street contractor. Others, including Patrick Meehan, J. Alba Davis, another wealthy real estate investor, and Alden Bartlett, a neighborhood real estate agent, were directly involved in real estate development. Many of the leaders of the movement had an interest in promoting the local growth through their involvement with the Jamaica Plain Gas Light Company and the Jamaica Plain Savings Bank.[32]

The neighborhood's working people also strongly supported annexation and turned out in large numbers for annexation rallies. At one such public meeting in the fall of 1873, Republicans Brown and Pratt introduced Patrick A. Collins, the young Irish-born leader of the Democratic party of Boston, to great musical fanfare and applause from the crowd. In his speech Collins articulated the progrowth philosophy. "Only those who are never in favor of improvement are opposed to annexation," he declared, and he promised that Boston would provide the Town of West Roxbury with pure water, more street lamps, public music, and access to the "renowned" public library. Collins anticipated that Boston would take the untaxed Bussey estate away from "that land-grabbing educational institution, Harvard College," and turn it into a park. He also pledged the construction of a complete drainage and sewer system, which would improve public health, especially among the families living in the Brookside area. He specifically addressed the desire of the Jamaica Plain Irish for employment when he predicted that the City of Boston would provide more "steady and permanent work" than that dispensed by "the picayune Town Government which now prevails."[33]

The leading opponents of annexation were large property holders, town officials, and longtime residents, who enjoyed the autonomy of town government. They included veterans of the West Roxbury secession campaign such as Arthur W. Austin and Moses Williams, as well as wealthy Pondside residents such as Joseph W. Balch, the president of the Boylston Insurance Company, and Edward N. Perkins, the owner of the Pinebank estate. Opponents such as Nelson Curtis, the contractor, Charles G. Mackintosh, a West Roxbury factory owner, and Samuel Jackson, a leather manufacturer, had received government contracts or had served as town officers. Well-to-do men such as Benjamin F. Wing, a doctor, and Calvin Young, a merchant, were longtime residents of Jamaica Plain.[34]

The opponents of annexation tended to minimize the problems of growth and to have confidence in the town's ability to handle them. Those who had been connected with town government asserted that the water and drainage difficulties were exaggerated. They felt that the worst sewerage and drainage problems related to the Stony Brook were located in Roxbury, now within Boston's jurisdiction, and that the city would take care of them by itself. Yet even the anti-annexationists admitted that the land Austin had once described as a place of rural beauty had outgrown town government and should adopt a city form of administration as soon as possible.[35]

Above all, the opponents of annexation worried about property taxes, the bane of large property holders. In a widely circulated anti-annexation pamphlet, an anonymous author charged that under Boston rule local residents would be forced to discharge Boston's enormous debts and pay for great expenditures in other sections of the city. On the other hand, locals would have to pay for their own local improvements, because it would be "mortifying and degrading for us to go hat in hand to the City Hall, and beg for expenditures in our territory." Unfamiliar with local conditions, Boston's assessors would overvalue local real estate and force property holders to sell their lands in order to pay taxes.[36]

In an effort to appeal to their fellow citizens, the anti-annexationists attempted to raise a grab bag of fears about Boston's government, most of which would later prove groundless. The city, they claimed, would ruin real estate investments by imposing jails and smallpox hospitals upon local neighborhoods and would never furnish gas and water to the sparsely settled outer districts. Local workers would lose because Boston's surplus labor force would be sent forth to construct local roads and buildings. And city government would not work, because local councilmen could not be trusted to defend local interests.[37]

During 1872 and 1873 town residents debated the annexation issue heavily. Exasperation with squabbles about town government and the apparent inability of the selectmen and the town meeting to overcome private political and neighborhood jealousies led increasing numbers of people to support union with Boston. The anti-annexationists did not help their cause with blatant appeals to wealthy property holders and statements casting doubts upon the competence of workers to decide the issue. As the time for a new election drew near, immigrants began registering to vote in noticeable numbers. On October 7, 1873, the day of the vote, an unprecedented number of townspeople cast their ballots. Annexation of the Town of West Roxbury to Boston carried by a vote of 720 to 613, and the following year Jamaica Plain, along with the other sections of West Roxbury, officially became part of the City of Boston. The legacies of the town-government phase of Jamaica Plain's history would be intense neighborhood localism, strong support for growth-related measures, and an aversion to property taxes.[38]

Once the local demand for progrowth measures and urban services had propelled it into the City of Boston, Jamaica Plain was no longer the politically dominant district of a small town. Now it was one of many neighborhoods striving to protect local interests within the framework of a great city. Despite the fears of some neighborhood residents, the City of Boston accommodated the demands of Jamaica Plain and other neighborhoods for improvements and services. Representing the emerging philosophy of activist urban administration, the process boosted government expenditures, debt, and taxation rates to what many considered shocking levels.

One reason for the city's willingness to gratify the demands of its districts was a governmental structure that responded to neighborhood pressures. In late-nineteenth-century American cities, the heart of government consisted of representative legislative bodies, the school committee, and the city council. These legislative bodies comprised representatives of local districts and functioned as the terminus of neighborhood requests. The school committee and the city council engaged in detailed administrative management (what would later be considered executive functions), but by the early twentieth century they had lost many of their original powers.[39]

The Boston School Committee governed the city's schools, which, as they had in the Town of West Roxbury, represented one of the two highest appropriation categories in the city's annual budgets. From 1875 until 1905 the school committee had twenty-four members (reduced from seventy-four members!) elected from different school districts. Working through standing committees and as individuals, district representatives exercised minute management of school operations. In 1881, for example, the committee authorized the use of Charles and Mary Lamb's *Tales of Shakespeare* as a textbook at West Roxbury High School and passed an order offered by Jamaica Plain's representative allowing a single session with two thirty-minute recesses at Jamaica Plain's Hillside Grammar School.[40]

Like its school committee, Boston's city council was dedicated to district representation and wide-ranging management. Although over time many responsibilities were removed from the council, increased governmental activity due to the growth of the city produced progressively thicker volumes of the council's annual proceedings. Until the 1909 charter, the city council comprised a lower house, the Common Council, whose members were elected by ward (three members from most wards), and an upper house, the Board of Aldermen, whose members were elected either at large or by district made up of two or three wards. A committee structure first established in early city charters controlled the business of the council. By the 1890s the council had developed a bewildering number of standing committees. As late as 1907 there were forty-two standing committees, although only twenty-eight of these were thought to be active.[41]

Originally the council oversaw a wide range of municipal activities. It functioned as the original body for city appropriations and thus paid for the gamut of city governmental duties, including the police, fire, water, streets, and parks departments, the public library, and the city's charitable and correctional institutions. The council served as a licensing board as well, dispensing licenses and permits to a wide variety of urban entrepreneurs, including concert hall and theater owners, professional baseball teams, saloon keepers, bootblacks, and newsboys. Until 1895, when a building commissioner took charge, the council issued building permits for factories, stores, and houses, as well as for additions such as bay windows and even signs and flags projecting from buildings. (On one occasion, the siting of a stable became the subject of heated debate.) It passed ordinances regulating streets, vehicles, passenger elevators, laundries, and steam engines. In its supervisory role, the council became involved in trivial matters, such as when it forbade the tying of horses to lampposts or when, in a measure offered by a Jamaica Plain alderman in 1897, it prohibited women attending a place of amusement from wearing a hat that obstructed another's view.[42]

As in other cities in the late nineteenth century, the tremendous growth of Boston and the scope of its administration inspired a series of governmental reorganizations. Over time the city council's power was diluted as its powers were redistributed and as new government agencies were created outside of its control. The fragmentation of urban jurisdictions complicated the job of influencing decisions concerning the home neighborhood. One competitor for the council's power, for example, was the mayor, whose responsibility was to set policy, veto bad laws, and, especially after the 1885 charter went into effect, to appoint many department heads.

The governor, the state legislature, and various regulatory commissions of the Commonwealth of Massachusetts also increasingly shared responsibility for Boston's administration. In theory, town and city governments were creatures of the state that allowed the state to encroach upon city jurisdiction. In 1875, for example, the state legislature established a debt limit for the City of Boston. This required the city council to request permission from the legislature to acquire loans beyond the debt limit. After 1885 the governor of Massachusetts appointed the chief of police and the heads of the metropolitan district commissions, which were established from 1889 to 1895 to manage the sewer, parks, and water systems that encompassed several municipalities, including Boston.

Some transportation and communications issues were decided by state regulatory commissions, such as the Board of Railroad Commissioners, which oversaw the state-chartered transportation companies. In 1907, for example, two Jamaica Plain citizens, Joseph J. Leonard and Robert W. Morville, spearheaded a drive for better telephone service and lower telephone rates, especially for outer-city suburban districts, through the Citizen's Telephone Reform Association. They brought their demand for a five-cent toll between outer-city districts and in-town exchanges to the state highway commission, and the following year rates were lowered. The increasing role of the state in municipal matters elevated the local importance of the state representatives and senators, who over time came to resemble city councilors in their relationship to the neighborhood.[43]

In general, however, as long as the city council represented relatively small geographic units, it retained its importance to neighborhood residents. Even after it was stripped of licensing and other functions, it was usually the place of first resort for those with requests, demands, and complaints for city government. City councilors thus served as governmental ombudsmen for neighborhood residents. The state legislature approved improvement loans beyond the city's debt limit, for example, but precise disbursement of appropriations was left to city government, in particular the council, which struggled to reconcile the requirements of the different neighborhoods.[44]

Neighborhood residents often called on councilors with complaints or requests concerning commissions, boards, and departments, even though their chiefs were appointed by the mayor or the governor. The members of the city council referred requests to appropriate city executive agencies, looked into the affairs of the departments, and if necessary admonished the agencies to modify their behavior. During the late nineteenth century, for example, the councilors represented their constituents' interests by sending to the park commissioners, a body that served independently of the council, a steady stream of requests and criticisms. The criticisms reached a crescendo in the mammoth city council investigation of the Parks Department in 1900.

Sometimes Jamaica Plain requests for better services took a circuitous route, from the neighborhood to the city council to the mayor, who then sent them on to the appropriate department head. In 1906, for example, Jamaica Plainers complained that the streets in their wards were not being watered often enough. The Board of Aldermen formally requested the mayor to ask the superintendent of the Street Watering Department to give better service to the Jamaica Plain area. The mayor passed the request along and then forwarded the superintendent's reply that the department was giving the wards "as good and frequent watering as is consistent with the means at our disposal."[45]

With its government built on the foundations of neighborhood representation, the City of Boston proved responsive to the wishes of Jamaica Plain and other neighborhoods. When it assumed control of city services in annexed areas, for example, the City of Boston did not dramatically change old patterns. In the area of waste disposal, Artemas Winchester, the offal collector for the Town of West Roxbury, continued to dispose of Jamaica Plain's offal until 1885. The following year the City of Boston hired Thomas Minton, a neighborhood contractor who also maintained the city stables in Jamaica Plain, to take over local offal collection.[46]

The city also maintained continuity in Boston's far-flung municipal service departments. When the City of Boston united with the Town of West Roxbury, the city took over the new police station in Jamaica Plain and converted the local constabulary into a new division, District 13, whose boundaries coincided with those of the former town. The former West Roxbury police chief, Alexander McDonald, became district captain, and two former town policemen were promoted to lieutenant and sergeant. Several policemen who served long terms in the local force provided the neighborhood with a sense of continuity. Of the veterans of the West Roxbury force, Chief McDonald, who had begun his service in Jamaica Plain in 1860, served as district commander until his retirement in 1885. Benjamin May, descendant of the ancient May family of Jamaica Plain, retired in 1908 after thirty-nine years as a police officer. Another Jamaica Plain resident and former town policeman, Andrew J. Chase, served a total of forty years in the local district before retiring in 1905.[47]

While the city maintained continuity in personnel, it provided more service than the former town government had supplied. The most noticeable change that annexation brought to the local police force, for example, was badly needed reinforcements. On the eve of annexation in 1874, the West Roxbury force comprised fifteen men (boosted from eleven the previous year); two years later twenty-seven police officers manned Boston's District 13. In 1890 an eighteen-box telegraph system was installed throughout the district, and citizen calls to the local police force, by then made up of forty-four officers, proliferated. By 1908 the local police force had grown to one hundred, and substations had been added in Roslindale and West Roxbury.[48]

The system of neighborhood policing that evolved during the late nineteenth century reflects the local basis of municipal governance. As in other American cities, both the Town of West Roxbury and the City of Boston required the neighborhood patrolman to circulate along a fixed route, inspecting the safety of street and sidewalk conditions and watching for suspicious people or circumstances. A District 13 patrolman's work journal for the year 1895 strongly suggests that the beat patrolman rarely discovered anything of note while on patrol. Instead, the complaints of citizens who lived on his route dictated most of his work assignments. Most frequently local residents called upon the policeman to protect their private property, although in the absence of a witness to a theft, he could usually do little. Much like nineteenth-century Philadelphians who resorted to their aldermen to resolve disputes, local residents used the patrolman to mediate and adjudicate the sometimes violent conflicts that arose between them and their neighbors.[49]

The patrolman also spent a great deal of time enforcing the city's licensing and permit regulations, but in this, too, he worked for the convenience of neighborhood residents. Citizens of Boston, like those in other cities, had to register their dogs and obtain permission for any building projects or street digging. To help them meet these requirements, the local patrolman provided blank permit forms to applicants at their home or place of business, carried the completed forms and license fee to the division station, and delivered the approved permits to the applicants. He also notified permit holders when their permits or licenses were about to expire.

It helped such locally oriented police to solve major crimes if the criminals were also local. About midnight on a Saturday night in 1907, for example, police officer McKinnon was badly beaten when he interrupted an attempted armed robbery in the working-class South Street section. McKinnon was familiar with neighborhood toughs from his beat patrol in the area and recognized two of his assailants, John J. and Edward B. Dolan, by name. Another member of the gang, whom McKinnon shot in the arm, was identified and later arrested when the robber went to the neighborhood health clinic, Faulkner Hospital, for treatment. In contrast, thieves who were strangers confounded the local constabulary. During the 1908 robbery of a Boylston Street saloon, armed "yeggmen" set off a bloody shooting spree that left three dead and eleven wounded. Hundreds of Boston policemen chased the suspects to Forest Hills Cemetery, where they killed one fugitive in a final shootout. After a few days and a series of mistaken arrests, the dead bandit was identified as a Lettish anarchist who had recently moved to Roxbury and had a sister in Jamaica Plain. Strangers to the neighborhood, the other bandits were able to escape.[50]

The transition brought by annexation was not as smooth in the area of firefighting, but in this area, too, the city demonstrated a respect for local traditions and a responsiveness to local needs. As with the police, after annexation the City of Boston absorbed both the physical plant and the personnel that had previously belonged to the Town of West Roxbury and expanded resources in both areas. Soon thereafter rising expectations about salaries, especially among the call members of the force, resulted in resignations and turnover in the local fire companies. In response to petitions from the permanent and call members of the Jamaica Plain force, in 1878 the Boston fire commissioners raised the firemen's salaries to the level of those in other outer-city neighborhoods. The membership of the force, predominantly lower-middle-class residents of Yankee, Irish, and German backgrounds, soon stabilized.[51]

Like the residents of neighborhoods in Boston and other American cities, the people of Jamaica Plain showered the city government with demands for services and in the process overthrew conservative municipal spending policies. Residents of Jamaica Plain, like other Bostonians, petitioned their government, usually by way of the city council, as individuals for specific measures or in groups for more general measures. Their demands varied widely but for the most part were related to local growth and improvements. In 1882 the president of the city council explained the recent rise in tax rates by pointing to the clamor from below. The city council held the ultimate responsibility for raising taxes, he admitted, but "the members of our City Government are in a large degree guided by the taxpayers themselves who so readily endorse petitions demanding great public improvements."[52]

Schools were a necessary service for the growing neighborhood population, many of whose members could not afford private schools. Jamaica Plain residents complained as their schools became overcrowded and looked to their representatives to expand local facilities. As early as 1876, for example, Jamaica Plain councilmen Levi Wilcutt and Benjamin H. Ticknor, responding to Egleston Square constituents, encouraged the Common Council to purchase a school construction site that was larger and more expensive than another under consideration. After Samuel Billings Capen, a member of the Boston School Committee from 1888 to 1893, succeeded in obtaining funds to replace the old Hillside girls' school, grateful local residents proposed naming the new building after him. In 1897 the principal of West Roxbury High School, George C. Mann, organized a drive to obtain appropriations for an addition to the old and increasingly crowded building. First Mann publicized the cause by distributing an information flyer with an endorsement from former school committee member Samuel Capen. Next he circulated a petition to send to the Boston School Committee. The effort was fabulously successful: instead of an addition, in 1900 he obtained an imposing new building for the school.[53]

Locals did their best to defend the neighborhood's schools, in particular the high school, which had a good academic reputation. In an incident in 1881 that foreshadowed later battles over centralizing the city government, a special committee of the school committee led by Henry P. Bowditch, a wealthy physician from Jamaica Plain, proposed abolishing four "district" high schools, in East Boston, Brighton, Roxbury, and West Roxbury. The purpose was to centralize the system in order to ensure full enrollments at the newly rebuilt Boston English and Latin schools in town. The affected sections immediately sent loud remonstrances to oppose the closing of their high schools. Soon after the proposal was made, a protest meeting was held near the West Roxbury High School, at the First Methodist Episcopal Church of Jamaica Plain. Within days George A. O. Ernst, a young attorney from Jamaica Plain and soon to be a Republican state representative, and 171 of his fellow citizens sent a petition of opposition, which Bowditch, as his district's representative, presented to the subcommittee. This outpouring of local protest had a pronounced effect on the subcommittee, which quickly abandoned its own plan and made the choice of high school optional, rather than by district. "When a nearly unanimous expression of opinion comes from the people that they desire the retention of a school," commented the majority, "it certainly is becoming the board to pay some heed to that opinion. We are but the representatives of the people."[54]

If the school committee was forced to listen to neighborhood requests, the city council was even more beholden to the neighborhood will. When in 1874 a number of local "gentlemen" personally requested that the council rename the former West Roxbury Town Hall after its builder, Nelson Curtis, the council happily obliged. In 1882, at the high-water mark of local prohibitionism, Protestant ministers and citizens sent petitions and letters of approval to the police commissioners by way of the council to obtain a crackdown on unlicensed liquor establishments.[55]

Jamaica Plain residents also sent a steady stream of individual requests for permits and licenses. The year after annexation came the petitions of Frank W. Reynolds to remove three trees from Orchard Street and of Timothy Gunning to move two horses into a stable on Lamartine Street; these and other such requests continued as long as the council had jurisdiction over such matters. Most such petitions were granted, although they could be refused where there was a health hazard, such as in Harry Jones's attempt in 1892 to store naptha on Jamaica Street, or where there was community opposition, such as in the case of Adam Mock's request in 1903 to project a bay window over the sidewalk in Hyde Square.[56]

The neighborhood demands for improvements that had taken up the time and expenditures of town government were also among the most expensive claims on the city government. Infrastructure appropriations far exceeded any other category of municipal expenditure. Within that general category the building and maintenance of streets ranked highest in annual budgets, occasionally even outpacing the allocations for schools. Street appropriations included straightening and otherwise integrating new roads into the existing street plan, as well as providing improvements such as paving, sewers, and sidewalks.[57]

The city government's acceptance of streets as public ways made them eligible for further city improvements. The elected (and therefore politically responsive) Board of Street Commissioners often accepted property owners' plans for new streets or extensions of old ones without much revision or thought to future patterns of development. The resulting patchwork meant that as streets were extended to meet crossroads, the city was frequently forced to adjust street lines and grades and, if necessary, to purchase and destroy obstructing buildings. The city council's committee on the laying out of streets complicated matters further by frequently suggesting to the street commissioners that they extend, align, or widen certain streets.

By the mid-1880s some Bostonians began to call for overall control of street planning. In 1890 Jamaica Plain's alderman proposed that the city extend Call Street, a project that involved the expensive acquisition and demolition of obstructing buildings. Another alderman attacked this typical attempt at constituent service as an example of the high cost of unplanned streets. He predicted that the extension would create a cul-de-sac that would have to be extended again, causing still more expensive demolitions. The following year the council created a Board of Survey to systematically assess Boston's street system in order to guide future planning, but intense political pressure from neighborhoods such as Jamaica Plain enabled the Board of Street Commissioners to absorb the Board of Survey in 1895.[58]

From the year of annexation onward, orders for street and sewer improvements in every section of Jamaica Plain flowed from the city council to the appropriate city departments. Driving the push for improvements were local property holders' petitions. In 1882, to name two typical examples, Hyde Square resident Alexander Mair petitioned for a sewer on Creighton Street and Thomas Caugley and others in the South Street district asked that the city grade, set edgestones, and pave gutters on the extension of Jamaica Street. The annual reports of the superintendent of streets record the impressive efforts of the streets department in excavating, draining, paving, laying and relaying gutters, edgestones, and sidewalks, and upgrading street pavements from macadam surfacing to granite blocks or asphalt. Of course not all local requests were granted. In 1875, with the economic slump of the 1870s depreciating real estate assessments, an order to widen South Street, an expensive proposition, was postponed, and it was still a neighborhood issue over twenty years later. At the same time that it postponed the South Street project, however, the Board of Aldermen did appropriate improvement funds for streets in the Pondside, Brookside, Egleston Square, Heath Street, and Forest Hills sections of Jamaica Plain.[59]

The Jamaica Plain area did relatively well in the competition among

Boston's neighborhoods for city street appropriations. Every year but one during the five-year period 1887–92, the West Roxbury district, which encompassed most of Jamaica Plain, received the third highest amount of appropriations, behind the central city and Roxbury. In order to impose some order on the annual competition among the representatives of the neighborhoods, during the late 1890s the city council adopted a policy of allocating twenty-five thousand dollars to each ward. Since wards differed in size and needs, this approach was not necessarily equitable or rational. Furthermore, the system did not prevent some wards from obtaining extra funds. In 1896, for example, Jamaica Plain's two wards received different shares. Ward 22 was allotted twenty-five thousand dollars, while Ward 23, which included West Roxbury, received twice that amount. In 1900 the council awarded both wards ten thousand dollars in excess of the basic allocation for streets.[60]

Jamaica Plain may have benefited from the appointment of neighborhood residents Michael Meehan and J. Edwin Jones as Boston superintendents of streets, but even without the political tug of city councilmen and resident commissioners, the streets department promoted neighborhood development. In 1889 and 1890, for example, two successive street superintendents requested higher annual appropriations so that the department could upgrade street paving around Boston to the more durable granite blocks or asphalt. During the early 1890s the deputy superintendent of the sewer division pointed to the necessity of more sewers in the South Street area in Jamaica Plain. Construction of a larger outlet sewer in nearby Washington Street, he suggested in 1893, would "open up much valuable land for building purposes, near the village of Jamaica Plain." The Street Laying-Out Department, which was under the supervision of the elected street commissioners, was just as enthusiastic about Jamaica Plain's development. In 1896 it proposed a series of new streets between Heath Street, Hyde Square, and the Jamaicaway that would offer "some of the best building sites within the city limits."[61]

During the late nineteenth and early twentieth centuries, Jamaica Plain residents also succeeded in obtaining funds from the city council for large-scale improvements related to growth. As with the requests for street work, the pressure for large-scale improvements began as soon as Jamaica Plain became part of Boston. As we have seen, Jamaica Plain obtained the lion's share of the city's new public open spaces. This achievement was all the more remarkable since, as Charles Huse pointed out, the establishment of a system of public parks during the 1870s and early 1880s "was one of the few extraordinary undertakings of this period of retrenchment."[62]

Local representatives were strong supporters of the park system, although one Jamaica Plain councilor, Henry F. Coe, displayed unbecoming neighborhood selfishness when he declared that on the grounds of its expense, he could not support the entire park system. Coe insisted that of all the parks, only the Jamaica Pond park was absolutely necessary. If long-term loans could be acquired, he supported a park along the Charles River, an inexpensive park at the South Bay, and Franklin Park, which, he added, was "the only Park recommended by the Commissioners, in the true sense of the word."[63]

In the 1860s and early 1870s, concern about the local water supply had led many Jamaica Plain residents to look to the City of Boston for relief. During 1874, the first year of Boston rule, Jamaica Plain's alderman, Francis A. Peters, the Boston banker who invested in Jamaica Plain real estate and the Haffenreffer brewery, urged the city council to buy the iron pipes needed to supply Jamaica Plain with water. The aldermen supported extension of the water system in principle, but a few were always reluctant to increase city expenditures. Peters argued strenuously for immediate appropriations, pointing out that the water supply had been one of the major reasons that West Roxbury residents had supported annexation. He went on to relate his own personal difficulties in living without a water supply. The aldermen were convinced, and in 1874 and 1875 they allocated funds for pipes and other materials to extend the city's water system to Jamaica Plain. By the mid-1880s, as street atlases reveal, a network of water pipes had been installed under the streets of Jamaica Plain.[64]

From 1874 to 1908, the Stony Brook Improvement, a difficult, large-scale project inherited from the governments of Roxbury and West Roxbury, cost the City of Boston the staggering sum of $2.5 million. The chief problem was that the construction of houses and factories filled in the water-storage areas along the Stony Brook and increased the hazard of floods. Poor drainage in the Brookside area created wet and unhealthy living conditions and prevented real estate development. In 1874, the year of West Roxbury's annexation to Boston, the state legislature empowered the city to improve the channel of the Stony Brook by deepening and widening it and in places altering its course. Work began in 1878 but was slowed until 1880 by a lawsuit filed by the Boston Belting Company, a Roxbury concern that claimed a mill right to the stream.

With Jamaica Plain residents and real estate investors affected by the outcome, the neighborhood's representatives naturally took great interest in the channeling project. In 1882, for example, Alfred S. Brown, Jamaica Plain's Republican councilor, helped push through a $50,000 appropriation for the Stony Brook and a few months later apologetically came back for an additional $20,000. By the following summer, work on the conduit had reached Green Street, where water was seeping under the shallow walls built by the Town of West Roxbury and threatening the channel and the foundations of nearby houses. In 1884 the improvements were completed at a cost of $370,000, but in February 1886 an early thaw combined with a rainstorm to create the worst flood in the history of the brook. The flood damage instigated a new round of lawsuits, and Boston's mayor, Hugh O'Brien, blamed "a most faulty piece of engineering" for wasting the earlier construction efforts.[65]

In 1886 a Commission on the Prevention of Floods in the Valley of Stony Brook recommended a completely new, covered channel, to be extended from Jamaica Plain through West Roxbury as the area was built up. The first part of the work was completed in 1889 at the breathtaking cost of $1.1 million dollars. In 1895 the culvert was extended by the New York, New Haven, and Hartford Railroad, successors to the Boston and Providence Railroad, to protect its track, which followed the river valley. The next year the city obtained from the state legislature the right to borrow outside the debt limit for funding to extend the rebuilt channel from Roxbury to a point beyond Boylston Street in Jamaica Plain. In 1897 Boston's street commissioners reported on the progress of the channel construction and recommended its further extension through Jamaica Plain to Neponset Avenue. The channel extension was intended not only to provide surface drainage for the street network but also to create a low-level outlet for the evolving sewage system in the South Street and Forest Hills subdistricts. In the lowlands near Washington Street the sewer was only two feet below street level, and a number of built-up streets, such as Williams and Keyes streets, lacked sewers altogether. "If this [channeling] is done," wrote the commissioners, "there will be opened up and developed a large territory that can be used for suburban residential purposes."[66]

A neighborhood lobbying campaign propelled the Stony Brook Improvement. In 1899 Roswell S. Barrows, the neighborhood newspaper publisher and real estate agent, wrote an act to allow the City of Boston to fund the extension of the Stony Brook channel to the Jamaica Plain railroad station. In February John Bleiler, a former city councilor and now a state representative from Jamaica Plain, introduced the Stony Brook Improvement bill in the legislature. In March the state legislature held hearings, at which a number of Jamaica Plain elected officials and residents testified. Barrows testified that the lack of good sewers between South and Washington streets was causing water to overflow into people's houses, creating a danger to public health and destroying private property. In May 1899 the bill was passed and signed into law, and by July construction had begun.[67]

Improvement, the powerful idea which had fueled growth and annexation sentiment in the Town of West Roxbury and had induced the City of Boston to spend hundreds of thousands of dollars, acted within the neighborhood of Jamaica Plain as a force for unity. Although middle-class in outlook, improvement tended not to be sectarian. Instead, it was a neighborhood booster ethos open to all who were interested in growth, respectability, and increased real estate values. Occasionally development threatened neighborhood property holders, such as in the late 1890s, when Pondside residents turned out in force to veto an attempt to extend Huntington Avenue through their fashionable district, but usually improvement was a banner under which all interested Jamaica Plainers could march.[68]

As in cities such as Worcester and, earlier, in the Town of West Roxbury, the supporters of neighborhood improvement represented a coalition of different social and economic classes. Many middle-class and upper-middle-class property holders in Jamaica Plain, of course, were investors in real estate. They were a part of a powerful outer-city prodevelopment coalition that during the 1890s fought off attempts to force subdividers and property holders to pay a greater share of the cost of street, sewer, and other local improvements from which they benefited. Others believed in improvement out of a sense of loyalty to a neighborhood they enjoyed living in and wished to see prosper. Similarly, local middle-class store owners took an interest in the welfare of the environment in which they worked. German and Irish ethnic entrepreneurs profited directly from the machinery of improvement. Because of its improvement projects, the city extracted gravel near Heath Street from Bleiler's Ledge, named after its owner, Frederick Bleiler, John Bleiler's brother, a German-born butcher, and hired local Irish-American construction contractors such as Patrick Ward, Owen Nawn, and Thomas Minton.[69]

Members of the working class and the lower middle class also continued to benefit from and support improvements. Improvements not only bettered living conditions in the less well-off precincts but also provided employment (from contractors or city departments) in an unstable urban economy. Thus during the late nineteenth century workers created political pressure to give government-funded construction jobs to local residents. The creation of Boston's park system inspired numerous proposals to restrict hiring to residents of City of Boston. In 1892 Frank F. Proctor, a Jamaica Plain city councilor, went further and proposed that the superintendent of streets hire only residents of his own Ward 23 to work on the sewer and street projects in that district. In his 1899 run for the state legislature, Roswell S. Barrows attempted to tap the political appeal of improvement to the working class when he claimed that the Stony Brook Improvement bill would keep 250 local workmen employed through the summer and winter. Depressions such as the Panic of 1893 only reinforced support for improvements and public works among workers in Jamaica Plain and elsewhere. Chronic underemployment increased the demands to expand the permanent city work force and provide city workers with union hours and wages.[70]

Support for improvement cut across party as well as class lines. Each fall Republican and Democratic candidates placed advertisements in the local paper stressing their commitment to local issues such as street improvements and cheaper and better transportation. In 1899 both of Jamaica Plain's state representatives, John M. Minton, a Democrat, and John Bleiler, a Republican, claimed credit for an amendment to an appropriation bill that had increased street-paving funds for Roxbury and West Roxbury from $200,000 to $350,000. A. S. Parker Weeks, a Ward 23 politician who switched allegiances from the Democratic to the Republican party, in 1905 campaigned successfully for the office of state representative on a local-improvement platform. "I'd like to know when there hasn't been a lot of strictly local issues in this ward," Weeks explained, "ever since we came in, away back in '74."[71]

Commitment to improvement was more important than even party loyalty, as a local Republican state representative, Frank W. Estey, discovered to his regret. In 1898 Estey introduced a bill to reform the procedure for laying out streets by eliminating the lobbying of street commissioners and by assessing abutters for the full value of the street improvements. Although Jamaica Plain's wards were considered to be Republican, the law was so unpopular among local property owners and real estate interests that in the following election many Republicans defected from Estey (who had tried to reverse his stand), and he lost his seat. In 1909 a Republican city councilor from Ward 23, George W. Smith, declared that he would run against his fellow Republican state representative, Earl Davidson, because Davidson had attacked Boston's Democratic street commissioners, James Gallivan and Salem D. Charles. In support of Smith, the Republican *Jamaica Plain News* explained that residents and improvement organizations of Ward 23 every week asked favors of the street commissioners and that, because of the attacks, they feared that they would not get many street improvements in the future.[72]

Like neighborhood improvement associations in Buffalo, Baltimore, and other cities, Jamaica Plain organizations set the agenda for neighborhood improvements on a nonpartisan basis. They lobbied for typical outercity measures: better services, street improvements, public works, neighborhood facilities such as municipal buildings and playgrounds, and less expensive and more efficient transportation and communication. For many years the Eliot Club, the neighborhood's prestigious literary club, took responsibility for matters of general neighborhood interest. Its permanent Outlook Committee reported to the full membership on questions of the day pertinent to the neighborhood and lobbied the appropriate government officials to take actions the club favored.[73]

Made up of businessmen, ministers, professionals, and other interested citizens, the Jamaica Plain Citizens' Association became the leading neighborhood improvement society at the turn of the century. It established committees on streets, public grounds, transportation, schoolhouses and education, police and public order, and other neighborhood concerns. In 1899, for example, the association launched an effort to lobby the legislature to repeal the laws governing assessments on new sewers and streets, to bring about the widening of South Street, and to obtain improvements in the local rapid-transit system.[74]

The importance of neighborhood issues sometimes prompted other prominent clubs to become involved in lobbying for local improvement. The Jamaica Club, a middle-class society devoted to entertainments, periodically became active. In 1903, for instance, the president of the Jamaica Club wrote a letter deploring unfinished streets, poor sidewalks, and the "miserable state of the cars" and suggested that a committee of the Jamaica Club combine with the Jamaica Plain Citizens' Association. The Tuesday Club, Jamaica Plain's elite women's literary club, now and then took public action on behalf of neighborhood issues such as clean streets. In 1903, after parties thrown by groups renting the city's municipal building, Curtis Hall, had resulted in destructive behavior by "hoodlums of both sexes, drunk and sober," the Jamaica Plain Citizens' Association coordinated a strategy with the Eliot, Jamaica, and Tuesday clubs to lobby the mayor to remedy the situation.[75]

Local politicians of both parties respected the importance of the clubs and came to them for instructions concerning the neighborhood agenda. In 1899 John Minton, the Democratic state representative, sent a letter to the Jamaica Plain Businessmen's Association asking which amendment the group wanted on a bill before the state legislature. On a November evening in 1900 the Republican alderman from Jamaica Plain, E. Peabody Gerry, reported to the members of the Jamaica Plain Businessmen's Association that if the street-loan bill passed, he would fight to see that the Jamaica Plain wards each got ten thousand dollars in addition to the twenty-five-thousand-dollar improvement allotments. He then asked that the association inform him of the best ways to spend the allotments in the neighborhood. Gerry asserted that he would heartily support new playgrounds, a bathhouse at Jamaica Pond, the extension of Huntington Avenue, and a nickel fare for local rapid transit, but only if the association agreed to the measures. More money for local improvements would be needed, however, and Gerry expressed the hope that neighborhood groups such as the association would help him obtain it. Soon it became a tradition for political candidates to present themselves to the association in the fall.[76]

Policies of growth and improvement, however, could also provoke opposition or differences of opinion within the neighborhood. The expense of growth encouraged resentment of the taxes that supported it. Immediately after the annexations of 1874, representatives of Jamaica Plain and other annexed districts opposed further incorporations by the City of Boston. A desire to avoid paying higher taxes to fund the extension of improvements in new areas fueled this sentiment. In the following decades anti-tax sentiments led to a suspicious attitude about city government, especially among better-off Republicans, who feared Democratic and Irish extravagances.[77]

At times local groups squabbled over who should benefit from improvement projects, although appeals to neighborhood unity usually quieted the controversies. In 1903 members of the Jamaica Plain Citizens' Association heatedly debated the location of a new playground to be built with a recent city appropriation of thirty thousand dollars. The difference of opinion separated residents of different wards until members were reminded that "they should unite in promoting the welfare of Jamaica Plain as a whole."[78]

In 1912 a city council appropriation for another new playground divided residents along religious and geographic lines. For several years the upper-middle-class Protestant reformers who ran the Neighborhood House Association had tried to get the city to take over the management of their supervised young children's playground on Carolina Street. Neighborhood Catholics and residents of Forest Hills, which lacked recreational fields, endorsed a different site, near Forest Hills, to be used for young men's baseball and football. By this time in the neighborhood's history, efforts to be inclusive in the decision-making process mitigated potentially divisive disagreements. Thus, even though the Protestant viewpoint prevailed in the playground dispute, the discussion was not embittered.[79]

Although a sense of neighborhood solidarity muted conflicts over improvements, rivalries between neighborhoods, which had provoked disputes under the old town government, did not abate. As Jamaica Plain began to reach a mature stage of urban development and its potential territory for real estate development began to diminish, the neighborhood became vulnerable to competition from "younger" neighborhoods undergoing more rapid development. Ironically, the southwestern districts that once had resented paying for urban improvements in Jamaica Plain now vigorously competed for improvement moneys and transportation services. In the early twentieth century the neighboring sections of Roslindale and West Roxbury collected large appropriations for local municipal halls, street construction, and other improvements.

The change in inter-neighborhood dynamics set the stage for one of the most bitter local controversies since annexation, the dispute over the construction of an elevated railroad through Jamaica Plain. This classic outer-city improvement battle over transportation services represented a conflict between progrowth residents, store owners, and property holders in Jamaica Plain and their counterparts in the neighboring districts to the southwest. It symbolized the maturing of the neighborhood of Jamaica Plain and the difficulty of opposing the improvement argument.

The fight began innocuously enough with an effort to redress a long-standing outer-city grievance, high street railroad fares. Beginning in the 1880s citizens of the neighborhoods and suburban towns southwest of Jamaica Plain tried to alter the anomalous situation in which the streetcar companies operating inside and adjacent to their borders demanded separate fares, without transfers. They complained that trips to and from such neighborhoods as Mount Hope, Roslindale, and West Roxbury and adjacent towns were more expensive than trips between points closer to the center city.

In the early 1900s a boisterous movement for a five-cent fare with transfers gathered momentum and galvanized several outer-city and suburban citizens' groups. Roslindale, the fast-growing neighborhood beyond Forest Hills, contributed several of the movement's most prominent leaders. They included John A. Coulthurst, whose leadership on the issue propelled him to the state legislature, Jean P. Nickerson, an enterprising real estate agent and subdivider, and Edward J. Bromberg, an attorney and city councilor. Despite some setbacks, the movement continued to roil the political waters; it climaxed with a petition to the Board of Aldermen signed by eleven thousand citizens demanding the revocation of the Old Colony Railroad Company's right to lay tracks on their streets. The board did not accede to this radical request, but sensing the political strength of the movement, in 1903 the parties involved agreed upon a nickel fare and a transfer system for the outer districts.[80]

Within days after this triumphant victory, the leaders of the five-cent-fare movement began pushing for quicker in-town transport. By extending the elevated tracks from the Dudley Street station in Roxbury to Forest Hills in southwestern Jamaica Plain (already the site of a railroad station and a street railway terminus), they hoped to give all neighborhoods and towns south of Forest Hills access to rapid transit to Boston. The Boston Elevated Railway Company cheerfully supported the idea and petitioned the government for permission to construct an elevated railroad through Jamaica Plain over Washington Street, a major commercial thoroughfare.[81]

Jamaica Plain residents were aghast over the prospect of the shadow and din of the elevated train. Joseph J. Leonard, a Jamaica Plain lawyer, attended a mass meeting organized by Nickerson and others to promote the elevated and protested vehemently. Building elevated tracks through Jamaica Plain, Leonard charged, would be like sticking a knife into the community. Neighborhood property owners and residents began calling their own mass meetings to derail the elevated project. They complained that the noise, darkness, and danger of the elevated would blight the Washington Street area. Conceding the ever-present need for "improvement" in the form of better transportation, some residents proposed other options, such as a subway to Forest Hills, lower railroad fares, or the widening of Washington Street into a boulevard with separate streetcar lanes. Supporters of the elevated, however, responded that the alternatives were not practical. The railroad would not carry enough passengers to replace the elevated, and a subway would be too expensive to build. The streetcars could not hope to move passengers as quickly as the elevated, and many Jamaica Plainers themselves were cool to the idea of a boulevard whose expense would be charged to abutting property owners.[82]

The dispute between the two groups of local improvers and boosters quickly turned personal and antagonistic. During the summer of 1903 a letter war broke out in the *Jamaica Plain News*. William H. Nitz, a Jamaica Plain bookkeeper and former city councilman, attacked the participants of a Roslindale rally for the elevated as selfish. They would ruin Washington Street and Jamaica Plain to benefit their own district. Another writer asked, "Why should Dedham, Readville, and other suburban towns get the advantage over us and rob us of our property for which we pay heavy taxes?" Nickerson of Roslindale responded that since the district south of

Forest Hills constituted one-quarter of the area of Boston, the elevated would bring the greatest good for the greatest number. It was the opponents of the elevated, he charged, who were selfish, because they were attempting to deprive an area of its natural growth.[83]

As the controversy raged in the following months, the attacks grew more vitriolic. People on both sides accused those on the opposite side of being led by real estate speculators looking solely for personal profit. Jamaica Plainers denounced the organizers of the five-cent-fare movement as "howlers" and political agitators bent on stirring up trouble and despoiling them of their property. A West Roxbury resident indignantly defended the Roslindale leaders. If Nickerson, Coulthurst, Bromberg, and the others who had delivered the nickel fare were howlers and agitators, he proclaimed, they acted in the tradition of the great heroes of the American Revolution. Upon hearing the comparison of the suburban boosters to John Adams, John Hancock, Benjamin Franklin, and Thomas Paine, a Jamaica Plain man wondered sarcastically "whether we do not over-reverence the revolutionary patriots who knew not Roslindale."[84]

As a matter of neighborhood improvement, the elevated was a sectional issue, not a partisan one. Among the supporters of the elevated, for example, Coulthurst was a Catholic Democrat and Bromberg was a German-American Republican. Roslindale's Catholic and Protestant pastors, improvement association leaders, and ordinary citizens all endorsed the elevated to get better transportation accommodations for their district. Within Jamaica Plain also, the *Jamaica Plain News* reported, party politics were thrown to the wind. Neighborhood Democrats such as Joseph Leonard and Republicans such as Roswell S. Barrows railed against the structure. In Jamaica Plain the opposition to the elevated included both those who were directly economically interested, such as real estate agents and property owners, and those who were not property owners. Among those in the latter category were Washington Street storekeepers who rented but did not own their shops. Unlike the property owners, the storekeepers complained, they would not be compensated for losses due to the elevated. In addition, many neighborhood residents objected to the noise and dirt it would inflict upon their homes.[85]

In the fall of 1903 the petitions for each side flew, and the battle spread to the political arena. The Jamaica Plain men nominated their own anti-elevated candidate to challenge Edward J. Bromberg, the Ward 23 councilor who was attempting to step up to the Board of Alderman. The effort to demonstrate political muscle behind the stop-the-el movement received severe blows in November, when Bromberg won the Republican nomination with majorities in both Ward 22 and Ward 23, and in December, when he was the only Republican candidate to survive a citywide Democratic landslide.[86]

In December the fight moved to the hearing rooms of the Board of Aldermen, where the railroad committee listened to the lengthy presentations of the disputants. The Jamaica Plain contingent brought numerous property owners and residents, who testified to the injuries that the elevated would bring and attempted to persuade the committee members to recommend a subway in their district. To dramatize their cause, the opponents presented people from Roxbury to affirm the damage that the elevated tracks had done in their neighborhood and a physician who testified that the train would contribute to the constant din that in large cities was "directly responsible for nervous diseases with a clear tendency to cause insanity."[87]

It was nonetheless difficult to counter the logic of improvement, which dictated that urban growth must be facilitated wherever possible. Nor was it easy to justify a subway as an alternative to the elevated. The city's first underground line had only recently been constructed in Boston's bustling downtown, and few would be willing to coerce the elevated company to pay the extraordinary sums for a subway in an area that would not be as heavily trafficked. The railroad committee reported favorably on the petition to build the elevated to Forest Hills Square. Admitting that the elevated railway's presence was undoubtedly "a serious detriment," the aldermen decided that "the interests of the few must be sacrificed for the general good." The extension would benefit the large population south of Forest Hills and "would open up for development a large territory for residential and other purposes which has been neglected to some extent in the past."[88]

In January 1904 the Board of Aldermen approved the extension of the elevated unanimously. The following week the order was signed by the mayor, Patrick A. Collins, the same man who thirty years earlier had helped persuade Jamaica Plainers to unite their town with the City of Boston in order to obtain improvements. Adding insult to injury, the Boston Elevated Railway Company then presented a plan to build the tracks without a local station for Jamaica Plain. Neighborhood residents were shocked to discover that they would be deprived of the only local advantage the elevated might bring. In the following years, while they campaigned for an elevated station at Green Street, Jamaica Plain residents continued to complain bitterly about the efforts of their neighbors to the south to improve their transportation systems at the expense of Jamaica Plain.[89]

The neighborhood progrowth coalitions of the late nineteenth-century city are sometimes criticized for inducing wasteful and inefficient municipal expenditures. Compared with the ideal of expert city planning, the localist approach, whether in the form of parochial rivalry between districts or the blank-check legislative logrolling of improvements across the city, seems a haphazard way to distribute resources. Yet the explosive growth of economic activity and population in American cities during the late nineteenth century required immediate responses. Even as government centralized its operations and improved its means of communications, officials downtown had difficulty keeping fully informed about the sprawling city. Who was better suited to set the agenda for municipal improvements than those familiar with local conditions? Without losing sight of the shortcomings of the system, it may be appropriate to consider the "unheralded triumph" of the locally based urban governments in the late nineteenth century. In a time of rapid urban expansion, city administrations built a complex and technologically advanced infrastructure on an egalitarian basis that allowed for competent residential development.[90]

It might also be said that neighborhood improvement represented a form of privatism, the selfish craving for the economic gains to be had from development. Clearly, self-interest played a large role in motivating the supporters of growth in the neighborhood, but it would be a mistake to dismiss the effort to improve the neighborhood as simple greed. Too many of the supporters of the local improvement association had no direct economic stake in the outcome. Much of the time and effort expended on the betterment of the home district also expressed allegiances to place. The improvement doctrine represented the political analogue to the sense of local attachments.

The fight over transportation in Jamaica Plain, however, demonstrated the limits of improvement as a force for unity within the neighborhood. It signified that as the opportunities for growth within the neighborhood waned, the progrowth policy of improvement would be replaced by increasingly defensive attitudes about the neighborhood and its fate. In the future, when Jamaica Plain experienced population and economic decline, attempts to preserve the status quo of the neighborhood's subdistricts would increasingly define the local sense of place.

During the 1890s and early 1900s the prospect of population and economic decline in the neighborhood still seemed distant or nonexistent. A frontal assault launched upon the localist governmental and political systems that had nurtured neighborhood growth posed a more immediate threat to the district. Surprisingly, Jamaica Plain residents were among those leading the charge.

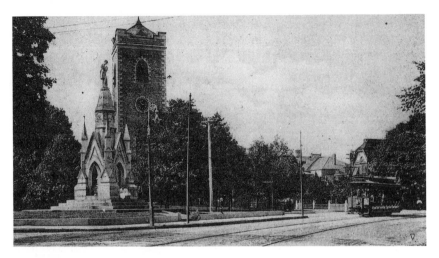

Centre Street and the Soldiers Monument, ca. 1906

The tower of the First Church of Jamaica Plain looms over the historic center of Jamaica Plain at the intersection of South and Centre streets.

Postcard published by the Metropolitan News Company, courtesy of Suzanne Presley.

Elm Street and the Central Congregational Church, ca. 1910

The Central Congregational Church, on tree-lined Elm Street, was one of the focal points of the Sumner Hill area.

Photograph by Thomson and Thomson, courtesy of the Society for the Preservation of New England Antiquities.

The St. John's Episcopal Church, c. 1885

To the rear at the left of this prestigious Sumner Hill church is the mansion of William H. Sumner, a Massachusetts adjutant general and real estate developer.

Photograph by Baldwin Coolidge, courtesy of the Society for the Preservation of New England Antiquities.

The Church of the Blessed Sacrament, ca. 1920

This mammoth Italianate Roman Catholic church dominated the Hyde Square area.

Glass plate negative by Leon Abdalian, courtesy of the Boston Public Library Print Department.

The Bowditch School and Green Street, ca. 1910

Built in 1891, the Bowditch School, for girls, replaced a much older school. Note the awnings of the Green Street stores in the rear.

Photograph by Thomson and Thomson, courtesy of the Society for the Preservation of New England Antiquities.

West Roxbury High School, ca. 1906

When the old Jamaica Plain high school on Sumner Hill (left) did not seem large enough, neighborhood residents petitioned for the extensive addition (front, right, and rear) that was built in 1900 and helped decorate the interior. The *Jamaica Plain News* regularly reported on the school's athletic teams, literary newspaper, alumni dances, and other activities.

Postcard published by the E. W. Clark Company, courtesy of Suzanne Presley.

Class Graduation Portrait, Jefferson Grammar School, ca. 1911

The Jefferson School was built in 1904 on Heath Street to accommodate the large numbers of school-age children who lived in northern Jamaica Plain. Of Irish, German, and other ethnic backgrounds, the local schoolchildren reflected the rich mixture of humanity in the area. According to Elsa Oberle (front row, third from left), the portrait shows the graduating class in costume for the class play, a version of the ancient Greek myth *Pandora's Box*.

Photograph courtesy of Marilyn Oberle.

District 13 Police Station and Municipal Court, ca. 1912

In the era of decentralized official administration, the headquarters of the local constabulary and court functioned as a center of neighborhood life. It served as a place not only to report crimes but also to obtain building and other permits and to adjudicate disputes between neighbors.

Postcard courtesy of Suzanne Presley.

The Jamaica Plain Post Office, 1920

The federal government workplace also served as a neighborhood social unit.

Glass plate negative by Leon Abdalian, courtesy of the Boston Public Library Print Department.

The Jamaica Plain Footlight Club Performance of *A Fool for Luck,* 1894

The productions of the amateur theater club were held at Eliot Hall, across the street from the First Church in Pondside, but the club attracted audiences from the neighborhood and from the City of Boston.

Photograph courtesy of the Houghton Library Theater Collection, Harvard University.

DIENSTAG, DEN 21. FEBRUAR 1905,

Subscriptions - Fancy - Dress - Party

Boylston Schul-Verein

Herbei, herbei, Ihr Narren all'	Wo Fiedel hell und Flöte klingt,
Ihr Närrinnen, Ihr schönen!	Wo Narr und Närrin lustig singt,
Wo hell bei unserm Maskenball	Die Sache wird ganz zweifellos
Die lust'gen Weisen tönen.	Famos !

Tickets für Mitglieder, Herr und Dame, 50 Cents. Nichtmitglieder $1.00. Extra-Dame 25 Cents.

B. E. A. DEMUTH, PRINTER, 683 WASHINGTON STREET.

Advertisement for the Boylston Schul Verein's Fancy Dress Party, 1905
The German social clubs held many annual events, such as this costume ball and a
Schlact-Fest, or sausage festival.
Courtesy of Karl Ludwig.

Dance at Linden Hall, ca. 1900

This formal ball, held at a historic Pondside mansion, was part of a three-day fair organized by the St. John's Episcopal Church.

Engraving by H. Learned, courtesy of the Boston Athenaeum.

The Jamaica Club House, ca. 1906

The elegant clubhouse, built about 1889 at Green and Elm streets, near the Jamaica Plain railroad station, was the locale for card games, billiards, and rehearsals for the annual minstrel show.

Postcard published by Reichner Brothers, courtesy of the Society for the Preservation of New England Antiquities.

Three Baseball Players, ca. 1919

The imagery of baseball clubs and lace curtains symbolizes a way of life in the outer city.

Glass plate negative by Leon Abdalian, courtesy of the Boston Public Library Print Department.

Trench for the Stony Brook Conduit, Columbus Avenue, 1896

Although it was an expensive project, the Stony Brook Improvement provided jobs for local workers and opened up new land for real estate development.

Photograph from *Annual Report of the Street Department of the City of Boston for the Year 1896* (Boston, 1897).

The Lucretia Crocker School, 1902

The construction of school buildings such as this one in the Heath Street district created both public works employment and facilities for the neighborhood. Note the adjacent tenements and row houses.

Photograph from *Annual Report of the School Committee of the City of Boston for the Year 1902* (Boston, 1902).

Washington Street at School Street, September 1906

As Jamaica Plainers complained bitterly, the construction of the elevated railway cast a shadow over the neighborhood below. Note the billboard advertisement for a local Democratic party candidate; such notices, like political activity in general, were a part of everyday life.

Photograph by the Boston Elevated Railway Company, courtesy of the Society for the Preservation of New England Antiquities.

Setting the Curbstones at Forest Hills
Square, March 1908

Street improvements such as this one boosted Boston's annual municipal expenditures to unprecedented heights.

Photograph by the Boston Elevated Railway Company, courtesy of the Society for the Preservation of New England Antiquities.

P. J. Brady and His Funeral Parlor, 1928

The proprietor, wearing a suit, stands in front of his establishment in Forest Hills. Brady was a local Democratic political leader who ran John Fitzgerald's mayoral campaign in his neighborhood ward.

Photograph by William T. Clark, courtesy of the Society for the Preservation of New England Antiquities.

7

The War against Localism

There will be a Declaration of Independence from all
partisan politics some day in all our cities, and then the
great curse at the present time of the local boss and the
ward politician will disappear.

—*Samuel Billings Capen, 1894*

J ust as municipal governments of
the late nineteenth century were planted in the soil of local representation,
urban political parties were rooted in city neighborhoods. During the late
nineteenth and early twentieth centuries, neighborhood ward and precinct
organizations constituted the units of political parties in the nineteenth-
century American city. These local party organizations belonged to the
social web of neighborhood society. They developed alongside other neighborhood organizations, adopted similar structures and rules of conduct,
and often shared members. Like the branch offices and local chapters, the
ward rooms and political clubs helped to foster local attachments to the
urban neighborhood.

Local political institutions also contributed to the sense of shared community in urban neighborhoods. Paralleling the spread of local voluntary
associations, neighborhood political organizations expanded to encompass
the diversity of urban society. In the late nineteenth century, the lower
middle and upper working classes penetrated neighborhood political party organizations and began regularly to elect their own candidates to city
offices. Although the political sphere expressed the animosities that naturally accompanied the heterogeneous urban population, it also harnessed

divisiveness and encouraged the building of coalitions across ethnic and class lines.

Into this system of urban assimilation stepped political reformers, who launched the great municipal reform crusades of the Progressive era. Heirs to the Mugwumps and civil-service reformers of earlier decades, they also applauded the modern accomplishments of business, science, and the professions. Driven by a fervent sense of moral mission, these city dwellers objected to the consequences of urban growth. They disliked the high cost of government services and scorned the participation in politics of those whom they considered unfit to rule. Thus, the reformers fought to vanquish governmental corruption by putting themselves or other like-minded members of the upper middle class in power.

Like the urban park proponents, urban political reformers were sophisticated thinkers who were guided by universal principles rather than local conditions. In order to design an administrative blueprint based upon fundamental principles of political science, they consulted diligently with experts and reformers across the nation. Pursuing a unified, moral, and efficient municipality based on centralized authority, the reformers declared war on the locally based governmental and political systems. The White City, the World's Columbian Exposition of 1893, entranced the reformers because they felt that it expressed the shining vision of civic and moral unity that they sought.

The outcomes of the struggles to restructure and purify America's cities depended upon prevailing social and political circumstances. In some cities, especially small and medium-sized jurisdictions, businessmen and professionals were able to impose virtual direct rule through the commission and city-manager forms of government. In large cities, where power was dispersed, reformers attempted to reorganize the form of government with strong mayors and at-large elections of councils. In Boston, for example, structural reformers succeeded in undermining the localist foundations of Boston's school committee and municipal government, although, unlike their New York and San Francisco counterparts, they immediately lost control of the newly strengthened office of the mayor. In other cities, such as Detroit and Chicago, reformers came to terms with emergent organized labor and ethnic constituencies and even tolerated local representation. In each city, however, the battles to reform city government recast the political culture for decades to come.

Although it has seldom been studied, political history at the neighborhood level illuminates the processes of urban reform and the impact reform had on neighborhood society. As elsewhere, local politics in Jamaica

Plain did not lack social tensions, but it tended to encourage accommodation of the diverse elements of neighborhood society to one another. A bastion of progressive urban reform in Boston, Jamaica Plain contributed important leaders to the municipal-reform movement and demonstrated the close links between moral, social, and structural types of reformers. As they pressed their case, neighborhood residents who believed in universal formulas of governmental centralization debated and ultimately prevailed against their neighbors who supported a locally based polity.

Unlike the universalist landscape reformers who had bestowed green-space amenities upon Jamaica Plain, universalist municipal reformers bequeathed troubling legacies to the neighborhood. By redrawing the political and governmental map of Boston, reformers made the process of government much more complicated and awkward for Jamaica Plain residents. As became painfully evident in the climactic mayoral race of 1910, reform also released the demons of class and race conflict, now unchecked by the ward-based party organizations. By attacking the framework in which local attachments flourished, moreover, the reformed political system ultimately helped to unravel the sense of a common neighborhood interest.

Historically in American cities, political activity reflected the localist structure of city government. In the eighteenth century, the neighborhood political caucus emerged out of the factional politics of Boston and other port towns to become a regular part of the colonial political process. In the early nineteenth century, factions and deference held sway as men of wealth dominated the political process. In antebellum Philadelphia, New York, and Boston, an array of political parties vied for the loyalties of neighborhood voters by tapping local clubs, militia companies, volunteer firemen's companies, and even street gangs. Responding to increased political competition and the growth of the urban population, enduring citywide political parties led by full-time politicians appeared. In the late nineteenth century, political parties built more formal and elaborate structures based on the neighborhood ward organizations. In Pittsburgh and other cities, as Samuel Hays writes, "the ward became the focus of politics."[1]

In certain urban centers, citywide political organizations and leaders were able to impose a measure of discipline upon the local districts. At various times during the late nineteenth century, city "bosses" emerged at the head of political "machines" in cities such as New York, Cincinnati, and San Francisco. The decentralized structure of politics and government, as well as attacks from political reformers, however, rendered the rule of nineteenth-century city bosses unstable. In some cities, such as Boston and Chicago, the parties were usually unable to restrain the ward organizations.

Thus, Boston city politics, like city government, was "bottom-heavy." The neighborhood wards chose representatives to the parties' central city committees and delegates to the city committees' conventions. This arrangement weakened the regular city party apparatus in two ways. When they were strong, local ward leaders could resist central control. When they were weak or disorganized, ward committees were vulnerable to forces outside the regular party organization. Republicans had to be wary of crusaders who entered politics to advance such causes as prohibition or anti-Catholicism and then threatened to run independent candidates who would compete for party votes. Similarly, the Democratic City Committee was obliged to keep close contact with the local ward committees to prevent successful insurgent challenges from taking them over.[2]

When the Town of West Roxbury was annexed to the City of Boston in 1874, Jamaica Plain's political organizations were integrated into Boston's locally based political structures. Under town government, the local political parties had participated in Norfolk County and Massachusetts caucuses and conventions. Now political-party ward organizations took their part in a hierarchy of Republican and Democratic party organizations in Boston, Suffolk County, and Massachusetts.

Building on a strong Whig legacy from early in the nineteenth century, Jamaica Plain maintained a tradition of voting Republican from the Civil War years. After Democrats won the first two post-annexation elections for seats on the Boston City Council, the numerically superior Republicans commanded the district for most of the next three decades. In 1895 the Republicans were able to increase their representation when the Jamaica Plain district was subdivided into Wards 22 and 23. They achieved their largest votes in the German-American and Protestant middle-class neighborhoods of Egleston Square, Boylston Street, and Cedar Hill and the older upper-middle-class Yankee districts of Pondside, Sumner Hill, Glenvale, and Parkside.

Toward the end of the nineteenth century, local Democrats became more competitive with the Republican party and occasionally captured seats in the city council and the state legislature. Most of Jamaica Plain's Democratic votes came from the concentrations of working- and middle-class Irish and Irish-stock citizens in the industrial and lower-middle-class districts, such as Heath Street, Brookside, and South Street, and the growing middle-class Forest Hills area.

In late-nineteenth-century American cities, local political organizations belonged to the network of voluntary associations that linked neighborhood residents to one another and encouraged attachments of place. From New York to San Francisco, big-city political parties relied on neighborhood political clubs to assemble their constituencies and organize electoral activity.[3] Like voluntary associations, ward organizations derived their internal structure from legislative bodies. Here, too, chairmen presided, and treasurers, secretaries, and subcommittees performed other duties. The rules-of-order manuals used by clubs and societies to run their meetings specifically addressed the problems of managing political ward meetings and party conventions.[4]

Like neighborhood clubs and societies, local political units were especially active in the "season," which in Boston lasted from autumn to spring. The political calendar included a series of neighborhood caucuses or other meetings to select ward officers and delegates to city, county, and state conventions (and every four years, national conventions). Of course, the annual municipal elections, biennial state elections, and the quadrennial presidential election added excitement to the regular political business. The constant round of activities kept political club members busy in local public life.

During the late nineteenth century, political activists in Jamaica Plain, as elsewhere, utilized the club form of organization. In Jamaica Plain's very first city election the Republicans formed a "citizens' club" to marshal the support of Yankee and German-American citizens. During the 1870s and 1880s local Republicans organized themselves in citizens' unions, ward committees, and, during presidential-election years, battalions for the great torchlight processions that marched through the neighborhood. In the late nineteenth century local Democrats came together in the Jefferson Club or the Cleveland Club.[5]

Throughout late-nineteenth-century Boston, Democratic ward bosses used independent political clubs to control the machinery of the ward committee. In Jamaica Plain political insurgents also organized local clubs outside the regular party ward committees. For example, the Democratic John R. Murphy Club of Ward 23 supported Murphy's renegade campaign for mayor of Boston in 1899, and Samuel L. Powers, a Newton attorney, organized a Powers Club in Jamaica Plain's Ward 22 to help him seize the Republican nomination for U.S. congressman in 1900.[6]

In the late nineteenth century, urban political organizations engaged in public activities that encouraged local attachments. From the Civil War era, local party organizations conducted spectacular parades replete with banners, torches, and fireworks that competed with theaters, fraternal organizations, and other urban amusements. Like Fourth of July festivities, these partisan rituals celebrated local community identity as much as they did national identity.[7]

Neighborhood political organizations enhanced the public life of the local community in other ways as well. Political organizations such as New York's Tammany Society had originated as social clubs, and in the late nineteenth century local political organizations in New York, San Francisco, and other cities continued to function as social clubs. Thus, they adopted the same forms of entertainment as other local voluntary associations. Reflecting this shift in Jamaica Plain, the company officers of an 1884 Republican torchlight parade took a logical step when they founded the Jamaica Club, an important neighborhood social club. Other Jamaica Plain political clubs retained their political purpose but held entertainments and dance balls similar to those of neighborhood church societies and fraternal lodges. In October 1899, for example, the John R. Murphy Club held a smoke talk attended by the candidate himself. Declining to speak about political matters until later in the campaign, Murphy instead entertained the club's members with a "very interesting talk on European travel and the customs of the different foreign countries" that he had recently visited.[8]

Given the social dimension of late-nineteenth-century political life, urban politicos not surprisingly became known for their convivial participation in clubs and other organizations that contributed to the sense of neighborhood identity and feelings of local attachments. In turn-of-the-century Cincinnati, for example, neighborhood ward leaders during the time of Boss George B. Cox were "well known bonifaces who liked a good joke or story and belonged to several social and fraternal organizations." The frequent affiliations of neighborhood politicians with neighborhood churches, lodges, and clubs suggests that such memberships were almost a requirement for political activity. On the nineteenth-century urban frontier and in twentieth-century society, research shows, members of voluntary associations usually knew about and participated in politics.[9]

In Jamaica Plain, too, participants in politics also joined local voluntary associations, usually more than one. An upper-middle-class candidate such as Sidney Cushing, a downtown businessman and Republican city councilor from 1888 to 1891, belonged to the Eliot Club, the Jamaica Club, and the Eliot Masonic Lodge. Frank Seiberlich, a neighborhood electrician and Republican politician, belonged to the Eliot Masonic, Quinobequin Odd Fellows, and Jager fraternal lodges, the Boston Turnverein, and the Jamaica Cycle Club. On the Democratic side, Mark Mulvey, a house decorator and painter who was elected to the state legislature in 1895, was a member of the Jamaica Plain chapters of the Catholic Order of Foresters and the Knights of Columbus. Local candidates, especially first-time candidates, pointed out their club and lodge affiliations in newspaper advertisements and fliers. In so doing, they made explicit the notion that participation in the neighborhood's associational life qualified a person to represent the community as a whole.[10]

For reasons of both visibility and sociability, Jamaica Plain politicians played prominent roles in local club entertainments and other public functions that celebrated the life of the neighborhood. The Jamaica Club minstrel show of 1909 starred the Democratic politicians Salem D. Charles and Joseph J. Leonard. In 1905 the Jamaica Plain Citizens' Association staged a mock trial, another popular type of vaudeville theatrical, which provided opportunities for local city officials and political activists to spoof both themselves and prominent Democratic and Republican politicians of the day. Sometimes politicians attended neighborhood functions as honored guests. At a dance thrown by the Jamaica Cycle Club, for example, former and present city councilors were among the invited company. Of course, city councilors, state legislators, and other politicians did not miss the opportunity to participate in the neighborhood's annual Memorial Day commemorations and Fourth of July festivities.[11]

Just as voluntary associations spread across the range of neighborhood society, local political organizations and offices also became more inclusive, encouraging the sense of neighborhood community. Jamaica Plain followed the downward social trend that prevailed in the politics of late-nineteenth-century Boston, New York, Pittsburgh, and other cities. Immediately following annexation, for example, Jamaica Plain sent downtown businessmen such as Alfred S. Brown and Henry F. Coe to the Boston Common Council, but by the 1880s middle-class insurance agents, salesmen, and real estate dealers served as local councilmen. Toward the end of the century, increasing numbers of low-white-collar and blue-collar workers captured the nominations for council seats. From the late 1890s, local Common Council offices went predominantly to skilled workers, small businessmen, clerks, and occasionally even to semiskilled workers. In 1909, the last year that the Common Council sat before it was abolished, the two wards that included Jamaica Plain were represented by a real estate agent, a salesman, a roofer, a butcher, a carpenter, and a fish merchant.[12]

At the same time, the age of local representatives was apparently decreasing. In 1908 Jamaica Plain's former state representative Walter A. Webster criticized the youth of city council members; according to his estimate, the average age of the members was below thirty. Adding credence to his complaint was the case of Frederic Andrew Finigan, an inspector and draftsman for the Boston and Northern Railroad. When he was eighteen years old, Finigan attended the 1892 Democratic convention as a member of the Massachusetts delegation. At age twenty-seven he ran for Eleventh District alderman and lost by six votes, but two years later he managed to win the at-large aldermanic election. Community-club affiliations may have compensated for lack of years: Finigan belonged to the Jamaica Plain Council of the Knights of Columbus, the Star of Jamaica Company of the Veteran Fireman's Association, and the John F. Fitzgerald Club of Ward 23.[13]

Local seats in the Massachusetts House of Representatives also diversified. After annexation, Jamaica Plain voters elected lawyers, businessmen, and owners of Boston stores and manufactories to represent them in the legislature. By the late 1890s clerks and salesmen also represented the district. In the early twentieth century the state representatives were a motley crew that included several lawyers, a dentist, two salesmen, an insurance agent, a clerk, a grocer, a restaurant owner, an electrician, a former blacksmith, a gas fitter, and even a bartender for one term.

Despite the democratization of neighborhood representation, inhabitants of America's late-nineteenth-century cities considered some governmental offices to be less plebeian. In Jamaica Plain an air of prestige still hung over the offices of alderman and state senator. Before the Board of Aldermen became an at-large body, Jamaica Plain and the other sections of the aldermanic district elected businessmen such as Henry F. Coe and Sidney Cushing or professionals such as Salem D. Charles, a lawyer, and E. Peabody Gerry, a local physician. State senators, whose districts were larger than those of either representatives or aldermen, tended to be lawyers or successful businessman. Positions in the U.S. Congress were more exclusive still, usually reserved for wealthy men. In the late 1890s, for example, the local congressional district elected Charles F. Sprague, a Harvard-trained attorney who married an heiress to the Weld fortune and lived on her Jamaica Hills estate.[14]

During the late nineteenth and early twentieth centuries, political parties in Boston, New York, and other American cities comprised and supported ethnic, class, and religious coalitions. Within neighborhood society, such coalitions functioned as local charitable and improvement organizations did to foster local attachments. They helped residents to cross social barriers and encouraged them to develop loyalties to the neighborhood as a whole. As in Boston, the Democratic party in Jamaica Plain represented an alliance between old-line New Englanders and Irish Catholics. Over the years, the local district elected wealthy and highly respectable Yankees such as Richard Olney, who in his youth served a term as the district's state representative, and Andrew J. Peters, scion to an old Jamaica Plain mercantile family, a U.S. congressman in the 1900s. Most of the local Yankee Democrats, however, were not blue bloods but unrenowned New Englanders such as Salem D. Charles, a lawyer who served as state representative in the 1890s and Boston building commissioner in the 1900s, and Frank F. Proctor, a manager at a Boston leather firm who was a local city councilor in 1891 and 1892. By the early twentieth century these Yankees shared the reins of the local party with middle-class Irish-Americans such as John M. Minton and John F. McDonald, both attorneys and powerful figures in the Ward 23 organization, and representatives of organized labor such as Fred J. Kneeland, a prominent member of the Boston Central Labor Union.[15]

No less diverse than the local Democracy, the Republican party in Jamaica Plain also bridged ethnocultural gaps in neighborhood society. Historically the party lay claim to a spectrum of New England–born Protestants who ranged from well-to-do Unitarians and Episcopalians to relatively more middle-class and fundamentalist Congregationalists, Baptists, and Methodists. Some of the local Republicans could claim distinctive lineage or great wealth. Benjamin H. Ticknor, for example, son of the founder of the publishing firm of Ticknor and Fields, served as city councilor in 1876 and participated in local party affairs for many years. Wealthy Boston lawyers such as William Minot, Jr., and Robert M. Morse, Jr., sprang from mercantile families with roots in antebellum Jamaica Plain and were elected to local offices as Republicans.[16]

More prevalent among the local Republican officeholders, however, were self-made Yankee businessmen such as William G. Baker, a native of Derry, New Hampshire, who worked in an upholstery and window-shade store in Boston and served three terms as a state representative, and Lewis L. P. Atwood, a local real estate agent, who won election to the Common Council in 1887. Neighborhood Republicans also included "swamp Yankees," New England migrants of obscure origins, such as Abram Jordan, a native of Maine who ran a carpentry shop near Boylston station for many years before winning elections to the ward committee and the Common Council in the late 1890s.[17]

Like the Democrats, the local Republicans also depended upon immigrant and immigrant-stock votes to buttress the Yankee office seekers. The neighborhood branch of the Grand Old Party benefited from the arrival of predominantly Protestant immigrant groups such as Scots, Canadians (from the Maritime Provinces), Swedes, and other Scandinavians. German-Americans participated in the neighborhood Republican voting coalition from before the annexation of West Roxbury but were able to elect few city or state officeholders until the 1890s. From the turn of the century Jamaica Plain sent to the Massachusetts State House such German-American Republicans as John Bleiler, a grocer and member of the Schwaben Verein social club, and Frank Seiberlich, an electrician and proprietor of a Forest Hills hotel. Thomas E. Johns, a Canadian-born carpenter from the Heath Street area, worked tirelessly for the Republican Ward 22 committee. When in 1900 a rival faction challenged his leadership of the ward, Johns accused his opponents of being disloyal Republicans and declared that he had given his time and money and even endangered his health for the sake of the local party. By 1900 there were enough politically active Swedes to help organize a Scandinavian Republican Club and elect Charles O. Engstrom, a Swedish-born lawyer and graduate of Boston's public schools, to the State House.[18]

As in other cities, socially charged controversies expressed ethnoreligious animosities between the groups that clustered in Boston's opposing political parties. In the 1880s, for example, religious and cultural hostilities broke out between Irish Catholics and middle- and lower-middle-class Protestants. With the election in 1885 of the city's first Irish-born mayor, Hugh O'Brien, and an increase in the number of Catholics on the school committee, Bostonians witnessed the apparent ascendancy of Irish Catholics over the old capitol of Puritan New England. The call of the 1884 Roman Catholic Plenary Council of Baltimore for parochial schools and a subsequent increase in the number of such schools added to Protestant fears.

Taking advantage of a recent law that allowed women to vote in school elections, in the mid-1880s prohibitionists and suffragists attacked the school committee for tolerating a saloon near a school. This campaign touched off a competition between Protestants and Catholics to register women voters and set the stage for a controversy in 1888 about the committee's disciplining of an anti-Catholic teacher. Feeding fuel to the fires, a nationalistic conflict between Canadian "British American" immigrants and Irish-American Catholics came to a head in disturbances connected with the celebration of Queen Victoria's Golden Jubilee at Boston's Faneuil Hall.[19]

Republicans could not resist exploiting this political opportunity and helped mobilize the anti–Irish Catholic vote. In 1888 a Republican party faction introduced a bill allowing school boards to inspect private schools, a measure that was aimed at harassing and perhaps suppressing the Catholic schools. With the help of large numbers of recently naturalized Canadian voters, prohibitionists, and fundamentalist Protestants, the Republicans swept the Democratic Irish Catholics out of City Hall and the school committee.

The competition between parties, however, tended to keep the political pendulum swinging back toward the center. Moderates on both sides deplored the controversies concerning the public schools. At the state legislature, members of the Boston elite, President Charles Eliot of Harvard, Edward Everett Hale, and Thomas Wentworth Higginson, spoke in opposition to the school-inspection act. Thomas Magennis, the pastor of Jamaica Plain's St. Thomas Church, testified for the Roman Catholics as one who had observed both the public-school system of West Roxbury and parochial schools. Drawing upon his experiences in Jamaica Plain, Magennis questioned the quality of the public schools, appealed to the Protestant sense of Christian morality, and invoked the separation of church and state.[20]

Faced with a lack of liberal support and the possibility of alienating non-Irish ethnic Catholics such as French-Canadians and Germans, the state Republican party retreated from the school-regulation issue. In Boston moderate Protestants, who were concerned that Catholics might leave the public-school system, backed away from flagrant anti-Catholicism in the school system. The Catholic clergy continued to establish parochial schools, but to avoid exacerbating religious tensions, they effectively urged Catholic women not to vote. In the 1890s Irish-American Democratic leaders restricted themselves to opposing any further extension of what was in effect the Protestant women's vote and, anxious for patronage, ran well-to-do Yankees for mayor. Thus, complexities of voting coalitions encouraged political parties to pull back from the brink of ethnic and class conflict.[21]

In late-nineteenth-century Jamaica Plain, the minority status of the Democratic party provided an incentive for ethnic cooperation. As in the rest of Boston, in the 1890s Irish-American support for Yankee candidates who could appeal to Protestant Republicans increased the Democrats' chances for electoral victory. Thus, in the 1890s Frank Proctor twice beat the odds by winning council elections against Republican Ward 23 Protestants, and Salem D. Charles was elected three times to the state legislature. With the help of local Irish-American political managers, in the early twentieth century Andrew J. Peters won elections to the Massachusetts house and senate and the U.S. Congress. The success of local Yankee Democrats paved the way in the early twentieth century for "respectable" Irish-American candidates in the same mold. Irish-stock Catholic candidates such as Joseph J. Leonard, an attorney, John J. Conway, a labor leader, and William M. McMorrow, a Boston College high-school teacher, won state legislature races in what was thought to be a Republican district by supporting neighborhood improvement and municipal reforms.

The law partnership of Keating and Brackett exemplified the kind of Anglo-Celtic collaboration that occurred within the neighborhood Democratic party. Patrick M. Keating was raised as a Catholic in Springfield, Massachusetts, where he attended public schools. He graduated from Harvard College in 1883, went on to study law, and two years later was admitted to the bar. In 1893 he became a partner in a law firm, developed a "large and lucrative practice," and moved to fashionable Pondside in Jamaica Plain. A leading Boston trial lawyer, Keating was a member of the bar associations of Boston and Massachusetts, and he served as president of the Charitable Irish Society and the Catholic Alumni Sodality of Boston. In the 1890s Keating participated in local party activities, and for several years he presided over the Democratic Ward 23 committee.

Sewall C. Brackett was born in Jamaica Plain, the son of a Yankee insurance agent, and attended local public schools, Roxbury Latin (preparatory) School, and Harvard College. He earned his law degree from Boston University in 1893, afterwards began practicing in Boston, and then joined the firm of Gargan, Keating, and Brackett (later Keating and Brackett) as a junior partner. An inveterate joiner of organizations, Brackett worked with Keating politically as well. He ran unsuccessfully for the city council in 1897 and 1898 and later became secretary of the Democratic ward committee.[22]

The Jamaica Plain Republican party also had to struggle with discordant constituencies. As a political home of fundamentalist Protestants (when they were not supporting independent party candidates), the local G.O.P. was naturally prone to anti-foreign and temperance sentiments. By the turn of the century, however, Yankee Republicans were forced to accommodate emergent ethnic groups, especially the German-Americans. With the creation in 1895 of a new ward in northern Jamaica Plain, where Republican ethnic groups concentrated, the local party began to nominate German-American candidates to oppose Irish-American Democrats. From this base, for example, the German-Americans were able to send John Bleiler to the state house of representatives for five terms. The political strength of the German-Americans naturally held in check the more extreme prohibitionist tendencies of the party. This policy of toleration became specific once German-Americans such as Bleiler took office and began defending the rights of beer drinkers.[23]

The German-Americans aggressively and blatantly supported their own kind, but the ideals of party allegiance and disinterested political leadership served as counterweights to ethnic chauvinism. In 1899, for example, Edward J. Bromberg, a German-American politician, decried the inference of an article in the *Jamaica Plain News* that "the Germans are so clannish as to ignore the virtues of any but their own candidate." Bromberg admitted that Andrew Brauer, a Roslindale Republican running for the position of state representative, was popular among his German friends but asserted that no group was more cosmopolitan or free from prejudice than the Germans. "Please don't lay the charge at our doors of attempting or in any way countenancing a 'race war' or encouraging even in the slightest the deplorable issue of one class against another. I assure you the German Republicans of Ward 23 will be thoroughly loyal to the Grand Old Party, and at the caucus or polls will vote on the question of merit and fitness, and in no way be governed by personal malice or spleen."[24]

Anti-foreign prejudice did not die among local Yankee Republicans, but it began to be publicly attacked. In 1904 ward organization leaders deserted John Bleiler for E. Peabody Gerry in a race for the state senate. Bleiler accused his fellow Republicans of supporting a discriminatory policy that prohibited German-Americans from any office higher than state representative. Despite Bleiler's charges, in 1907 Edward J. Bromberg, an attorney, was elected to the state senate either because the Republicans had grown more tolerant or, what is just as likely, because a lawyer was more acceptable than a grocer as a candidate for the senate.[25]

Local Republicans even considered Irish-Americans as potential candidates. In 1903 Republicans in Jamaica Plain and elsewhere around Boston seriously discussed giving the mayoral nomination to Michael J. Murray, a Catholic resident of Jamaica Plain. Some doubted that the party would go so far as to nominate a Catholic, and in the event it did not. The subsequent Democratic landslide, however, suggested that tolerance was a more practical electoral strategy. The Republican *Jamaica Plain News,* which had supported the local son Murray, blasted the party for choosing candidates for mayor and street commissioner whose only qualifications were "American names."[26]

Such efforts underscore how the localist system of politics offered incentives for ethnic cooperation. As anomalous as it might seem, Boston Republicans more than once attempted to attract Irish-Americans after the Civil War. Although on the ethnocultural spectrum the Irish stood opposite the party's fundamentalist Protestant constituency, their numbers in the population made them too important to ignore. By the turn of the century some Republicans were ready to try again to incorporate the city's Celtic element into the party coalition. If the masses of Irish-Americans were beyond the immediate reach of the Republicans, the reform traditions of the Irish and an increase in the numbers of middle- and upper-middle-class Irish-Americans created a potential group to tap in neighborhoods such as Jamaica Plain. In an increasingly immigrant-stock city, the small group of prominent Irish-American Republicans, such as Murray, an attorney with reformer credentials, or Stephen O'Meara, a Boston newspaper editor, suggested a promising way for Republicans to maintain their party as a creditable alternative to the Democrats.[27]

During the Progressive era, urban reformers in Boston in pursuit of a unified polity severely damaged the decentralized political and governmental systems that had evolved during the late nineteenth century. By centralizing governmental authority and weakening the party organizations, reformers diminished the importance of the political clubroom, which had encouraged neighborhood attachments. They unintentionally reduced the incentives for class and ethnic accommodation within the party system and opened a Pandora's box of class and ethnic hostilities.

Historians have studied progressive urban reform exhaustively. Some have distinguished between moral, social, and structural types of reform. In this scheme, moral reformers especially aimed to eradicate urban vice, structural reformers mobilized to overhaul what they believed were inefficient and corrupt municipal governments, and social reformers concentrated on welfare measures such as housing reform, labor legislation, and municipal ownership. Similarly, historians have identified progressive reformers variously as old-stock Yankee Protestant heirs to the Mugwumps, members of the new upper middle class of urban professionals and businessmen, and middle-class ethnics responsive to working-class needs.[28]

Although these distinctions help to explain the complexities of the era, in practice no clear line separated reformers from one another. The moral impulse, as Paul Boyer has shown, seldom lay far below the surface of any type of nineteenth-century urban reform. Inspired by such disparate sources as the Protestant social gospel, the business corporation, modern science, and high art, progressives fashioned a complex set of ideals that encompassed morality, efficiency, expertise, and aesthetics. With such a diverse ideology to draw upon, progressives of all stripes employed the ideas they found most congenial to state their case. Who supported which reforms, especially governmental reforms, often depended upon particular circumstances, including which group was in power at the moment. Whether in support of neighborhood improvement, or labor legislation, or some other crusade, political interest groups appropriated the language of progressivism to explain and advance their cause.[29]

During the late nineteenth and early twentieth centuries, Jamaica Plain uplifters ran the gamut of urban reform. During the Gilded Age, conservative Congregationalists and Baptist Protestants represented the tradition of moral uplift by fighting for prohibition and supporting missionaries at home and abroad. In the Progressive era, neighborhood reformers pushed for a broad array of social reforms, including women's rights, playgrounds, manual training, and sex education. At the First Church, members formed "social action organizations" in such fields as "International Justice and Peace," "Welfare of the Community," and "Social Justice and Progress," which covered child labor, the work of the consumers' league, and working conditions in Jamaica Plain shops and factories.[30]

Individual Jamaica Plainers exemplified all the varieties of reformers to be found in Boston. Charles F. Dole, pastor of the First Church, advocated free speech for anarchists and opposed the United States' entry into World War I on pacifist grounds. His protégé, Emily Greene Balch, first went into settlement-house work and later went on to win the Nobel peace prize for her efforts at arbitrating international conflicts. The daughter of John Boyle O'Reilly, the Irish nationalist leader, Catholic newspaper editor, and toast of Brahmin Boston, maintained the Irish Catholic liberal tradition. Mary Boyle O'Reilly served as a trustee on the State Board of Prisons and the City Board of Children's Institutions, on which Balch had also once served. Edmund Billings, a professional social worker, directed Boston philanthropic institutions and helped organize the first municipal baths in Boston. Representing the trade-union wing of Progressive reform were Boston labor leaders such as Charles G. Wilkins, a Scottish immigrant and colleague of the prominent labor reformer, Frank K. Foster. Wilkins, a leader of the Boston Typographical Union and the State Federation of Labor, pioneered the idea of a municipally owned printing plant to set union standards in the trade.[31]

At the inner core of Jamaica Plain's reform culture, and of Jamaica Plain society in general, were a group of upper-middle-class residents whose abiding sense of family, heritage, and leadership rivaled their commitment to the neighborhood. Most of these reformers were connected to the Unitarian First Church of Jamaica Plain and had strong associations with New England abolitionism and the causes of the Civil War. For example, Charles F. Dole, the pastor of the First Church, came from a Whig and Free Soil lineage in Maine. In his adolescence, Dole served in the Massachusetts state militia in what he considered to be a holy war to destroy slavery and preserve the Union. By the turn of the century, Dole's intellectual journey in Protestant liberalism led him to reject war and imperialism, but his New England background represented a secure and familiar starting point.[32]

Some of Dole's parishioners were direct heirs to the moral-reform legacy of the antebellum and postwar eras. Emily Greene Balch and Francis N. Balch inherited a missionary passion for reform from their father, Francis Vergnies Balch, a prominent Boston title and trust attorney. After graduating from Harvard College, the senior Balch enlisted as a private in the Union army. Stricken ill almost immediately, in 1863 Balch became personal secretary to Charles Sumner, the famous abolitionist senator, who greatly influenced his political views. Balch helped lay the groundwork for postwar reform when he drew up for Sumner the country's first civil-service bill. The father of another local reformer, E. Peabody Gerry, had given speeches in the abolitionist cause (Gerry remembered on one occasion sitting in Charles Sumner's lap as his father spoke) and in 1875 founded the Society for the Prevention of Cruelty to Children to protect the young from immorality and physical abuse. In the 1840s and 1850s, Sarah Ernst, the mother of George Alexander Otis Ernst, had helped lead the anti-slavery movement in Cincinnati and corresponded with William Lloyd Garrison. Her son, who later chaired the First Church's Parish Committee, cut his political eyeteeth on the issue of civil-service reform, a favorite Gilded Age cause. As a delegate of the Young Republicans of Massachusetts he pressed the 1880 Republican National Convention to adopt the reform in the party platform.[33]

For neighborhood reformers, as for progressives elsewhere, the attractions of modernity balanced the moral legacies of the past. Like urban reformers in other cities, Jamaica Plain's leading reformers held the kinds of high-white-collar occupations that had multiplied in Boston and the rest of urban America during the late nineteenth century. They also belonged to the professional networks that spread across the country during the same period. Brimming with self-confidence, these businessmen, lawyers, physicians, social workers, and ministers looked forward to the future. The power and efficiency of the modern business corporation, the

exciting developments in the fields of social and natural science, the expertise of the newly organized professions, and the spread of an aesthetic high
culture all represented appealing aspects of an emergent new order.[34]

In common with progressive reformers across the United States, Jamaica Plain's reformers believed that the "problem of the cities" represented a
crisis comparable to that which precipitated the Civil War. In their minds,
saloons, prostitution, gambling, slums, crime, and even the ugliness of the
streets were moral evils that were in some way connected. Most reformers
believed that political corruption was a prime cause of the urban dilemma,
or at the very least a major obstacle to its solution. For municipal reformers, the restructuring of city governments along universal principles
was an essential step in solving the moral problems of the city.

The movement for fundamental municipal reform in Boston first
emerged in the public-school arena as a by-product of the conflicts of the
1880s. Historically, school reformers had envisioned city public schools as
moral environments that would instill virtuous character and republican
virtues in the urban masses. During the Progressive era, reformers in New
York, Philadelphia, St. Louis, and other American cities became convinced that politics had polluted these environments and launched efforts
to save them by restructuring and centralizing the administration of public
education. Many of these efforts at centralization succeeded and, as in
Boston, encouraged reformers to tackle the larger problem of the city
government.[35]

The public career of Samuel Billings Capen, a longtime Jamaica Plain
resident and prominent leader in the school- and municipal-reform movements, demonstrates the close links between moral reform and structural
reform. Unlike the well-to-do and liberal Unitarians, Capen came from a
Boston Congregationalist family of modest means and a Calvinist outlook
that frowned upon dancing, theater, and novels as too worldly. Starting as
an office boy in a Boston carpet business, Capen worked his way up to
partner in the firm of Torrey, Bright, and Capen. In Jamaica Plain, Capen
became a deacon of the Central Congregational Church and taught the
men's Bible class.

The Sunday school movement expressed the strong missionary and
moral-reform impulses of the Protestant church, and leading Congregationalists hoped to strengthen their church's role in this area. In 1882 the
new secretary of the Congregational Sunday School and Publishing Society
recruited Capen to be the organization's president. Because of his work
with the Congregational Sunday schools, Capen became interested in
Boston's public-school system. Capen was convinced that Catholics in city

government were trying to undermine the school system by withholding construction funds. As part of the Protestant backlash of 1888, Capen ran and was elected to the Boston School Committee.[36]

Despite his fervent Protestantism, Capen showed himself to be a moderate moral reformer rather than a fundamentalist fanatic. A leader on the school committee, which tried to find a middle ground between the beliefs of Catholics and those of militant Protestants, Capen pressed for an aggressive expansion of the public-school system in order to accommodate Boston's growing and increasingly Catholic population. His highest goal for the public schools, as he stated in an 1889 address to public-school masters, was to mold young minds by teaching morals. Thus he effectively advocated such educational reforms as manual training—in 1891 he oversaw the establishment of the Mechanic Arts High School—and the reform school, both of which he believed offered moral direction to youth in danger of going astray. Like other moral reformers, Capen was prepared to use coercion when environmental influence failed. He resisted curbs on capital punishment and was until late in his life a leading supporter of immigration restriction.[37]

Like school reformers in other cities, Capen concluded that political influence on hiring and building policies corrupted the integrity of the school system. Capen, like school reformers elsewhere, felt that the practice of renewing teacher appointments annually subjected the teachers to harmful political pressures. To protect the teachers, Capen obtained permanent tenure of office for them. Applying the Gilded Age remedy to the problem of patronage jobs, Capen helped persuade the state legislature to place the jobs of janitors on the civil-service rolls. On the school building subcommittee, Capen worked to prevent conflicts of interest in the purchase of land for school buildings.[38]

Capen resigned from the school committee in 1893 but continued to be interested in school affairs. Beginning in 1895, he met with prominent Boston progressives such as attorney Louis Brandeis, women's-rights advocate Mary Morton Kehew, and the settlement-house activist Robert A. Woods to suggest reform candidates for the school board to the political parties. When two years later the parties refused to accept the suggestions, Capen and his colleagues organized the Public School Association (PSA) to run their own candidates. At first electoral victories were intermittent, but by the turn of the century the PSA was able to elect candidates such as George A. O. Ernst and George W. Anderson, both lawyers and Jamaica Plain residents, and A. Lawrence Lowell, Robert Treat Paine, John Farwell Moors, and James Jackson Storrow, wealthy Boston philanthropists. In 1901, aided by an alliance with Democratic reform mayor Josiah Quincy, the PSA obtained a majority on the twenty-four-member school committee.[39]

The members of the PSA were dedicated to eliminating the influence of politicians in school affairs and professionalizing the school system. The reformers were convinced that a corrupt and inefficient school committee hopelessly distorted the management of the schools. Overlapping meetings, secret deliberations, logrolling, and the consideration of petty details weighed down the many subcommittees of the school board. Reformers felt that neighborhood representatives on the committee displayed extreme provincialism by insisting on a say in the purchase of textbooks and other matters. Worse yet in the reformers' view was the corruption of political influence. Teachers lobbied to get jobs for their friends. Politicians decided which building lots to purchase and who should be hired for every position from janitor up. The shadow of the neighborhood ward committeeman had fallen over the entire public educational system. The PSA raised the battle cry to "keep the schools out of politics."[40]

To restructure the management of school systems in Boston and elsewhere, reformers applied universal principles of administration. The centralized bureaucracy of the business corporation and the expertise of the professional provided the models for their reforms. In the late 1890s, Boston reformers attempted to replace "the inherently vicious system of sub-committees," as George A. O. Ernst called it, with a management by independent experts, especially a strong central officer, the superintendent. The reformers felt that such neutral administration would transcend the bitter sectarianism of the Irish Catholics and militantly Protestant British-Americans and remove the sources of political corruption.[41]

Unfortunately for the reformers, the effort to impose a moral and nonsectarian meritocracy on the Boston school system boomeranged. When the reformers attempted to transfer the powers of appointment from the school board subcommittees to the superintendent of schools and establish other mechanisms of independent consultation, they met stiff opposition from entrenched school board members. The PSA had never freed itself from its anti-Catholic roots, and in 1902 and 1903 Catholic politicians led by Mrs. Julia Duff, a school committee member from the neighborhood of Charlestown, attacked the hiring practices of the PSA-dominated school committee as discriminatory. Under Duff's influence, the Democrats nominated anti-reform candidates, and the PSA soon lost its majority on the school committee. By 1904, PSA committee members were outnumbered by the anti-reformers and were unable to prevent the ouster of the school superintendent.[42]

Frustrated by political defeat, the reformers turned to the kind of structural corrections that had been adopted in New York City and were tried in other cities. They hoped that an administrative structure based on principles of moral behavior and business efficiency would overcome the sectarian differences that had roiled school affairs for so long. In 1904 school committeeman Storrow proposed a plan to transform the elected school committee of twenty-four members into a board of five members appointed by the mayor and to centralize business and educational management under the authority of the superintendent. Fellow PSA members such as Robert Treat Paine opposed an appointed board as undemocratic, and so the plan was modified to incorporate an at-large election of the five board members. In 1905 Storrow, Capen, and the PSA succeeded in obtaining a charter that eliminated the neighborhood and partisan basis of the school committee.[43]

Although the new form of school-system administration was supposed to engender a sense of common civic virtue, it failed to unify those associated with the Boston school system. The first election after the adoption of the nonpartisan reforms brought public charges of anti-Irish discrimination against the reformers. Because of his record of hiring qualified Catholics as a school committeeman, Storrow was able to effectively rebut these charges, but once again reform had stirred up, not calmed, ethnic and religious discord. Already in 1903 the PSA had cut its ties with the Independent Women Voters, a militant Protestant group, and experimented with a balanced ticket of Yankee Protestant, Irish Catholic, and Jewish candidates. To protect itself from charges of discrimination, the PSA now adopted a permanent policy of endorsing ethnically and religiously mixed slates. The new superintendent of schools, a man nominated by Storrow and elected by the reform members of the school committee, turned out to be a rigid administrator who soon alienated a large portion of the system's underpaid teachers.[44]

The efforts to overhaul the administration of the Boston school system added momentum to the growing urge to do something about the government of Boston. By the late nineteenth century, the belief that Boston's political and governmental life was diseased had become commonplace among reformers. Jamaica Plain's Samuel B. Capen and George W. Anderson and other veterans of the school wars blamed the problems of the schools on a city government that they assumed was riddled with graft and corruption.[45]

Reformers who made such charges had an eager audience. Dissatisfaction with big spending and high taxes fueled efforts to restructure municipal government in such cities as New York, Philadelphia, and Milwaukee. As elsewhere, the soaring cost of government led many Bostonians to be concerned about its efficiency, cost, and honesty. In 1884 the rate of taxation in Boston jumped to an unprecedented height, and the following year Boston taxpayers supported a new city charter that gave the state government responsibility for some city services. Still, the infrastructure and services that they demanded were expensive, and the political pressures to expand government employment opportunities for laborers did not help matters. In the late nineteenth century, both Yankee and Irish mayors found it difficult to hold the budget down in the face of the voracious appetite for improvement. Holding politicians in low repute, reformers were quick to conclude that only a sick and corrupt polity could cause such large expenditures and high taxes.[46]

Municipal reformers, however, sought a loftier goal than the mere reduction of property tax rates. Fusing moralism, class biases, and a desire for administrative efficiency, they pursued a vision of a city unified by civic virtue. Nothing symbolized the urban reformer's vision more than the World's Columbian Exposition held in Chicago in 1893. Urban reformers in Boston and elsewhere were captivated by the image of its monumental buildings, designed by the country's best-known architects and filled with exhibits of the latest technological achievements, gleaming above the lagoons and wooded parkland landscaped by Frederick Law Olmsted. They associated the White City, as the great fair was known, with the progressive ideals of efficiency, expertise, morals, and aesthetics.

Many observers credited the Columbian Exposition with creating the City Beautiful movement, the effort to elevate the aesthetic and functional qualities of the modern urban environment by means of planning. In fact the movement had many antecedents, but the fair did energize and focus it. The large-scale physical elements typically associated with the City Beautiful included Olmsted-style parks, circulation systems with imposing boulevards or graceful parkways, and civic centers of monumental neoclassical architecture. Like the earlier park proponents, City Beautiful advocates such as Daniel Burnham believed in universalist principles and attempted to impose similar features on such disparate cities as Cleveland, Washington, D.C., Denver, and San Francisco.[47]

Boston's accomplishments in design had contributed to the White City and the City Beautiful, and their glittering images in turn influenced Boston's physical development. Charles McKim's Renaissance-style design for the Boston Public Library had contributed to the national fashion for neoclassicism that climaxed in the Court of Honor buildings at the White

City. After the fair, new classically styled museums, hotels, and other structures appeared in downtown, Back Bay, and other sections of Boston. Nor did Jamaica Plain residents have to look far to find elements of the City Beautiful. Olmsted's parks adorned the neighborhood, and his parkways, the Jamaicaway and the Arborway, gracefully wound through the district. The Pondside mansions built during the 1890s and 1900s proudly displayed the columns and pediments of neoclassical architecture, and down the parkway, in the Fenway neighborhood, a series of institutions reiterated the monumental structures of the White City.[48]

Although usually relegated to the specialized field of planning history, the City Beautiful movement might better be considered as a wing of the progressive urban-reform movement. Not merely an exercise in physical planning, the movement also expressed the moral environmentalism that characterized the parks movement and such urban-uplift efforts as tenement and sanitation reform. City Beautiful exponents such as Daniel Burnham felt that their work had a social and moral dimension, and municipal reformers such as Frederic C. Howe included the City Beautiful in their prescriptions for improving the American city. Indeed, as made explicit on the covers of the reform journal *New Boston,* the neoclassicist image of the City Beautiful represented the face of progressive urban reform.[49]

Thus, reformers in Chicago and other cities concerned with morals as well as aesthetics found inspiration in the Columbian Exposition. To them, the White City represented the ideal that should be reproduced in every city in the United States. The fair, wrote Richard Harding Davis in *Harper's Weekly,* offered a "model of how to run the modern city— efficiently, without corruption or scandal, and in the best interests of all its citizens."[50]

In Boston, reformers dissected the Columbian Exposition to learn "what a great city might be." To the Reverend Charles G. Ames, the White City offered Boston an example of the City Beautiful and the City of God, a moral metropolis that was planned and cultured, possessing tasteful architecture and the most modern engineering. Unified in purpose, it was a city that transcended the chaotic competition and petty self-interest that plagued modern Boston. In his *New England Magazine,* Edwin D. Mead, the crusading editor and close ally of Samuel B. Capen, celebrated the White City because it possessed "the charm of a noble unity, a beautiful adaptation of great means to great ends . . . conceived, constructed, and controlled upon the principles of beauty and reason." The White City was the "one place where beauty and fitness and efficiency had been achieved."[51]

can Local History," in *The Past before Us: Contemporary Historical Writing in the United States,* ed. Michael Kammen (Ithaca, 1980), 288–91; Patricia Mooney Melvin, "Changing Contexts: Neighborhood Definition and Urban Organization," *American Quarterly* 37 (Bibliography 1985), 357, 367.

For a related subject, the evolution of the intellectual *concept* of neighborhood, see Jean B. Quandt, *From the Small Town to the Great Community: The Social Thought of Progressive Intellectuals* (New Brunswick, N.J., 1970); Patricia Mooney Melvin, *The Organic City: Urban Definition and Community Organization, 1880–1920* (Lexington, Ky., 1987).

12. Keller, *Urban Neighborhood,* 87–88; Hunter, *Symbolic Communities,* 67–94.

13. This study uses the boundaries of modern Jamaica Plain as established by the Boston Redevelopment Authority. These boundaries coincide with those referred to in the local newspaper at the turn of the century and with those commonly recognized by neighborhood residents today.

14. Max R. Grossman, "Jamaica Plain—It Has Everything," *Boston Post,* Jan. 26. 1941.

15. African-American Bostonians, who were concentrated in the South End, were especially underrepresented within the neighborhood population from 1850 to 1920.

Chapter 1 On the Urban Fringe

Epigraphs: Thomas Gray, *Half Century Sermon, Delivered on Sunday Morning, April 24, 1842, at Jamaica Plain* (Boston, 1842), 16; George William Curtis, *Trumps, Harper's Weekly,* Apr. 16, 1859, 253.

1. *Application of Samuel D. Bradford and Others to Set Off Wards Six, Seven, and Eight, of the City of Roxbury, as a Separate Agricultural Town* (Boston, 1851); *Report of the Joint Special Committee on Division and Annexation,* City of Roxbury City Doc. No. 5 (Roxbury, 1851), 7.

2. Gray, *Half Century Sermon,* 31–32; Sam Bass Warner, Jr., *Streetcar Suburbs: The Process of Growth in Boston, 1870–1900* (Cambridge, Mass., 1962), 41–42.

3. Gray, *Half Century Sermon,* 16. These proportions are similar to those of Boston and its neighboring communities in 1850. See Oscar Handlin, *Boston's Immigrants: A Study in Acculturation* (Cambridge, Mass., 1941; rev. ed., New York, 1974), 244, 250–52. Before 1850 the Bureau of the Census did not record an individual's birthplace.

4. Francis Z. Blouin, *The Boston Region, 1810–1850: A Study of Urbanization* (Ann Arbor, 1980); Robert G. Leblanc, *Location of Manufacturing in New England in the Nineteenth Century* (Dartmouth, 1969); Allan Pred, *Urban Growth and City Systems in the United States, 1840–1860* (Cambridge, Mass., 1980), 65–84; John B. Sharpless, "The Economic Structure of Port Cities in the Mid-Nineteenth Century: Boston and Liverpool, 1840–1860," *Journal of Historical Geography* 2, no. 2 (1976), 131–43.

5. Henry C. Binford, *The First Suburbs: Residential Communities on the Boston Periphery, 1815–1860* (Chicago, 1985).

6. Francis S. Drake, *The Town of Roxbury: Its Memorable Persons and Places, Its History and Antiquities* (Roxbury, 1878), 11, 46, 48–49, 393–94, 399–402; Ellis, *History* (intro., n. 1), 138–40; Harriet Manning Whitcomb, *Annals and Reminiscences of Jamaica Plain* (Cambridge, Mass., 1897), 9–10; Record Commissioners of the City of Boston, *A Report of the Record Commissioners, containing the Roxbury Land and Church Records* (Boston, 1881), passim.

7. Record Commissioners, *Report*, 35, 46; Drake, *Town*, 398, 438–39; Town of Roxbury, "Town Records," Rare Books and Manuscripts Department, BPL, vol. 1, Feb. 23, 1652, Jan. 29, 1654.

8. Charles Frederick Robinson, *Weld Collections* (Ann Arbor, 1938), 35–45, 56–58; Drake, *Town*, 158–59.

9. Benjamin P. Williams, *Address Delivered on the Dedication of Eliot Hall, on Jamaica Plain, January 17, 1832* (Boston, 1832), 5–6; SRD, *Suffolk Deeds* (Boston, 1899), bk. 10, 75–76.

10. Town of Roxbury, "Town Records," vol. 1, Oct. 10, 1683, Oct. 2, 1706, Mar. 11, 1717; vol. 2, Aug. 10, 1739, June 5, 1746.

11. Ellis, *History*, 32–33; Drake, *Town*, 447–50; Town of Roxbury, "Town Records," vol. 1, Mar. 1, 1703, Feb. 7, 1710/11. The northeastern boundary for the new parish was drawn through what is now southern Jamaica Plain: Walk Hill and South, Eliot, and Prince streets.

12. Samuel C. Clarke, *Records of Some of the Descendants of William Curtis, Roxbury, 1632* (Boston, 1869), 10; Drake, *Town*, 86. Curtis lived from 1722 to 1792.

13. Gray, *Half Century Sermon*, 31–32; Binford, *First Suburbs*, 32–33.

14. Gray, *Half Century Sermon*, 31–32.

15. Carl Bridenbaugh, *Cities in Revolt: Urban Life in America, 1743–1776* (New York, 1955; rev. ed., Oxford, 1971), 337–40.

16. Drake, *Town*, 207, 255–56; Hugh Morrison, *Early American Architecture from the First Colonial Settlements to the National Period* (New York, 1952), 484–85; William H. Cordingley, "Shirley Place, Roxbury, Massachusetts, and Its Builder, Governor William Shirley," *Old Time New England (Bulletin of the Society for the Preservation of New England Antiquities)* 12, no. 2 (1921), 51–63.

17. Drake, *Town*, 407–11, 415–17; Walter K. Watkins, *The Pemberton Family* (Boston, 1892), 7; Eva Phillips Boyd, "Jamaica Plain by Way of London," *Old Time New England* 49, no. 4 (1959), 87–89; Robert Hallowell Gardiner, *The Early Recollections of Robert Hallowell Gardiner, 1782–1864* (Hallowell, Maine, 1936), 5–7.

18. Edward Channing and Archibald Cary Coolidge, eds., *The Barrington-Bernard Correspondence and Illustrative Matter, 1760–1770, Drawn from the "Papers of Sir Francis Bernard"* (Cambridge, Mass., 1912), 49, 78; Drake, *Town*, 431.

19. Drake, *Town*, 407, 412, 415, 426–27, 429, 435–36.

20. For these and other estates, see Drake, *Town*, 386–90, 399, 412–16, 425–28;

Whitcomb, *Annals,* 27, 54–55; Cynthia Zaitzevsky, "Victorian Jamaica Plain," in *Victorian Boston Today,* ed. Pauline Chase Harrell and Margaret Supplee Smith (Boston, 1975), 80–81; Francis S. Russell, *The Knave of Boston* (Boston, 1987), 71; and Hamilton Perkins Greenough, *Some Descendants of Captain William Greenough of Boston, Massachusetts* (Santa Barbara, 1969), 56, 239–45. Perkins was the brother of Thomas Handasyd Perkins, one of the richest merchants in New England.

21. Samuel Griswold Goodrich, *Recollections of a Lifetime,* 2 vols. (New York, 1856), 2:283; Whitcomb, *Annals,* 28–29; John G. Hales, surveyor, *Map of the Town of Roxbury,* 1832; Daniel Roselle, *Samuel Griswold Goodrich, Creator of Peter Parley: A Study of His Life and Work* (Albany, 1968), 86, 138; Drake, *Town,* 231; Emily Goodrich Smith, "Peter Parley as Known to His Daughter," *Connecticut Quarterly* 4 (July–Sept. 1898), 304–15, and ibid. (Oct.–Dec. 1898), 406.

22. Grindall Reynolds, *A Discourse Preached on the Occasion of Leaving the Old Meeting House at Jamaica Plain, West Roxbury, Mass.* (Boston, 1853), 26–27.

23. Fred Seaver, *The Founders and Incorporators of the Third Parish in Jamaica Plain* (Jamaica Plain, 1917), 4–11, map; Ellen Lunt Frothingham Ernst, *First Congregational Society of Jamaica Plain, 1769–1909* (Boston, 1909), 34–37; Drake, *Town,* 428; Luther M. Harris, *Robert Harris and His Descendants, with Notices of the Morey and Metcalf Families* (Boston, 1861), 49; Robinson, *Weld Collections,* 106.

24. For secessionist campaigns, see below, chapter 6.

25. Gray, *Half Century Sermon,* 32. At a minimum, ten of the sixteen clerks and tellers listed in the 1850 census worked in Boston, according to *The Roxbury Directory for 1850* (Roxbury, 1850); a work address was shown for only one of the remaining cases.

26. For the early phases of American suburbia, see Robert Fishman, *Bourgeois Utopias: The Rise and Fall of Suburbia* (New York, 1987), 116–54; Kenneth T. Jackson, *Crabgrass Frontier: The Suburbanization of the United States* (New York, 1985), 45–102; and John R. Stilgoe, *Borderland: Origins of the American Suburb, 1820–1939* (New Haven, 1988), 21–161.

27. Binford, *First Suburbs,* table 5.3.

28. Whitcomb, *Annals,* 13–14; George Rogers Taylor, "The Beginnings of Mass Transportation in Urban America: Part II," *Smithsonian Journal of History* 1, no. 2 (1966), 40–43. For early commuting in Charlestown and Cambridge, see Binford, *First Suburbs,* 85–90.

29. *Bulletin of the Railway and Locomotive Society,* Mar. 1924, 1–2.

30. Binford, *First Suburbs,* 84–101; Eric H. Monkkonen, *America Becomes Urban: The Development of U.S. Cities and Towns, 1780–1980* (Berkeley and Los Angeles, 1988), 79–81, 158–76; Charles J. Kennedy, "Commuter Services in the Boston Area, 1835–1860," *Business History Review* 36 (Summer 1962), 157–58; Robert Morse, Jr., *First Congregational Society of Jamaica Plain Reminiscences* (Boston, 1917), 3.

31. Kennedy, "Commuter Services," 161; Binford, *First Suburbs,* 128–29; *Rox-*

bury Directory, 1850, 165–66; Frederic J. Wood, *The Turnpikes of New England* (Boston, 1919), 92–93; C. H. Warren, "Report," *Report of the Directors of the Boston and Providence Railroad Presented at the Annual Meeting of the Stockholders,* 1856 (Boston, 1856), 4.

32. *Roxbury Directory, 1850;* BLC, JP 157A: 28–30 Lakeville Place; Whitcomb, *Annals,* 19; Abner Forbes and J. W. Greene, *Rich Men of Massachusetts* (Boston, 1851), 175; Binford, *First Suburbs,* 98–100.

33. Whitcomb, *Annals,* 19, 27–28; BLC, JP 222: 20 Robinwood Avenue.

34. BLC, JP 34: 9 Brewer, 41: 44 Burroughs; Henry F. Walling, *Map of the County of Norfolk, Massachusetts,* 1859; *WRN,* Oct. 10, 1891. For bank employees as early commuters, see Binford, *First Suburbs,* 131–34.

35. Drake, *Town,* 412, 439; Robert M. Morse, Jr., *Memoir of Hon. Stephen Minot Weld* (Boston, 1868), 6–7.

36. *JPN,* Feb. 23, 1907.

37. NRD, 111:220, 115:226; Grantor, grantee indexes for Samuel G. Goodrich, Mary B. Goodrich, Theophilus Parsons, and John Ashton. Board of Street Commissioners of the City of Boston, *A Record of the Streets, Alleys, Places, Etc., in the City of Boston* (Boston, 1910), 218. BLC, JP 120: 33 and 35 Green Street. United States Bureau of the Census, manuscript schedules for Roxbury, Mass., 1850 (hereinafter cited as Census Bureau, Roxbury schedules). *Roxbury Directory, 1850.*

38. *Roxbury Directory, 1850;* Census Bureau, Roxbury schedules, 1850. James's store was another neighborhood fixture. See Ellen Morse, "A Paper Read by Miss Ellen Morse on her Eightieth Birthday at the Tuesday Club," 1921, typescript, JPL, 2.

39. Gray, *Half Century Sermon,* 16.

40. Binford, *First Suburbs,* 30–41, 157–62; Arthur J. Krim, *Survey of Architectural History in Cambridge, Report Five: Northwest Cambridge* (Cambridge, Mass., 1977), 18–30; William I. Davis, "Industrial History of Suffolk County," *Professional and Industrial History of Suffolk County, Massachusetts,* vol. 3 (Boston, 1894), 428–30, 452; Drake, *Town,* 52; Francis S. Drake, "Roxbury in the Last 100 Years," in *Memorial History of Boston,* ed. Justin Winsor, vol. 3 (Boston, 1881), 578.

41. Drake, *Town,* 386, 428. In 1848 the City of Boston changed its water source to Cochituate Pond. See ibid., 405–6; Acts of the Commonwealth of Massachusetts, 1857, ch. 135, 1886, ch. 199.

42. *Roxbury Directory, 1850,* 128.

43. NRD, 115:240; *Roxbury Directory, 1850;* Charles Whitney, *Map of the Town of Roxbury Surveyed in 1843,* 1843; Walling, *Map of Norfolk County;* BLC, JP 267: 3313 Washington.

44. *Roxbury Directory, 1850;* Census Bureau, Roxbury schedules, 1840, 1850; BLC, JP 133: 14 Grenada Park.

45. Binford, *First Suburbs,* 161–62; Handlin, *Boston's Immigrants,* 91–94, table 7; Ronald Dale Karr, "Brookline and the Making of an Elite Suburb," *Chicago History* 13 (Summer 1984), 37.

46. Gray felt that the most credible explanation was that many Indians who traveled to Roxbury to buy rum were called Jamaica folks after their preferred beverage and that over time the name was applied to the Pond Plain part of town. Although Roxbury's surviving records occasionally mention Indians, the scarcity of references in a town whose minister, John Eliot, was especially interested in native Americans tends to undermine this explanation. Although no more documented than the other theories, the explanation of Francis S. Drake was the most probable. Drake held that the Roxbury Puritans were in some way honoring their fellow Puritan Oliver Cromwell, whose conquest of the Caribbean island took place shortly before residents first made official note of the name. See Thomas Gray, *Half Century Sermon*, 32–33; and Drake, *Town*, 405.

47. Binford, *First Suburbs*, 112–24, 225.

Chapter 2 The Making of an Urban Place

Epigraph: The Church Militant, Oct. 1904, 69.

1. Warner, *Streetcar Suburbs* (ch. 1, n. 2). See also Charles N. Glaab and A. Theodore Brown, *A History of Urban America* (New York, 1967), 155–57, 159; Raymond A. Mohl, *The New City: Urban America in the Industrial Age, 1860–1920* (Arlington Heights, Ill., 1985), 28–29, 37–40; David R. Goldfield and Blaine A. Brownell, *Urban America: A History,* 2d ed. (Boston, 1990), 261–63; Samuel P. Hays, "The Changing Political Structure of the City in Industrial America," in Hays, *American Political History* (intro., n. 6), 328–31. Stuart M. Blumin offers a revisionist version of Warner in *The Emergence of the Middle Class: Social Experience in the American City, 1760–1900* (Cambridge, Mass., 1989), 275–85.

2. Warner, *Streetcar Suburbs*, 15–29, 40, 52–56, 58–64, 67–68, 77–78, 81, 158. Ernest W. Burgess, a founding member of the Chicago school of urban sociology, earlier propounded the theory that urban areas formed homogeneous concentric zones. See Burgess, "The Growth of the City: An Introduction to a Research Project," in *The City* (intro., n. 9), 47–62.

3. Warner, *Streetcar Suburbs*, 42, 53, 62; Margaret Marsh, *Suburban Lives* (New Brunswick, N.J., 1990), 50–51.

4. Alfred D. Chandler, Jr., "The Structure of American Industry in the Twentieth Century: A Historical Overview," *Business History Review* 43 (Autumn 1969), 258–60, 268–69; Harold G. Vatter, "The Position of Small Business in the Structure of American Manufacturing, 1870–1970," in *Small Business in American Life*, ed. Stuart W. Bruchey (New York, 1980), 143–47; Harold G. Livesay, "Lilliputians in Brobdingnag: Small Business in Late-Nineteenth-Century America," in ibid., 338–51; United States Bureau of the Census, *Social Statistics of Cities: New England States, Boston, Massachusetts* (Washington, D.C., 1880), 159–62.

5. Stephan Thernstrom, *The Other Bostonians: Poverty and Progress in the American Metropolis, 1880–1970* (Cambridge, Mass., 1973), 10–21, 38–42. See also Ste-

phan Thernstrom and Peter R. Knights, "Men in Motion: Some Data and Speculations about Urban Population Mobility in Nineteenth-Century America," *Journal of Interdisciplinary History* 1 (1970), 7–35; and Howard P. Chudacoff, *Mobile Americans: Residential and Social Mobility in Omaha, 1880–1920* (New York, 1972).

6. Thernstrom, *Other Bostonians*, 130–38.

7. Warner, *Streetcar Suburbs*, 179.

8. Stilgoe, *Borderland* (ch. 1, n. 26), 151–61; Douglass Shand-Tucci, *Built in Boston: City and Suburb, 1800–1950* (New York, 1978; reprint ed., Amherst, 1988), 73–130.

9. For American suburban history, see ch. 1, n. 26, and Peter G. Rowe, *Making a Middle Landscape* (Cambridge, Mass., 1991). For the working class in Boston's elite suburbs, see Jackson, *Crabgrass Frontier* (ch. 1, n. 26), 99–100; and Karr, "Brookline" (ch. 1, n. 45), 36–47.

10. Theodore Hershberg, Alan N. Burstein, Eugene P. Ericksen, Stephanie W. Greenberg, and William L. Yancey demonstrate a steady shift in the number and proportion of manufacturing jobs to the outer rings of Philadelphia from 1850 to 1970 in "A Tale of Three Cities," in *Philadelphia: Work, Space, Family, and Group Experience in the Nineteenth Century* (New York, 1981), ed. Theodore Hershberg, table 7. See also Olivier Zunz, *The Changing Face of Inequality: Urbanization, Industrial Development, and Immigrants in Detroit, 1880–1920* (Chicago, 1982), 292–302; Harold M. Mayer and Richard C. Wade, *Chicago: Growth of a Metropolis* (Chicago, 1969), 120–23, 234–50, 348–52; and Walter Firey, *Land Use in Central Boston* (Cambridge, Mass., 1947), 84–86.

11. Theodore Hershberg, Dale Light, Jr., Harold E. Cox, and Richard R. Greenfield, "The 'Journey-to-Work': An Empirical Investigation of Work, Residence, and Transportation, Philadelphia, 1850 and 1880," in Hershberg, *Philadelphia*, 128–73; Graham Romeyn Taylor, *Satellite Cities: A Study of Industrial Suburbs* (New York, 1915), 91–164. For ethnic dispersion, see Rudolph J. Vecoli, "The Formation of Chicago's 'Little Italies,'" *Journal of American Ethnic History* 2 (Spring 1983), 5–20; Zunz, *Changing Face*, 136–37, 350.

12. Jon C. Teaford, *City and Suburb: The Political Fragmentation of Metropolitan America, 1850–1970* (Baltimore, 1979), 11–23, quote on 11. See also Joel Schwartz, "Evolution of the Suburbs," in *Suburbia: The American Dream and Dilemma*, ed. Philip C. Dolce (Garden City, N.Y., 1976), 1–36, reprinted in *American Urban History*, ed. Alexander Callow, Jr., 3d ed. (New York, 1982), 499–502.

13. Stilgoe, *Borderland*, 136–38, 143–45; Alan N. Burstein, "Immigrants and Residential Mobility: The Irish and Germans in Philadelphia, 1850–1880," in Hershberg, *Philadelphia*, 178. Taking into account that Philadelphia had more artisans than Boston, the occupational distributions in the northwestern and northeastern outlying areas were roughly comparable to those in Jamaica Plain. In Milwaukee during the same period, physicians, teachers, railroad workers, foremen, and mechanics were overrepresented in the same wards (see Roger D.

Simon, "The City-Building Process: Housing and Services in New Milwaukee Neighborhoods, 1880–1910," *Transactions of the American Philosophical Society* 68 [1978], 22–25). In San Francisco the Mission District and the Western Addition represent relatively heterogeneous neighborhoods (see William Issel and Robert W. Cherny, *San Francisco, 1865–1932: Politics, Power, and Urban Development* [Berkeley and Los Angeles, 1986], 63–68).

14. Robert A. Woods and Albert J. Kennedy, *The Zone of Emergence: Observations of the Lower Middle and Upper Working Class Communities of Boston, 905–1914* (Cambridge, Mass., 1962), 64–65, 122, 165–70; Warner, *Streetcar Suburbs*, 40–41, 106–16.

15. Kennedy, "Commuter Services" (ch. 1, n. 30), 160–61; *Report of the Committee of the Citizens of Dedham Relative to an Advance in Fares* (Dedham, 1856), 8; Warren, "Report," *Report of the Directors* (ch. 1, n. 31), 4.

16. *Report of the Directors,* 1867, 7; Beth Anne Bower, Constance Crosby, and Byron Rushing, Museum of Afro-American History, with Kaiser Engineers, Inc., and Fay, Spofford, & Thorndike, Inc., MBTA SCP, *Report on the Phase II Archaeological Subsurface Testing of the Southwest Corridor Project Area: Part II, Site Reports* (1984), 429.

17. Byron Rushing and Beth Anne Bower, MBTA SCP, *Archaeological Reconnaissance Survey of the Southwest Corridor Project Area (Part One)* (1979), 23. *Report of the Directors,* 1870, 7–8; 1871, 1872; 1873, 6. Warner, *Streetcar Suburbs,* 56.

18. William J. Cunningham, "Transportation in Massachusetts," in *Commonwealth History of Massachusetts,* ed. Albert Bushnell Hart, vol. 5 (New York, 1930), 401–3; George W. Bromley and Walter S. Bromley, *Atlas of the County of Suffolk, Massachusetts* (Philadelphia, 1884), vol. 5, and (1897), vol. 6.

19. Prentiss Cummings, "The Street Railway System of Boston," in Davis, *Professional and Industrial History* (ch. 1, n. 40), 288; Town of West Roxbury, "Selectmen's Records," Rare Books and Manuscripts Department, BPL, vol. 1, Jan. 5, 1857, June 3, 1861, Oct. 5, 27, 1863; *The Brookline, Jamaica Plain, and West Roxbury Directory for 1868* (Boston, 1868), 160. The first horsecar line opened in 1852 and ran from Harvard Square, Cambridge, to Union Square, Somerville.

20. Cummings, "Street Railway System," 290–96; *WRN,* Oct. 10, 1891; *JPN,* Feb. 19, 1910, Sept. 14, 1912.

21. *Brookline, Jamaica Plain, and West Roxbury Directory, 1868;* Taylor, *Satellite Cities,* 18–19, 98–100, 141.

22. William Minot, Jr., *Private Letters of William Minot (1817–1894)* (Boston, 1895), 50, cited in Rocky Lee, "The Role of Real Estate in the Development of 'Woodbourne'" (Seminar paper, Harvard College, May 1989).

23. *JPN,* Sept. 26, 1903, Sept. 29, 1906; August Becker, interview with author, Jamaica Plain, Jan. 18, 1982.

24. *JPN,* Feb. 21, 1903, Aug. 25, 1900, June 25, 1904.

25. For the lower middle class in the historians' model, see Warner, *Streetcar Suburbs,* 53, 62–63. Although the *Brookline, Jamaica Plain, and West Roxbury Di-*

rectory, 1868 included only residents of the Town of West Roxbury, census records from 1860 and 1870 reveal a similar increase in the proportion of middle-class and blue-collar workers in the part of Jamaica Plain that still belonged to the City of Roxbury. Out of 177 work addresses listed for Jamaica Plain residents in the 1880 *Boston City Directory* (Boston, 1880) 61 percent were in Boston, 33 percent in Jamaica Plain, and 6 percent in Roxbury. Although directories overreported the work addresses of white-collar residents, who were most likely to be employed in Boston, they indicate that a large number of residents were locally employed.

26. Thernstrom, *Other Bostonians,* 50; Reed Ueda, *Avenues to Adulthood: The Origins of the High School and Social Mobility in an American Suburb* (Cambridge, 1987), 70. I am grateful to Stephan Thernstrom for providing data on the occupational distribution in Brighton in 1910: high-white-collar, 29 percent; low-white-collar, 13 percent; skilled, 21 percent; low-blue-collar, 29 percent; no occupation, 8 percent.

27. Thernstrom, *Other Bostonians,* table 6.1.

28. Handlin, *Boston's Immigrants* (ch. 1, n. 3), 261. According to the Census Bureau, in 1910 the Irish-born made up 9.8 percent of the total city population of 670,585. *Thirteenth Census of the United States . . . 1910, Volume 2, Population, Reports by States* (Washington, D.C., 1913), 890.

29. Firey, *Land Use in Central Boston,* 78.

30. Walling, *Map of Norfolk County* (ch. 1, n. 34); G. Morgan Hopkins, *Atlas of the County of Suffolk, Massachusetts,* vol. 5 (Philadelphia, 1874); BLC, JP 42: 50 Burroughs. Exceptions to the upper-class tendency were the buildings of the Jamaica Pond Ice Company and the market gardens of George and Joseph Curtis.

31. BLC, JP 94: 28, 96: 48 Eliot, 43: 54, 44: 60 Burroughs, 154: 350 Jamaicaway.

32. BLC, JP 215: 10 Roanoke; Eva Phillips Boyd, *The History of the Loring-Greenough House* (Jamaica Plain, 1957), 7; Greenough, *Descendants of Greenough* (ch. 1, n. 20), 56, 239–45; William H. Sumner, *A History of East Boston* (Boston, 1858); SRD, Grantor, grantee indexes.

33. Eva Phillips Boyd, "Loring-Greenough Appointment Calendar 1940," 1940, typescript, JPL, 4; NRD, 155:230, 233:202, 249:39, 259:293; BLC, JP 4: 20, 5: 28 Alveston, 24–26: 9, 13, 15 Bishop, 241: 109 Sedgewick, 106: 73 Elm, 214: 6 Roanoke; *Boston Transcript,* June 6, 1904.

34. BLC, JP 107: 83 Elm, 212: 10 Revere, 129: 15 Greenough Avenue; see also JP 108–10: 6, 8, 22 Everett, 127–28, 130: 7, 9, 21 Greenough Avenue, 131: 1–2, 132: 5 Greenough Park, 258: 2 Storey Place. The other church on Sumner Hill, the Jamaica Plain Methodist Episcopal Church, was built in 1870.

35. SRD, 2425:9; BLC, JP 124: 2 Greenough Avenue. Lakeville was constructed in 1905, Beaufort Terraces in 1908. See BLC, JP 158: 7–17, 23–33 Lakeville, 6–16, 24–30 Beaufort; *JPN,* May 27, 1905; Shand-Tucci, *Built in Boston,* 101–6, 115–20; Elizabeth Collins Cromley, *Alone Together: A History of New York's Early Apartments* (Ithaca, 1990).

36. Forbes and Greene, *Rich Men* (ch. 1, n. 32), 177; *The Bowditch Family of*

Salem, Massachusetts (Boston, 1936), 7–8, 10; *Brookline, Jamaica Plain, and West Roxbury Directory, 1868; Boston Evening Transcript,* Feb. 20, 1889; Mercedes M. Randall, *Improper Bostonian: Emily Greene Balch* (New York, 1964), 27–28; BLC, JP 62: 991, 63: 1011 Centre, 268: 32 Woodland, 227: 96 Rockwood.

37. BLC, JP 3: 165 Allandale, 22: 22 Avon St.; Edward A. Jones, ed., *Blue Book of Roxbury, Jamaica Plain, and West Roxbury* (Cambridge, Mass., 1899); United States Bureau of the Census, manuscript schedules for Boston, Mass., 1900 (hereinafter cited as Census Bureau, Boston schedules); Robinson, *Weld Collections* (ch. 1, n. 8), 173–74; Isabel Perkins Anderson, *Under the Black Horse Flag* (Boston, 1926); Hopkins, *Atlas;* Bromley and Bromley, *Atlas,* 1884, 1897.

38. Drake, *Town* (ch. 1, n. 6), 230–31; *Roxbury Directory, 1850* (ch. 1, n. 25); BLC, JP 111: 106, 115: 235 Forest Hills; Hopkins, *Atlas;* Greenough, Jones, and Co., *Boston Business Directory, Supplementary Edition* (Boston, Nov. 1872); Robinson, *Weld Collections,* 178; *JPN,* Mar. 9, 1907. Weld was also the treasurer of a New Hampshire cotton mill.

39. *JPN,* Mar. 9, 1907; Alexander Wadsworth, "Glenvale Park," May 16, 1848, NRD, Plan Book 2:17; BLC, JP 73–76: 195, 199, 223, 233 Chestnut Avenue. Weld collaborated with property owner Nehemiah Williams.

40. Bromley and Bromley, *Atlas;* BLC, JP 225: 22 Rockview, 223: 52, 224: 95 Robinwood.

41. BLC, JP 248: 64 Sigourney, 220: 11 Robeson (and see also JP 247: 32 Sigourney, 219: 58, 218: 22–38, 221: 31 Robeson); SRD, 2112:182.

42. Hopkins, *Atlas; Brookline, Jamaica Plain, and West Roxbury Directory, 1868;* BLC, JP 145: 16, 146: 22, 24, 26, 147: 50, 148: 43, 45, 47, 49 Holbrook, 61: 801 Centre, 135: 47 Halifax; City of Boston Listing Board, *List of Residents,* 1922, Ward 22, Precinct 1, Halifax and Moraine Streets.

43. Nearby Roxbury subdistricts included Parker Hill (known today as Mission Hill) and Highland Park.

44. Edwin L. Rand, NRD, 415:296; Edwin Brown, NRD, 405:308; Edmund Farnsworth, NRD, 383:8; Clark Waters, NRD, 422:108; N. B. Chamberlain, NRD, 395:318; BLC, JP 84: 41 Clive; NRD, 415:96; JP 252: 8 Spring Park; *Brookline, Jamaica Plain, and West Roxbury Directory, 1868; Boston City Directory,* 1868–75. For subsequent development, see Census Bureau, Boston schedules, 1880, 1900, 1910, and also JP 27: 16, 28: 18, 29: 33 Boylston, 192: 55, 190: 38, 194: 127, 191: 142–46 Paul Gore, 510: 45 Danforth. For Egleston Square, see BLC, JP 17: Arcadia, 18: 1–5 Atherton Place, 19: 18 Atherton; Hopkins, *Atlas; Boston City Directory,* 1874.

45. For Hyde Square, see NRD, 283: 42; BLC, PH 35: 10, 36: 12–14, 40: 40, 39: 38 Creighton, 58: 3, 11, 15–17, 60: 29 Evergreen, 38: 20 Creighton, 47: 86 Day, 56: 24 Evergreen, 44: 43, 46: 53, 41: 46 Creighton, 48: 120, 122, 124 Day, 1 Mark. For Cedar Hill, see BLC, JP 270: 41 Wyman, 86: 18, 87: 17 Cranston, 244: 34–40 Sheridan, 23: 11 Belmore Terrace, 179: 31, 178: 38 Oakview Terrace.

46. BLC, JP 242: 14 Sheridan; City of Boston Listing Board, *List of Residents,* 1898; *Boston City Directory,* 1866–87.

47. Census Bureau, Boston schedules, 1910; City of Boston Listing Board, *List of Residents*, 1922, Ward 22, Precincts 10 and 11; Peter Rowe and Alexander von Hoffman, "Woodbourne: An Early Garden City Experiment in Affordable Living" (1992).

48. Fred Seaver, "An Address by Fred Seaver before the Jamaica Plain Board of Trade on April 1, 1931," in "Sumner Hill Association Historical Data," typescript, JPL, 13; *JPN*, Mar. 3, 1906; *Brookline, Jamaica Plain, and West Roxbury Directory, 1868*.

49. Walling, *Map of Norfolk County;* NRD, 249:247; *Brookline, Jamaica Plain, and West Roxbury Directory, 1868;* Hopkins, *Atlas*.

50. BLC, JP 707: 172–78, 708: 180 Green, 702: 14 Bismarck, 705: 128 Brookside, 163: 325R Lamartine; Buff and Buff Manufacturing Company, *A Quality Talk* (Boston, n.d.), in author's possession.

51. Orra L. Stone, "The Industries of Metropolitan Boston," in *Metropolitan Boston: A Modern History*, ed. Albert P. Langtry, vol. 2 (New York, 1929), 631–33; Davis, "Industrial History of Suffolk County" (ch. 1, n. 40), 484–85; *JPN*, Mar. 19, May 21, 1904.

52. Walling, *Map of Norfolk County;* Charles Whitney, "Plan of Land at Jamaica Plain, Roxbury, belonging to David S. Greenough, Esq," Aug. 12, 1850, NRD, 343:206; BLC, JP 168: 85, 169: 101–3 McBride, 151: 34, 152: 53 Jamaica; NRD, 221:49; Census Bureau, Boston schedules, 1880, 1900.

53. *Saint Thomas Aquinas, Jamaica Plain, Massachusetts* (Hackensack, N.J., 1970), 4–7.

54. Bromley and Bromley, *Atlas*, 1884, 1897.

55. Hopkins, *Atlas;* Davis, "Industrial History of Suffolk County," 476–77; Gallus Thomann, "The Brewing Industry in New England," in *The New England States*, ed. William T. Davis (Boston, 1897), 2288–93; Bower et al., MBTA SCP, *Report on Phase II Testing, Part II, Site Reports*, 280–312, 331–46; Beth Anne Bower and Sheila Charles, MBTA SCP, *The Highland Foundry Site, Roxbury, Massachusetts* (1988); Beth Anne Bower, Sheila Charles, and John Cheney, MBTA SCP, *The Guild and White Company Tannery Site, Roxbury, Massachusetts* (1987); *JPN*, Aug. 1, 1903. Bradley later moved to a church at Walden and Centre streets (later St. Andrew's Methodist Episcopal Church on Heath Street).

56. Thomann, "Brewing Industry"; BLC, PH 705: 123–25, 706: 294A, 704: 31 Heath; *JPN*, July 14, 1900; Bromley and Bromley, *Atlas*, 1884.

57. Drake, *Town*, 398; BLC, JP 700: 55–71 Amory, 701: 76 Atherton; *JPN*, Mar. 24, 1906.

58. BLC, JP 12: 223–41, 248–60 Amory, 704: 21–35 Bismarck; *Boston Transcript*, July 5, 1916; Hopkins, *Atlas;* Census Bureau, Boston schedules, 1880.

59. Prescott Farnworth Hall, "The Building Situation in Brookline" (address to the Brookline Civic Society, May 31, 1916), in Hall, *Immigration and Other Interests of Prescott Farnworth Hall* (New York, 1922), 42; Marion C. Balch, "History of the Jamaica Plain Neighborhood House," 1953, typescript, JPL, 28; BLC, PH 501: 361 Centre.

60. Shand-Tucci, *Built in Boston*, 120–27; Krim, *Survey* (ch. 1, n. 40), 76–78; idem, *Three-Deckers of Dorchester: An Architectural Historical Survey* (Boston, 1977); BLC, JP 61: 801 Centre/6 Holbrook, 36: 66, 68 Brookside.

61. *Roxbury Directory, 1850;* Morse, "Paper" (ch. 1, n. 38), 5.

62. *JPN,* Mar. 7, 1903, 3.

63. Walling, *Map of Norfolk County; Brookline, Jamaica Plain, and West Roxbury Directory, 1868;* Hopkins, *Atlas.*

64. *WRN,* Oct. 10, 1891; *JPN,* June 3, 1899; BLC, JP 403: 45 Green.

65. *Brookline, Jamaica Plain, and West Roxbury Directory, 1868.*

66. Hopkins, *Atlas;* Bromley and Bromley, *Atlas,* 1884; *Brookline, Jamaica Plain, and West Roxbury Directory, 1868;* Sanborn Map and Publishing Company, *Boston, Roxbury, West Roxbury, and Parts of Brighton and Brookline, Vol. 3* (New York, 1888); Sanborn-Perris Map Company, *Insurance Maps of Boston, Mass., Vol. 7* (New York, 1898); BLC, JP 7: 3 Alveston, 400: 701–5, 401: 707–11, 402: 743–45 Centre; BLC, PH 400: 331–33 Centre; SRD, 2257:495.

67. *Brookline, Jamaica Plain, and West Roxbury Directory, 1868;* Hopkins, *Atlas;* Bromley and Bromley, *Atlas,* 1884, 1897; *JPN,* 1899–1912, passim; BLC, JP 122: 183–87, 123: 189–95 Green.

68. *WRN,* Oct. 10, 1891; *JPN,* June 3, 1899; BLC, JP 403: 45 Green. Cahill designed the Hotel McKinley and also 701 Centre Street. See BLC, JP 123: 189–95 Green.

69. *JPN,* Dec. 23, 1899, June 16, 1900.

Chapter 3   *The Paradox of Parks*

Epigraphs: [William Augustus Crafts,] *Forest Hills Cemetery: Establishment, Progress, Scenery, Monuments, Etc.* (Boston, 1860), 159; *Twenty-second Annual Report of the Board of Commissioners of the Department of Parks for the Year Ending January 31, 1897* (Boston, 1897), 59–60, hereinafter cited as *[Twenty-second] Annual Park Commissioners' Report for [year].*

1. David Schuyler, *The New Urban Landscape: The Redefinition of City Form in Nineteenth-Century America* (Baltimore, 1986).

2. Stephen Hardy, *How Boston Played: Sport, Recreation, and Community, 1865– 1915* (Boston, 1982), 64–84; Rosenzweig, *Eight Hours* (intro., n. 4), 127–52; Couvares, *Remaking of Pittsburgh* (intro., n. 4), 106–8.

3. Tamara Plakins Thornton, *Cultivating Gentlemen: The Meaning of Country Life among the Boston Elite, 1785–1860* (New Haven, 1989), 21–56; Frederic Cople Jaher, *The Urban Establishment: Upper Strata in Boston, New York, Charleston, Chicago, and Los Angeles* (Urbana, 1982), 29–37, 56–65, 222–45; Paul Goodman, "Ethics and Enterprise: The Values of a Boston Elite, 1800–1860," *American Quarterly* 18 (Fall 1966), 437–51.

4. Thornton, *Cultivating Gentlemen,* 57–77.

5. Stilgoe, *Borderland* (ch. 1, n. 26), 93–123; Ulysses Prentiss Hedrick, *A History*

of Agriculture in the State of New York (Albany, 1933), 384; Henry Boyd, *A History of the Pennsylvania Horticultural Society, 1827–1927* (Philadelphia, 1929), 34–40, 382–83; Luther Farnham and Robert Manning, *History of the Massachusetts Horticultural Society, 1829–1878* (Boston, 1880), 47, 498–501.

6. Henry Alexander Scammel Dearborn, *An Address Delivered before the Massachusetts Horticultural Society, on the Celebration of the First Anniversary, September 19, 1829* (Boston, 1833), 4; "Report of the Corresponding Secretary of the Pennsylvania Horticultural Society, 1832," *American Farmer,* Dec. 7, 1832, 309, reprinted in Boyd, *Pennsylvania Horticultural Society,* 62.

7. Dearborn, *Address,* 4, 10–11; Malthus Ward, *An Address Pronounced Before the Massachusetts Horticultural Society in Commemoration of its Third Annual Festival, September 21, 1831* (Boston, 1833), 14; John Lewis Russell, *A Discourse Delivered before the Massachusetts Horticultural Society in Celebration of Its Seventh Anniversary, September 17, 1835* (Boston, 1835); John C. Gray, *An Address Delivered before the Massachusetts Horticultural Society at their Sixth Anniversary, September 17, 1834* (Boston, 1834), 9; Alexander Everett, *An Address Delivered before the Massachusetts Horticultural Society at their Fifth Annual Festival, September 18, 1833* (Boston, 1833), 4.

8. Thornton, *Cultivating Gentlemen,* 147–72. For moral philosophy and the theory of the sublime in nineteenth-century America, see Daniel Walker Howe, *The Unitarian Conscience: Harvard Moral Philosophy, 1805–1861* (Cambridge, Mass., 1970); William Charvat, *The Origins of American Critical Thought, 1810–1835* (Philadelphia, 1936; New York, 1961); Roger B. Stein, *John Ruskin and Aesthetic Thought in America, 1840–1900* (Cambridge, Mass., 1967), ch. 1; Barbara Novak, *Nature and Culture: American Landscape and Painting, 1825–1875* (New York, 1980).

9. Russell, *Discourse,* 7; George Lunt, "An Address Delivered before the Massachusetts Horticultural Society on the Dedication of Horticultural Hall, May 15, 1845," in *Transactions of the Massachusetts Horticultural Society for the Years 1843–4–5–6* (Boston, 1847), 7–8; Ward, *Address,* 33.

10. For the influence of English landscape styles in nineteenth-century America, see Andrew Jackson Downing, *A Treatise on the Theory and Practice of Landscape Gardening Adapted to North America; with a view to the Improvement of Country Residences* (New York, 1841); Robert Morris Copeland, *Country Life* (Boston, 1859); Norman T. Newton, *Design on the Land: The Development of Landscape Architecture* (Cambridge, Mass., 1971), 207–32, 259–306 ff.; and Cynthia Zaitzevsky, *Frederick Law Olmsted and the Boston Park System* (Cambridge, Mass., 1982), 19–32 ff.

11. Drake, *Town* (ch. 1, n. 6), 231; Farnham and Manning, *History,* 52, 246–47; Walter Muir Whitehill, "Francis Parkman as Horticulturist," *Arnoldia* 33 (May–June 1973), 173–74; Whitcomb, *Annals* (ch. 1, n. 6), 28.

12. Smith, "Peter Parley" (ch. 1, n. 21), 304–15; NRD, 130:23, 40; Downing, *Treatise on Landscape Gardening,* 4th ed. (1850), 54–56.

13. "Benjamin Bussey," *Dedham Historical Register* 10 (July 1899), 71–75; "Will of Benjamin Bussey, of Roxbury," reprinted in *Report of the Special Committee of the Common Council on the Arnold Arboretum,* City of Boston City Doc. No. 134-1881 (Boston, 1882), 21; Thomas Gray, *Tribute to the Memory of Benjamin Bussey, Esq.* (Boston, 1842); Inventory of Benjamin Bussey's Estate, Administration 3016, Norfolk County Registry of Probate, Dedham, Mass. (Apr. 30, 1842), 3–14. See also the depiction of Bussey as Christopher Burt in George Williams Curtis's *Trumps* (serialized in *Harper's Weekly,* Apr. 9, 1859–Jan. 21, 1860; published, New York, 1861); *JPN,* Feb. 18, 1899.

14. Gray, *Tribute;* "Will of Benjamin Bussey," 5–6, 19–20.

15. "Benjamin Bussey," 74; Whitcomb, *Annals,* 52–53.

16. Richard F. Fuller, "Memorial of Mrs. Margaret Fuller," in *Memoirs of Margaret Fuller Ossoli,* William Henry Channing, Ralph Waldo Emerson, and James Freeman Clarke, 2 vols. (Boston, 1884; reprint ed., 2 vols. in 1, New York, 1972), 1:381–82; William Henry Channing, "Jamaica Plain," ibid., 2:34–35.

17. William Morton Wheeler, "The Bussey Institution, 1871–1929," in *The Development of Harvard University since the Inauguration of President Eliot, 1869–1929,* ed. Samuel Eliot Morison (Cambridge, Mass., 1930), 508–10.

18. Wheeler, "Bussey Institution," 508–9, 512–17; *Annual Report of the President and Treasurer of Harvard College, 1870–1871,* 26–28, *1871–1872,* 32, *1878–1879,* 34–36; Karl Sax, "The Bussey Institution," *Arnoldia* 7 (1947), 13–16.

19. Farnham and Manning, *History,* 101–2, 110–11. For the history of Mount Auburn Cemetery and rural cemeteries in general, see Stanley French, "The Cemetery as Cultural Institution: The Establishment of Mount Auburn and the 'Rural Cemetery' Movement," in *Death in America,* ed. David E. Stannard (Philadelphia, 1975), 69–91; Blanche Linden-Ward, *Silent City on a Hill: Landscapes of Memory and Boston's Mount Auburn Cemetery* (Columbus, 1989); David Charles Sloane, *The Last Great Necessity: Cemeteries in American History* (Baltimore, 1991), 44–64, 73–75.

20. [Crafts,] *Forest Hills Cemetery,* 17–23, 173–74; Drake, *Town,* 95–97, 211. For a brief account of the establishment of Forest Hills Cemetery, see Linden-Ward, *Silent City,* 331–32.

21. Dearborn also hoped to acquire the landscaped estate of John Collins Warren for the cemetery. [Crafts,] *Forest Hills Cemetery,* 18–20, 187–89.

22. Carl Seaburg and Stanley Paterson, *Merchant Prince of Boston: Colonel T. H. Perkins, 1764–1854* (Cambridge, Mass., 1971), 318–19; Henry A. S. Dearborn, *A Report of the Trustees of the Roxbury Athenaeum, made to the Proprietors at the Annual Meeting, Held on the First of January, 1849* (Roxbury, 1849), 8–9. Dearborn (1783–1851), a minor but fascinating figure in American political and cultural history, has not yet found a biographer. See *Dictionary of American Biography,* s.v. "Dearborn, Henry Alexander Scammell"; George Putnam, *Address Delivered Before the City Government and Citizens of Roxbury on the Life and Character of the Late Henry A. S. Dearborn* (Roxbury, 1851); Henry A. S. Dearborn, Collected

Works, New York Public Library, New York, N.Y.; Henry A. S. Dearborn Correspondence, Rare Books and Manuscripts Department, BPL; Henry A. S. Dearborn Correspondence, Massachusetts Historical Society. See also Linden-Ward, *Silent City,* 123 and passim.

23. Dearborn, *Writings on Horticulture and Other Branches of Rural Industry* (Roxbury, 1844), introduction and passim; idem, "Agriculture in Norfolk," Dec. 18, 1848, in *Writings on Various Subjects,* vol. 7 (Roxbury, 1849), item 19, New York Public Library.

24. Dearborn, *An Address Delivered on the VII of October, MDCCCXXX, the Second Centennial Anniversary of the Settlement of Roxbury* (Roxbury, 1830), 5–38.

25. Farnham and Manning, *History,* 72–73, 86–90, 95; Linden-Ward, *Silent City,* 199–203; Schuyler, *New Urban Landscape,* 42–50; *Guide to Laurel Hill Cemetery Near Philadelphia* (Philadelphia, 1847), 15.

26. [Crafts,] *Forest Hills Cemetery,* 25–26; *First Annual Report of the Board of Commissioners of Forest Hills Cemetery* (Roxbury, 1849), 14–15; idem, *Second Annual Report* (Roxbury, 1850), 2–3.

27. "Address of Joseph Story," in Jacob Bigelow, *A History of the Cemetery of Mount Auburn* (Boston, 1860), 156–57; [Crafts,] *Forest Hills Cemetery,* 152.

28. Joseph Addison, "Westminster Abbey" and "Reflections on Bills of Mortality," *Spectator,* nos. 26 (Mar. 30, 1711) and 289 (July 31, 1712); Washington Irving, *The Sketchbook of Geoffrey Crayon, Gent.,* rev. ed. (New York, 1864), 198–99; Zebedee Cook, *Address Pronounced before the Massachusetts Horticultural Society in Commemoration of its Second Annual Festival, the 10th of September, 1830* (Boston, 1830), 27; Linden-Ward, *Silent City,* 131–48; George Putnam, "Address," in [Crafts,] *Forest Hills Cemetery,* 63–64; [Crafts,] *Forest Hills Cemetery,* 66, 180.

29. Dearborn had intended to build a monument to George Washington on the highest hill in Mount Auburn Cemetery. *Report of the Joint Standing Committee on Burial Grounds,* City of Roxbury City Doc. No. 7 (Roxbury, 1847); Marchant de Beaumont, *History of Père la Chaise,* trans. H. A. S. Dearborn, in "Proceedings of the Massachusetts Horticultural Society, 1833," in *Transactions of the Massachusetts Horticultural Society, 1829–1838* (Boston, 1847); *First Annual Report of the Commissioners of Forest Hills Cemetery,* 5–6; John Collins Warren to Henry A. S. Dearborn, Feb. 9, 1849, Dearborn Correspondence, BPL; [Crafts,] *Forest Hills Cemetery,* 186, Linden-Ward, *Silent City,* 65–130..

30. Ann Douglas, "Heaven Our Home: Consolation Literature in the Northern United States, 1830–1880," in Stannard, *Death,* 49–68; [Crafts,] *Forest Hills Cemetery,* 136, 140; *Boston Almanac,* 1858, 40.

31. Most of Craft's examples of those who felt the moral influence of the cemetery, however, were upper-middle-class types. See [Crafts,] *Forest Hills Cemetery,* 10–11, 152. Cf. Cook, *Address,* 27–28; and Amy Louise Reed, *The Background of Gray's Elegy: A Study in the Taste for Melancholy Poetry, 1700–1751* (1924; reprint ed., New York, 1962), 113–87.

32. *Third Annual Report of the Commissioners of Forest Hills Cemetery* (Roxbury,

1851), 68; *Fifth Annual Report of the Commissioners of Forest Hills Cemetery* (Roxbury, 1853), 1.

33. [Crafts,] *Forest Hills Cemetery,* 162–63, 210–11. Misconduct also plagued Mount Auburn. See Bigelow, *History of Mt. Auburn,* 202; and Andrew Jackson Downing, "Public Cemeteries and Public Gardens," *Horticulturist* 4 (July 1849), 9–10.

34. *First Annual Report of the Commissioners of Forest Hills Cemetery,* 9; *Thirty-second Annual Report of the Trustees of the Proprietors of Forest Hills Cemetery* (Boston, 1900), 4–5, 38–39; Sloane, *Last Great Necessity,* 109.

35. Schuyler, *New Urban Landscape,* 101–46.

36. Linden-Ward, *Silent City,* 175–78, 250–53; Zaitzevsky, *Olmsted,* 141–44.

37. Hugh M. Raup, "The Genesis of the Arnold Arboretum," *Bulletin of Popular Information,* 4th ser., 8 (Apr. 26, 1940), 1–3; Downing, *Treatise on Landscape Gardening,* 57; Forbes and Greene, *Rich Men* (ch. 1, n. 32), 177.

38. Raup, "Genesis," 7–9; George B. Emerson to Charles W. Eliot, Dec. 8, 1869, Charles W. Eliot Collection, Harvard University Archives, Cambridge, Mass.; Charles Sprague Sargent, "The First Fifty Years of the Arnold Arboretum," *Journal of the Arnold Arboretum* 3 (Jan. 1922), 127.

39. Raup, "Genesis," 3–4; *Dictionary of American Biography,* s.v. "Emerson, George Barrell."

40. George B. Emerson, *A Report on the Trees and Shrubs Growing Naturally in the Forests of Massachusetts* (Boston, 1875), 8–12, 42–43.

41. Stephanne B. Sutton, *Charles Sprague Sargent and the Arnold Arboretum* (Cambridge, Mass., 1970), 3–7, 19–49, 109–14, 124–25, 190–92.

42. Sargent, "Arnold Arboretum," 4; Zaitzevsky, *Olmsted,* 60; Sutton, *Sargent,* 55–57, 60–62; *PCCB,* Oct. 13, Nov. 7, Dec. 1, 15, 1881.

43. Sargent, *Annual Report of the Arnold Arboretum to the President and Fellows of Harvard College for 1884–1885* (Cambridge, Mass., 1886), 3; idem, "Arnold Arboretum," 2; "Letter to the President of the Horticultural Club of Boston," *Horticulture* 14 (Oct. 21, 1911), 559; W. T. Councilman, "Charles Sprague Sargent, 1841–1927," in *Later Years of the Saturday Club, 1870 to 1920,* ed. M. A. DeWolfe Howe (Boston, 1927), 289; Sutton, *Sargent,* 38–39, 184, 186.

44. *Garden and Forest,* Feb. 6, 1889, 61–62. See also the work of Sargent's friend Mariana G. Van Rensselaer, *Art Out-Of-Doors* (New York, 1893).

45. Sutton, *Sargent,* 68–71, 183–84; Zaitzevsky, *Olmsted,* 63. For a detailed analysis of the plan and its precedents, see ibid., 141–47.

46. "The Administration of Public Parks," *Garden and Forest,* Feb. 6, 1889, 61–62; *Boston Evening Transcript,* Mar. 23, 1927; Sutton, *Sargent,* 53–54, 338–39.

47. *JPN,* July 8, 1899. The *Jamaica Plain News* reprinted an "excellent suggestion" that the plants at the Arnold Arboretum be labeled with their common names as well as their botanical ones so that the ordinary people could understand them (July 14, 1900).

48. *Parks for the People: Proceedings of a Public Meeting held at Faneuil Hall, June*

7, *1876* (Boston, 1876); *Second Annual Park Commissioners' Report for 1876,* 30.

49. For a detailed account of Olmsted's intentions for Franklin Park, see Alexander von Hoffman, "'Of Greater Lasting Consequence': Frederick Law Olmsted and the Fate of Franklin Park, Boston," *Journal of the Society of Architectural Historians* 47 (Dec. 1988), 339–50. For Olmsted as a sophisticated moral reformer, see Thomas Bender, *Toward an Urban Vision: Ideas and Institutions in Nineteenth Century America* (Lexington, Ky., 1975), 164–87; and Paul Boyer, *Urban Masses and Moral Order in America, 1820–1920* (Cambridge, Mass., 1978), 237–40.

50. Charles Capen McLaughlin, "Biographical Directory," in McLaughlin, ed., *The Papers of Frederick Law Olmsted: Volume I, The Formative Years, 1822–1852* (Baltimore, 1977), 77–79; Olmsted to John Hull Olmsted, June 23, 1845, ibid., 219; Olmsted to Frederic Kingsbury, June 12, 1846, ibid., 243.

51. Geoffrey Blodgett, "Frederick Law Olmsted: Landscape Architecture as Conservative Reform," *Journal of American History* 62, no. 4 (1976), 871–77; Laura Wood Roper, *FLO: A Biography of Frederick Law Olmsted* (Baltimore, 1973), 19–20, 59–75.

52. Olmsted designed Prospect Park in Brooklyn (1866–67), Delaware Park in Buffalo (1868), the South Parks in Chicago (1871), and Belle Isle Park in Detroit (1882). For a survey and chronological selection of Olmsted's works, see Albert Fein, *Frederick Law Olmsted and the American Environmental Tradition* (New York, 1972).

53. Two works that greatly influenced Olmsted were Johann Georg von Zimmermann, *Solitude* (London, 1800), and John Ruskin, *Modern Painters,* 5 vols. (London, 1843–60). See Roper, *FLO,* 10–11, 35, 345, 408, 521n; Olmsted to John Hull Olmsted, Feb. 2, 1845, *Olmsted Papers, Vol. I,* 203. The quotation is from Frederick Law Olmsted, "Public Parks and the Enlargement of Towns," *Journal of Social Science* 3 (1871), 24.

54. Olmsted to Parke Godwin, Aug. 1, 1859, *The Papers of Frederick Law Olmsted: Volume III, Creating Central Park, 1857–1861,* ed. Charles Beveridge and David Schuyler (Baltimore, 1983), 201; Frederick Law Olmsted, "The Justifying Value of a Public Park," *Journal of Social Science Containing the Transactions of the American Association of Social Science* 12 (1880), 163; Blodgett, "Olmsted," 869–89.

55. Olmsted, "Public Parks," 14–15; idem, "Justifying Value," 162–63; idem, *Notes on the Plan of Franklin Park and Other Related Matters* (Boston, 1886), 41–46.

56. Olmsted, "Public Parks," 24, 34; idem, *Notes,* 101, 103.

57. Olmsted, *Notes,* 46–47.

58. Ibid., 47–48; Elizabeth Gaskell, "Libbie Marsh's Three Eras," originally published in *Hewitt's Journal* in 1847, republished as "A Lancashire Tale" in 1850, in *The Works of Mrs. Gaskell,* 8 vols. (London, 1906; reprint ed., New York, 1972), 1:lxxiv, 474–79.

59. Olmsted, "Public Parks," 14–15, 22–24; Frederick Law Olmsted and Calvert Vaux, "A Review of Recent Changes, and Changes Which Have Been Projected, in the Plans of the Central Park," in *Forty Years of Landscape Architec-*

ture: Central Park, ed. Frederick Law Olmsted, Jr., and Theodora Kimball (1928; reprint ed., Cambridge, Mass., 1973), 250.

60. Olmsted, "Public Parks," 22–24; idem, *Notes,* 46.

61. Olmsted, *Notes,* 46; Zaitzevsky, *Olmsted,* 77, 176–81; *Sixteenth Annual Park Commissioners' Report for 1890,* 36–37.

62. Olmsted, *Notes,* 43, 45, 53, 60–61, 114.

63. Ibid., General Plan, 53, 56–61; Olmsted to A. Hyatt, Mar. 24, 1889, cited in Zaitzevsky, *Olmsted,* 234 n. 50; Schuyler, *New Urban Landscape,* 121–22, 124–25; Francis R. Kowsky, "Municipal Parks and City Planning: Frederick Law Olmsted's Buffalo Park and Parkway System," *Journal of the Society of Architectural Historians* 46 (Mar. 1987), 52–60.

64. Olmsted, *Notes,* 49; Zaitzevsky, *Olmsted,* 70.

65. *JPN,* Oct. 14, 1899, July 14, 1900; Minutes of the Board of Commissioners of the Department of Parks of the City of Boston, Sept. 11, 1899, Records of the Boston Parks Department, Boston City Hall.

66. *Fourteenth Annual Park Commissioners' Report for 1888,* 29; *Fifteenth Annual Park Commissioners' Report for 1889,* 44–47; Minutes of the Board of Commissioners of the Department of Parks of the City of Boston, May 12, 1890; George H. Sargent, "Golfing Around The Hub," *Outing* 34 (May 1899), 131–32. For golf links and golfers, see, e.g., *JPN,* Apr. 7, 1900, Apr. 21, Aug. 29, 1903; Rosenzweig, *Eight Hours,* 127–52; and Hardy, *How Boston Played,* 64–84.

67. *Boston Globe,* July 5, 1891; Hardy, *How Boston Played,* 158; *JPN,* Sept. 9, 23, Oct. 4, 7, Nov. 4, 1899; *Twenty-second Annual Park Commissioners' Report for Year Ending January 31, 1897,* 59–60.

68. *JPN,* May 16, July 11, ("baseball crazy") Aug. 29, Sept. 26, 1903; *Thirtieth Annual Park Commissioners' Report for Year Ending January 31, 1905,* 19.

69. Hardy, *How Boston Played,* 85–106; *JPN,* Jan. 2, 1909.

70. Zaitzevsky, *Olmsted,* 83–86. Leverett Park, half of which belonged to the Town of Brookline, centered on two small ponds, Leverett Pond and Ward's Pond. In his design of 1892, Olmsted placed paths around the ponds and a large meadow between them.

71. Drake, *Town,* 404–5, 415–17, 426–29; *Report of a Committee of the Town of West Roxbury in Relation to Jamaica Pond* (Boston, 1859), 10–13; Howard Chandler Robbins, *The Life of Paul Revere Frothingham* (Boston, 1935), 1–5, 9; Morse, "Paper" (ch. 1, n. 38), 8; *Boston Globe,* July 6, 1876; Seaver, "Address" (ch. 2, n. 48), 9–10. According to Fred Seaver, he and his father and brother had once secretly transplanted pickerels in the pond from the Charles River.

72. *Second Annual Park Commissioners' Report for 1876,* 29–30.

73. *Seventeenth Annual Park Commissioners' Report for Year Ending January 31, 1892,* 21; *Eighteenth Annual Park Commissioners' Report for . . . January 31, 1893,* 21; Zaitzevsky, *Olmsted,* 88–90.

74. Zaitzevsky, *Olmsted,* 88–89.

75. Frederick Law Olmsted, "A Healthy Change in the Tone of the Human

Heart," *Century Illustrated Monthly Magazine* 32 (Oct. 1886), 964–65; "Quiet in West Roxbury," *Boston Globe,* July 5, 1894.

76. *JPN,* July 8, Oct. 7, 1899, Sept. 4, 1900.

77. *Opinion of the Board of Park Commissioners on Advisability of Locating a Bathhouse at Jamaica Pond,* City of Boston City Doc. No. 69-1902 (Boston, 1902), 2; *JPN,* Mar. 3, June 16, Dec. 1, 1900, Feb. 27, 1904.

Chapter 4 Neighborhood Business Ties

Epigraph: Thirty-first Annual Report of the Jamaica Plain Gas Light Company for the Year Ending March 31, 1886 (Boston, 1886), 5–6.

1. Park and Burgess mention the creation of sub-business centers only briefly (p. 52) in their seminal work on the structure of urban society, *The City* (intro., n. 9). Similarly, reviews of economics and geography literature such as Alan W. Evans, *Urban Economics* (Oxford, 1985), and David Ley, *A Social Geography of the City* (New York, 1983), stress other issues.

2. Stuart W. Bruchey, *Enterprise: The Dynamic Economy of a Free People* (Cambridge, Mass., 1990), 317–19; James H. Soltow, "Origins of Small Business and the Relationships between Large and Small Firms: Metal Fabricating and Machinery Making in New England, 1890–1957," in Bruchey, *Small Business* (ch. 2, n. 4), 192–211; Roland I. Robinson, "The Financing of Small Business in the United States," ibid., 287–89.

3. Town of West Roxbury, "Mortgages," 2 vols., Rare Books and Manuscripts Department, BPL.

4. West Roxbury, "Mortgages," 1:129, 131, 139–40. For investment patterns of nineteenth-century commercial merchants in general, see Glenn Porter and Harold C. Livesay, *Merchants and Manufactures: Studies in the Changing Structure of Nineteenth-Century Marketing* (Baltimore, 1971), 72–77.

5. Peter R. Decker, *Fortunes and Failures: White Collar Mobility in Nineteenth-Century San Francisco* (Cambridge, Mass., 1978), 100; Michael B. Katz, *The People of Hamilton, Canada West: Family and Class in a Mid-Nineteenth-Century City* (Cambridge, Mass., 1975), 190–91; West Roxbury, "Mortgages," 1:10, 156, 574.

6. Katz, *People of Hamilton,* 193; West Roxbury, "Mortgages," 1:166, 168, 176, 285.

7. West Roxbury, "Mortgages," 1:272, 456. It took Byron eight years to pay off his mortgage and recover the ownership of his factory.

8. Ibid., 1:407, 526.

9. Clyde Griffen and Sally Griffen, *Natives and Newcomers: The Ordering of Opportunity in Mid-Nineteenth-Century Poughkeepsie* (Cambridge, Mass., 1978), 103–17; Blumin, *Urban Threshold* (intro., n. 8), 207–11.

10. Rudolf F. Haffenreffer, *Letters to Home, 1864–1879* (Privately printed, 1967), 5–7, 13–45 passim.

11. Ibid., 39–40, 49, 62.

12. Davis, "Industrial History" (ch. 1, n. 40), 476–77.

13. Ibid.; Census Bureau, *Social Statistics of Cities* (ch. 2, n. 4).

14. Haffenreffer, *Letters,* 58, 62.

15. Ibid., 59, 62–65, 70, 72–73, 75, 93, 117.

16. Haffenreffer, *Letters,* 70–71, 73, 93; West Roxbury, "Mortgages," 2:242. In 1874 Haffenreffer invited his parents to move from Germany to Jamaica Plain because it was "lovelier here in almost every way, especially also in religion." Mrs. Franz von Euw, a widow, of the same address as Franz von Euw, ran a saloon, which was no doubt the connection between the two men.

17. Haffenreffer, *Letters,* 71, 74–75, 77; West Roxbury, "Mortgages," 2:287; *Boston Transcript,* Feb. 15, 1916; Boston city directories; Hopkins, *Atlas* (ch. 2, n. 30); Massachusetts, vol. 16, p. 71, R. G. Dun and Company Collection, Baker Library, Harvard University, Graduate School of Business Administration, Boston, Mass.

18. Haffenreffer, *Letters,* 8, 80, 87, 92, 107, 121; Hopkins, *Atlas;* Bromley and Bromley, *Atlas* (ch. 2, n. 18), 1884, 1897.

19. Mansell G. Blackford, "Small Business in America: A Historiographic Survey," *Business History Review* 65 (Spring 1991), 4; Soltow, "Origins of Small Business," 201; *American Shoemaking* 3, no. 14 (1910), 741. For the extensive Plant Company employee programs, see below, chapter 5, and Barry H. Rodrigue, "Thomas G. Plant: The Making of a Franco-American Industrialist, 1859–1941" (Master's thesis, University of Maine, 1992), 83–93.

20. Census Bureau, Roxbury schedules, 1850, 1860; Hopkins, *Atlas;* BLC, JP 133: 14 Grenada Park; Haffenreffer *Letters,* 69–70, 73, 76.

21. *Roxbury Directory, 1850; Brookline, Jamaica Plain, and West Roxbury Directory, 1868;* Boston city directories; J. B. Shields, *Map of the City and Vicinity of Boston, Massachusetts* (1852); Walling, *Map of Norfolk County* (ch. 1, n. 34); Hopkins, *Atlas;* Bromley and Bromley, *Atlas,* 1884, 1897; "Tax List for the Year 1872," in Town of West Roxbury, *Assessors' Report* (Boston, 1872); BLC, JP 109: 8 Everett, 76: 233 Chestnut; Haffenreffer, *Letters,* 9, 70, 103; *JPN,* Jan. 7, 1911.

22. *Official Reports of the Town of West Roxbury,* 1851–74, hereinafter cited individually as *West Roxbury Reports for [year].* Jackson also served for many years as town assessor, and Dolan served as official sealer of leather.

23. [Robert H. Marshall, Jr.,] *Trinity Lutheran Church Souvenir History, 100th Anniversary, 1871–1971* (Framingham, Mass., 1972), 7, 9, 53; Herbert Pierce to David Wolkoff, private communication, May 18, 1988; *JPN,* Nov. 4, 1899, Jan. 7, 1911.

24. Massachusetts Bureau of Labor Statistics, "Trade Union Directory," *Massachusetts Labor Bulletin* 24 (Nov. 1902), 112–15. The directory list changed from year to year, but Jamaica Plain was consistently one of the neighborhoods given as an address for local business agents.

25. Herbert Gutman, "Class, Community, and Power in Nineteenth-Century

American Cities: Paterson, New Jersey, a Case Study," in, *Work, Culture, and Society in Industrializing America* (New York, 1977), 234–60; *JPN,* Dec. 23, 1899, Jan. 27, 1900, Mar. 3, 1906; *Boston Globe,* Apr. 3, 12, 13, 1902.

26. *JPN,* Sept. 5, 1903, Jan. 5, 1907, Apr. 30, 1910.

27. Gans, *Urban Villagers* (intro., n. 7), 117, 160–61. In her classic critique of urban planning, *The Death and Life of Great American Cities* (New York, 1961), Jane Jacobs equated the presence of local shops with the vitality of neighborhood life.

28. St. John's (Episcopal Church), *Centenary Celebration, 1841–1941* (Jamaica Plain, 1941), 2, 15; *Boston Transcript,* Feb. 15, 1888; West Roxbury, "Mortgages," 2:49–50; Boston city directories; BLC, JP 400: 701–5 Centre; *Leading Businessmen of the Back Bay, South End, Boston, Highlands, Jamaica Plain, and Dorchester* (Boston, 1888), 217; *JPN,* Aug. 21, 1912. Until it went out of business in the 1970s, Charles B. Rogers and Company was said to be the longest continually operating drug store in the United States.

29. Stephan Thernstrom, *Poverty and Progress: Social Mobility in a Nineteenth Century City* (Cambridge, Mass., 1964), 80, 142–44, 177–78; idem, *Other Bostonians* (ch. 2, n. 5), 111–44; Griffen and Griffen, *Natives and Newcomers,* 121–22.

30. Lewis Atherton, *Main Street on the Middle Border* (Bloomington, 1954), 43–49; Seaver, "Address" (ch. 2, n. 48), 13; Morse, "Paper" (ch. 1, n. 38), 2.

31. West Roxbury, "Mortgages," 2:394. For debts to grocers Alden Bartlett, Robert Seaver, and George James, see ibid., 2:80, 102, 284, 333.

32. *Boston Transcript,* Mar. 14, 1928; Walter Bleiler, interview with author, North Abington, Mass., June 6, 1978; August Becker, interview, Jan. 18, 1982; Boston city directories.

33. Census Bureau, Boston schedules, 1880; Boston city directories; *JPN,* Apr. 1, 1899; Perry Duis, *The Saloon: Public Drinking in Chicago and Boston, 1880–1920* (Urbana, 1983), 135–37; Jon M. Kingsdale, "The 'Poor Man's Club': Social Functions of the Urban Working-Class Saloon," *American Quarterly* 25 (Oct. 1973), 472–89. The lists of applications for liquor licenses published in local newspapers give locations and proprietors of establishments allowed to sell and serve alcohol. Relatively few saloon keepers were elected to Boston's city council, and none were ever elected to representative office from Jamaica Plain.

34. *Roxbury Almanac and Business Directory, 1847* (Boston, 1847); *West Roxbury Reports,* 1853–72; *Boston Transcript,* Mar. 14, 1928; *JPN,* May 16, 1903; *Blue Book of Roxbury, Jamaica Plain, and West Roxbury* (Cambridge, Mass., 1899), opp. 179; St. Paul's Universalist Church, "Church Record," 1888–1922, Manuscripts and Archives Department, Andover-Harvard Theological Library, Harvard University Divinity School, Cambridge, Mass.

35. Homer Hoyt, *One Hundred Years of Land Values in Chicago* (Chicago, 1933), 163–65, 168–73, passim.

36. Warner, *Streetcar Suburbs* (ch. 1, n. 2), 124.

37. Morse, *Memoir of Weld* (ch. 1, n. 35), 4, 6–7; NRD, Grantor, grantee indexes,

178:253–55, 179:165–67, 195–96; BLC, JP 24–26: 9, 13, 15 Bishop, 106: 73 Elm, 79: 305–7 Chestnut; Hopkins, *Atlas; Boston Transcript,* Nov. 2, 1884; SRD, 1561:640, 1620:514, 1652:640. See also Woodman subdivision of 1872 in NRD, 419:210.

38. Boston city directories; *Boston Transcript,* July 5, 1916; SRD, Grantor index; NRD, Grantor index, 397:35, 409:188, 410:177; Hopkins, *Atlas;* BLC, JP 12: 223–41, 248–60 Amory, 702: 14 Bismarck.

39. Boston city directories; SRD, 2140:458, 470.

40. SRD, Grantor index, 2112:181, 3706:325–26; [Samuel May,] *A Genealogy of the Descendants of John May* (Boston, 1878), 37; BLC, JP 201: 48 Peter Parley Road. The long-term nature of the investment is shown by the fact that twenty years later the company was still paying out the proceeds of lot sales to shareholders. Other shareholders were in all likelihood family members also.

41. "Tax List for 1872"; SRD, 1909:143, 2025:435; BLC, JP 203: 12–14 Pond / 15–17, 19–21 Grovenor Road; *JPN,* Dec. 26, 1903, Jan. 19, 1907.

42. BLC, JP 261: Warren Square; SRD, Grantor, grantee indexes; City of Boston Assessing Department, "Assessor's Records," 1885, Research Library Office, BPL; Suffolk County Registry of Probate, Administration 13160 (1905); SRD, 1881:255, 2136:31; Boston city directories.

43. Edward Oberle, interview with author, West Roxbury, Mass., June 21, 1978. This would have been an extraordinary bargain. Sam Bass Warner found that from the 1880s the price for land in Roxbury, Parker Hill, and West Roxbury averaged ten to thirty cents per square foot. See Warner, "Residential Development" (Ph.D. diss., Harvard University, 1959), app. D.

44. Warner, *Streetcar Suburbs,* 126–27; Boston Landmarks Commission, "Jamaica Plain Survey Area Architects and Builders," 1982, typescript; Flyer for William B. Heath, Henry A. May Collection, File Folder 6: Miscellaneous, Rare Books and Manuscripts Department, BPL; BLC, JP 86: 18 Cranston, 244: 34–40 Sheridan; Boston city directories. The lawyer Charles B. Sargent previously had lived nearby in Roxbury.

45. Hopkins, *Atlas,* "Business Notices"; Edwin M. Bacon, *Men of Progress: One Thousand Biographical Sketches and Portraits of Leaders in Business and Professional Life in the Commonwealth of Massachusetts* (Boston, 1896), 541; BLC, JP 246: 107–9 Sheridan; *JPN,* Mar. 16, 1912.

46. *West Roxbury Reports for 1872–73,* 30; BLC, JP 104 1/2 Williams Street; *Annual Report of the Superintendent of Streets for the Year 1887,* City of Boston City Doc. No. 19-1890 (Boston, 1888), 91; *Annual Report of the Street Department for the Year 1899,* City of Boston City Doc. No. 38-1900 (Boston, 1900), 43, 57, hereinafter cited as *Annual Report of Boston Street Department for [year]; WRN,* Oct. 10, 1891 (advertisements). Minton also was in the real estate business. Minton Street, which runs between Amory Street and Brookside Avenue, commemorates his name.

47. Hopkins, *Atlas,* "Business Notices"; *WRN,* Oct. 10, 1891. Some Jamaica Plain real estate subdividers and agents resided outside the neighborhood but

concentrated their suburban work in a particular area. For example, Charles Morris, a downtown real estate agent, worked extensively in Roxbury and northern Jamaica Plain.

48. BLC, JP 4: 20, 5: 28 Alveston, 213: 7 Revere; 238: 18, 240: 84, 88, 90 Seaverns; NRD, 284:320, 309:173, Grantor index.

49. Drake, *Town* (ch. 1, n. 6), 418–19; Ernst, *First Congregational Society* (ch. 1, n. 23), 55; Morse, "Paper," 7; Massachusetts, vol. 56, p. 165, R. G. Dun and Company Collection.

50. *JPN,* Jan. 12, 1907, Oct. 22, Dec. 3, 1910, Sept. 9, 16, 1911.

51. Daniel J. Boorstin, *The Americans: The National Experience* (New York, 1965), 115–23. Kevin Starr refers to Otis as "the city's ultimate booster" in *Inventing the Dream: California through the Progressive Era* (New York, 1985), 72.

52. Morse, *Memoir of Weld,* 7–10; *West Roxbury Reports for 1864,* 45; Town of West Roxbury, "Selectmen's Records" (ch. 2, n. 19), vol. 1, Dec. 1, 1856. Weld served on the board of overseers of Harvard College, as a member of the Massachusetts governor's executive council in 1858 and 1859, and as a presidential elector for Abraham Lincoln in 1860 and was a leading fundraiser for Harvard's Memorial Hall. Weld also headed a committee to recruit the townsmen of West Roxbury as soldiers for the Union cause. In 1858 the West Roxbury Railroad Company was incorporated; after overwork brought on a severe illness, Weld resigned from the presidency of the Metropolitan Railroad Company in 1859.

53. *Report of a Committee in Relation to Jamaica Pond* (ch. 3, n. 71), 10–11.

54. Morse, "Paper," 8.

55. Bacon, *Men of Progress,* 541; *WRN,* Oct. 10, 1891; SRD, Grantor, grantee indexes; *JPN,* Dec. 23, 1899.

56. *Brookline, Jamaica Plain, and West Roxbury Directory, 1868,* 160; *JPN,* Jan. 19, 1907; *WRN,* Oct. 10, 1891. A resident of the Pondside area of Jamaica Plain from the 1850s, Pratt invested in a few Jamaica Plain properties. In the 1890s the company officers and directors were still downtown and neighborhood businessmen.

57. NRD, 221:49, 122; *Report of the Receipts and Expenditures of the Town of West Roxbury,* 1854–73; *Boston Transcript,* June 7, 1888; Massachusetts, vol. 6, p. 310, R. G. Dun and Company Collection; *Thirtieth Annual Report of the Jamaica Plain Gas Light Company for the Year Ending March 31, 1885,* 6–7; *Thirty-first Annual Report of the Jamaica Plain Gas Light Company for the Year Ending March 31, 1886,* 5–7. In 1903 the Jamaica Plain Gas Light Company was consolidated with seven other companies to form the Boston Consolidated Gas Company.

58. *Norfolk County Gazette,* June 15, 1872; *Brookline, Jamaica Plain, and West Roxbury Directory, 1868;* Russell, *Knave of Boston* (ch. 1, n. 20), 71. The other vice-presidents besides Brewer were Seaver, the local grocer, and Henry A. Church, a downtown businessman. The trustees of the bank were Balch, president of the Boylston Insurance Company, Francis Minot Weld, a Central Wharf commission merchant, Andrew J. Peters, the scion of a wealthy family in the wholesale lumber

business, Bartlett, the local real estate agent, George James, a Centre Street grocer, and Joseph Stedman, a neighborhood physician.

59. *WRN,* Oct. 10, 1891; *JPN,* Mar. 24, 1906, Dec. 4, 1909.

60. *Directory of Directors* (Boston, 1905), 559.

61. Janowitz, *Community Press* (intro., n. 7).

62. *WRN,* Oct. 10, 1891; *JPN,* July 1883, reprinted July 25, 1908.

63. *JPN,* Jan. 3, 1903.

64. *Boston Globe,* July 5, 1897, July 5, 1898; *JPN,* June 24, July 8, 1899, Apr. 28, 1900, July 11, 1903, July 8, 1905; Boston city directories.

65. *JPN,* Feb. 4, 11, 25, 1899, Jan. 6, 1900, and advertisements passim; Boston city directories; *WRN,* Oct. 10, 1891. According to the *Jamaica Plain News* (Aug. 24, 1912), the Jamaica Plain Citizens' Association had grown from the "old Carnival Association of Jamaica Plain."

66. Atherton, *Main Street,* 330–35; David Hammack, *Power and Society: Greater New York at the Turn-of-the-Century* (New York, 1982), 88.

67. *JPN,* Feb. 11, Mar. 18, 25, Apr. 15, Nov. 18, 1899, Mar. 17, June 16, 1900.

68. Ibid., June 20, 1903, May 2, 1908, Apr. 1, 1911.

Chapter 5 The Web of Neighborhood Society

Epigraph: *JPN,* Mar. 3, 1900.

1. Warner, *Private City* (intro., n. 3); Richard Sennett, *Families against the City: Middle Class Homes of Industrial Chicago, 1872–1890* (Cambridge, Mass., 1970; reprint ed., 1984); Barth, *City People* (intro., n. 4).

2. *JPN,* May 9, 1903.

3. John S. Gilkeson, *Middle-Class Providence, 1820–1940* (Princeton, 1986); Blumin, *Emergence of the Middle Class* (ch. 2, n. 1), 206–29.

4. Blumin, *Urban Threshold* (intro., n. 8), 160–65, 220–22; Doyle, *Social Order* (intro., n. 8), 178–93; Thernstrom, *Poverty and Progress* (ch. 4, n. 29), 168–70.

5. Arthur M. Schlesinger, "Biography of a Nation of Joiners," *American Historical Review* 50, no. 1 (1944), 1–25; Rowland Berthoff, *An Unsettled People: Social Order and Disorder in American History* (New York, 1971), 254–74, 444–54. For an excellent synthesis of social-science literature on this subject, see Constance Smith and Anne Freedman, *Voluntary Associations: Perspectives on the Literature* (Cambridge, Mass., 1972).

6. Sydney E. Ahlstrom, *A Religious History of the American People* (New Haven, 1972), 379–83.

7. Ronald G. Walters, *American Reformers, 1815–1860* (New York, 1978), 21–37; Bertram Wyatt-Brown, *Lewis Tappan and the Evangelical War against Slavery* (Cleveland, 1969); Gregory H. Singleton, "Protestant Voluntary Organizations and the Shaping of Victorian America," in *Victorian America,* ed. Daniel Walker Howe (Philadelphia, 1976), 47–58.

8. Nancy Cott, *The Bonds of Womanhood* (New Haven, 1977); Ann Douglas, *The Feminization of American Culture* (New York, 1977); Mary P. Ryan, *Cradle of the Middle Class: The Family in Oneida County, New York, 1790–1865* (Cambridge, Mass., 1981); Paul E. Johnson, *A Shopkeeper's Millennium: Society and Revivals in Rochester, New York, 1815–1837* (New York, 1978).

9. In the early twentieth century a few small Jewish synagogues also located briefly in northern Jamaica Plain.

10. The elite Harvard College, for example, was a Unitarian bastion.

11. Unitarian Church and Society, Greenfield, to Unitarian Church and Society, Jamaica Plain, Sept. 25, 1837, Andover-Harvard Library, Harvard University Divinity School, Cambridge, Mass.

12. An attempt in the 1860s to replace the word *Congregational* with *Unitarian* in the church's name was beaten back in favor of "the more liberal and broad term." See Thomas Gray, *Religious Opinions of the Present Day . . . delivered September 23, 1821* (1822); and Ernst, *First Congregational Society* (ch. 1, n. 23), 49–50, 62–63.

13. Charles F. Dole, *My Eighty Years* (New York, 1927), 200, 239–46.

14. Robert Morse, *First Congregational Society Reminiscences,* 8. All but 3 of 200 family addresses listed in the 1880 parish manual were located in Jamaica Plain. Of 119 business addresses of First Church members, 111 were located downtown and only 6 were located in Jamaica Plain. By 1915 their proportion of the employed male congregation had slipped, but professionals and large proprietors still dominated.

15. J. Vaughn Morrill, "Some Recollections of Saint John's Church, Jamaica Plain, in the Early 60s," St. John's Church file, Episcopal Diocesan Archives, Boston, Mass., 3–4, 6–9, 11–12.

16. Ahlstrom, *Religious History,* 630; "Father's residence" list in St. John's Parish Register, Marriages, 1910–1912, Episcopal Diocesan Archives.

17. *A Brief History of the Jamaica Plain Baptist Church, of West Roxbury* (Boston, 1871), 3–11.

18. *Brief History,* 11; Herb Pierce and Hollis Blue, interviews with author, Jan. 12, 1991; Bacon, *Men of Progress* (ch. 4, n. 45), 633–34.

19. Joseph Bourne Clark, *An Historical Discourse Commemorative of the Twenty-fifth Anniversary of the Gathering of the Central Congregational Church* (Boston, 1878), 6–15.

20. *Rules, Confession of Faith, and Covenant of the Central Congregational Church, Jamaica Plain, Massachusetts with a Catalogue of its Officers and Members* (Boston, 1870; Jamaica Plain, 1878, 1898); *JPN,* Nov. 23, 1912, 3.

21. James Mudge, "Address at the Fiftieth Anniversary of the Foundation of the First Methodist Episcopal Church of Jamaica Plain," 1909, typescript, JPL; *JPN,* Nov. 6, 1909; Records of St. Paul's Universalist Church (ch. 4, n. 34).

22. Robert L. Lord, John E. Sexton, and Edward T. Harrington, *History of the Archdiocese of Boston, 1604–1943,* vol. 3 (New York, 1944), 258–59; *St. Thomas Aquinas* (ch. 2, n. 53), 4–6.

23. Donna Merwick, *Boston's Priests, 1848–1910: A Study of Social and Intellectual Change* (Cambridge, Mass., 1973); Census Records, St. Thomas Aquinas Parish, Archives, (Roman Catholic) Archdiocese of Boston, Brighton, Mass.

24. Boylston Congregational Church, *Our Year of Jubilee, 1879–1929* (Jamaica Plain, 1929), 7, 9–10; *Manual of the Boylston Congregational Church, Boston, Mass., 1896* (Boston, 1896), 2–3, 39–45.

25. "St. Peter's Church, Jamaica Plain," *The Church Militant,* Oct. 1904, 70; St. Peter's Register, baptisms and marriages, 1900, 1901, 1909, 1910, Episcopal Diocesan Archives; 1900 and 1910 census manuscript. St. Peter's was also the church for at least one African-American, Lyde W. Benjamin, a real estate agent who hailed from South Carolina.

26. Lord, Sexton, and Harrington, *History,* 258; Episcopal Register, Feb. 3, May 22, June 7, 1891, Archives, Archdiocese of Boston. Charles Greco, a Cambridge architect who specialized in institutional buildings, designed the Church of the Blessed Sacrament.

27. Kathleen Neils Conzen, *Immigrant Milwaukee, 1836–1860: Accommodation and Community in a Frontier City* (Cambridge, Mass., 1976); Miller, *Boss Cox's Cincinnati* (intro., n. 3), 29; Trinity Lutheran Church, *100th Anniversary: 1871–1971, Souvenir History* (Boston, 1971), 3–23.

28. Francis X. Weiser, *Holy Trinity Parish, Boston, Mass., 1844–1944* (Boston, 1944), 9–33; Petition for establishment, proposed parish, General Parish Records, Archives, Archdiocese of Boston.

29. St. Paul's Methodist Church, "History of St. Paul's Methodist Church, One Hundredth Anniversary Celebration, November 5, 1952," JPL; *JPN,* Jan. 13, 1900, Aug. 27, 1904. In addition, in 1904 a German Reformed Church was established on Cedar Hill (*JPN,* Feb. 13, 1904).

30. Protestant churches banded together to fight for prohibition in the 1880s and for community work in 1910. See *JPN,* Feb. 12, 1910.

31. *St. Thomas Aquinas,* 6; "Report of the School Committee," *West Roxbury Reports for 1872–73,* School Committee report. Child also sold the land upon which St. Thomas was located. Other Protestant supporters of St. Thomas included wealthy individuals such as Andrew J. Peters, Sr., Dr. George Faulkner, Moses Williams, and members of the Bowditch family, as well as local businessmen such as the druggist Charles B. Rogers and grocers Robert and Fred Seaver and Isaac Myrick.

32. Ernst, *First Congregational Society,* 42, 65–68; *First Congregational Society Manual and Parish List* (Jamaica Plain, 1915), 11. Prior to the opening of Parish House, the First Church had rented Eliot Hall, located across the street, for its activities.

33. *JPN,* July 23, 1910.

34. Ibid., Sept. 17, 1904.

35. Ueda, *Avenues* (ch. 2, n. 26), 40–58, 89–118; D. S. Smalley, "History of the Eliot School," *West Roxbury Reports for 1872–73,* 13, 16; *Annual Report of the School Committee of the City of Boston for the Year 1898* (Boston, 1898), 34, *1901,* 302, *1902,*

111–12, hereinafter cited as *Annual Report of Boston School Committee for [year]*. Some local public-high-school students, however, commuted to Boston English High School on the train, where the girls offended riders with their "lack of etiquette" by talking loudly about a risqué French novel and the "fellers." See *WRN,* Oct. 10, 1891.

36. William Augustine Leahy, "Archdiocese of Boston," in *History of the Catholic Church in the New England States,* ed. William Byrne, vol. 2 (Boston, 1899), 150–51; *Saint Thomas Aquinas,* 10; *Fifty-fifth Annual Report of the Massachusetts Board of Education, 1890–1891* (Boston, 1892), 148–49; "An Account of the School from 1900 to 1907," Record, Blessed Sacrament School, Jamaica Plain, 8, 35; Louis S. Walsh, *Historical Sketch of the Growth of Catholic Parochial Schools in the Archdiocese of Boston* (Newton Highlands, Mass., 1901), 9–10; *JPN,* Mar. 2, 1912; Sister Margaret Patricia Donahue, interview with author, Jamaica Plain, Apr. 12, 1978; Arthur T. Connolly file, Deceased Priests Correspondence Files, Archives, Archdiocese of Boston. The pastors' commitment to education can be seen in Magennis's founding of a school for deaf-mutes and Connolly's appointment to be a trustee of the Boston Public Library. In some parishes Catholic parents showed considerable initial reluctance to send their children to a parochial school; this may explain why the local schools did not charge tuition. Ambitious Catholics, on the other hand, could leave the neighborhood to attend Boston College High School and Boston College.

37. Ueda, *Avenues,* 119–52; *Clarion,* vols. 1–9 (1893–1900), JPL; Dorothy Halder, interview with author, Jamaica Plain, Apr. 21, 1978.

38. For example, the Harvard Alumni Association was founded in 1842.

39. *JPN,* Feb. 18, 1899, Feb. 9, May 4, 1907.

40. Mark C. Carnes, *Secret Ritual and Manhood in Victorian America* (New Haven, 1989), 24–29; Mary Ann Clawson, *Constructing Brotherhood: Class, Gender, and Fraternalism* (Princeton, 1989), 119–21, 157–64.

41. Carnes, *Secret Ritual,* 1–9; Clawson, *Constructing Brotherhood,* 123–44.

42. Clawson, *Constructing Brotherhood;* Carnes, *Secret Ritual;* Berthoff, *An Unsettled People,* 273–74.

43. Frederic G. Bauer, "History of Eliot Lodge," *Proceedings of the Most Worshipful Grand Lodge of Ancient Free and Accepted Masons of the Commonwealth of Massachusetts for the Year 1941* (Boston, 1941), 95–104; *Proceedings . . . of Masons . . . for the Year 1921* (Boston, 1921), 286–88; *JPN,* May 5, 12, 1900, Mar. 2, 1907.

44. Bauer, "Eliot Lodge," 97, 102–4; *JPN,* Nov. 28, 1903. See also Roy Rosenzweig, "The Lower Middle Class in a Divided Society," *Journal of Voluntary Research* 6 (July–Oct. 1977), 119–26. According to Frederic Bauer, the historian of the Eliot Lodge, the original members were men of the "substantial middle class—chiefly merchants, with a sprinkling of professional men, bankers, farmers, tradesmen, and master artisans." The occupations of the officers at the turn of the century (*Blue Book of Roxbury, Jamaica Plain, and West Roxbury* [ch. 4, n. 34], 214) suggest that the lodge still retained the loyalty of local professionals, but its

leadership also included local shopkeepers and middle-level white-collar workers.

45. *JPN,* Mar. 2, 1907. At the turn of the century the membership had hit a plateau of about 165 men. An occupational analysis of 18 members listed in the local newspaper showed that 11 were skilled workers, 6 were semiskilled workers, and 1 was an unskilled worker. See ibid., May 5, 12, 1900.

46. Alvin J. Schmidt, *Fraternal Organizations* (Westport, Conn., 1980), 356–58; Albert C. Stevens, ed., *The Cyclopedia of Fraternities* (New York, 1899), 193–94; *JPN,* Jan. 3, Mar. 11, 1903, Nov. 7, 1907. Despite its working-class roots, the A.O.U.W. was conservative in its social philosophy, hoping to reconcile the interests of capital and labor. In 1899 ten of eleven officers of the Marion Lodge (listed in the *Blue Book*) worked in blue-collar occupations.

47. Schmidt, *Fraternal Organizations,* 176–78; *JPN,* Mar. 25, Dec. 30, 1899, Jan. 6, 1900, Mar. 4, 1905. Of thirty-two members listed in the *Jamaica Plain News* as participating in a ladies' night or as officers in late 1899 and early 1900 there were five professionals, twenty-two low-white-collar workers, five skilled workers, and two low-blue-collar workers.

48. Rosenzweig, *Eight Hours* (intro., n. 4), 74–78, 86–87; Schmidt, *Fraternal Organizations,* 158; *JPN,* Apr. 8, 22, 1899, June 23, 1900, Apr. 18, 25, 1903. Of twenty organizers of the annual social dance thrown by A.O.H. Division 15 in 1899, nine had low-white-collar jobs (seven of these were relatively low-paid local store clerks), six were skilled workers, and five were unskilled workers.

49. Carnes, *Secret Ritual,* 85–88; Clawson, *Constructing Brotherhood,* 178–210.

50. Morse, "Paper" (ch. 1, n. 38), 4; "Jamaica Plain, Mass.," Regional Theater Files, Theater Collection, Pusey Library, Harvard University, Cambridge, Mass., hereinafter cited as Harvard Theater Collection. For an analysis of parlor theatricals in the context of changing middle-class culture, see Karen Halttunen, *Confidence Men and Painted Women: A Study of Middle-Class Culture in America, 1830–1870* (New Haven, 1982), 174–82.

51. MacGregor Jenkins, *Some Reflections on the Footlight Club* (Privately printed, 1937), 6–7; *The Footlight Club Constitution and By-Laws* (Jamaica Plain, 1911), 5. Caroline H. Morse died about 1879. She probably was not immediately related to Robert M. and Ellen C. Morse, although the memoirs of the Footlight Club indicate that she came from an educated and cultivated background. Ticknor began at his father's firm and then in 1883 worked for J. R. Osgood and Co. and finally worked for the Houghton, Mifflin, Co. Another original Footlighter was Ellen Frothingham, a member of a prominent local Pondside family.

52. Footlight Club, "100th Performance, 1877–1906," JPL; Footlight Club Files, Harvard Theater Collection. The Footlight Club is still located in Eliot Hall, Eliot Street.

53. Morse, "Paper," 4; *WRN,* Oct. 10, 1891.

54. *JPN,* Dec. 21, 1907.

55. Jaher, *Urban Establishment* (ch. 3, n. 3), 66–67, 110; *JPN,* Feb. 25, May 20, Nov. 11, 1899, Jan. 20, 1900, Mar. 20, Dec. 4, 1909, Feb. 26, 1910. Eliot Club lecture

subjects were eclectic. In 1910–11 they included such topics as forestry, the Cape Cod Canal, forms of workmen's compensation in Europe, and a comparison of commercial port facilities in Europe with those of Boston. See ibid., Nov. 26, Dec. 24, 1910, Feb. 25, Mar. 25, June 24, 1911.

56. Theodora Penny Martin, *The Sounds of Our Own Voices: Women's Study Clubs, 1860–1910* (Boston, 1987); Karen J. Blair, *The Clubwoman as Feminist: True Womanhood Redefined, 1868–1914* (New York, 1980).

57. *JPN*, Dec. 30, 1899, Mar. 3, Apr. 28, Nov. 17, 1900; *Blue Book of Roxbury, Jamaica Plain, and West Roxbury* (ch. 4, n. 34), 213. The Tuesday Club still preserves the Loring-Greenough house as a museum and lecture hall for the club.

58. Alexander Williams, *A Social History of the Greater Boston Clubs* (Barre, Mass., 1970), 7–29; Jaher, *Urban Establishment*, 246–48, 277.

59. *JPN*, Jan. 10, Oct. 15, 1903, Dec. 10, 1904.

60. As early as 1891 the popular show ran for four nights in Eliot Hall; in 1904 twelve hundred Jamaica Plain residents bought tickets to see the production. See *WRN*, Oct. 10, 1891; and *JPN*, Apr. 16, 1904.

61. Research about twenty-three original members revealed three downtown wholesale merchants or manufacturers, one lawyer, one draughtsman, sixteen clerks, and two skilled workers. In the early 1900s the club continued to attract some prominent local residents, such as Charles F. Sprague, a Boston lawyer and U.S. congressman, and Eugene N. Foss, heir to the Benjamin F. Sturtevant Company and governor of Massachusetts. See *JPN*, Dec. 10, 1904.

62. Hardy, *How Boston Played* (ch. 3, n. 2), 130–31; Williams, *Social History*, 77–80; Stephen A. Reiss, *City Games: The Evolution of American Urban Society and the Rise of Sports* (Urbana, 1989), 25–26; *Boston Evening Traveler*, July 6, 1874, 2; *Boston Globe*, July 6, 1876, July 6, 1880; *Boston Herald*, July 5, 1878; *JPN*, July 4, 1908.

63. Hardy, *How Boston Played*, 131–32, 139–40; Williams, *Social History*, 52–76; Gilkeson, *Middle-Class Providence*, 147–48; *The Country Club, Constitution, By-laws and List of Members* (Boston, 1910).

64. *JPN*, July 29, 1899, Apr. 7, Sept. 1, 1900; *WRN*, Oct. 10, 1891. Social occasions such as the large dance the Jamaica Cycle Club held in February 1900 extended the opportunities for ethnic mixing. Of thirty-three traceable members of the Cycle Club dance committee and guests (some of whom were members) present at the dance thirteen were clerks, twelve were skilled blue-collar workers, five were semi- or unskilled workers, and one, Annie Dooley, was a neighborhood schoolteacher. Of twenty-two members and guests at the dance or mentioned in an 1899 newpaper article, two each were of Irish, Canadian, English, and Scottish birth, and twelve had been born in New England or New York, but of these twelve, three had German parents, one had Irish parents, and one, Canadian parents. Untraceable common names such as Kelly and Lutz indicate even greater diversity. See *JPN*, July 22, 1899, Feb. 10, 1900.

65. *JPN*, Sept. 16, 1899, May 23, June 27, Aug. 29, 1903. Locals played other sports as well. The Hyde Square Athletic Association, for example, was organized to play football. See ibid., Oct. 6, 1900.

66. Lewis A. Erenberg, *Steppin' Out: New York Nightlife and the Transformation of American Culture, 1890–1930* (Chicago, 1981), 8, 10, 12–13; Handlin, *Boston's Immigrants* (ch. 1, n. 3), 156.

67. *WRN,* Oct. 10, 1891; *JPN,* Jan. 3, Feb. 21, Apr. 25, May 2, 23, 1903, Feb. 11, 1905. For much of the twentieth century, the dance classes conducted by Jamaica Plain resident Marguerite Souther in Eliot Hall were a Boston institution for learning ballroom etiquette.

68. Conzen, *Immigrant Milwaukee,* 154–91; Miller, *Boss Cox's Cincinnati,* 35; Stephen J. Ross, *Workers on the Edge: Work, Leisure, and Politics in Industrializing Cincinnati, 1788–1890* (New York, 1985), 173, 256–57; *Geschichte des Boylston Schulverein, 1874–1924* (Boston, 1924), 29.

69. Hardy, *How Boston Played,* 136–37; Ross, *Workers,* 174–75; Conzen, *Immigrant Milwaukee,* 179–80.

70. *JPN,* Sept. 9, 1899, Sept. 17, 1910; Edward Oberle, interview with author, West Roxbury, June 21, 1978; August Becker, interview, Jan. 18, 1982. Longtime members remembered that Boylston Schul Verein men felt superior to the workers in the other clubs, while the members of the Arbeiter Turnverein looked down on the club members who did not earn as much as they did.

71. *JPN,* Apr. 25, 1903, Feb. 17, 1906, May 25, 1907, Sept. 12, 1908, June 5, 1909.

72. Ibid., Nov. 18, 1899.

73. Ibid., May 23, 1903. For Roxbury residents at a Jamaica Cycle Club dance in 1900, see ibid., May 23, 1900.

74. Ibid., July 28, 1900, Feb. 14, May 16, 1903; Balch, "History of the Jamaica Plain Neighborhood House Association" (ch. 2, n. 59), 12–13, 28; Suttles, *Social Construction* (intro., n. 7), 198–201.

75. A worshipful master and senior and junior wardens led the Eliot Masonic Lodge, the Odd Fellow lodges were directed by noble and vice grands or chief patriarch, high priest, and scribe; regents and vice-regents directed the Daughters of the American Revolution and the Royal Arcanum. Perhaps because of its importance, the office of treasurer was usually not renamed.

76. Robert M. DeWitt, *Webster's Chairman's Manual and Speaker's Guide, Showing Plainly and Clearly How To Preside Over and Conduct Every Kind of Public Meeting* (New York, 1871), 9; Harriette R. Shattuck, *The Woman's Manual of Parliamentary Law* (Boston, 1891; rev. ed., 1897), iv.

77. Quotation italicized in the original text. Sarah Corbin Robert et al., *Robert's Rules of Order, Newly Revised* (Glenview, Ill., 1970), xxxix; Doyle, *Social Order,* 192. Between the first publication in 1876 and the 1915 revision, the pocket edition of *Robert's Rules of Order* sold over half a million copies.

78. Gilkeson has labeled this development "the club idea" in *Middle-Class Providence,* 136–74.

79. Joseph Boskin, *Sambo: The Rise and Demise of an American Jester* (New York, 1986), 85–86.

80. Carl J. Ludwig, "The Boylston Schul Verein," in *Germans in Boston,* ed. Paul Kurt Ackermann (Boston, 1981), 87–88; *Geschichte des Boylston Schulverein,* 30–

31; *JPN,* May 27, 1905. At times German club theatrical productions could be quite elaborate. Edward Oberle (interview, June 21, 1978) remembered that the Schwaben Verein once produced Gilbert and Sullivan's *Mikado.*

81. Samuel B. Capen, "Golden Jubilee," *JPN,* Feb. 28, 1903.

82. Boylston Congregational Church, *Our Year of Jubilee,* 11–12; *JPN,* Sept. 29, 1900.

83. *Saint Thomas Aquinas,* 7; *JPN,* Oct. 15, 1907; Lord, Sexton, and Harrington, *History,* 258.

84. *JPN,* Mar. 19, 1904, Mar. 9, 1907.

85. Ibid., Mar. 11, Apr. 8, 1899, Dec. 11, 1909, Feb. 19, 1910. See also *Manual of the Boylston Congregational Church.*

86. *JPN,* Mar. 2, 1907; Gilkeson, *Middle-Class Providence,* 159.

87. *JPN,* Mar. 11, 1899, Apr. 18, 1903, Mar. 4, 1905, Nov. 7, 1907.

88. Ibid., Apr. 8, 1899, June 23, 1900, Apr. 18, 1903.

89. Allen F. Davis, *Spearheads for Reform: The Social Settlements and the Progressive Movement, 1890–1914* (New York, 1967), 76–83; Marvin Lazerson, *Origins of the Urban School: Public Education in Massachusetts, 1870–1915* (Cambridge, Mass., 1971), 204–23.

90. *West Roxbury Reports for 1872–73; Annual Report of Boston School Committee for 1902,* 21–23, 32–33, *1904,* 51–53; *JPN,* Mar. 19, 1904.

91. Lazerson, *Origins,* 223–32; *Annual Report of the Boston School Committee for 1902,* 81–83; *JPN,* Jan. 5, Feb. 2, 1907.

92. *JPN,* Mar. 28, 1903, Aug. 20, 27, 1904, Oct. 19, 1907, Apr. 4, 1908; *Bath Independent,* June 4, 1910. The Plant Company also maintained an infirmary and two full-time barbers.

93. Doyle, *Social Order,* 186–87; *Catalogue of Members,* 71; Capen, "Golden Jubilee."

94. *JPN,* Mar. 14, 1903, Jan. 23, 1904.

95. Ibid., Oct. 19, 1907; *First Congregational Society Manual;* "Marriages," Blessed Sacrament Church, 1892–1910, Archives, Archdiocese of Boston; Edward Oberle, interview, June 21, 1978; Marion Cleary, interview by Margaret Pendlebury, Boston, Mar. 28, 1978; Peter A. Alemi, interview with author, Boston, May 14, 1978.

96. August Becker, interview, Jan. 18, 1982; *Geschichte des Boylston Schulverein,* 18.

97. *JPN,* Feb. 7, 14, 1903, Apr. 20, 1907.

98. Ibid., June 30, Aug. 11, 1900, Jan. 29, 1910.

99. Ibid., May 23, Sept. 5, 1908. For patronizing humor about local "Celestial" laundry wars, see ibid., June 16, 1900.

100. Thomas B. Ticknor to the Footlight Club, Jan. 3, 1894, Footlight Club Files, Harvard Theater Collection; *Saint Thomas Aquinas,* 11–12; *Geschichte des Boylston Schulverein,* 30.

101. August Becker, interview, Jan. 18, 1982; see also Alice Woodall, "William

Stanley Parker," n.d., typescript, Footlight Club File, Harvard Theater Collection.

102. *JPN,* Mar. 2, 1907; Clark, *Historical Discourse,* 19; Capen, "Golden Jubilee." See also the obituary of Arthur Connolly, pastor of the Blessed Sacrament Church, *Boston Globe,* Nov. 11, 1933.

103. *Our Year of Jubilee,* 12–15; *JPN,* Oct. 3, 1903. Church members established a memorial church endowment fund and, appropriately for the organizing minister, a new church group, the Mendell Brotherhood. The show of neighborhood sentiment convinced the school committee to name the school after Mendell.

104. For the theory of an anti-urban upper middle class, see Sennett, *Families against the City.*

105. Nathan Irvin Huggins, *Protestants against Poverty: Boston's Charities, 1870–1900* (Westport, Conn., 1971); *JPN,* May 5, 1900.

106. *Report of the West Roxbury Relief Society* (Boston, 1872), 1, 4–7. At the group's first meeting, the theme of interdenominational cooperation was underscored by a dramatic gift of one hundred dollars from Father Magennis, the pastor of St. Thomas Aquinas Church.

107. The analysis presented here and below is based upon annual reports of the Jamaica Plain Employment and Temporary Relief Society, 1874–84, and the Jamaica Plain Friendly Society, 1885–90, 1900–1920, Massachusetts State Library, Boston, Mass., hereinafter cited as *[First] Annual Report of Friendly Society, [year].* For a history of this society, see Terri Ellen Gerstein, "The Jamaica Plain Friendly Society: Care and Oversight of 'Our Poor'" (Senior honors thesis, Committee on Degrees in History and Literature, Harvard College, 1990).

108. Boyer, *Urban Masses and Moral Order* (ch. 3, n. 49), 86–94, 144–48.

109. *First Annual Report of Friendly Society, 1874–75,* 9, 11, *Fourth Annual Report, 1877–78, Tenth Annual Report, 1883–84,* 3. In the 1880s, Mrs. Bradley and her husband, the Reverend William Bradley, a relief society vice-president, ran a Heath Street–area mission, appropriately named the Union for Christian Work, where access to the soup kitchen was gained by chopping wood in the workyard. See *JPN,* Aug. 1, 1903.

110. *Eleventh Annual Report of Friendly Society, 1884–85,* 4–5, *Twelfth Annual Report, 1886–87,* 2–3; Gerstein, "Friendly Society," 37–38, 40–41, 53–56.

111. *Fifth Annual Report of Friendly Society, 1878–79,* 2; Ellen C. Morse, "Case Committee Report," in *Thirty-ninth Annual Report of Friendly Society, 1912–13,* 6–9; Gerstein, "Friendly Society," 39. The society later added social-work and public-health organizations to its referral matrix.

112. *Fifth Annual Report of Friendly Society, 1878–79,* 2; *JPN,* Feb. 14, 1903. The original officers of the W.C.T.U. included as president, the wife of the pastor of the Baptist church; as vice-president, the wife of a neighborhood physician; and as members of the executive board, two members from each of the participating Protestant churches.

113. Morris J. Vogel, *The Invention of the Modern Hospital, Boston, 1870–1930* (Chicago, 1980), 19–20; Judith Walzer Leavitt, *The Healthiest City: Milwaukee and*

the *Politics of Health Reform* (Princeton, 1982), 67–68; *JPN,* May 14, 1904.

114. Faulkner Hospital, *Eighth Annual Report* (Boston, 1912), 6–15; *Faulkner,* special ed., June 1976. See also Archives, Faulkner Hospital, Jamaica Plain. Named in honor of George Faulkner's late daughter, Faulkner Hospital officially opened in 1903, on Centre Street near the Arnold Arboretum. Its history vividly illustrates the developments traced in Vogel, *Invention,* and Paul Starr, *The Social Transformation of American Medicine* (New York, 1982), 145–79.

115. Sam Bass Warner, Jr., *Province of Reason* (Cambridge, Mass., 1984), 90–115; Randall, *Improper Bostonian* (ch. 2, n. 36), 23–49; Balch, "History of the Jamaica Plain Neighborhood House Association," 1–4.

116. *JPN,* Apr. 1, 1899, Apr. 7, 1900, Dec. 4, 1909, Feb. 19, 1910; Balch, "History of the Jamaica Plain Neighborhood House Association," 3–5.

117. *JPN,* Aug. 22, 1903, Apr. 20, 1907. For settlement houses, see Boyer, *Urban Masses and Moral Order,* 155–58; Davis, *Spearheads for Reform;* and Jane Addams, *Twenty Years at Hull-House* (New York, 1910; reprint ed., 1960). Classes at the Helen Weld House included clay modeling, paper sloyd, carpentry, cobbling, cane-seating, printing, and gymnastics for boys; sewing, embroidery, knitting, housekeeping, and singing for girls.

118. *JPN,* Aug. 22, 1903, Jan. 12, 1907. The charter of incorporation declared that the organization's purpose was to maintain "reading and classrooms, gymnasium, and places for social meetings, and such other educational, charitable, and benevolent purposes as may tend to the education and improvement of the working people of the community." See Balch, "History of Jamaica Plain Neighborhood House," 5.

119. *JPN,* Mar. 24, 1900.

120. Ibid., May 16, 1903, Aug. 3, 1907.

121. Ibid., Mar. 3, 1900. For the popularity of local hits, see also ibid., Mar. 25, 1899, Feb. 24, 1900, Feb. 13, 1909.

122. *WRN,* Oct. 10, 1891. By the turn of the century, the paper also devoted pages to the adjacent neighborhoods, Roslindale and West Roxbury.

123. For the use of the term *orbits* and a thoughtful discussion of perceptions of urban space, see Anselm Strauss, *Images of the American City* (New York, 1961), 52–67.

124. *JPN,* Sept. 16, 1906.

125. Blumin, *Emergence of the Middle Class,* 285.

126. *JPN,* Sept. 17, 1910, June 3, Aug. 12, 1911.

127. Ibid., June 13, 1908.

128. "The Old Home Town," *Boston Sunday Herald,* 1941, reprinted in The Boston 200 Corporation, *Jamaica Plain,* Boston 200 Neighborhood History Series (Boston, 1976), 5.

Chapter 6 Improvement and the Politics of Place

Epigraph: JPN, Oct. 13, 1900, Feb. 29, 1908.

1. See, e.g., Christine Rosen, "Infrastructural Improvement in Nineteenth-Century Cities: A Conceptual Framework and Cases," *Journal of Urban History* 12 (May 1986), 211–56.

2. See, e.g., Hammack, *Power and Society* (ch. 4, n. 66); and Harold L. Platt, *City Building in the New South: The Growth of Public Services in Houston, Texas, 1830–1915* (Philadelphia, 1983).

3. Teaford, *City and Suburb* (ch. 2, n. 12), 12–13; Michael Ebner, *Creating Chicago's North Shore* (Chicago, 1988), 55; Karr, "Brookline" (ch. 1, n. 45), 41.

4. Arthur W. Austin, *Address at the Dedication of the Town House at Jamaica Plain, West Roxbury* (Boston, 1868), 20–21. As early as 1817 a Jamaica Plain committee concluded that local taxes would be reduced if both the second (West Roxbury) and third (Jamaica Plain) precincts were set off as a separate town. They included West Roxbury in the scheme only because they believed that the Massachusetts General Court would reject the idea of establishing Jamaica Plain by itself. See Committee Report, May 5, 1817, Records of the Congregational Society of the Third Church, Roxbury (The First Church, Jamaica Plain).

5. *Report of a Committee of the Third Parish in Roxbury, Respecting a Division of the Town* (Roxbury, 1838), 4. The members of the 1838 committee were the great landholders, Benjamin Bussey and William H. Sumner, Francis C. Head, an independently wealthy son-in-law of Bussey, Joseph Curtis, and David S. Greenough. No one who examines the town books, the report goes on to say, "can avoid being struck with the enormous proportion of the town expenses for these purposes, the benefits of which are exclusively confined to the first parish."

6. Ibid.; Austin, *Address,* 21.

7. See Austin, *Address,* 21–23. Residents of Jamaica Plain sent petitions in 1843 and 1844 and prepared another in 1845. The report of the committee of 1843, for example, signed by the large property holders Samuel G. Goodrich and Stephen Minot Weld stated that the separatists "feel that they are controlled by a majority, thickly settled at one extremity of the Town. Imputing no evil design, no ungenerous feeling to any one, they still think that they are in a state of practical servitude."

8. Ibid., 23–24, 30.

9. *Application of Samuel D. Bradford and Others* (ch. 1, n. 1); *Speech of Hon. Rufus Choate before the Joint Legislative Committee on Towns, Boston, April 4, 1851* (Boston, 1851), 27–28.

10. *Speech of Hon. Rufus Choate,* 33. One resident had told Austin that he was unable to sell his land while it was part of a city because "people would not emigrate to a city" and that his lands were therefore "large unproductive estates." See Austin, *Address,* 24.

11. *West Roxbury Reports for 1854–55,* 22–23, 34.

12. The citizens of the western part of the town, Austin claimed, "cheerfully acquiesced." Austin, *Address,* 36.

13. *West Roxbury Reports for 1866–67,* 8–9, *1867–68,* 9, 12, 14; *Norfolk County Gazette,* May 4, 1872. See, e.g., support for the reconstruction of Walk Hill Street in Town of West Roxbury, "Selectmen's Records" (ch. 2, n. 19), vol. 1, July 6, 1863.

14. *West Roxbury Reports for 1866–67,* 13, *1867–68,* 30, *1870–71,* 57–59; *Opening Arguments of Arthur W. Austin, Esq., on behalf of the Jamaica Pond Aqueduct Corporation before the Committee on Mercantile Affairs* (Boston, 1867), 18–21; *Report of a Committee of the Town of West Roxbury Appointed to Examine the Sources of Water Supply for the Town, February, 1871* (Boston, 1871).

15. *West Roxbury Reports for 1867–68,* 18–19.

16. Ibid., *1860,* 21–22, *1867–68,* 20–21, *1870–71,* 10–11.

17. "Report of the Chief of Police," ibid., *1870–74,* 70; "Reports of the Overseers of the Poor," ibid., *1866–74.* In the area of poor relief, as shown in chapter 5, the inability of the town overseers of the poor to deal with local poverty led Jamaica Plain residents to form a volunteer relief society.

18. "Report of the School Committee," ibid., *1866–67,* 47, 52, *1867–68,* 68, *1871–72,* 127—28. For harsh discipline, see Michael S. Morton, "Our Public Schools," *JPN,* Mar. 5, 1904.

19. West Roxbury School Committee, minutes of meetings, Rare Books and Manuscripts Department, BPL, vol. 1, Oct. 14, 1858, vol. 2, July 7, Aug. 4, Sept. 1, 1873. After the Drake incident, the school committee attempted to ease the stringent classroom code of behavior when it told teachers to allow students to freely change position and not force them to "walk upon their toes, to place their hands behind their backs while sitting or walking or to assume any other unnatural or constrained position."

20. "Report of the School Committee," *West Roxbury Reports for 1871–72,* 123, 129–32, *1872–73,* 3–8.

21. "Report of the Memorial Committee," ibid., *1869–70,* 47–49; "Report of Town House Committee," ibid., *1866;* "Selectmen's Report," ibid., *1868–69,* 22–25; "Report of the Chief of Police," ibid., *1873–74,* 93–94.

22. Town of West Roxbury, "Selectmen's Records," vol. 1, June 18, July 1, 1861, Nov. 6, 19, 1863.

23. *West Roxbury Reports for 1865–66,* 9, *1867–68,* 29–30, *1871–72,* 8–9; *PCCB,* Mar. 9, 1874.

24. *West Roxbury Reports for 1871–72,* 5–6, 12.

25. *Norfolk County Gazette,* June 15, 1872.

26. "Report of Town House Committee," *West Roxbury Reports for 1866,* 4–5, 7–9; "Selectmen's Report," ibid., *1867–68,* 24–26.

27. *Norfolk County Gazette,* May 4, 1872.

28. Ibid.

29. William Whiting, *Report of the Committee in Favor of the Union of Boston and Roxbury* (Boston, 1851); *Report of the Joint Special Committee on Division and*

Annexation (ch. 1, n. 1), 13; "Argument of Hon. John H. Clifford," *Argument on the Question of the Annexation of Roxbury to Boston before the Legislative Committee, Thursday, February 23, 1865* (1867); *Argument of Nathaniel F. Safford, Esq., In the Matter of the Petition for the Annexation of Boston and Roxbury* (1865); *Report of the Commissioners Appointed by the City Councils of the Cities of Roxbury and Boston, respectively on the Union of the Two Cities Under One Municipal Government* (Roxbury, 1867); Drake, *Town* (ch. 1, n. 6). For election results, see "Memorabilia," *The Municipal Register . . . of the City of Roxbury* (Roxbury, 1867), 121–24. For annexations, see Teaford, *City and Suburb,* 32–63; Jackson, *Crabgrass Frontier* (ch. 1, n. 26), 138–48; and James Anthony Merino, "A Great City and Its Suburbs: Attempts to Integrate Metropolitan Boston, 1865–1920" (Ph.D. diss., University of Texas at Austin, 1968), 7–23.

In 1868 the Town of Dorchester was also united with Boston. In 1874, Charlestown, West Roxbury, and Brighton followed.

30. *Norfolk County Gazette,* Mar. 2, 1872. A city form of government offered an alternative to annexation. It could be obtained when the state population requirement for a city charter had been met by increasing the town's population or by uniting with the neighboring Town of Brookline.

31. Ibid., Nov. 23, 1872.

32. *Boston Globe,* Oct. 8, 1873. Pratt, Brewer, Seaver, and Bartlett were officers of the Jamaica Plain Savings Bank, which gave out real estate mortgage loans. Dolan had invested in Haffenreffer's Jamaica Plain brewery.

33. Geoffrey Blodgett, *The Gentle Reformers: Massachusetts Democrats in the Cleveland Era* (Cambridge, Mass., 1966), 53–55; *Boston Globe,* Oct. 8, 1873.

34. *Norfolk County Gazette,* Mar. 1, 1873; *Boston Globe,* Oct. 8, 1873.

35. *Norfolk County Gazette,* Mar. 1, 1873; *Independence to be Preferred to Annexation!* (West Roxbury, 1873), 2–4.

36. *Independence,* 3–7, 13.

37. Ibid., 7–9.

38. *Norfolk County Gazette,* May 4, June 15, 1872, Apr. 20, 1873; *Boston Globe,* Oct. 7, 8, 1873.

39. Jon Teaford, *The Unheralded Triumph: City Government in America, 1870–1900* (Baltimore, 1984), 15–41, 77–79.

40. *Proceedings of the School Committee of Boston for the Year 1881* (Boston, 1881), 26, 41.

41. Boston Finance Commission, *Final Reports, January, 1909* (Boston, 1909), 24. The members of the Board of Aldermen were elected at large prior to 1885 and from 1894 to 1900, and by district from 1885 to 1893 and 1900 to 1909. The 1909 charter eliminated the two chambers and created a nine-member at-large council. A limited degree of geographic representation was reintroduced in 1924, when the city charter was amended to allow the election of councilors from five boroughs, each of which comprised from four to seven wards. These changes can be traced in the City of Boston's annual *Municipal Register.*

42. *PCCB,* July 7, 1874, May 24, 1897.

43. *JPN,* Jan. 7, 1907, Feb. 1, Apr. 11, 1908. Although the state was generally cooperative in fiscal matters, large appropriations ran a complicated gauntlet, starting with the city council, moving to the General Court, and then returning to the council.

44. Teaford notes that even with diminished powers the American city council "survived as the voice of the neighborhoods" and the "channel" for neighborhood requests. *Unheralded Triumph,* 15.

45. *PCCB,* Sept. 29, 1906.

46. *Annual Report of the Auditor of the City of Boston,* 1880, 97, 1884, 129, 1885, 272, 1886, 94, 1887, 94, cited in Kristina Hill, "Growing Pains: Municipal Administration of the 'Garbage Problem' in West Roxbury, 1853–1900" (Seminar paper, Harvard University Graduate School of Design, 1990), 18–19.

47. *Annual Report of the Chief of Police for the City of Boston for 1876,* City of Boston City Doc. No. 7-1876 (Boston, 1877), 7; *JPN,* Jan. 11, Feb. 15, Nov. 28, 1908.

48. "Report of the Chief of Police," *West Roxbury Reports for 1873–74,* 91; *Annual Report of the Chief of Police for . . . 1876; Sixth Annual Report of the Board of Police for the City of Boston, December 1890* (Boston, 1891), 62; *JPN,* Nov. 28, 1908.

49. Alexander von Hoffman, "An Officer of the Neighborhood: A Boston Patrolman on the Beat in 1895," *Journal of Social History* 26, no. 2 (1992); Allen Steinberg, *The Transformation of Criminal Justice, Philadelphia, 1800–1880* (Chapel Hill, 1989). The routes of the patrolman covered the West Roxbury Village and Roslindale neighborhoods.

50. *JPN,* June 13, 1903, Apr. 27, 1907, July 25, Aug. 1, 1908.

51. Arthur Wellington Brayley, *A Complete History of the Boston Fire Department . . .* (Boston 1889), 301, 308, 312, 672–76, 684–87; *JPN,* Aug. 1, 1908 (reprint from 1883). In the 1880s Jamaica Plain engine and ladder companies included veterans of the old West Roxbury fire department.

52. *PCCB,* Dec. 30, 1882.

53. Ibid., Sept. 21, 1876; *JPN,* May 7, 1904; George C. Mann, Flyer (1897), Henry A. May Collection, File Folder 5: West Roxbury ephemera, Rare Books and Manuscripts Department, BPL.

54. *Annual Report of the Boston School Committee for 1881,* 9–11, *1901,* 301; *Majority and Minority Reports of the Special Committee on Discontinuance of Suburban High Schools,* City of Boston School Doc. No. 8-1881 (Boston, 1881), 3, 4 (quotation), 5; *Proceedings of the School Committee for 1881,* 53, 55, 92–93; *Boston Globe,* Apr. 2, 13, May 11, 25, 1881.

55. *PCCB,* Mar. 9, 1874, July 31, 1882.

56. Ibid., Oct. 19, Nov. 30, 1874, Apr. 11, 1892; *JPN,* Jan. 10, 1903.

57. Charles Phillips Huse, *The Financial History of Boston from May 1, 1822 to January 31, 1909* (Cambridge, Mass., 1916), app. 1.

58. Ibid., 192–93, 260–61; *PCCB,* Oct. 27, 1890.

59. *PCCB,* Dec. 13, 1875, Apr. 10, 1882; *JPN,* Mar. 25, 1899.

60. *Annual Report of Boston Street Department,* 1887–1900.

61. Meehan served from 1884 to 1886, Jones from 1889 to 1891. *Annual Report of Boston Street Department for 1888,* 121–22, *1889,* 114, *1893,* 108; *Annual Report of the Street Laying-Out Department for the Year 1896,* City of Boston City Doc. No. 30-1897 (Boston, 1897), 58. Note also the comments of the superintendent of sewers in 1892: "In the rapidly growing districts there is a great demand for new sewers, which should be heeded, as it is shown repeatedly that the failure to build sewers petitioned for has greatly delayed the development of these localities, and consequently prevented the great increase in valuation which would have resulted." See "Report of the Deputy Superintendent of Sewer Division," *Annual Report of Boston Street Department for 1891,* 315.

62. Huse, *Financial History,* 187.

63. *Report of Special Committee on Subject of Parks for Boston,* City of Boston City Doc. No. 44-1877 (Boston, 1878), 14–18, quotation on 15.

64. *PCCB,* Sept. 8, Dec. 23, 1874, Dec. 20, 1875. In 1883 another drought lowered the water level of local wells and helped popularize the city's Cochituate water distribution. See *JPN,* Aug. 22, 1908.

65. *PCCB,* Sept. 21, 1882; *JPN,* Aug. 22, 1908 (reprint of Aug. 18, 1883); Huse, *Financial History,* 197.

66. *Acts and Resolves Passed by the General Court of Massachusetts in the Year 1896* (Boston, 1896), ch. 530; *Annual Report of Boston Street Department for 1896,* 17–20, quotation on 19; *JPN,* Mar. 4, 1899.

67. *Acts and Resolves Passed by the General Court of Massachusetts in the Year 1898* (Boston, 1898), ch. 262, *Acts and Resolves . . . 1899* (Boston, 1899), ch. 397; *JPN,* Mar. 4, May 27, July 15, 22, 1899, Aug. 15, 1908; Huse, *Financial History,* 266–67. In the 1890s the construction project was again delayed by law suits and arbitration with the Boston Belting Company.

68. *JPN,* Feb. 11, 1899.

69. Robert J. Kolesar, "The Politics of Development: Worcester, Massachusetts in the Late Nineteenth Century," *Journal of Urban History* 16 (Nov. 1989), 15–16; *The Valedictory Address of the Honorable Nathan Mathews,* City of Boston City Doc. No. 220-1894 (Boston, 1895), 89–92; *JPN,* Feb. 25, 1899.

70. *PCCB,* Feb. 18, 1892; *JPN,* Nov. 4, 1899; Alexander Keyssar, *Out of Work: The First Century of Unemployment in Massachusetts* (New York, 1986), 211–13 and passim.

71. *JPN,* Sept. 23, Nov. 4, 1899, Nov. 4, 1905.

72. Ibid., Feb. 11, 25, 1899, June 12, 1909.

73. Ibid., Dec. 30, 1899, Feb. 24, 1906, Dec. 24, 1910. Goldman, "Buffalo's Black Rock" (intro., n. 10); Joseph L. Arnold, "The Neighborhood and City Hall: The Origin of Neighborhood Associations in Baltimore, 1880–1911," *Journal of Urban History* 6 (Nov. 1979), 3–30; Patricia Mooney-Melvin, "'With Interests Common to All': Neighborhood Improvement Associations, Civic Federations, and City Planning, 1880–1920" (Paper delivered at the Fourth National Conference on American Planning History, Richmond, Va., Nov. 8, 1991).

74. *JPN,* Feb. 4, 11, 25, Mar. 18, 25, Nov. 18, 1899, Mar. 17, June 19, 1900, June 20, 1903.

75. Ibid., Jan. 31, Feb. 14, Mar. 28, June 13, 1903.

76. Ibid., Mar. 4, 1899, Nov. 17, 1900, Jan. 31, 1903, Oct. 26, Nov. 30, 1907, Dec. 12, 1908.

77. *PCCB,* Mar. 3, 1874; Merino, "A Great City," 24–28.

78. *JPN,* Sept. 26, 1903.

79. Ibid., Jan. 6, 1912. An example of neighborhood inclusiveness was the 1909 committee to set up guidelines for facilities at a new Curtis Hall, which included prominent Catholics and well-known local Protestants. See ibid., May 15, 1909.

80. Ibid., July 4, 1903.

81. Ibid., July 11, 18, 1903.

82. Ibid., July 18, 25, Aug. 8, 1903.

83. Ibid., July 25, Aug. 1, 1903.

84. Ibid., Aug. 8, 15, 1903.

85. Ibid., July 25, Dec. 5, 1903.

86. Ibid., Oct. 31, Nov. 21, Dec. 19, 1903.

87. Ibid., Dec. 5, 12 (quotation), 26, 1903.

88. Ibid., Jan. 2, 1904.

89. Ibid., Jan. 9, 1904, Apr. 8, Sept. 30, Oct. 7, 1905, Feb. 1, 1908, May 28, 1910. A final appeal to the Massachusetts Board of Railroad Commissioners for a veto of the elevated was dropped because the commission did not have jurisdiction over the matter. In 1910 Jamaica Plain residents finally achieved approval for an elevated station at Green Street. In 1988–89 the entire elevated structure was torn down, and the transit line was moved to the old railroad corridor.

90. For critiques of the unplanned city, see Warner, *Streetcar Suburbs* (ch. 1, n. 2); and Arnold, "The Neighborhood and City Hall." The quotation comes from the title of Jon Teaford's reevaluation of late-nineteenth-century municipal government.

Chapter 7 The War against Localism

Epigraph: Samuel Billings Capen, "How to Bring Public Sentiment to Bear Upon the Choice of Good Public Officials . . . ," *Proceedings of the National Conference for Good City Government* (Philadelphia, 1894), 201.

1. G. B. Warden, "The Caucus and Democracy in Colonial Boston," *New England Quarterly* 43 (Mar. 1970), 19–45; Ronald P. Formisano, *The Transformation of Political Culture: Massachusetts Parties, 1790s–1840s* (New York, 1983); Bruce Laurie, *Working People of Philadelphia, 1800–1850* (Philadelphia, 1980), 152; Amy Bridges, *A City in the Republic: Antebellum New York and the Origins of Machine Politics* (Ithaca, 1984), 61–82; Hays, "Changing Political Structure" (ch. 2, n. 1), 334.

2. Paul Kleppner, "The Dissolution of Boston's Majority Party, 1876–1908," in

Boston, 1700–1980: The Evolution of Urban Politics, ed. Ronald P. Formisano and Constance K. Burns (Westport, Conn., 1984), 117–18; Dale Baum, *The Civil War Party System: The Case of Massachusetts, 1848–1876* (Chapel Hill, 1984), 76–77, 134; Richard Harmond, "Troubles of Massachusetts Republicans during the 1880s," *Mid-America* 56 (Apr. 1974), 85–99.

3. Martin Shefter, "The Electoral Foundations of the Political Machine: New York City, 1884–1897," in *The History of American Electoral Behavior,* ed. Joel H. Silbey, Allan A. Bogue, and William H. Flanigan (Princeton, 1978), 263–98; William A. Bullough, *The Blind Boss and His City: Christopher Augustine Buckley and Nineteenth-Century San Francisco* (Berkeley and Los Angeles, 1979), 58–59, 63, 89–91.

4. Benjamin Matthias, *Rules of Order: A Manual for Conducting Business in Town and Ward Meetings, Societies, Boards of Directors and Managers, and Other Deliberative Bodies* (Philadelphia, 1846), 11–23, 26–27; DeWitt, *Webster's Chairman's Manual* (ch. 5, n. 76), 24–29.

5. *Boston Globe,* Dec. 4, 1873; *PCCB,* Sept. 26, 1892.

6. Kleppner, "Dissolution," 121–22; *JPN,* Sept. 1, 1900.

7. In 1868 Rudolf F. Haffenreffer, then living in Roxbury, witnessed local Republicans marching for Grant in a torch parade that extended over five miles and had fifty-four bands! See Haffenreffer, *Letters* (ch. 4, n. 19), 51, 108–9.

8. *JPN,* Feb. 11, Nov. 4, 1899.

9. Miller, *Boss Cox's Cincinnati* (intro., n. 3), 87; Doyle, *Social Order* (intro., n. 8) 190; Smith and Freedman, *Voluntary Associations* (ch. 5, n. 5), 86–97.

10. *Boston Transcript,* May 11, 1912; *JPN,* Sept. 22, 1900, Feb. 14, 1903; "A Souvenir of Massachusetts Legislators," 1895, Massachusetts State Library, Boston.

11. *JPN,* Feb. 10, 1900, Mar. 11, 1905, Feb. 13, 1909. See also the description of the Roslindale Cycle Club's minstrel show in ibid., Jan. 27, 1900.

12. Occupations compiled from Boston city directories, 1874–1910, "Souvenir" and obituaries in the *Boston Transcript,* the *Boston Herald,* and the *Boston Globe.*

13. *JPN,* Jan. 12, 1907, Mar. 28, 1908.

14. Teaford, *Unheralded Triumph* (ch. 6, n. 39), 42–82.

15. Blodgett, *Gentle Reformers;* idem, "Yankee Leadership in a Divided City: Boston, 1860–1910," *Journal of Urban History* 8 (Aug. 1982), 371–96.

16. *Boston Transcript,* Jan. 17, 1914.

17. "Souvenir," 1892; *JPN,* Sept. 23, 1899.

18. *JPN,* Sept. 23, 1899, Sept. 22, Nov. 24, 1900; "Souvenir," 1903.

19. Lois Merk, "Boston's Historic Public School Crisis," *New England Quarterly* 31 (June 1958), 172–99; Harmond, "Troubles," 95–97; *Boston Transcript,* Dec. 12, 1888.

20. Katherine E. Conway and Mabel Ward Cameron, *Charles Francis Donnelly: A Memoir* (New York, 1909), 29–82 ff.

21. Merk, "Public School Crisis," 196–99; Harmond, "Troubles," 98–99; Peter

K. Eisinger, "Ethnic Political Transition in Boston, 1884–1933: Some Lessons for Contemporary Cities," *Political Science Quarterly* 93 (Summer 1978), 217–39. French-Canadians were concentrated in the mill towns of Massachusetts.

22. *JPN,* Jan. 23, 1904, Aug. 5, 1911. In 1911 Governor Eugene Foss appointed fellow Jamaica Plainer Brackett to the Massachusetts Superior Court. Keating later became Boston's ballot commissioner.

23. Ibid., Jan. 27, 1900. Bleiler served on the house liquor committee.

24. Ibid., Sept. 16, 1899.

25. Ibid., Sept. 17, 1904.

26. Ibid., June 20, Aug. 29, Dec. 19, 1903.

27. For Murray as reformer, see ibid., Dec. 9, 1899. For discussion of O'Meara as a candidate for the U.S. Congress, see ibid., Sept. 17, 1904. Democratic factionalism created further opportunities for the minority Republican party to siphon off Irish-American votes. On occasion Martin Lomasney, the Democratic ward boss of the West End, supported Republican candidates to defeat his Democratic rivals.

28. Melvin Holli delineated the concept of structural reform in *Reform in Detroit: Hazen S. Pingree and Urban Politics* (New York, 1969). For a recent synthesis of the types of Progressive reform, see Mohl, *The New City* (ch. 2, n. 1), 108–37.

29. Boyer, *Urban Masses and Moral Order* (ch. 3, n. 49). A good example of interest-group politics cloaked in the mantle of progressive reform is the Citizens' Telephone Reform Association, a Boston outer-city group that worked for improved phone service and lower rates. *JPN,* Jan. 12, 1907. The elastic language of reform confused one scholar, who mistook James Michael Curley for a Boston progressive reformer and his Good Government Association opponent for a machine candidate. Martin J. Schiesl, *The Politics of Efficiency: Municipal Administration and Reform in America, 1880–1920* (Berkeley and Los Angeles, 1977), 158–60.

30. *JPN,* Jan. 1, 1910.

31. Arthur Mann, *Yankee Reformers in an Urban Age: Social Reform in Boston, 1880–1900* (Cambridge, Mass., 1954; reprint ed., New York, 1966); on Billings, A. N. Marquis, ed., *Who's Who in New England* (Chicago, 1916); *JPN,* Apr. 8, 1911. Boston's reform mayor Josiah Quincy instituted both the municipal baths and the printing plant. Wilkins later became president of the Forest Hills Improvement Association.

32. Dole, *My Eighty Years* (ch. 5, n. 13), 26, 56–58 ff.

33. *Boston Transcript,* Feb. 7, 1898; Randall, *Improper Bostonian* (ch. 2, n. 36), 34–36; *JPN,* Jan. 7, June 24, 1911; Boyer, *Urban Masses and Moral Order,* 142–43, 331 n. 2; Sarah (Otis) Ernst to Anne Warren Weston, June 18, 1849, July 28, 1850, Feb. 1, 1852, June 13, 1856, and Sarah (Otis) Ernst to William Lloyd Garrison, Jan. 8, 1853, Rare Books and Manuscripts Department, BPL. The great legacy imbued the consciousness of the Unitarian reformers. At an Eliot Club meeting in 1903, for example, George W. Anderson angrily compared the treatment of immigrant Chinese by the Boston police to the hunting down of fugitive slaves in antebellum Boston. See *JPN,* Dec. 26, 1903.

34. Hays, *American Political History* (intro., n. 6), 201–356; Wiebe, *Search for Order* (intro., n. 3), 111–95.

35. David B. Tyack, *The One Best System: A History of American Urban Education* (Cambridge, Mass., 1974), 126–76; Paul E. Peterson, *The Politics of School Reform, 1870–1940* (Chicago, 1985); Hammack, *Power and Society* (ch. 4, n. 66), 259–99.

36. Chauncey J. Hawkins, *Samuel Billings Capen: His Life and Work* (Boston, 1914), 20–36.

37. Ibid., 53–62; Lazerson, *Origins* (ch. 5, n. 89), 32–33, 80; Constance Burns, "The Irony of Progressive Reform, 1898–1910," in Formisano and Burns, *Boston,* 139.

38. Hawkins, *Capen,* 63–66; Tyack, *One Best System,* 97–104.

39. Hawkins, *Capen,* 75–77; Alice Woodward Karl, "Public School Politics in Boston, 1895–1920" (Ed.D. diss., Harvard University, 1969), 25–31; Burns, "Irony," 139–40.

40. George A. O. Ernst, "The Movement for School Reform in Boston," *Educational Review* 28 (Dec. 1904), 433–43; George W. Anderson, "Politics and the Public Schools," *Atlantic Monthly* 87 (Apr. 1901), 433–47.

41. Tyack, *One Best System,* 142–47; Ernst, "School Reform in Boston," 433; Anderson, "Politics," 437–39, 443.

42. Karl, "Public School Politics," 32–34; Burns, "Irony," 140–41.

43. Karl, "Public School Politics," 81–89; Hawkins, *Capen,* 73.

44. Karl, "Public School Politics," 35–38, 90–93; *JPN,* Nov. 11, 1903; Burns, "Irony," 142–43; James W. Fraser, "Mayor John F. Fitzgerald and Boston's Schools, 1905–1913," *Historical Journal of Massachusetts* 12 (June 1984), 120–25. Storrow was defended by a Catholic school committeeman, endorsed by the diocesan newspaper, and nominated by the Democrats.

45. See, e.g., Anderson, "Politics," 434, 443–45.

46. Boston Finance Commission, *Final Reports* (ch. 6, n. 41), 14–15; Schiesl, *Politics,* 41–42. Irish-American mayors Hugh O'Brien and Patrick Collins were fiscally conservative and thus earned a grudging respect from Yankee voters.

47. Mel Scott, *American City Planning since 1890* (Berkeley and Los Angeles, 1969), 31–109; Jon A. Peterson, "The City Beautiful Movement: Forgotten Origins and Lost Meanings," *Journal of Urban History* 2 (Aug. 1976), 415–33; William H. Wilson, *The City Beautiful Movement* (Baltimore, 1989).

48. Shand-Tucci, *Built in Boston* (ch. 2, n. 8), 131–54. The neoclassical structures in the Fenway included the Museum of Fine Arts, the Harvard Medical School complex, and Fenway Court, the home of Isabella Stewart Gardner.

49. Boyer, *Urban Masses and Moral Order,* 266–76; Frederic C. Howe, *The City: The Hope of Democracy* (New York, 1905; reprint ed., Seattle, 1967), 239–48.

50. Boyer, *Urban Masses and Moral Order,* 182–83; Davis, *Spearheads for Reform* (ch. 5, n. 89), 187–93; Richard Harding Davis, quoted in David F. Burg, *Chicago's White City of 1893* (Lexington, Ky., 1976), 338.

51. Charles G. Ames, "Boston—The City of God," *New England Magazine,* n.s.

10 (Aug. 1894), 769–77; Edwin D. Mead, "Editor's Table," ibid., n.s. 10 (Mar. 1894), 387–88. See also John Colman Adams, "What A Great City Might Be—A Lesson From the White City," ibid., n.s. 14 (Mar. 1896), 3–13.

52. Ames, "Boston—The City of God," 774.

53. Capen, "Public Sentiment," 194–95; Hawkins, *Capen,* 81–86; Mead, "Editor's Table," *New England Magazine,* n.s. 9 (Jan. 1894), 666–67. Capen intended the Boston Municipal League to be nonsectarian, and thus one of the vice-presidents was an Irish-American, Thomas B. Fitzpatrick, a wealthy downtown businessman.

54. Hawkins, *Capen,* 82; Ames, "Boston–The City of God," 775.

55. Kleppner, "Dissolution," 116–18, 127; Josiah Quincy, "Address to the City Council," *PCCB,* Jan. 4, 1897; *JPN,* Jan. 24, Mar. 7, June 27, Sept. 26, 1903; Boston Board of Election Commissioners, *Digest of Laws in Force Relating to the Registration of Voters and the Conduct of Caucuses and Elections in the City of Boston* (Boston, 1895), 33–46.

56. *JPN,* Apr. 21, May 26, Nov. 17, 1900. In 1891 William G. Baker overwhelmed his Republican rival by sending in barges of supporters from his home area of Egleston Square. See *WRN,* Oct. 10, 1891.

57. *JPN,* Nov. 24, 1900.

58. Ibid., Feb. 7, May 16, 1903.

59. Capen served as the National Municipal League's first vice-president. The First Church's Charles F. Dole participated in both the Boston Municipal League and the National Municipal League. Capen, like many Gilded Age and Progressive era reformers, used the phrase "the best men." See John G. Sproat, *"The Best Men": Liberal Reformers in the Gilded Age* (Chicago, 1968).

60. *Proceedings of the Indianapolis Conference for Good City Government and of the Fourth Annual Meeting of the National Municipal League* (Philadelphia, 1898), 256.

61. Capen, "Public Sentiment," 201.

62. *Proceedings of the Fourth National Conference for Good City Government and of the Second Annual Meeting of the National Municipal League held at Baltimore* (Philadelphia, 1896), 240.

63. Samuel B. Capen, "Shall We Have One or Two Legislative Chambers?" ibid., 248–49, 251; Schiesl, *Politics,* 69.

64. National Municipal League, *A Municipal Program* (New York, 1900), iv–v, 164, 167–69, passim. See also Frank Mann Stewart, *A Half Century of Municipal Reform: The History of the National Municipal League* (Berkeley, 1950). In addition, the Program incorporated strong home rule provisions, another popular cause of municipal reformers.

65. *JPN,* Feb. 7, 1903, Nov. 19, 1904.

66. Ibid., Feb. 22, 29, Mar. 28, 1908.

67. Ernst was appointed as a representative of the city's United Improvement Association, a league of groups such as the Jamaica Plain Citizens' Association.

68. Boston Finance Commission, *Final Reports,* 22–23.

69. Ibid., 25–26.

70. For the proposed charter, see ibid., 96–114; for the adopted charter, see City of Boston, *Municipal Register for 1910 . . . ,* City of Boston City Doc. No. 43-1910 (Boston, 1910), 18–33; and for a synopsis, Schiesl, *Politics,* 104–6. The provision for removal of the mayor had been implemented by the governor in the National Municipal League's model charter.

71. Recent city charters such as those of Baltimore and New York had also informed the formulation of the Fin Comm charter. At the 1909 National Municipal League conference Robert Treat Paine championed nonpartisanship as the best method to avoid the subordination of municipal issues to the selfish interests of the parties.

72. *JPN,* Oct. 2, 23, 1909.

73. Ibid., Oct. 23, 1909.

74. Ibid., Nov. 6, 1909.

75. For an insightful discussion of "political culture," see Maureen A. Flanagan, "Charter Reform in Chicago: Political Culture and Urban Progressive Reform," *Journal of Urban History* 12 (Feb. 1986), 109–30.

76. *JPN,* Oct. 9, 1909.

77. There continued to be disgruntlement in the reformers' ranks, however. In Jamaica Plain, Mary Boyle O'Reilly, the Irish-American progressive, was upset by the aggressive tactics of Storrow's campaign committee. See *Boston Globe,* Nov. 22, 23, 1909. Both Ernst and the Waldos lived in Jamaica Plain.

78. *JPN,* Apr. 10, 1909; *Boston Evening Globe,* Sept. 10, 1909.

79. *JPN,* Dec. 4, 11, 1909; *Boston Globe,* Nov. 22, 29, 1909, Jan. 9, 1910.

80. *Boston Globe,* Jan. 1, 1910.

81. *JPN,* Aug. 28, 1909.

82. *Boston Globe,* Jan. 6, 10, 1910. In fact, Storrow was a well-known philanthropist who helped found an inner-city youth club, the West End House, and lead the City Club, which brought together leaders of Boston's important social groups.

83. Ibid., Jan. 8, 10, 1910; *Boston Evening Globe,* Jan. 8, 1910.

84. *JPN,* Jan. 15, 1910; *Boston Globe,* Jan. 12, 1910.

85. *Municipal Register for 1910,* 242–45.

86. In some years none of the at-large city councilors came from Jamaica Plain.

87. *JPN,* Feb. 19, 1910, Feb. 18, 1911, Apr. 6, 1912. Two weeks after his neighborhood meeting in 1912, Fitzgerald returned to Jamaica Plain and addressed the Eliot Club, Jamaica Plain's reform-minded literary club. The club members related their local concerns, such as preserving the pond in Franklin Park and cleaning up the garbage on Forest Hills Street, and then settled back to hear the garrulous mayor recite the virtues of the new Metropolitan District Commission (a regional governmental authority) and the advantages of the Panama Canal for the Port of Boston. He completed his presentation with a rendition of his theme song, "Sweet Adeline." Unfortunately the reaction of the club mem-

bers to his performance was not recorded. See ibid., Apr. 20, 1912.

88. Ibid., Dec. 21, 1912.

89. Ibid., Mar. 5, May 28, 1910, Feb. 25, 1911.

90. Ibid., Aug. 27, 1910.

91. The deterioration of political life was not lost on some Jamaica Plain reformers, who complained that the new charter divided the citizenry along ethnic and religious lines and that the Citizens' Municipal League was neither geographically, ethnically, nor politically representative. Ibid., Dec. 10 1910, Mar. 11, 1911.

92. Charles H. Trout, "Curley of Boston: The Search for Irish Legitimacy," in Formisano and Burns, *Boston*, 165–95; Jack Beatty, *The Rascal King: The Life and Times of James Michael Curley, 1874–1958* (Reading, Mass., 1992); Burns, "Irony," 158–59; John D. Buenker, *Urban Liberalism and Progressive Reform* (New York, 1973), 123.

93. *Boston Herald*, Feb. 28, 1919; Boyd, *Loring-Greenough House* (ch. 2, n. 32), 8–9.

94. Henry Keaveny, "Those Were the Days . . . A History of Jamaica Plain in the 1920s," c. 1980, typescript, JPL; Henry Keaveny, interview with author, Jamaica Plain, July 1, 1982; Balch, "History of Jamaica Plain Neighborhood House" (ch. 2, n. 59), 12; James Lenihan, interview with author, Cambridge, Mass., Feb. 17, 1982; Sister Margaret Patricia Donahue, interview, Apr. 12, 1978; Marion Bradley, "'Prosit': Long Ago in Jamaica Plain," *Jamaica Plain Chronicle* (c. 1978), clipping in author's possession; August Becker, interview, Jan. 18, 1982.

95. Charles H. Trout, *Boston, the Great Depression, and the New Deal* (New York, 1977), 300.

96. *Boston Herald*, Jan. 14, 21, 1938, Jan. 26, Dec. 12, 1940, Jan. 26, 1941; Sumner Hill Association Records, JPL.

Chapter 8 Conclusion: The Waning of Neighborhood Society

1. William Tuttle, *Race Riot: Chicago in the Red Summer of 1919* (New York, 1972).

2. *Boston Herald*, Apr. 6, 1933; Boston Redevelopment Authority, *Jamaica Plain District Profile* (Boston, 1979), 6.

3. *JPN*, Nov. 14, 1908; *Boston Herald*, June 24, 1924.

4. Davis, *Spearheads for Reform* (ch. 5, n. 89), 60, 75–76, 84, 148. The first settlement house founded in the United States was named Neighborhood Guild. Neighborhood Houses later were organized in Chicago and Louisville, as well as Jamaica Plain. The movement's journal, started in 1928, was titled *Neighborhood*.

5. Melvin, *Organic City* (intro., n. 11); Robert Fisher and Peter Romanofsky, eds., *Organization for Urban Social Change: A Historical Perspective* (Westport, Conn., 1981).

6. National Commission on Neighborhoods, *Neighborhoods, People, Building Neighborhoods* (Washington, D.C., 1979).

7. Gans, *Urban Villagers* (intro., n. 7); Roger S. Ahlbrandt, Jr., *Neighborhoods, People, and Community* (New York, 1984).

Index

301

Centre Street, 4, 5, 9, 10, 14, 15, 16, 32, 49, 52, 60–62, 102–4, 109, 111, 126–28, 131, 172, 175, 176, 234, 244
Centre Street Baptist Church, 131
Champion, Levi, 94
Chandler, Harry, 110
Channing, William Henry, 70
charitable reform organizations, 157–63
    and women, 157–59
Charles, Salem D., 193, 207, 208, 209, 211
Charlestown, 7, 21, 28, 38, 96, 166
charter, City of Boston, 170, 181, 221, 228–31, 234, 236, 238
chattel mortgages and local investment patterns, 92–95
Chicago, 26, 27, 29, 30, 81, 103, 104, 110, 114, 145, 158, 161, 170, 202, 204, 221, 222, 243, 245
Chickering, Caroline, 158
Chickering and Sons Company, 31
Child, Abner, 56, 133
Chinese, 155
Choate, Rufus, 171
churches, 122–34, 163–64
    interdenominational cooperation, 133
    members' organizations, 133–34, 150–51, 154–55
    membership transfers, 153
    ministers and congregations, 156–57
    and women, 122–23, 126, 127, 128, 133–34, 154
Church of Our Lady of Lourdes (Roman Catholic), 131, 236
Church of the Blessed Sacrament (Roman Catholic), 58, 131, 132, 134, 135, 150, 154
Cincinnati, 110, 145, 216, 246
cities
    communities in, xvi–xviii
    historians' views, xvi–xvii
    sociologists' views, xvii–xviii
    See also urban development
City Beautiful movement, 221–22
city governments and spending policies, 167–69, 180, 185–92
city planning, 187, 188, 200, 236
Clark, Eugene W., 101, 104, 113, 115, 116, 128, 158
clubs, 120, 121, 140–46, 148, 149, 152, 154, 163, 166, 207, 234, 236–37, 241, 245
    amateur theater, 120, 140, 155, 156. See also Footlight Club

dance, 120, 145, 149
    literary, 120, 140–42, 151, 154, 194, 238
    military-drill and patriotic clubs, 146
    political, 201, 205–8, 210, 214, 224, 233, 234
    reform, 154, 161–62, 194, 223
    social, 85, 100, 101, 103, 120, 134, 136, 138, 140–43, 153, 154, 163, 164, 194
    sports, 120, 121, 143–46, 149, 163
Coe, Henry F., 190, 207, 208
Collins, Patrick A., 178, 199, 224
commerce, 2, 3, 5, 12, 15–16, 23, 25–26, 27, 28, 54, 59–62, 90–92, 101–3, 105, 114, 117, 122
    in preindustrial city, 23
    as real estate development. 104–10
commercial areas, 15, 16, 25, 27, 28, 43, 59–62, 65, 106, 197
commercial buildings, 61–62, 102, 108, 234
commuters, 11
    low blue-collar, 36, 57, 243
    skilled workers, 31, 36, 52, 53
    white-collar, 2, 4, 11–12, 14–15, 19, 24–25, 29–31, 36, 51–52, 59–60, 123–24, 141, 146–47, 171, 178, 228, 241
commuting, 11–15, 24–25, 30–33, 52, 141, 146–47, 171, 243–44
    crosstown, 32–33, 36, 53, 57
Connolly, Arthur T., 135, 150
Converse, James W., 93, 126
Coulthurst, John A., 196, 198
Country Club (Brookline), 144
country houses, 8–10, 47, 66, 69. See also estates
Cox, George B., 206
Crafts, William Augustus, 64, 74
Croly, Jane C., 142
Curley, James Michael, 48, 238
Curtis, George William, 1, 80
Curtis, Joseph, 7, 11, 52
Curtis, Mary, 9
Curtis, Nelson, 94, 175, 179, 187
Curtis, William, 5, 9
Curtis Hall, 150–56, 175, 194
Cushing, Sidney, 206, 208

Danforth Street Chapel, 129
Daughters of the American Revolution, Mary Draper chapter, 146
Daughters of Veterans, Betsy Ross Tent, 146
Davis, J. Alba, 105, 161, 178
Davis, Richard Harding, 222

industrial areas, 16–18, 28, 29–30, 38, 43,
    47, 55–58, 91, 96, 131, 134, 190
  real estate development of, 109
  saloons in, 103
  voters in, 204
  See also industry; manufacturers
industry, 3, 25–26, 28, 29–30, 55–58, 90, 91,
    92, 95–98, 105, 106, 122, 138, 153, 161,
    165, 166, 234, 238, 242
  departure of, 35, 56, 240, 243
  at Jamaica Pond, 87
  and neighborhood life, 100–101
  on urban fringe, 3, 4, 5, 16–19
insurance associations, 138–39
interdenominational cooperation, 133
investment sources, 92–94
Irish, 18, 27, 30, 38–39, 41, 42, 50, 55, 57,
    58, 62, 98, 102, 103, 107–9, 133, 135,
    139, 144, 150–51, 158, 160, 161, 174,
    175, 178–79, 183, 185, 192, 195, 196,
    198, 204, 209, 211, 212, 213, 214, 219,
    221, 224, 232–33, 239, 243, 244
  in churches, 125, 129, 130, 131, 132, 133,
    134
  and ethnic politics, 210–11, 212, 213–14,
    219
  occupations, 3, 18, 19, 27, 42, 43, 50, 100,
    102, 103, 108, 130, 185, 192
  and politics, 196, 178–79, 195, 198–99,
    204, 209, 210–12, 213–14, 215, 221,
    224, 232–33, 235, 239
  as recipients of charity, 158, 160
  residential areas, 38–39, 56, 58, 129, 244
  and voluntary associations, 139, 144, 150–
    51, 212
Italians, 27, 29, 39, 154, 243

Jackson, Samuel, 18, 100, 179
Jacobs, Jane, xix, 246
Jamaica Boat Club, 143
Jamaica Club, 142, 143, 153, 154, 163, 194,
    206, 207
Jamaica Cycle Club, 85, 144, 163
Jamaica Park (Olmsted Park), 48, 64–66,
    86–89
  and Jamaica Plain, 87–89
Jamaica Plain
  birthplace of residents, 2, 19, 38–42
  conflicts between resident groups, 195
  description, xx–xxi
  early lack of neighborhood identity, 6,
    19–20

early roads, 4–5
as heterogeneous urban neighborhood,
    24–25, 30–62
name, 6–7, 20, 259n.46
occupational groups, 2–3, 7–8, 11–12, 15,
    19, 35–43
population, 2, 33–34, 243
as postal district, 63
settlement, 5–6
as telephone exchange district, 63
topography, 4
See also specific subdistricts
Jamaica Plain Businessmen's Association,
    115, 194. *See also* Jamaica Plain Citi-
    zens' Association
Jamaica Plain Carnival Association, 88, 115,
    163
Jamaica Plain Citizens' Association, 116,
    153, 154, 194, 195, 207, 228, 236, 237,
    239. *See also* Jamaica Plain Business-
    men's Association
Jamaica Plain Dispensary, 157, 160, 161
Jamaica Plain Friendly Society, 157, 158
Jamaica Plain Gas Light Company, 56, 90,
    112, 113, 159
Jamaica Plain Neighborhood House Asso-
    ciation, 157, 161–63, 238–39. *See also*
    Helen Weld House
Jamaica Plain News, 61, 63, 112, 114, 193,
    197, 198, 213, 225, 235
Jamaica Plain Savings Bank, 113, 178
Jamaica Plain Station, 14, 15, 31–32, 51, 56,
    61, 102, 108, 191, 234
Jamaica Plain Tuesday Club, 142, 143, 194,
    238
Jamaica Plain Women's Christian Tem-
    perance Union, 160
Jamaica Plain Working Girls' Club, 161
Jamaica Pond, 1, 4, 6, 7, 9, 17, 33, 47, 48, 50,
    52, 55, 62, 69, 77, 86–89, 93, 111, 143,
    173, 190, 195, 236
  as recreation site, 1, 86, 87, 88, 111, 115,
    143, 195
James, George, 16, 126
Janowitz, Morris, xviii
Jewish Citizens Association, 234
Jews, eastern European, 27, 39
Johns, Thomas E., 210, 224

Keating, Patrick M., 212
Kehew, Mary Morton, 218
Kenny, James, 58

Sumner Hill subdistrict, 48, 49, 51
Suttles, Gerald, xviii

Teaford, Jon C. (quoted), 30, 200
Thomas G. Plant Company, 33, 55, 57, 86,
    99, 153, 234, 243
    as social center, 153
Thompson, Albert, 51
three-decker apartment building, 59
Ticknor, Benjamin, 186, 209
Ticknor, Thomas D., 140, 155–56
Ticknor, William D, 14
Tonnies, Ferdinand, xvii
Town House, 172, 175, 176
trade unions, 100–101, 120, 146, 153, 160,
    193, 209, 215
transportation, 12–14, 24, 30–32, 59, 244.
    See also elevated railroads; railroads
Trimount Manufacturing Company, 58
Trinity Lutheran Church. *See* German
    Evangelical Lutheran Trinity Church
Troutbeck, John, 9
Tuckerman, Joseph, 159

United Order of Pilgrim Fathers, General
    Warren Colony, 139
unskilled workers, 3, 18, 19, 25–30, 36–38,
    42–43, 58–59, 103, 124, 125, 128, 130
    residential areas, 19, 28, 29, 37–38, 55, 58
urban development, xv, xix, xxi, xxii, 2, 3,
    20, 23, 24–30, 64, 90, 107, 167–68, 174,
    181, 182, 202, 240–41, 246
    models of, xvi–xviii, 23–24, 36–37, 47, 62
    and neighborhood rivalry, 196–99
    opposition to, 169–72, 109–10
    response to, 174–75, 195
    role of transportation in, 30–33, 37, 43,
    54, 244
    support for (progrowth), 110–14, 117,
    177–80, 185–89, 200
    See also real estate development; boosters
urban growth. *See* urban development

Vaux, Calvert, 81
Vogel, Leopold, 102, 159
voluntarism movement, 122
voluntary associations, 120–21
    activities, 149–53
    and affective feelings, 155–57
    and citywide networks, 146–47
    and gender barriers, 154
    and neighborhood loyalty, 157–66

and politics, 206–8, 233–34
and racial attitudes, 155
and rules of order, 148–49
and shared culture, 147–55
von Euw, Franz, 97, 98

Waldo Brothers Company, 48, 232
Wallace, David, 47
Ward, Patrick, 165, 166, 192
Ware and Van Brunt architectural firm, 49
Warner, Sam Bass, Jr., 2, 23, 104, 261n.25
Warren, John Collins, 10
Washington, Booker T., 155
Washington Street, 4, 15, 19, 32, 50, 54, 57,
    169, 189, 191, 197–98, 244
waste disposal, 173, 183. *See also* sewers
water supply, 4, 6, 17, 55, 58, 96, 173, 175,
    177–79, 181–82, 190–91, 236
wealthy, 2, 3, 7–12, 14–15, 19, 35, 49, 66–
    67, 69, 73, 75–79, 88, 93–94, 120–25,
    129, 133–34, 140, 141, 143–44, 157,
    168, 170–72, 175, 180, 209, 238, 241
    residential areas, 3, 8, 11, 25, 28, 29, 47,
    51, 99, 104–6, 179
Webster, Walter A., 167, 207, 225, 227, 229
Weeks, A. S. Parker, 193
Weld, Annie Coffin, 142, 157, 161
Weld, Asa Spaulding, 109, 125
Weld, Christopher, 56
Weld, Francis Minot, 50
Weld, Helen C., 161
Weld, John, 6
Weld, Joseph, 6
Weld, Stephen Minot, 15, 50, 56, 105, 109,
    111, 112, 172
Weld, William Fletcher, 50, 166
Weld Academy, 5, 15, 105
Weld (estate), 50, 166
Weld House. *See* Helen Weld House
West End Street Railway Company, 32
West Roxbury (neighborhood), 6, 9, 32, 39,
    54, 109, 112, 113, 132, 133, 170, 171,
    179, 184, 189, 191, 193, 196, 198
West Roxbury, Town of, 4, 6, 129, 169
    annexation to Boston, 33, 169, 177–80,
    204
    civic buildings, 175–76
    growth of agencies, 174–75
    police, 173
    schools, 135–36, 173–75, 177
    secession from Roxbury, 1–2, 19, 20, 169–
    71, 176–77, 179

About the Author

A native of Chicago, Illinois, Alexander von Hoffman has lived in the Boston area since 1972. He received a B.A. in English and a M.A. in history from the University of Massachusetts at Boston and a Ph.D. in history at Harvard University. He is an associate professor at Harvard University, where he teaches urban history under a joint appointment by the Graduate School of Design and the Department of Visual and Environmental Studies.

Books in the Series

The American Backwoods Frontier: An Ethnic and Ecological Interpretation
    Terry G. Jordan and Matti Kaups

The City Beautiful Movement
    William H. Wilson

The Rough Road to Renaissance: Urban Revitalization in America, 1940–1985
    Jon C. Teaford

Greenways for America
    Charles E. Little

Bravo 20: The Bombing of the American West
    Richard Misrach, with Myriam Weisang Misrach

The Spanish-American Homeland: Four Centuries in New Mexico's Rio Arriba
    Alvar W. Carlson

Nuclear Landscapes
    Peter Goin

The Last Great Necessity: Cemeteries in American History
    David Charles Sloane

Measure of Emptiness: Grain Elevators in the American Landscape
    Frank Gohlke, with a concluding essay by John C. Hudson

To Build a New Land: Ethnic Landscapes in North America
    Edited by Allen G. Noble

Jens Jensen: Maker of Natural Parks and Gardens
    Robert E. Grese

The Pennsylvania Barn: Its Origin, Evolution, and Distribution in North America
    Robert F. Ensminger

Pride in the Jungle: Community and Everyday Life in Back of the Yards Chicago
    Thomas J. Jablonsky

The Four-Cornered Falcon: Essays on the Interior West and the Natural Scene
    Reg Saner

Cities and Buildings: Skyscrapers, Skid Rows, and Suburbs
    Larry R. Ford

Figures in a Western Landscape: Men and Women of the Northern Rockies
    Elizabeth Stevenson

Local Attachments: The Making of an American Urban Neighborhood, 1850 to 1920
    Alexander von Hoffman

Library of Congress Cataloging-in-Publication Data

Von Hoffman, Alexander.
   Local attachments : the making of an American urban
neighborhood, 1850 to 1920 / Alexander von Hoffman.
       p.   cm. — (Creating the North American landscape)
   Includes bibliographical references and index.
   ISBN 0-8018-4710-9 (alk. paper)   ISBN 0-8018-5393-1 (pbk. : alk. paper)
   1. City and town life—Massachusetts—Jamaica Plain (Boston)—
History.   2. Cities and towns—Massachusetts—Jamaica Plain
(Boston)—Growth.   3. Neighborhood—Massachusetts—Jamaica
Plain (Boston)—History.   4. Jamaica Plain (Boston, Mass.)—
History.   5. Jamaica Plain (Boston, Mass.)—Politics and
government.   I. Title.   II. Series.
HT384.U52J357   1994
307.76'09744'61—dc20   93-37367
                                                                CIP